Urban Agri-Cultural Heritage

This book and the preceding Herrenhausen Conference
"Urban Agricultural Heritage and the Shaping of Future Cities"
in Hanover in 2019 were supported by VolkswagenStiftung.

Institute of Landscape Architecture | RWTH AACHEN UNIVERSITY

VolkswagenStiftung

Birkhäuser
Basel

Urban Agri-Cultural Heritage

Frank Lohrberg
Katharina Christenn
Axel Timpe
Ayça Sancar
(Eds.)

Introduction

Linking Urban Agricultural Heritage to Historical Research and Food Policies

Linking Urban Agricultural Heritage to the Concept of Cultural Memory and Practice

Linking Urban Agricultural Heritage to the Concept of Cultural Landscape

Showcasing and Reflecting Active Heritage Approaches

Informal and Local Approaches to Urban Agriculture Heritage

Appendix

Introduction

Urban Agriculture as Heritage

Frank Lohrberg

Urban Agriculture Is Thriving ...

Since 2010 urban agriculture has turned out to be an important tool in city planning. Addressing global challenges such as rapid urbanization and food security, a lot of initiatives emerged all over the world promoting the production of agrarian goods within the city. Also, the United Nations Food and Agriculture Organization (FAO) is engaging in urban agriculture to establish it as a "recognized urban land use and economic activity, integrated into national and local agricultural development strategies, food and nutrition programs, and urban planning." In its Growing Greener Cities initiative, the FAO (2010) is funding micro-gardens in numerous cities in developing countries to enhance food security and urban greenery as a double benefit.

Most urban agriculture initiatives focus on creating new systems like the FAO micro-gardens. The qualities of inherited and existing systems of agricultural production have not been explored systematically yet. The same is true for media coverage, which is very much interested in urban agriculture but often narrows its reports to high-tech solutions such as vertical farming or edible green facades.

... but a Look Back Is Missing

While focusing on new and cutting-edge forms of urban agriculture, its historic continuity or discontinuity within the city has not been a subject of investigation. With this book we will point out for the first time that urban agriculture is not an invention of the twenty-first century. Its roots are much older, going back to the very first cities that were founded in regions such as Mesopotamia or the Nile River Valley, with their high agricultural productivity. However, agriculture in urban history has been treated as a footnote. Furthermore, the scientific discourse often presents it as an antithesis to the city: while agriculture is associated with rural areas, the city is defined by infrastructure, industries, power, culture or arts—and by overcoming a primary production (Siebel 2015).

However, with a closer look one could see that agriculture has been linked to the city throughout history—think, for example, of farming citizens' towns in medieval Europe or small-scale, agriculture-oriented workers' housing estates which emerged during the Industrial Revolution. As well as in planning—think of the highly influential Garden City concepts of Ebenezer Howard or Frank Lloyd Wright's Broadacre City, which both highlighted a crucial role for agriculture in cities of the future (Lohrberg 2001).

Lessons Can Be Learned from History ...

Today, being aware of this past is more relevant than ever. Sustainable economies have to turn away from a fossil-based energy supply. This will lead to considerable changes in the metabolism of cities and their agriculture in the long term. Acting at the city-regional scale is becoming more important as shown by the concepts of the circular urban economy, regional food policies, or urban-rural partnerships. In this transition it is helpful to revisit historical examples of urban agriculture, especially if they have survived up to today. How could forms of agriculture in Tokyo, Granada, or other cities of the world persist for centuries? How did they survive the test of time (Koohafkan, Altieri 2011), and what lessons are to be learned from this? What has been the role of agricultural systems in ancient Mexican cities and how should we treat the remnants of this traditional form of production today?

... and Put into Practice by Heritage

Answering these questions will transcend a purely historical interest and approach urban agriculture as heritage. From a heritage perspective we expect a more reflective practice in urban agriculture, an attitude that considers it not as a new and ahistorical phenomenon but as one that has shaped cities over millennia and in different forms. By exploring this heritage, we will gain a stock of multiple knowledge and illustrative material on urban agriculture. As will be shown, the notion of heritage will also allow us to highlight specific historical settings and unravel their values—both universal and local—and act toward a sustainable development of cities.

Understanding the Process of Heritagization

This volume is the first undertaking to digest approaches dealing specifically with urban agricultural heritage. There is little academic experience in this field. The current situation is reminiscent of the early 1990s, when urban agriculture was conceptualized (Smit et al. 1996). It took more than two decades for it to turn from a phenomenon experienced as exotic to a globally recognized instrument for sustainable urban development. To unfold the heritage dimensions of urban agriculture will also afford a long run.

But how about the roadmap for this long run? And what is the starting point represented by the contributions of this volume? To figure out this baseline it is helpful to realize that heritage is a subject of processual construction.

Heritage is made explicitly a subject of understanding and doing by processes of discovering, describing, attributing, and valorizing that we summarize as *heritagization*. According to Kalakoski et al. (2020, 791) "heritagisation encompasses the production of the cultural meanings of the heritage and the framing and explaining [of] the fragments of history to the contemporary audience." Understanding the process of heritagization helps "tracing the meaning-making process" and uncovering underlying "social-cultural premises" (791). Also Bernbeck (2013) and Sánchez-Carretero (2015) elaborate on heritagization as a concept of a reflective heritage thinking.

Kalakoski et al. (2020) have collated different models which explain heritagization as a phased procedure, namely from Davallon (2014) and Bonta (1975, 1979), the latter author introducing canonization as a central part of collective narrative processes.

In order to frame the heritagization in the field of urban agriculture, **Fig. 1** combines both models. While Kalakoski et al. (2020) analyzed the heritagization process retrospectively (on the subject of Nordic wooden towns) by analyzing its phases, this book's approach is to operate with heritagization, therefore distinguishing the steps to be conducted in such a process. Hence, our aim is twofold, making clear the heritagization phases in general, thereby also identifying different entry points for stepping into this process, and matching this book's contribution accordingly to better understand their relevance and potential impact to promote urban agriculture as heritage.

As **Fig. 1** clearly reveals to designate a specific site as heritage is only one step (step 5) in a wider process encompassing also activities of knowledge building, canonization and, later on, mainstreaming and reinterpretation.

It is to be mentioned that the model considers heritagization as an expert-driven process. We acknowledge that heritage can also be promoted by local communities—a crucial aspect especially for urban agriculture as we will show. However, also in such processes a professional knowledge is needed to frame and stimulate activities and to enhance their impact. We as editors agree with the findings of Kalakoski et al. (2020, 791) who state, "that the accumulation of experts' attention on a specific heritage object, site or category plays a major role in how heritage becomes recognised by the wider society."

Baselining of Heritagization in the Field of Urban Agriculture

With regard to ongoing activities in the field of urban agricultural heritage and this book's essays in particular, we can clearly state that heritagization of urban agriculture is in its initial phases. We can identify the 2019 Herrenhausen Conference on *Urban Agricultural Heritage and the Shaping of Future Cities* as a pioneering activity (step 1) in this field. As a follow-up, this book can mainly contribute to a precanonical knowledge-building (step 2) by presenting contributions from various disciplines that deal with urban agricultural heritage: from historical science to planning, from geography to sociology, from agriculture to landscape architecture. We take the diverse contributions that have reached us not as something to be streamlined but as a richness to be interpreted. We deem them all as relevant pieces of a puzzle and try to unfold their cross-fertilizing potential. However, we will also try to promote a consensual

	Bonta phases	Davallon phases	This book's activities
Pioneering	*Blindness*: few pioneers recognize [the heritage's] significance	[early] *Recognition* of value of the object	(Herrenhausen Conference)
Precanonical knowledge-building	*Precanonical responses*: different but equal interpretations	*Production of knowledge* about the object	Linking urban agricultural heritage to historical research, concepts of cultural memory and practice, and of cultural landscape
Canonical interpretation	*Canonical interpretation*: a consensus about the object of study		Integrative introduction to urban agricultural heritage
Authoritative interpretation	*Authoritative interpretation*, where the prestige of a recognized authority affirms the correctness of the interpretation		Showcasing and reflecting active heritage approaches, both universal and local
Activation and designation of heritage		(official) *Declaration* of the heritage status, *Public access* to a site or object	Showcasing and reflecting active heritage approaches, both universal and local
Mainstreaming	*Dissemination*, where the canonical interpretation breaks free from the academic circles to the consciousness of the general public	*Transmission* of the object to the future generations	
Reiteration and reinterpretation	*Silence or oblivion*, as the reiteration of the same interpretation/ reinterpretation, which restarts the interpretation process		

Fig. 1 Steps of heritagization

understanding of urban agricultural heritage (step 3). This is done by highlighting contributions as valuable or even ground-breaking, and by presenting approaches to conceptualization (like this introduction).

We can also present contributions dealing with an activated and designated heritage (step 5), mainly case studies, and the underlying authoritative interpretations (step 4). To this end we present high-level interpretations and actions, namely from the United Nations Educational, Scientific and Cultural Organization (UNESCO) and the FAO, but also from local-level authorities, as it turned out that the particularities and specific potentials of urban agriculture also require elaboration on heritage at the local level.

As spearheads of the current heritagization, these cases are quite valuable. However, as will be shown, they often represent isolated or even exceptional practices and should not blind us to the fact that the general heritagization of urban agriculture is in its early stages.

Taking this baseline into account, this volume is outlined to stimulate heritagization in the field of urban agriculture by two main actions:

1. Knowledge-building by linking urban agricultural heritage to different research arenas, namely historical research (on urban food policies) and research on cultural memory and practice, and cultural landscapes.
2. Showcasing and reflecting an activated heritage, both on the universal and the local levels.

In the following we will describe these actions in more detail, locate the book's contributions therein—although most of them fit into more than one category—and show how their heritage approaches can benefit the future of urban agriculture.

Knowledge-Building: Linking Urban Agricultural Heritage to Historical Research, Especially on Food Policies

Urban agriculture's past is examined by different disciplines. Historical science and archaeology address a history of urban agriculture which has only survived in documents like books, maps, and illustrations or in archaeological remnants. Disciplines such as social science or natural science process the information of a still living past which can be experienced as part of everyday life, often described following the metaconcepts of cultural memory and practice, and cultural landscape.

The work of historical sciences is of great importance, as it can provide us with a source of knowledge on former forms and phenomena of urban agriculture. However, research on urban agriculture's past is quite dispersed and far away from mainstream activities in historical research. The book on the history of urban agriculture is still to be written. Up to now few scholars have focused on the subject. Landsteiner and Soens (2020) have recently edited the volume *Farming the City: The Resilience and Decline of Urban Agriculture in European History,* a pioneering work underpinning both the necessity of concerted research in this field and the blind spots to be tackled.

In this volume Ansgar Schanbacher sheds light on these blind spots when describing "Early Modern Urban and Peri-Urban Horticulture in German

Territories." He delivers manifold evidence that urban agriculture has been an integral part of many German cities during the early modern era. Moreover, he reveals that "urban gardens were also centers of innovation that imparted horticultural knowledge and practices [...] to the surrounding countryside."

These findings are clearly underpinned by Sibylle Küttner and Frank Lohrberg's case study on the city of Erfurt, a German city with a rich urban horticultural history. They give evidence that Erfurt has not only been provided by its hinterland with food and fiber, but has played an active role as a "Driver of Regional Agriculture" throughout the centuries.

Another informative branch of urban agriculture's history is that of food policies. While spatial information has not been recorded systematically, food policy activities are mirrored in documents like laws, regulations, treaties, and court files. Daviron et al. (2019) offer an overview on the "History of Urban Food Policy in Europe, from the Ancient City to the Industrial City," thereby shedding light also on the history of urban agriculture. Among multiple interesting facets, they point out that "medieval and modern cities [...] made sure of their [food] supplies by setting up exclusive catchment areas" (48). In these perimeters of several kilometers around the city, food products were not allowed to be traded other than directly to the city itself—another striking hint as to the intense integration of local agriculture in the urban life of former times.

In her contribution Dona Pickard also focuses on food policies when elaborating on "The Role of Centralized Policy Planning for Bulgarian Urban Agricultural Heritage from the Socialist Period." Similar to Daviron et al., who focus on Mediterranean and Western European cities, Pickard gives evidence that urban agriculture played a prominent role in Sofia's socialist policies. This ranked from the allowance for each citizen to grow food on unused land to city-wide analysis and zoning concepts for the establishment of a vegetable belt in the city's northeastern territory. Showing the socialistic period's policies, Pickard can inform today's urban agriculture policies in two ways: questioning the "dominant discourse on urban agriculture [that] views it as a novelty, driven by postmaterialist values for environmental sustainability and social cohesion," and outlining "a lesson as to the many ways in which urban agriculture can fit into the daily rhythm of the city that can be in line with a contemporary democratic policy making process."

Explaining the development of urban agriculture through urban food policies—this is also a key notion of three other contributions to this book. Attila Tóth gives a brief overview of allotment gardening in Europe, pointing out the active role of municipalities and states in promoting this form of agriculture in the city. This study is complemented by Johanna Altendorf, Jay Heydecke, Katharina Christenn, and Axel Timpe, who delve into the Russian experience of dachas. Although they are different phenomena, in both contributions the authors discover tangible and especially intangible heritage worth consideration when it comes to making today's cities more resilient. This is also the point of Giles B. Sioen and Makoto Yokohari's elaboration on urban agriculture in Tokyo. They explain why Tokyo—a city with more than 6,000 inhabitants per square kilometer—still has a significant share of agricultural land, which is of increasing importance to ensure the resilience of the city.

Knowledge-Building: Linking Urban Agricultural Heritage to the Concept of Cultural Memory and Practice

Urban agriculture is quite different from other potential heritage carriers like buildings, statues, or other artifacts. It is a living practice, handed over from one generation to the next. Hence, the past activities do have an impact on what is going on today. They are inscribed in collective memories and practices, and the spatial structure of the site. According to Barthel et al. (2010, 255–56) it was Maurice Halbwachs who in 1926 introduced the concept of collective memory to underline that there are "supra individual means shared with others, such as language, symbols, events, and cultural contexts" by which groups construct their "own images of the world through agreed-on versions of the past—versions constructed through negotiation, not private remembrance." It is this process of negotiation and mediation and its cultural means such as language and commemorative rituals that—according to Misztal (2003)—causes other scholars to use the term *cultural memory*.

Describing cultural memory and practice is also of high relevance here, where much of urban agriculture's heritage is rooted. In this volume, Slavica Čepić, Dragana Ćorović, and Jelena Tomićević-Dubljević dig for such a root when describing garden colonies in Belgrade as a place "Where Memory, Nature, and People Meet." They point out how processes of postwar socialist industrialization and migration led to a special form of urban agriculture—the garden colonies—which are still shaping relevant parts of the postsocialism city. Their interest is dedicated to the garden colonies as part of a vernacular landscape. It is not an active heritage approach they are claiming; however, their investigations are basic to uncover the garden colonies as a result of the "needs, social interactions, traditions, and agricultural practices of the people who established them and those who still use them today."

Uncovering more and more of such processes of collective memory and practice is essential to promote the heritagization in the field of urban agriculture. Regarding urban agricultural heritage as a living heritage, these sociocultural features contribute much to explain its significance. This is clearly demonstrated by Leandra Brunet, Nicole Laufhütte, Axel Timpe, and Katharina Christenn, who describe two "almost unique" urban market gardening areas in French cities that can be traced back to the Middle Ages. The authors draw a fascinating picture of the gardening practices, not only how they transformed the natural setting to shape the urban landscape, but also how professional knowledge and practice shaped the community of gardeners, its identity, organization, language, and rituals. Notably, the market gardeners developed their own names for their professional groups, which are called *Maretiers* and *Hortillons*.

Belgrade's garden colonies and French horticultural areas—most of the cases presented in this book are European ones. Obviously, this volume is trapped in a Eurocentric perspective which is—of course—rooted in the editors' backgrounds and affiliations but also in the circumstance that historical science and heritage approaches in particular are very much anchored in the European context. Thus we are all the more happy to include case studies from other global regions. Notably, these also focus on aspects of cultural memory and practice as an approach to heritage. Mengyun Chen and Guangsi Lin criticize the ongoing practice of wetland restoration in Guangzhou, China, which focuses on maintaining ecological benefits but is blind to the traditional wetland agriculture of the Wanmu Orchards being replaced by wetland parks. This destroys the unique local knowledge and the conservation of "memory from the people."

Mariana Sanchez Salvador in her case study of Lisbon sheds light on another heritage aspect of urban agriculture bound to cultural practices: its biodiversity in respect of its genetic resources. It has been Shackleton, Pasquini, and Drescher (2009) who laid the groundwork for this line of thinking in *African Indigenous Vegetables in Urban Agriculture*, therein showing a rich biodiversity in vegetables cultivated in and around African cities. In this book, Sanchez Salvador reports from urban agriculture in Lisbon, outlining that the rich heritage is not an issue of the city's policies, except for "one dimension [...] [its] agricultural biodiversity." In fact, a survey in some horticultural areas of the city has revealed "an impressive variety of vegetables, fruits, and pulses." The author links this diversity to cultural practices, especially the fact that migrants brought species from their homelands with them. Bossima I. Koura, Eric Boenecke, Frank Lohrberg, and Luc H. Dossa take a similar approach when elaborating on a traditional agro-sylvo-pastoral system in Cotonou, Benin—the "Coconut-Lagune system." Focusing on the Lagune cattle as a robust African land race, they clearly state that urban agriculture can play a decisive role to safeguard valuable genetic resources.

We highlight such research as paramount and path-breaking for identifying the diverse heritage potential of urban agriculture, and encourage academics in all regions of the world to follow these examples.

Knowledge-Building: Linking Urban Agricultural Heritage to the Concept of Cultural Landscape

Cultural memory and practice is also inscribed in space, a process framed by the concept of cultural landscapes (Sauer 1925). As urban agriculture has a strong spatial impact (by scale and by function, for example, irrigation of the land), it is worth taking the cultural landscape concept into particular consideration. Cultural landscapes are defined by UNESCO as "cultural properties [that] represent the combined works of nature and of man" (UNESCO 2012, 14). Having entered the Anthropocene with a postulated almost global impact of man on nature, cultural landscapes have to be considered as a ubiquitous phenomenon. Hence, UNESCO highlights three forms of outstanding cultural landscapes,

1. Highly and intentionally designed ones,
2. Organically evolved ones, and
3. Associative ones, the latter meaning landscapes highly attributed by cultural meaning.

Urban agriculture landscapes mainly fit into the second category, as they have emerged over time and represent the impact of generations of farmers on the land.

In this volume, a number of contributions make cultural landscapes into subjects of investigation and the basis of contemporary approaches, for example,

Anna Kerfers and Ardiana Rahimi, Axel Timpe, and Katharina Christenn in their inspiring description of "La Vega de Granada: A Cultural Landscape Built Around Irrigation." The former swampy marshland has been reclaimed by complex irrigation systems that have turned it into a rich landscape with linear canals, fields, and trenches—but which need to be used properly in order to be maintained. Kerfers and Rahimi analyze the many dimensions of this horticulture area near the city of Granada and outline it as a cultural landscape. Until today, the Vega has faced different challenges but these could be handled by adaptation, thanks to the fact that producers and citizens have always been aware of the system's value and of the rich heritage surrounding them in the production landscape.

Nerea Morán and Marian Simón Rojo take a similar approach when describing the Manzanares River area southeast of Madrid as a "Hidden Urban Agricultural Heritage." The cultural landscape dates back to Moorish times and was mainly influenced by the building of a hydraulic infrastructure in the eighteenth century that still structures the landscape in some parts. However, in recent decades, the area was heavily impacted by urbanization and gray infrastructure, which has destroyed much of the formerly intact agrarian landscape. In this situation, Morán and Simón Rojo propose a combined approach: planning and design should turn the area into a meaningful part of Madrid's green infrastructure, a "green edible corridor."

Other contributions to this book also reveal the relevance of addressing urban agricultural heritage as a part of cultural landscapes, such as Anna Lei's well-informed elaboration on the Campagna Romana and her plea for "reviving urban agricultural heritage for landscape protection."

These contributions give strong evidence that urban agriculture has played a significant role in shaping the urban landscape, underpinning the need to further link the discourse on urban agricultural heritage with the one on cultural landscapes and their preservation. However, it would be too shortcoming to limit this thinking to the legitimate question of how to sustain cultural landscapes by means of urban agriculture—an aspect touched upon here by Xavier Recasens, Dolors Nieto, Clara Forn, and Oscar Alfranca in their contribution on urban gardening as a practice to safeguard historical agricultural sites and their heritage. We deem it necessary to delve deeper into the history of urban agriculture itself and investigate how this has shaped the urban fringe's cultural landscapes, its land use, physical structure, ecology, metabolism, and so on. Such further research and practice is needed and will greatly benefit for a sustainable territorial development.

Showcasing and Reflecting Active Heritage Approaches

So far, we have touched upon contributions that uncover heritage-relevant knowledge but do not actively operate with heritage as outlined in step 5 of our heritagization model. In the following, and based on some selected contributions, we will focus on that core step of the heritagization process and the underlying authoritative interpretations (step 4). Doing so, we want to shed light on the range of approaches—from global to local ones—and the heritage values and benefits aimed for.

Defining and designating heritage needs a value-ascribing action. High-level institutions or local initiatives can allocate values to the tangible and intangible carriers of heritage. The main high-level institutions in the field of urban agricultural heritage are UNESCO, targeting World Heritage, and the FAO, highlighting Globally Important Agricultural Heritage Systems (GIAHS). However, heritage can also be activated and valorized starting at the local level. When it comes to agriculture, heritage needs to be understood in a more contextual, ecosystematic way. Hence, the local stakeholders—farmers, artisans, vendors, and others keeping the heritage alive—move into the center of consideration.

Considering this, for the development of urban agriculture, two contrary but complementary approaches have to be considered:

1. A universal heritage approach focusing on outstanding national or global heritage approach, which is framed by UNESCO, and
2. A local heritage approach focusing on values and benefits for local communities.

Recently, Jiang (2021) has explained how to identify and activate both forms of heritage by outlining selection criteria and how to apply them to potential heritage sites. She makes clear that for urban agriculture, both approaches, local and universal, are relevant and often to be combined to fully unlock the heritage potential. In this book Paola Branduini takes a similar claim when focusing on "Intangible Agricultural Heritage as a Resource for Sustainable Contemporary Cities."

Universal and Official Heritage Approaches to Urban Agriculture

How is urban agriculture represented in the institutionalized heritagization process of UNESCO and the FAO? UNESCO started its heritage initiatives focusing on built monuments (ICOMOS 1964), and it took several decades to widen the perspective. Today, while UNESCO addresses cultural landscapes as heritage, it still neglects the term *agriculture* in its 2021 Operational Guidelines (UNESCO 2021). This is highly surprising, as agriculture is the driving force shaping most cultural landscapes. Obviously, UNESCO restricts itself to the term *land use*, as *agriculture* is claimed by the FAO. Consequently, agricultural heritage is not in the focus of UNESCO and, all the more, addressing urban agriculture is quite exceptional.

Such an exception is the "Bamberg Market Gardeners' District" in the city of Bamberg (Germany), which Diana Büttner is describing in this volume. It was the medieval structure of the city, its winding lanes and squares, its baroque churches and townhouses that were the focus of UNESCO when declaring Bamberg as a World Heritage Site back in 1993. However, the City of Bamberg realized that the market gardeners' houses in the east of the city were only part of a bigger urban agricultural heritage that encompasses backyard fields and rich traditions in market gardening. Step by step this heritage was explored, documented, and addressed as a living heritage: Market gardeners are supported to keep and update their businesses. The City of Bamberg has recognized it is the community-in-practice safeguarding and keeping alive this urban agricultural heritage.

Bamberg was not only a pioneer in addressing urban agriculture as an intangible heritage, it was also successful in getting the city's gardening tradition included in the German Inventory of Intangible Cultural Heritage. For urban agriculture as a living heritage, intangible features are especially relevant. To keep the heritage alive, tangible and intangible features have to be addressed in their interplay, for example, seeds in principle are tangible and can be conserved in a seed bank, but without the intangible knowledge of traditional cultivation techniques—and their ongoing practice—the heritage will be lost.

While Bamberg's World Heritage approach seems to offer urban agriculture as a successful development, we know of other World Heritage Sites, like the Theodosian Walls of Istanbul, where urban agriculture is neither highlighted nor promoted (Shopov 2019). Along the same lines, in this book Alexander Kader reports from a UNESCO World Heritage Site—the Oman *falaj* irrigation system—which neglects the role of urban agriculture for its formation and future development.

The agriculture gap of UNESCO heritage activities is partly compensated by the GIAHS program. The FAO launched it in 2002, aiming to highlight the dramatic loss of agricultural diversity due to a globalized industrial agricultural production. The program wants to counterbalance this negative trend. It brings attention to the manifold values of traditional, local, or regional production systems for local communities and their benefits for a sound environment and genetic variety in agricultural crops and animals.

To this end, FAO makes use of a universal heritage approach highlighting globally outstanding sites. However, while UNESCO works with *landscape* as an overall term, FAO uses *system* to protect the heritage of traditional farming methods, techniques, and cultivated species. In contrast to UNESCO, it does not operate with a predominantly spatial approach—for example, a protected zone—but takes an integrative approach addressing the "totality of the functionalities, goods and services provided by the system" (FAO 2017). GIAHS are selected according to five criteria:

1. Food and livelihood security,
2. Agro-biodiversity,
3. Local and traditional knowledge systems,
4. Cultures, value systems, and social organizations, and
5. Landscapes features.

The criteria underline that the GIAHS program is also working with a living heritage approach with the communities-in-practice as the main carrier of heritage. For a further development of urban agricultural heritage we consider this approach as fundamental.

The GIAHS at present covers more than 60 agricultural heritage systems worldwide (FAO 2021). However, a specific approach to urban agriculture is missing. Today, only two GIAHS are situated in (peri)urban settings. First was the Xuanhua urban grape garden in Zhangjiakou city, Hebei Province, China, which highlights a traditional funnel-framed grape production area (People's Government of Xuanhua District 2013). Second is the Chinampas Agricultural System of Mexico City, certified as GIAHS in 2018 and also part of the UNESCO World Heritage Site Historic Center of Mexico City and Xochimilco, designated already in 1987. This highly fascinating agricultural system reveals the full significance and potential of addressing urban agriculture as heritage as Laura Camacho Latz, Sophie Laukemper, Katharina Christenn, and Axel Timpe demonstrate in their contribution. Chinampas are described as artificial islands that are of high fertility and productivity. The Chinampa tradition dates back to the Aztecs and is assumed to have been a cornerstone of the flourishing Aztec capital of Tenochtitlan. Today, the remaining Chinampas area is experiencing a renaissance based on cultural tourism, biodiversity appreciation, and a growing demand in Mexico City's markets for fresh food and flowers perceived as traditional and authentic.

Based on these encouraging experiences of safeguarding and showcasing urban agricultural heritage in China and Mexico, former GIAHS program manager Parviz Koohafkan (2019) declared the program's openness to include further urban agriculture systems. It is hoped that multiple initiatives will emerge to this end. With reference to the Chinampas of Xochimilco, we claim that these artificial agricultural systems located in urban areas are not exceptional but generic. As Thebo et al. (2014) have pointed out, 60 percent of the global irrigated croplands are located in and around a 20-kilometer buffer for cities exceeding 50,000 inhabitants. Many of these irrigation systems are deeply rooted in the past, indicating a rich agricultural heritage in today's urban world.

Local and Informal Heritage Approaches to Urban Agriculture

As we can see, concepts of universal heritage have opened to agriculture. The GIAHS program, in particular, asks for a systemic heritage approach and the involvement of local stakeholders. Their collective practice in its tangible and intangible features is seen as crucial knowledge to keep the heritage alive.

In addition, this volume offers another interpretation of a local heritage approach. In this, the local community is not seen mainly as carrier of a universal agricultural heritage but as an agency to unfold local heritage potentials informing sustainable development. In this approach *heritage* takes on a different notion: it is not seen as a target of safeguarding activities, but as a tool for territorial development. Consequently, the local heritage is not intended to uncover universal values of heritage, although it may do so; moreover, it should open doors for multiple stakeholders of sustainable development to rethink and agree upon history-informed territorial strategies.

In this respect Rafael Mata Olmo, Carolina Yacamán Ochoa, and Esther Sanz Sanz describe a "participatory heritage creation process" making reference to the work of the Agrarian Park of Fuenlabrada in the south of the metropolitan region of Madrid, Spain. There, the authors conducted a research project together with local farmers and other stakeholders in order to start a process of social reappropriation that moves away from traditional heritage approaches. Based on archival work, joint field trips, interviews with farmers, and workshops, they used heritage not as subject of inventorying but as a medium to facilitate the collaborative work among stakeholders. The aim was to achieve "agreed-upon practices [for] the enhancement of the living landscape between public and private bodies" and also to grant "strategic value to food as a cultural asset, which recognizes the singularity and quality of local production with a historical background."

What the authors describe can be generalized as an important approach to heritage—especially in the field of urban agriculture—complementing the established procedures of UNESCO and the FAO. This local heritage again ties in the living heritage with its close links to the community, but also the fact that agricultural products—mainly food—shape urban life in a close and vivid way, thereby generating another path of sociocultural development to be traced back and explored henceforth toward local values such as capacity building, income generation, food security, aspects of traditions, local identity, and more.

This specific heritage potential of urban agriculture is also reflected in the case of the "Murs à Pêches de Montreuil," elaborated by Ayda Hamid Kargari, Kevin C. Wehnert, Katharina Christenn, and Axel Timpe. In this case a former espaliered/wall-based fruit production system in the east of Paris has been rediscovered by local initiatives. They are attracted by the rich history of the site and the remaining wall gardens, creating a unique place offering multiple opportunities to restore its former uses but also to integrate new ones like environmental education or urban gardening.

Ole Oßenbrink, Birte Mehrkens, Andreas Ulbrich, and Cord Petermann describe two extended production areas and cultural landscapes near the city of Hamburg, and their fading links to the city's markets. Both horticultural areas date back to the twelfth century, when Dutch migrants turned a swampy marshland into a rich landscape with linear villages, fields, and trenches. Right from the beginning, these areas delivered to the Hamburg market, using rivers and channels for transport. In reverse, the production areas were under the influence of the city, for example, taking expression in urbanized farmhouses that mirrored architectural vogues of the metropolis. Today, the horticultural areas—representing some of the largest in Germany—are hardly connected to urban life, and the city's society is not aware of their rich horticultural heritage. Oßenbrink et al. describe a pilot project that analyzed the actor's needs and formulated ideas on how the fading link between farmers and urban society could be reinvented.

We round off this volume with Andrea L'Erario, Paola Branduini, Raffaella Laviscio, G. Matteo Mai, Lionella Scazzosi, and Francesco C. Toso's inspiring and promising description of a Milanese museum called MUSA, which has been established as cultural hub to engage local stakeholders in the preservation and development of the city's agricultural landscape. MUSA is a valuable endeavor to make the history and future of urban agriculture a subject of joined engagements of planners, farmers, and citizens.

In all these approaches, the local stakeholders' engagement is not merely dedicated to an official listing of the heritage but its utilization and bottom-up valorization. This line of thinking is different to UNESCO's approaches but bears rich potential for a local commitment with the heritage. In addition, this procedure is a low-threshold one: it can start at any place of interest, even if it seems to be an undistinguished and ordinary one. This also makes a local heritage approach a promising strategy to broaden the idea of urban agricultural heritage, raise its impact, and mainstream its significance, thereby reaching a next stage (step 6) in the heritagization of urban agriculture. So, globally, a local heritage approach to urban agriculture should be explored further in its opportunities and challenges, and methods to be applied.

Summary

With regard to the process of heritagization in the field of urban agriculture, we consider further knowledge-building vitally important. Urban history can supply a source of knowledge which is key to better understanding urban agriculture and also to better anticipate its future. Moreover, the deepened insights in the role of agriculture in urban history have already revealed the twentieth century's separation of agriculture and the city as an exception to the rule. Also, other research conceptualizing cultural memory, practice, and cultural landscapes is highly relevant, as these concepts offer a theoretical and methodological access to address values inherited in urban agricultural systems.

When it comes to active heritage approaches, we stated that agriculture in general has been recognized as heritage due to UN initiatives and especially the FAO GIAHS program. The latter underlines that agriculture has to be approached as a living heritage. It is kept alive by dynamically evolving practices and based on active local communities. However, UNESCO or GIAHS initiatives focus only on a "universal heritage" and do not cover urban agriculture systematically, yet.

On the other hand, grassroots movements increasingly address urban agriculture as local heritage and explore its potentials for a sustainable development. Both approaches have their place. Addressing the local heritage offers vast potential for sustainable development—especially by engaging local stakeholders—and can be applied to a wide range of urban-agricultural settings, thereby mainstreaming the idea of urban agriculture as heritage. The universal heritage approach is also to be extended as it flagships urban agricultural heritage's potential and raises public awareness in general. Also, it can provide intellectual resources and political support for urban agriculture, in turn supporting grassroots initiatives and their work on local heritage.

This volume is dedicated to promoting the heritagization in the field of urban agriculture. To this end we offer a first edited collation of elaborations and case studies on the subject, and also models for their comprehensive understanding. We thank all authors for their tremendous work and the full range of approaches they provided. Editing the articles, we experienced urban agricultural heritage as a fascinating phenomenon full of potential. The subject merits deeper analysis. May this volume support and stimulate such further research and inspire initiatives to safeguard and develop urban agriculture as heritage. ▪

Linking Urban Agricultural Heritage to Historical Research and Food Policies

Early Modern Urban and Peri-Urban Horticulture in German Territories

Ansgar Schanbacher

Horticulture: Multifaceted but Underestimated

Urban agriculture in Central European early modern cities (that is, between circa 1500 and 1800) stands out for its great variety. Within the city walls or close to the town—regarded as urban and peri-urban agriculture—there were fields, fish ponds, pastures, sometimes with beekeeping, and gardens, whose forms of usage could differ widely. Being situated behind the house or beyond the city walls, gardens could contribute fruit and vegetables to the livelihood of city dwellers and enhance their food security, while often helping them to avoid the market (Soens 2020, 14–16). This subsistence use of gardens was paralleled by peri-urban commercial horticulture and by the increasing use of gardens for leisure activities in the eighteenth century, which was not only practiced by the upper class (Rosseaux 2015, 142–43).

Since the Middle Ages, the garden has been an intermediary between the open field and the town buildings. It was an area that gave the owner or tenant, who usually had to pay low taxes, more cultivation options, because it was not part of the fields cultivated jointly. But usually this form of use until the nineteenth century was limited to the middle and upper classes, directing the demand of landless city dwellers to the market (Hofmann 2015, 76; Soens 2020, 20). Whereas research on urban agriculture had been rather neglected for a long time in the historiography of premodern cities in Europe, the production of food by urban dwellers has gained more attention over the last few years (Imbert 2015; Landsteiner and Soens 2020; Häberlein and Zink 2015; Petersen 2020). Combined with recent source findings and actual research, it is thus possible to give an outline of the importance of this form of agriculture by analyzing the urban conditions successively with regard to space, actors, plants, and trade.

Of Diligence and Vermin: Early Modern Horticultural Knowledge

Most accessible to historical research are early modern printed sources such as journals, treatises, and encyclopedias, which abounded in the polycentric German landscape of knowledge especially during the Age of Enlightenment (Schindling 1999, 3). Authors usually linked their own practical experience with results made from other experts, which were often based on works on gardening from France and Italy. As a rule, their recommendations on kitchen and herb gardens were valid for urban and rural gardens but rather directed to upper-class readers (Hiebner 1664, 174; Anon. 1799, 152–206). Only in a few cases were they explicitly addressed to urban horticulture or female gardeners from the middle class (Schröder-Lembke 1984, 120–22, 127). One of the most influential authors of German *Garten-Wissenschaft* (garden science) with connections to the urban sphere was the Erfurt-based magistrate and gardener Christian Reichart (1685–1755), who contributed to the establishment of Erfurt as a hub of horticulture (Müller 2003;

Figs. 1a–b Wolfgang Kilian, “Augusta Vindelicorum/Augspurg,” 1626 (detail)

Schaier 2009, 61). In his seminal works he emphasized the need for professionalism but also admonished the gardener to be diligent and faithful and to combine aesthetics with practical aspects (Reichart 1758, 28–34, 53). Also, in connection with cities, there were specialized journals such as the *Annalen der Gärtnerey*, which was published in Erfurt between 1795 and 1800, and almanacs such as the *Haus-, Garten- und Land-Kalender* (1712–80) from Leipzig, which recommended how to tend the garden, for example to plant cucumbers, pumpkins, and beans in April. Many of these journals and almanacs are today accessible via the Internet—for example at www.zeitschriftendatenbank.de. Most usefully, encyclopedias such as Johann Heinrich Zedler's *Grosses vollständiges Universal Lexicon* (1731–54) and Paul Jacob Marperger's *Curieuses und Reales ... Lexicon* (1731), summarized different aspects of urban agriculture such as dealing with vermin. Next to the gardens of noblemen, where new techniques were used and new species of plants were cultivated, urban gardens were also centers of innovation that imparted horticultural knowledge and practices—often preserved in tracts and journal articles—to the surrounding countryside (Düselder 2009, 23; Liebster 1984, 143). Similar to journals, printed German tracts and broadsheets from the seventeenth and eighteenth centuries are widely accessible via www.vd17.de and www.vd18.de. A searchable version of Zedler's encyclopedia can be found at www.zedler-lexikon.de. The importance of urban knowledge and practices leads to the question of what role garden areas played in the setting of the early modern city.

Needed and Disturbing: Gardens in the Urban Topography

Before 1800, a surprisingly large part of city areas within the walls of Central European cities consisted of gardens which were completed with orchards and vegetable gardens just outside the city, forming a belt of green space which corresponds to the first circle in Johann Heinrich von Thünen's ideal-type model (von Thünen 1842, 2–3; Schott 2014, 65–67). This can be observed for example in Augsburg, where a map made by Wolfgang Kilian (1581–1662) from 1626 **[Figs. 1a–b]** convincingly shows the great presence of open areas within the city, which could be cultivated or be a place of leisure and which were protected from enemies by the city walls (Roeck 1989, 490–91, 501–2). On the other hand, as early as in the sixteenth century, land in densely populated cities such as Leipzig was so expensive that only a few houses possessed small gardens (Schwarz 2016, 687), so cheap access to fruit and vegetables was strictly limited.

Urban agriculture, however, was not uncontested. Military conflicts such as the Thirty Years' War and the Napoleonic Wars led to the destruction of gardens and trees (Hofmann 2014, 150; Ahrens 2008, 558). Growing city populations with rising demand for more dwellings and the space-consuming erection of fortifications in the French style reduced open spaces as well. This was the case in many cities, for example, in Hamburg, Vienna, and Breslau (Wrocław). Although city inhabitants quickly made use of niches that the fortifications of the cities offered, and cultivated accessible soils, in cases of conflicts military purposes usually prevailed. Sometimes changes in military engineering also favored horticulture. In Braunschweig, unused ramparts were cultivated again (Moderhack 1997, 131–32) and in 1788 defortification began in Goslar, a small imperial town southeast of Hanover. There, in 1797, the city was again surrounded by 200 gardens (Werner 1967, 131–35). City councils, monarchs, and cameralist science perceived the loss of fertile land and the growing demand for food, and took countermeasures that were backed up explicitly by the growing administrative, financial, and technological capacity of the state in the Enlightenment and the goal to bring wastelands into cultivation. In Berlin, for example, King Frederick II in 1763 ordered the founding of agricultural settlements such as Wedding near the city to improve Berlin's supply of fruit and vegetables. Manure would come directly from the streets of the capital, recognizing contemporary concepts of a circular economy. The growth of the early modern city led to the extension and displacement of garden areas away from the city center, which can be well observed by comparing Berlin city maps from the seventeenth and eighteenth centuries (Aust and Stark 1992, 15–22, cf. for the digitized version: https://fbinter.stadt-berlin.de/fb/index.jsp, Historische Karten). Also in Vienna, Empress Maria Theresa and her son Joseph II made new areas for gardens in the south and southeast

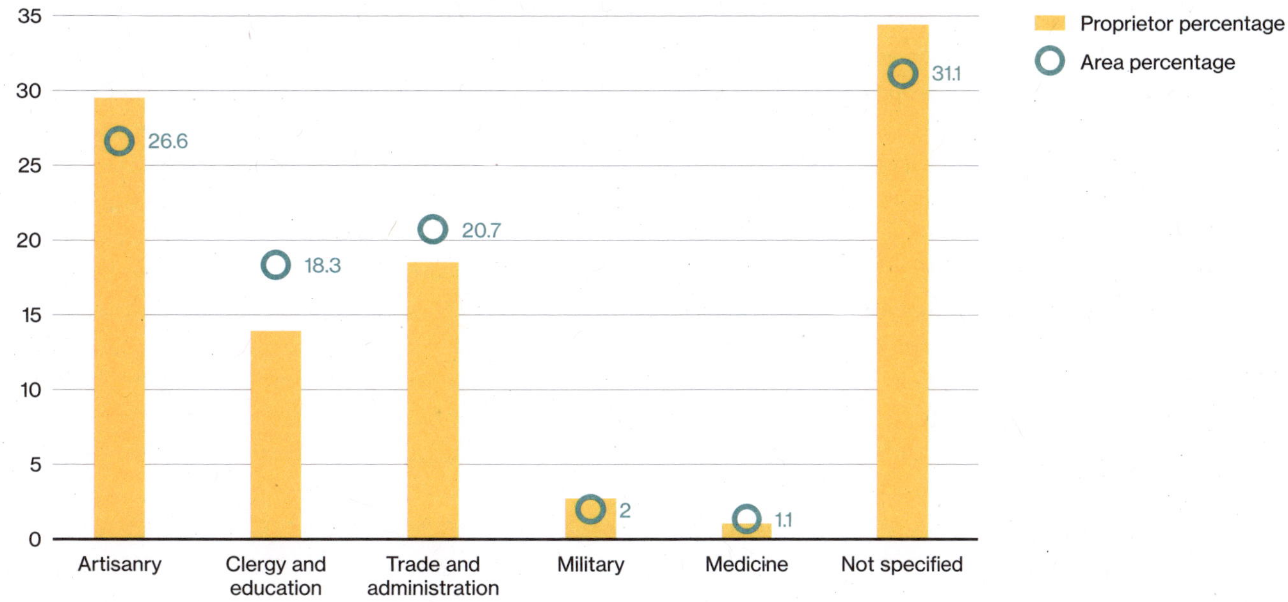

Fig. 2 Professional background of garden proprietors in Braunschweig, 1750s

of the city available, which can be observed on a military map of Lower Austria from around 1800 (Schanbacher 2019, 115–17; Peterson and Meindl 2005, 220). During the early modern period, in many cases, horticulture persisted within the cities, but often gardens in or near the cities gave way due to military or commercial interests and had to be moved to suburban areas. Such challenges for garden spaces shift the focus to the people who owned and worked in the gardens.

Patricians and Chimney Sweeps: The Social Distribution of Garden Ownership

Archival documents from the municipal archives in Braunschweig allow a closer look at the social background of garden proprietors from a medium-sized Northern German town which in 1758 had approximately 22,500 inhabitants (Pingel 1992). In the 1750s the Duke of Braunschweig, Carl I, instructed the engineer Andreas Carl Haacke to survey the city and principality of Braunschweig (Meibeyer 2008). As a result, a comprehensive land register of Braunschweig was created and has been preserved in the municipal archives (C VIII, no. 323). Apart from fields, ponds, and meadows, gardens both inside and outside the city were recorded. The total number of them, which partly exist in the same areas today, exceeded 1,200, and at least two-thirds of them can be assigned to proprietors with their occupation mentioned **[Fig. 2]**.

Most gardens belonged to craftsmen and were on average usually slightly smaller than the plots of proprietors who were not manual workers. Nevertheless, and regardless of the soil quality of the gardens, the register shows the great variety of garden ownership. Not only patricians, merchants, and lawyers had their gardens, but also day laborers, chimney sweeps, and carters. Although most gardens belonged to men—a few widows and prioresses were exceptions—and the horticultural literature mainly appealed to the male gardener, there is some evidence that wives and maids were the ones responsible for kitchen and flower gardens (Schröder-Lembke 1984, 129; Soens 2020, 23). Unfortunately, garden owners and workers provided historians with scarce information regarding the plants cultivated in their gardens.

Between Tradition and Innovation: Variations of Garden Uses

Since the Middle Ages, horticulture—usually with vegetables and herbs planted in rectangular formed beds and orchards surrounded by wicker fences (Willerding 1987, 459–60)—had begun to replace farming in and around the cities. In Nuremberg, burghers from circa 1400 onward bought farmland in the direct vicinity of the city, laying out gardens for fruit and vegetables, which they enclosed in wicker fences (Hofmann 2014, 385). But garden spaces were not always marked off. While traveling along the Rhine, the English physicist and inventor Adam Walker (1790, 53–54) noticed in Cologne: "neither hedge or ditch marks out or secures the property of the gardeners: it is all a plain, with high and foot-roads running through all parts of this vast plantation."

With regard to the usage of gardens, it is often difficult to prove the forms of cultivation in individual and subsistence gardens and distinguish agricultural from nonagricultural use. Thus, as early as in the late sixteenth century, well-to-do inhabitants of Leipzig possessed flower gardens on the outskirts of the city, which were further developed until the eighteenth century and became famous, such as Apel's Garden in the west of the city (Mundus 2016, 596; Schwarz 2016, 708–10). Books of account, inventories, diaries, and archaeological findings allow a closer look at the use of the land. Findings of weeds in soils in Göttingen indicate gardens in backyards in the city center and the use of manure (Willerding 1987, 460). In Nuremberg, the patrician Paulus Behaim ordered the planting of 25 sour cherry trees in November 1559 (Hofmann 2014, 390). Peter Lauremberg (1585–1639), the professor of medicine and author of the Latin tract *Horticultura*, possessed several gardens in Rostock. In 1628, one of his orchards alone contained 329 fruit trees, including quinces, peaches, and walnuts, and he planted a wide range of vegetables, for example cabbages, radishes, leeks, and melons (Schröder-Lembke 1984, 120–21). In the eighteenth century, too, gardens within the city had to provide food. Advertisements in papers such as the *Wirzburger Intelligenzblatt* (no. 14, February 23, 1787) exemplify this: "A garden within the city and enclosed with a wall, which possesses fruit trees of the best kind, four big cased and manured beds, a spacious summer house with a cellar and a water well with pump is for sale."

Together with the higher demand for fruit and vegetables and the spread of horticultural activity, the self-employed gardener became a profession of its own. In Augsburg and Quedlinburg, commercial horticulture existed as early as in the sixteenth century (Seitz 1984, 364). The plants cultivated in commercial gardens are better documented than in subsistence gardens. In Bamberg, a decree for the gardeners' guild from 1670 mentioned vegetables and seeds which the gardeners were allowed to sell. This list included cauliflowers, artichokes, kohlrabi, nasturtium, onions, different kinds of salad, celeriac, sugar beets, and parsnips (Scheinost 2009, 29). This survey shows the great variety of plants cultivated in home food and commercial gardens in central Europe. Here, especially the sixteenth and seventeenth centuries brought decisive changes when new plants from the Mediterranean area, Africa, and as part of the Columbian Exchange from America found their way to German territories. For these new species, botanical gardens and affluent urban plant enthusiasts such as the merchant Johann Fugger (1531–1598) from Augsburg were especially important intermediaries (Schröder-Lembke 1984, 114–15; Schmölz-Häberlein 2015, 39–42; Crosby 1973, 168–82).

Although difficult to find in archival sources, tracts on horticulture often included recommendations as to the most useful garden tools and techniques (Wimmer 2008). In the seventeenth century already, garden tools such as spades, rakes, hoes, and pruning shears had gained the forms and variety which remain the standard today **[Fig. 3]**.

However, the practices of garden work and the different plants mentioned give only indirect hints as to what happened to fruit and vegetables after they were harvested.

Mostly at Short Distance: The Trade in Fruit and Vegetables

Presumably, most fruit and vegetables which were grown in individual gardens complemented the provision of their owners and were only sold in small amounts, leaving no archival trails. Concerning agricultural flows, often only assumptions are possible; further research is necessary. Full-time or part-time commercial gardeners sold their products at greater distances, which was often made possible by waterways (von Thünen 1842, 273; Schott 2014, 66). In 1544 turnips, radishes, and parsley from Bamberg were sold in Coburg, which is 40 kilometers away in linear distance (Habel 2015, 98). As early as in the 1640s the surplus of garden products from Erfurt

Fig. 3a Petri Lavrembergii Rostochiensis, *Horticultura*, 1631

was sold in other Thuringian towns, whereas commercial gardening and the selling of plants and seeds started in the eighteenth century. Then professionals such as Christian Reichart cultivated areas close to town and exported seeds as far as Sweden and Denmark (Schaier 2009, 61). But in most cases, and similar to other European cities, fruit and vegetables reached townspeople from their direct vicinity and—as in the case of fruit in Nuremberg—foremost between September and December (Hofmann 2014, 294; Abad 2002). In the seventeenth and eighteenth centuries so-called *Kohlgärten* (cabbage gardens) near Leipzig produced cabbages, turnips, onions, and fruits (Mundus 2016, 604); since around 1750 professional gardeners from Wolfenbüttel had supplied the market in Braunschweig with fresh vegetables; and Frankfurt am Main inhabitants bought from nearby Oberrad and Sachsenhausen, where half of the taxpayers around 1750 were gardeners (Seitz 1984, 372). So distances between production and consumption were small, and seasonal fresh food easily reached the tables of the city inhabitants.

Conclusion: The Revived Appreciation of Urban Horticulture

Partly written in Latin for an explicitly European audience, but always in intellectual contact with thinkers and researchers from other European countries, German tracts represent horticultural knowledge and experiences from large parts of the continent. Although mainly aimed at the landed gentry, some treatises also referred to the urban sphere and give hints to everyday practices and the appearance of tangible components such as tools and plants. Urban gardening took place inside and outside the city and was influenced by population growth, the development of the manufacturing trade, and developments in warfare and fortification architecture. Whereas each city had its own condition, early modern horticulture in general expanded and shifted, usually with the support or pressure of the authorities, to a greater distance from the city center, a phenomenon which continued by the spread of the cities during the nineteenth and twentieth centuries. The analysis of the professional background of garden owners in eighteenth-century Braunschweig shows a broad social distribution of garden plot ownership and the inclusion of women and people from lower classes. Together with population growth and a new understanding of and esteem for nature during the Enlightenment, more proprietors used their gardens for nonagricultural activities. Nonetheless, also at the end of the eighteenth century, home food production inside the cities can be proved. Owing to the "horticultural revolution" (Soens 2020, 18), which from the end of the sixteenth century onward gave more weight to commercial gardening and the arrival of new plants from other world regions, the commercialization and diversification of horticulture intensified in the early modern period and continued until the nineteenth and twentieth centuries. This development was paralleled by an increasing market integration of horticulture, although it is hardly possible to quantify the flows of fruit and vegetables.

Finally, when looking at the place of gardens in early modern and twenty-first-century urban

Fig. 3b Petri Lavrembergii Rostochiensis, *Horticultura*, 1631 (detail)

society, one can clearly perceive more continuities than ruptures. Similar to early modern gardens, horticultural areas of the twenty-first century could become the point of origin for small but substantial innovations like the introduction of new plant species. Individual gardeners and city authorities both in the eighteenth century and today tried to enhance the land use in or near the city to increase food security, using sometimes tiny spaces of soil. Although today's gardeners can make use of industrial products and devices such as fertilizers, pesticides, and lawn mowers, they still have to work the soil and wait for the fruits to ripen. Early modern horticulturists had to manage vermin and weather extremes in a traditional way, adapted to regional conditions. Moreover, they were part of a network that reached different social strata. With the desire to combine social dialogue, recreation, and eco-friendly production of homegrown food, today's gardeners face similar challenges as their early modern counterparts, whose history and experiences are worth being considered when aiming at a sustainable horticultural food production that takes part in a circular urban economy, at a short distance to cities and their inhabitants. ■

The City as a Driver of Regional Agriculture: Erfurt and Its Horticultural Heritage

Sibylle Küttner and Frank Lohrberg

The relationship between urban development and agriculture has been a long-neglected topic within historical research. Fortunately, in recent years, this theme has begun to receive greater attention from researchers and academics, thereby highlighting the complex historical interconnections between cities, agriculture, and their food resources (for example, Daviron et al. 2019). This essay, focusing on the city of Erfurt and its unique horticultural heritage, aims to provide some additional insights into these topics. The case of Erfurt clearly demonstrates that it has not merely been a passive recipient, nourished by the agricultural produce from the surrounding hinterland. In many places throughout its history, Erfurt has played a proactive role, consciously driving the pace of agricultural development and horticultural activities on a regional scale. It has promoted and commercialized agricultural production through the development of unique trading opportunities and also through its administrative and educational systems.

The role of cities as drivers of innovation in agriculture and the highlighting of such connections in greater detail offers considerable potential for gathering new insights. This is also increasingly relevant in the present day, as in recent years, stakeholder groups in many cities have been repositioning themselves and are calling for a radical rethink of our food supply and its functioning. Erfurt shows that municipalities do not have to start from scratch, but can also draw upon traditions, collective practices, and experience.

Historical Outline

Erfurt is one of the oldest cities in Germany. By the early Middle Ages, the city had already developed into the political and economic center of the Thuringian Basin, a natural region sheltered between the low mountain ranges of the Thuringian Forest and the Harz Mountains. The region possesses a warm, dry climate and boasts fertile loess soils, making it highly favorable for agriculture. In the first documented reference from AD 742, Erfurt was described as a fortified settlement predominantly of pagan farmers. In 1133, documents specifically mention horticulture within the city for the first time, referring to a special form of agriculture that was scaled up to provision the city directly with fresh fruit and vegetables (Czekalla 2011, 271).

Erfurt developed a special interconnection with regional agriculture between the thirteenth and the seventeenth centuries. This was the period of peak production for *Färberwaid* (dyer's wood, *Isatis tinctoria*), a flowering plant whose leaves can be used for the extraction of glycoside indican, one of the few possibilities during the Middle Ages for obtaining blue dye. Stimulated by a huge demand for blue-dyed textiles, woad was cultivated in more than 300 towns and villages within the Thuringian Basin and was sold around the region's urban markets (Müllerott 1991). Due to its considerable economic power, Erfurt was able to secure the majority of the regional harvest of woad and developed into a European center of woad processing and trade, ahead of other competing towns such as

Fig. 1 How alive the memory of woad cultivation is in the Thuringian Basin is shown by the woad mill in the municipality of Ballstädt, Gotha county, which was reconstructed here and erected in 2014. In 1991, 152 original millstones still existed in the region. One of them can still be found in front of the German Horticultural Museum on the grounds of the egapark.

Arnstadt or Gotha. The City Council actively helped in this process, issuing a decree in 1351—which was probably copied from an older document—that required all farmers around Erfurt to sell their woad harvest exclusively through the main Erfurt Market (see Noll-Reinhardt 2017; Selzer 2011, 24ff.). Thus, the city merchants—so-called *Waidjunker* (woad lords)—received their supply of woad leaves from far and wide and not just from the immediate vicinity. The leaves were first ground up **[Fig. 1]**, formed into balls, and then dried for transport and storage. Despite the accompanying stench, processing and refining these semifinished products took place within the city walls (Selzer 2011, 30). The high profit margins of 25 percent for the dye, which was traded mainly to the economic centers of northern Germany and the Netherlands, apparently made the "stinking rich" woad lords so influential that stinky woad-processing was tolerated within the city center (Müllerott 1991). Large woad storehouses in Erfurt's Old Town still bear witness to this former economic phase **[Fig. 2]**. The urban wealth acquired through the woad trade certainly also played an important part in the founding of Erfurt University as early as 1392. At the beginning of the seventeenth century, the demand for woad decreased due to cheap imports of indigo from India. Farmers in the Thuringian Basin therefore had to look for new alternative crops to ensure their continued livelihoods. Although there are no detailed studies on this period of agricultural transformation, it can be assumed that parts of the agricultural production system were re-localized and returned to traditional subsistence farming for local needs. It is also interesting to note, however, that the long-standing interregional character of farming, with its emphasis on specialist commodity production, appears to have originated during the phase of woad cultivation in Erfurt. This later influenced the development of a highly commercialized and specialist horticulture in following centuries (Herz 2021, 11). In fact, the first resulting commercial market gardens can be traced back to the end of the seventeenth century. Among others, Johann Peter Haage, mentioned for the first time in 1685, founded the Erfurt horticultural dynasty Haage, which still exists today (Schalldach 2011, 76).

An important pioneer of Erfurt's commercial horticulture was the Councilor Christian Reichart (1685–1775). From today's perspective Reichart might be considered an innovative practitioner, who developed and tested numerous new horticultural methods and equipment. In particular, his method of cultivating the Erfurt speciality, *Brunnenkresse* (watercress, *Nasturtium officinale*), which is still practiced today (Fischer et al. 2017) **[Figs. 3 a–c]**. Reichart used indigenous wild watercress, turned it into a horticultural product, and thus paved the way for

Fig. 2 New uses could be found for some of the still existing former *Waidspeicher* (wood storages). The cultural use as theater, museum, or gallery predominates. The picture shows the Waidspeicher Theater, Domplatz 18.

Fig. 3a Cress cultivation at the Haage company in Dreienbrunnen, ca. 1930. Between the basins are strips for vegetable beds.

Fig. 3b Harvest on the Haage cress basin fields after modernization, ca. 1961. To increase yields, the strips between the basins were removed.

Fig. 3c Unique horticultural craft: watercress cultivation as developed by Christian Reichart in the mid-eighteenth century

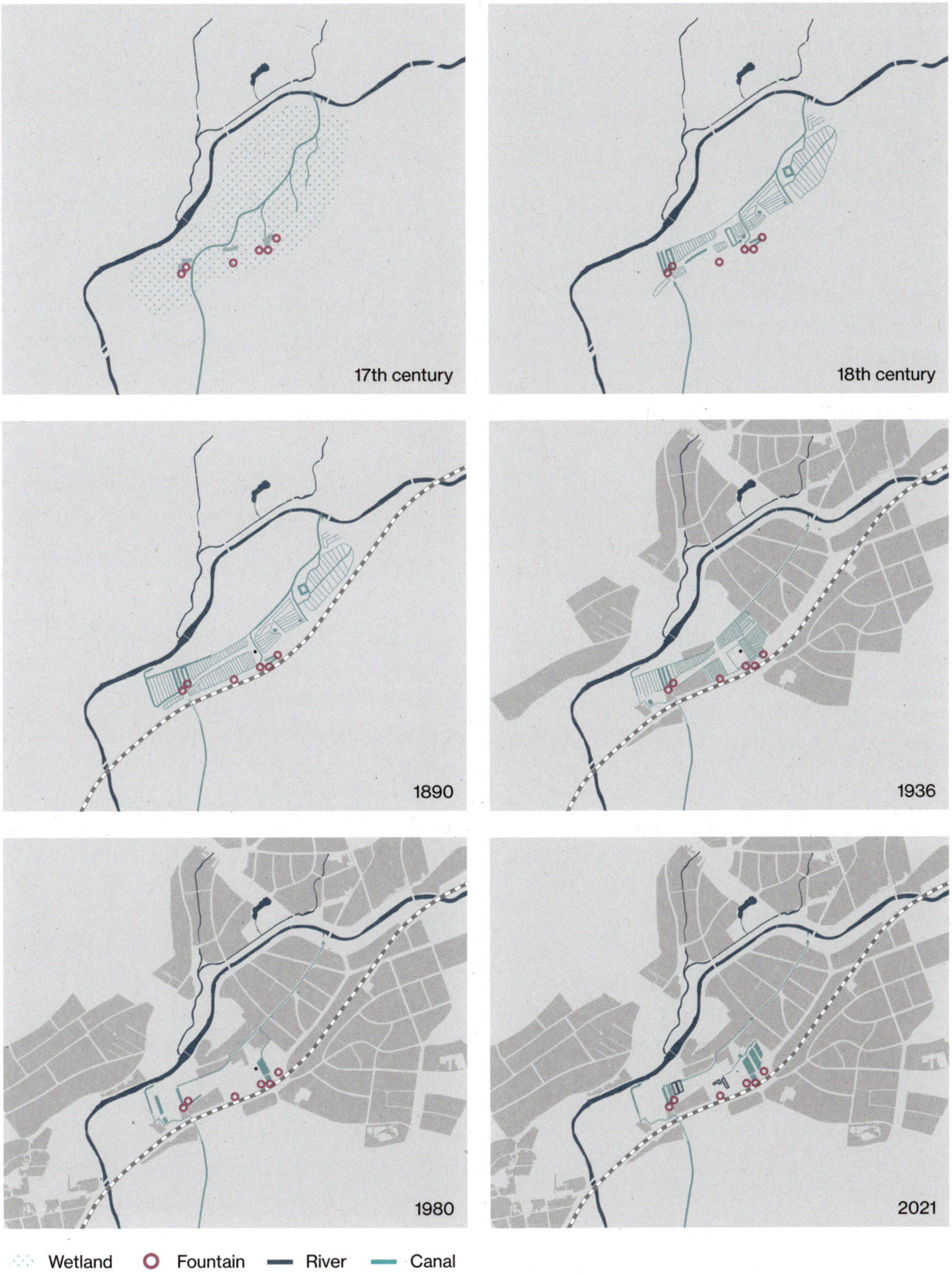

Figs. 4a–f Spatial development of cress basins, canals, and water bodies in Dreienbrunnen, seventeenth century until today

watercress to be regionally and internationally marketed as an Erfurt delicacy, which was appreciated even in ruling houses. Based on Reichart's invention, it was undertaken in long, shallow basins with fresh spring water flowing through them, the so-called *Kresseklingen* (cress basins with flowing water). The alternating parallel layout of basins and *Jähnen* (strips of land) regulates irrigation and allows the cultivation of various other vegetables. This integrated, multilayered structure proved to be very efficient and high-yielding, so that the former wetlands were gradually drained and transformed into a distinctive horticultural landscape from the eighteenth until the end of the nineteenth century **[Fig. 4]**.

In addition, Reichart's development of the 18-year, without fallow, rotation system was significant. According to this model, ten years of vegetable cultivation were followed by eight years of cultivation of various other crops (Reichart 1754). These innovations testify to his scientific approach to systematizing and optimizing local cultivation methods. He also laid the foundation for the Erfurt seed-breeding tradition with his flower and vegetable breeding programs—among other things, he acclimatized and bred cauliflower (Reichart 1753). Moreover, Reichart not only practiced but also published textbooks on horticulture, making use of the extensive publishing resources available in Erfurt. The city's postal network also offered him the opportunity to exchange scientific information with like-minded experts; within Erfurt itself, in Germany, and beyond. Seeds and cuttings were sent over great distances for this purpose. Reichart's work not only strengthened Erfurt's commercial horticulture internally, but also gave it considerable external impact through his publications and far-reaching connections (Pontius et al. 1985, Czekalla and Prass 2011).

Building on Reichart's fundamental work, Erfurt's commercial horticulture experienced its heyday in the nineteenth and early twentieth centuries. The Erfurt directory of 1894 lists 119 market gardens (Moritz 2021, 4). A large number of these specialized in the breeding of fruit, vegetables, and flowers. Over time, Reichart's postal distribution of seeds gradually developed into a profitable worldwide seed-trading business. Seed-breeding techniques benefited from the dry climate of the Thuringian Basin, which allowed the plants to retain and develop their seeds to full maturity. The seeds harvested in Erfurt were therefore of high quality and high

Fig. 5 This picture postcard from around 1910 shows a very typical postcard motif for that time: a city view of Erfurt, embedded in fields of flowers, with a woman with a basket of flowers (a gardener or flower seller) standing to the side in the foreground of the picture.

yield. Fields of flowers and vegetables blossomed and fruited all around Erfurt—an image that was also exploited by the local tourist industry for promotion of the city. In addition to its existing titles of "Cathedral City" and "Luther City," Erfurt was given the title of "City of Flowers" at the end of the nineteenth century, a title that has shaped Erfurt's self-image and is still used today **[Fig. 5]**.

The horticultural tradition was continued after 1945 under Socialist economic policies, which, in the majority of cases, were responsible for the involuntary merger of agricultural and horticultural enterprises into larger production cooperatives *Landwirtschaftliche Produktionsgenossenschaften* and *Gärtnerische Produktionsgenossenschaften* (LPG/GPG; agricultural/horticultural production cooperatives). The transformation into LPGs, GPGs and *Volkseigene Betriebe* (VEB; People's Own Enterprises) took place through a series of incremental steps between 1946 and 1979.

With the Volkseigene Gartenbaubetrieb (VEG) Saatzucht Zierpflanzen, founded in 1956, various horticultural cooperatives for fruit and vegetables, and the establishment of research and teaching institutes, Erfurt became an important center for horticulture in the GDR, especially floriculture (Czekalla 2011, 275).

A wide range of species and varieties was produced, serving markets within West Germany too.

There were also close economic ties with the countries of the former Eastern Bloc. These Eastern Bloc states not only served as potential markets for produce, but also worked in the role of production partners. Romania, for example, was home to the parent plants for chrysanthemums, whose cuttings were then grown in Erfurt. The importance of Erfurt as a center of floriculture was expressed by regular "Flower Days," which included parades of flower-decorated floats **[Fig. 6]**.

The establishment of such large cooperatives further reinforced the ongoing development and commercialization of horticulture as an important feature of Erfurt. However, the emphasis later changed from specialized niche products such as watercress toward more industrial-scale mass production. The Socialist view of modernity was also reflected in the creation of the extensive garden showground, the Internationale Gartenbauausstellung (IGA) Erfurt (International Horticultural Exhibition), which was established in 1961 (Baumann 2011). Here, periodic exhibitions took place to showcase the latest agricultural and horticultural products, machines, and techniques of the Eastern Bloc and to promote the image of the Flower City on an international stage (Karn 2011). A horticultural museum was also built on the site to highlight historical horticultural themes to a wider audience (Bischoff 2011). It is still run today as the German Horticultural Museum Foundation. Following the political upheavals of the 1990s, the nationalized enterprises were subsequently dissolved. However, some continued their work under their previous ownership; including Haage, the city's oldest remaining nursery, which was founded in 1822 and which then went on to specialize entirely in the cultivation of cacti (Schalldach 2011). The wholesale nursery N.L. Chrestensen, founded in 1867, also reestablished itself under its former ownership and continued production. However, this company has now completely stopped its own seed production and instead concentrates exclusively on sales (Blüthner 2011). Erfurt's seed-breeding tradition is now continued on a large scale by one remaining company: Rose Saatzucht.

In 2020 the Office for Economic Development recorded a total of 28 horticultural businesses within Erfurt. Despite this seemingly low number, the horticulture and foodstuff sector is still listed as one of the city's five key economic sectors. In addition to the city's long-standing horticultural tradition and the existence of the large associated companies, the skilled labor supply available in Erfurt is also cited as providing a locational advantage for the city.

Much of this labor force has been trained by the local Teaching and Research Institute, the neighboring University of Applied Sciences (including departments of horticulture, landscape architecture, and forestry) and the Research Centre for Horticultural Crops (Landeshauptstadt Erfurt 2021; Landeshauptstadt Erfurt 2011). Erfurt can therefore still be considered as a center of competence for horticulture.

Fig. 6 Flower Days Parade 1958: float with a cauliflower tower

Celebrating the Horticultural Tradition

Erfurt is well aware of its special horticultural traditions. Street names refer to the great gardening dynasties; indeed, Christian Reichart is still considered one of the city's most important sons. His work has been commemorated since 1867 by a monument located within a prominent public space (Kahl 1985) **[Fig. 7]**. Furthermore, an additional monument was erected in front of the horticultural school in Leipziger Straße (now the Landscape and Horticultural College) to mark the 300th anniversary of Reichart's birth in 1985.

However, a more comprehensive assessment of Erfurt's unique horticultural legacy—especially within the context of the Socialist economic system of the GDR—has yet to be fully undertaken. During the preparations for the 2021 Federal Horticultural Show (BUGA), the theme was resurrected by Erfurt's Economic Development Department. Indeed, the horticultural tradition has been chosen as the main theme of the show, including the cultivation of vegetable varieties grown in Erfurt and a special exhibition in the German Horticultural Museum celebrating the history of Erfurt's horticultural businesses.

It is to be hoped that a heightened awareness of Erfurt's horticultural legacy will also lead to the emergence of more sensitive urban development policies. Erfurt has applied several times for listed status as a UNESCO World Heritage Site, with a particular focus on the outstanding historic buildings in the Old Town, including its ancient surviving medieval synagogue. Despite this, a similar policy has yet to be adopted for its unique horticultural heritage.

Some of the historic woad warehouses have, however, been renovated and put to new uses, such as municipal galleries. In addition, the Garden Show grounds of the former IGA are also now listed. Despite this, fertile horticultural land on the outskirts of the city continues to be steadily consumed through incremental urban development. Meanwhile, horticultural businesses experience difficulties and a lack of support to maintain their production areas, or indeed, to lease new ones. Through such a lack of support, historic gems such as Reichart's watercress fields have been neglected and misappropriated.

It therefore remains to be seen how Erfurt's horticultural tradition can not only be documented but also maintained and developed as a living heritage for the benefit of its residents. Does Erfurt's horticulture then have a future?

Perhaps the best solution to this question can be found in Erfurt itself. For example, private efforts maintain the last remaining Kresseklinge and the unique horticultural craftsmanship, while a crowdfunding campaign has been launched to revive this cultivation tradition in an adjoining basin (Riehm 2021).

Fig. 7 The Reichart monument, erected in 1867 on the Anger, at its second location on a green strip on the Wilde Gera between Vogelsbrücke and Grimmigbrücke

Fig. 8 Prospective Erfurt horticulture, a mood board of an innovative mixed-use approach developed by Jay Heydecke in his master's thesis

Furthermore, a master's thesis by Jay Heydecke, supervised by the Institute of Landscape Architecture at RWTH Aachen University, has recently illustrated/carved out the significance of watercress cultivation within the city of Erfurt. Based on historical analysis, it proposes strategies to preserve this legacy and develop this cultural heritage as a driver or focal point for sensitive approaches to sustainable urban planning. It outlines ways to further develop and complement former production sites and traditional cultivation techniques, and introduces the transfer of knowledge to younger generations as a winning approach in order to implement the meaning of the watercress cultivation as an urban agricultural heritage in urban planning concepts and to strengthen Erfurt's awareness of its rich horticultural history. In an exemplary design to the former watercress hotspot Dreienbrunnen (three-well area), educational, productional, and recreational functions are merged by means of a living museum and transparent horticultural production processes, forming a versatile green public space integrated into the city's fabric.

In particular, the thesis emphasizes the importance of increasing the adaptability to changing socio-cultural and economic contexts in order to preserve the city's urban agricultural heritage and its tangible and intangible components. Heydecke's work proposes approaches to launch and promote bottom-up initiatives and to combine them with city-led strategic planning measures which have the impact to send a clear signal to the urban population and thus revive public interest and encourage citizens to participate **[Fig. 8]**.

It is to be hoped that such civil society initiatives and academic activities will help Erfurt's horticulture to reinvent itself and thus create a unique and innovative profile for the city—it would certainly not be for the first time in Erfurt's long history. ■

The Role of Centralized Policy Planning for Bulgarian Urban Agricultural Heritage from the Socialist Period

Dona Pickard

Contemporary urban agriculture in Bulgaria has been driven by bottom-up citizens' initiatives since the beginning of the 2010s, and no top-down policies on urban agriculture have been implemented so far. The dominant discourse on urban agriculture views it as a novelty, driven by postmaterialist values for environmental sustainability and social cohesion (Koleva and Pickard 2015). Little attention is paid to the predemocratic history of urban agriculture, probably because it is all too easy to dismiss the practices that resulted from totalitarian rule, to which there are too many obvious objections related to centralized power and the often oppressive regime. On the other hand, many of the urban agriculture demands that citizens have toward policymakers today correspond to policies implemented by the regime before 1989, which included agriculture in its vision of a modern Socialist city. Undoubtedly, the social dynamic was much different then—urban agriculture policies from the beginning of the 1970s were dictated by the need to ensure a regular supply of fresh food to citizens in urban centers that grew fast and drew human resources from the countryside (Fol et al. 1981, 452–62). Thus policies that fostered practices of urban agriculture were not based on environmental or social values, but regardless of the motives behind them, they indirectly led to such results.

Three goals that urban agriculture activists have today and were enacted during the Socialist regime are presented here. They can give clues as to how they can affect the contemporary urban communities in Bulgaria. This is done on the basis of data gathered during the research project Urban Agriculture as a Strategy for Improving the Quality of Life of Urban Communities (2016–20, funded by the Bulgarian National Science Fund) and a desktop study of archival documents.

The key demand concerning urban agriculture that civil society has of policymakers today and which has not been met, is to legally recognize urban agriculture as a public priority. What the activists want is a legal act or an article in existing municipality bills that defines urban agriculture as an activity with public benefits, hence eligible for public support. Astonishingly, in Socialist Bulgaria such legal acts were introduced as early as 1963. They stated that "every acre of land" (State Gazette [SG] 1963), including the land in the urban peripheries, along rivers and canals, around airfields, and on the grounds of schools and enterprises, needs to be put to full use by people for personal use, contributing to the households' food self-sufficiency (SG 1963; SG 1978a; SG 1978b; SG 1982; SG 1987).

The land was to be given out to individuals and households by demand and for free, "for eternal use, 1 to 2 decares [1,000–2,000 square meters] per household" (SG 1963). This right of use was to be transferred to their heirs, provided they continued to cultivate it. If any plot of land was not cultivated for two years, the regional institutions were responsible for taking it away from its users. Users had to observe strictly the officially outlined good practices for protecting the land from erosion and pollution; there were also set norms for animal welfare and veterinarian and hygienic standards.

Figs. 1a–b Private peri-urban vegetable and fruit garden near Sofia in 1976 at the time of constructing a small cottage on the plot

Until the end of the 1970s these lands could not be built upon and had to be dedicated only to agricultural activities, which corresponds to the modern demands of urban agriculture activists to protect agricultural land from construction works.

The regulations that were passed from the 1960s to the 1980s made it possible for a large share of urban dwellers to obtain a plot of land for food production in peri-urban areas. As the policies addressed all family holdings, already existing household gardens and micro-farms, which were very common inside many cities (Yoveva and Mishev 2001, 14), were also covered by these new policies, including new norms and standards ensuring that every food producer, no matter how small and whether they produced only for their family, had access to good quality seeds, breeding animals, and agricultural services.

This policy line was built upon until the end of the 1980s and led to the creation of self-organized communities in the newly created allotment areas. In the peripheries of large cities, the state provided land, but the tasks of drilling water wells, getting connected to the electricity network, and building roads and other community facilities were organized by the new plot owners, who often democratically chose managers and treasurers of the community activities. Unlike the family gardens on private land within cities, those new territorial formations developed stronger social cohesion. From the end of the 1970s, when building houses on the plots was allowed and when the land could be bought from the state, these plots gradually lost their food production primary role and in the long run, in most cases, turned to residential and recreational areas. Older interviewees share their observations that the communities they built have now disintegrated as younger generations are not interested in tending the plots and either sell them off or keep them as summer houses without maintaining close connections with the neighbors **[Figs. 1a–b]**.

A second demand that bottom-up initiatives have toward policymakers in Bulgaria today is to ensure not only land, but also materials for agriculture—soil, seeds, tools, etc. especially for socially responsible initiatives such as educational or socially integrative urban gardens. To provide such materials and support, the Socialist regime set in its decrees a responsibility of state agricultural holdings and local institutions to include in their yearly plans additional amounts of seeds, fruit trees, fertilizers and chemicals, animal feed, veterinarian products, as well as the needed advisory and veterinarian services for private gardens and farms. Additionally, to secure the "faster introduction of new technologies, highly productive animal breeds and plant hybrids as well as other achievements of the scientific and technological progress in agriculture" (SG 1982), research institutions had to extend their knowledge and services to all holdings, including small family ones. Although this regulation was not specifically targeted at urban agricultural holdings, they made use of it just as much as the rural ones. Special attention was given to creating experimental fields in schools where pupils could learn through experience. With such state support and official policies, there was no place to dwell on the question of whether agriculture belongs to cities or not. Of course, the lack of pluralism in the vision of how urban communities should develop cannot be commended. But the present situation is also not one that gives great freedom to unconventional urban development visions, in this case, to ones that include urban agriculture as part of the urban environment. Today, urban agriculture in schools and kindergartens has no policy protection from neighbors who object to the "rural" nature of agriculture and the sight of vegetables and compost bins where they feel only low-cut grass and flowers are appropriate. Even scientific forms of urban agriculture are neglected today, an example being the Forestry University experimental field on the outskirts of Sofia, which lost a large chunk of its area to a new road junction and has been waiting for the municipality to keep its promise to build a fence along the new border since 2017. Still, this field exists and performs its urban agricultural role today, as do a few other academic agricultural fields around Sofia, Plovdiv, and some other towns in the country **[Fig. 2]**.

A third demand that seems elusive at present, is for urban agriculture to be integrated as fully as possible in urban planning and other sectors, such as educational institutions, green infrastructure, providing fresh food for company canteens, etc. It seems elusive because of a general disagreement between different actors about the compatibility of agriculture with the characteristics of the modern city. In the time of centralized party policy, it was easier to act on the ambition to industrialize agriculture and make it modern and innovative by resting it on the urban industrialization wave. What this means is that agriculture was squeezed into every niche, where it could use the advantage of interaction with compatible activities as the state was the common owner of all enterprises. A famous example is building greenhouses at thermal power stations in cities to utilize the available energy for heating these facilities. One of the first hydroponic systems in Bulgaria was developed in the greenhouses of Bulgarplod, the state vegetable and fruit production and processing enterprise, and built at the thermal power station Sofia, just north of the capital city center. By 1979 there were 70 decares of six-meter-tall glass and steel greenhouses heated by the thermal station. Today only a few of those greenhouses remain, and they are let out to private businesses **[Fig. 3]**.

Fig. 2 The Forestry University experimental field's cows risk being run over by the heavy traffic along the new road that cut through its territory without the fence along the new border having been reinstated by the municipality.

Fig. 3 Cucumber production at the Sofia thermal power station greenhouse, 1981

Cities became agri-science centers with a focus on veterinarian science, plant and animal genetics, soil research, and agricultural technology research and development. It must be said that urban agriculture was not specifically the aim, but resources of the urban centers were deliberately used—the urban research institutes employed workers and highly skilled and experienced researchers from the cities.

The industrialization of the cities also led to a concentration of workers, changing the food needs of large settlements. The capital city's hinterland was subjected to a climate and soil analysis which served as the basis to specialize the region in the production of carrots, leeks, cauliflowers, cabbages,

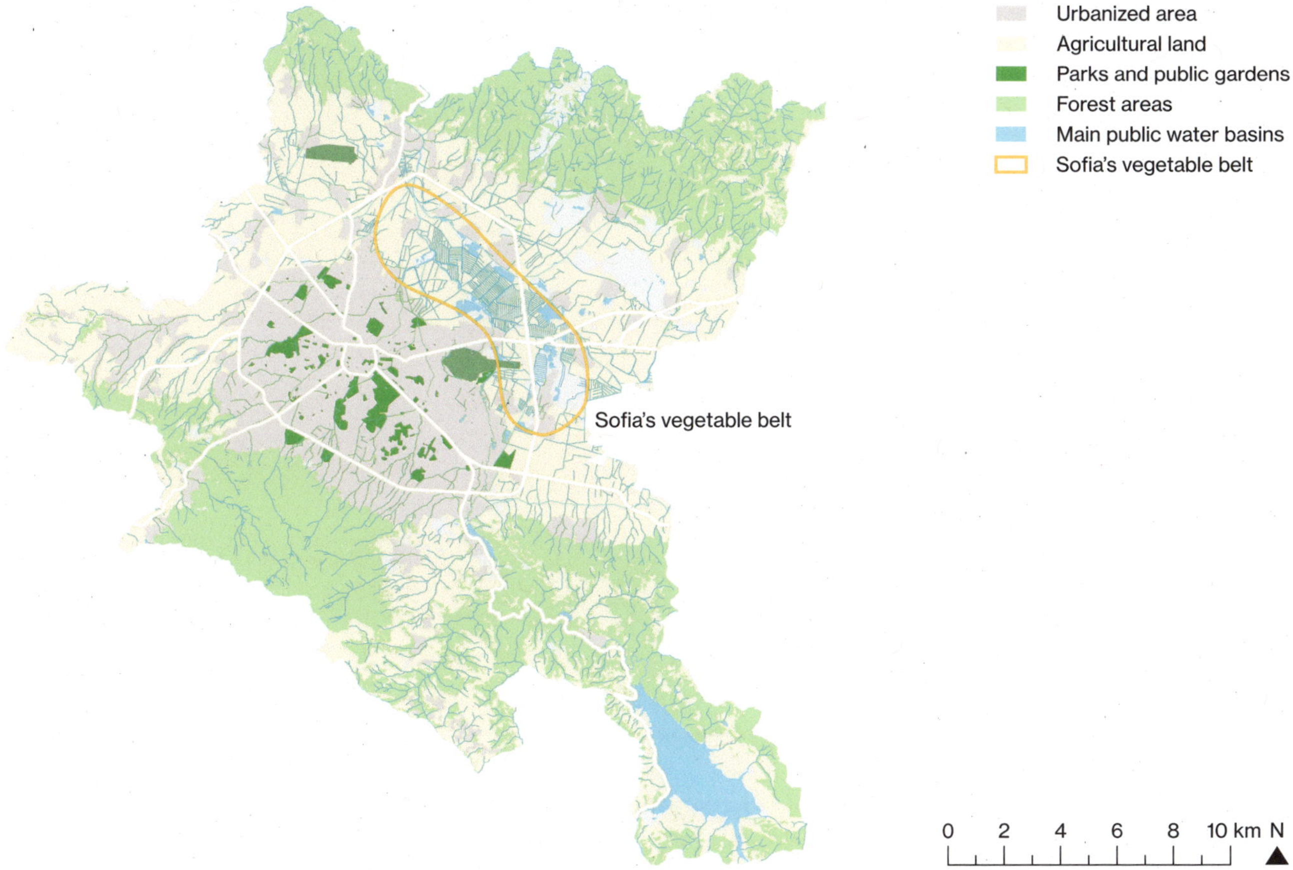

Fig. 4 Agricultural land and Sofia's green belt

and strawberries, as well as developing a dairy sector to provide for the needs of the city. The area that was dedicated to this agricultural production was called the "vegetable belt of Sofia." It covered the northeast periphery of the city and was managed by agro-industrial complex in Sredets **[Fig. 4]**.

It was common practice for all Socialist agricultural holdings to use seasonal workers recruited from high schools or state enterprises—groups of students or workers who spent a few days to a few weeks of their holidays or off work on the farm picking fruit, helping with cultivation, etc. At the end of the 1990s the land within the old vegetable belt was restituted to its pre–Socialist era owners and today is used mainly for monoculture cereal production.

Looking back at the totalitarian history of urban agriculture in Bulgaria demonstrates that integrating agriculture into the fabric of the cities could have positive social effects on the urban communities, as well as increased efficiency when combining agriculture with other compatible economic activities. The policies of the Socialist regime that stimulated the development of urban agriculture are very controversial and guided by complex motifs that cannot be analyzed here, and we can definitely not propose their direct implementation today. On the other hand, they provide a lesson as to the many ways in which urban agriculture can fit into the daily rhythm of the city, which can be in line with a contemporary democratic policymaking process. Most urban agriculture practices that were thriving in the Socialist city have died out and very little living urban agricultural heritage from that period can be found at present. Still, their legacy can teach policymakers today that top-down support and protection of urban agriculture could contribute to the quality of urban life and the urban environment through improving social cohesion and food security, and boosting optimal use of resources in different economic sectors. Focusing on the benefits might help build a vision of future urban development that transcends the fear of unwanted political connotations and builds upon a discontinued tradition with proven positive impacts. ■

Heritage at the Urban Fringe: Allotment Gardening in Europe as Urban Agricultural Heritage

Attila Tóth

Allotment Gardens and Industrial Revolution Hand in Hand

The origins of urban allotment gardening in Europe date to the end of the eighteenth and first half of the nineteenth century, when the first allotments were established in the United Kingdom (1795), followed by Prussia/Germany (1814), Denmark (1821), and the Netherlands (1838). This trend continued in Luxembourg (1886), Sweden (1895), Belgium and France (1896), Poland (1897), Finland (1900), Austria (1904), among others, especially Western and Central European countries (Keshavarz and Bell 2016). The allotments' origin is strongly linked to the Industrial Revolution, which caused a rapid and often unplanned and unregulated growth of industrial towns and cities, which were a sprawling mix of industry, housing, railway corridors, canals, and other infrastructure elements (Hall and Tewdwr-Jones 2010, 11–26). These cities offered poor environmental and living conditions (King 2007, 47–49; Bell et al. 2016, 1–7), accompanied by lack of fresh food (Keshavarz and Bell 2016, 8). During industrialization, a significant part of the poor and landless rural population moved to modern industrial cities for work, which by Barthel et al. (2013) is referred to as the "transformation from feudal agrarianism to urban industrialism." The need for food was growing together with the expanding urban population, while the food transport system was not fully able to cover this new and more concentrated demand for food in urban areas (Grantham 1989; Keshavarz and Bell 2016, 11).

While the need for fresh food was one of the major drivers for the establishment of allotment gardens, urban residents also had important social and cultural motivations for establishing and using allotments. One of the main cultural aspects was that formerly rural agricultural workers who moved from the countryside to industrial cities for work in factories did not have the mindset to fully abandon agricultural activity, which was part of their identity and culture (Tóth et al. 2018, 165). In most countries, from the very beginning, allotments were recognized and supported also for their pedagogical function (Duží et al. 2014, 98) and health benefits (Keshavarz and Bell 2016, 16). As a result of these

Fig. 1 An allotment garden in Stockholm, Sweden, in 1915

processes in urban society, allotment gardens appeared at the urban fringes and in the vicinity of factories, and gradually became integral and characteristic components of industrialized cities in the nineteenth century (Van den Berg et al. 2010) [Fig. 1].

The Rise of Allotment Gardens across Europe from the Late Eighteenth to the Early Twentieth Century

Keshavarz and Bell (2016) identified four main development phases of urban allotment gardening in Europe:

1. Industrialization (1700–1910)
2. The world wars and Great Depression (1911–50)
3. Postwar decline (1951–72)
4. The revival of urban allotment gardens (since 1973)

Having been one of the main functions of urban allotment gardening during the abovementioned phase of industrialization, during the world wars and economic depression, food production gained further importance. During this phase, allotments as well as other urban green spaces and brownfields functioned as pure kitchen gardens for citizens.

The first allotment site established in the United Kingdom was located at Long Newnton and was followed by an allotment garden in Kappeln, Germany, established by the priest Christian Friedrich Heinrich Schröder (1744–1818), who divided some church land into small plots and leased them to the poor to grow their own food. After the death of popular orthopedist and outdoor exercise advocate Moritz Schreber (1808–1861), a gardening association with 100 family gardens was created along a playground in Leipzig and named after Schreber. This name became popular and widespread and since then *Schrebergärten* has been used as a synonym for allotment gardens in German-speaking countries.

From the beginning of the twentieth century, allotments continued to develop in other countries across Europe too, and gradually became characteristic components of most urban (fringe) landscapes [Fig. 2]. In the early twentieth century, war- and poverty-induced gardening campaigns were initiated in the USA (Lawson 2005, 111–22) and influenced

Fig. 2 Allotments at the interface of industry and housing at a factory in Duisburg, Germany

Europe during both world wars and the economic depression, when allotments were implemented as an effective solution to hunger and unemployment in many European countries (Glotter 2007, 22–30). Allotments also developed in the new states that had been founded after World War I, for instance in Czechoslovakia, where garden colonies were established in the 1920s in Prague, in addition to allotments in other towns and cities across the region (Tvardková and Rolfová 2013; Tóth et al. 2018, 161–66).

Allotment Garden Associations as Intangible Heritage

Urban allotment gardening developed hand in hand with local and national associations (known under different names, such as allotment societies, clubs, leagues, federations, unions, councils, among others) that have persisted to this day and have grown into significant intangible heritage over time. They have helped urban allotment gardening to evolve and continue to support it. Allotment associations had an organized and hierarchical structure and played an important role in the self-organization of the new urban working class. National associations have had an important role in organizing nationwide educational events with practical training, as well as exhibitions, competitions, annual meetings, and award ceremonies. They have been active in establishing a distinctive social status for allotment gardening and gardeners, for instance through publishing their own periodical publications, magazines, or even television shows. Local associations have been important mainly in organizing small-scale and less formal meetings for defining common rules, sharing knowledge and experience, organizing voluntary brigade work, exchanging garden products, and networking.

Thanks to local and national associations, allotment gardeners have developed their own identity and sense of belonging. The associations' organizational structure developed both top-down and bottom-up, depending on the overall political and societal system. Allotment associations, with their long-term history, societal significance, and widespread presence, can be considered an important intangible heritage element of urban agriculture in Europe. They have made allotments visible in the public life at local, regional, national, or even international levels, constituted a platform for the formation and development of collective memory and practices, and provided ways of organization and self-government.

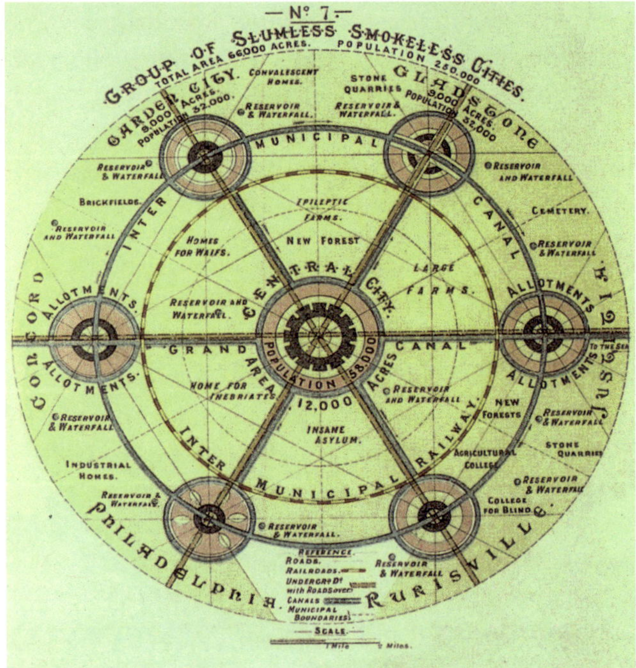

Fig. 3 The Garden City concept by Ebenezer Howard (1850–1928)

Allotment Gardens and Their Legacy in Urban Planning

Beside local allotment movements and national associations, allotments also made their way into the formal planning system and professional planning and design practice. Late nineteenth and early twentieth-century architects and urban planners alongside engaged politicians and philanthropic factory owners were looking for novel urban planning models to reshape industrialized cities and improve their environment (Hall and Tewdwr-Jones 2011, 27–54; Keshavarz and Bell 2016, 8–17). Allotment gardens were featured in the broader visions about the place of nature in cities (Drilling et al. 2016). Perhaps one of the most famous concepts was Ebenezer Howard's *Garden Cities* published as *To-Morrow: A Peaceful Path to Real Reform* (1898) and reprinted as *Garden Cities of To-Morrow* (1902). Howard's Garden City diagram clearly indicates that allotments were considered an integral part of an ideal garden city **[Fig. 3]**.

After 1945, when Europe divided into East and West, planners in both parts still included allotments in urban plans and planning concepts as an important component of cities. However, planners in the West did so only until the economic situation recovered and started flourishing again. After that they gradually lost interest in allotment gardens, as did gardeners themselves. This was mainly because allotments were associated with poverty, crisis, charity, and wartime needs. Western allotments shifted their focus from mere self-sufficiency to active recreation in second homes with summer houses and hobby gardens. Conversely, in countries of the Eastern Bloc, the development of allotments took a rather different course. Allotments were included in the Soviet Food Program and information campaigns were organized to promote food growing in allotments and collective (cooperative) gardens. Allotments complemented the centralized food supply by the state that often turned out to be inefficient, resulting in chronic food shortages. They enriched the offer of fresh food by selling surpluses and supplying the state with scarce horticultural commodities (Tóth et al. 2018, 167). Just as important was the recreational function of allotments in the context of limited traveling options and the lack of private or semiprivate open spaces in the large-scale housing estates in which a significant part of urban residents lived.

In Socialist countries, allotments were strongly influenced by centrally regulated planning and standardized design (166–68). Especially allotments established in the 1970s (the so-called Normalization period) reflect the intentions of the government to unify design morphology and features of allotments (Dekánek, 1971; Tóth et al. 2018, 168) **[Fig. 4]**. In the 1950s and 1960s, allotments were included in municipal zoning plans, while also highlighting their importance for recreation, well-being, and motivation to work. Allotments had therefore gained importance and allotment associations were integrated into the national, centrally organized political framework (Tóth et al. 2018, 167).

Allotment Gardens as Urban Agricultural Heritage Sites

Allotment gardens as a specific form of urban agriculture in Europe have become important cultural heritage with tangible and intangible heritage elements. According to Branduini et al. (2016), tangible heritage of urban agricultural landscape pertains to its material elements, historical authenticity, and physical permanence through time. Intangible heritage of urban agricultural landscapes, on the other hand, pertains to the significance attributed by people to specific places, techniques, and skills that have enabled the creation of urban agricultural landscapes and to features dictated by economic and behavioral factors.

In light of this definition, the tangible heritage of urban allotment gardens can be observed and perceived at three different levels and scales—the urban landscape scale, the allotment colony scale, and the allotment parcel scale:

1. At the scale of urban landscape, the heritage value of allotments consists in the fact that they have a long-term physical permanence in the urban fringe and as such have coformed its visual and structural character for decades. Allotments were usually located at the edges and in the gaps of the built environment and were later enclosed by residential areas, railways, highways, and other infrastructure elements (Appel et al. 2011, 23–24). Nowadays many of these allotments can be

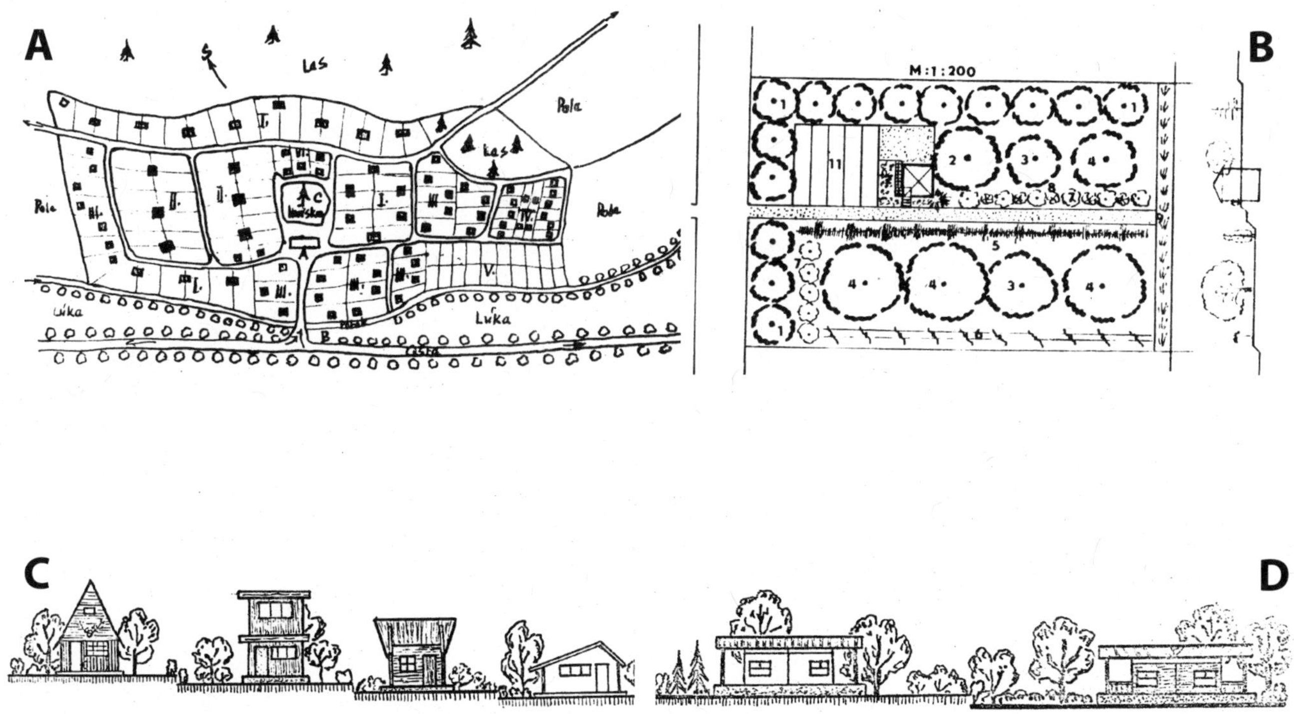

Fig. 4 Czechoslovakian allotment planning in the 1970s: recommended models of a site plan (A) and planting design (B); sketches of unsuitable/diverse (C) and suitable/unified (D) cottage architecture

Fig. 5 Allotment settlement Mojšová Lúčka, near Žilina in Slovakia, with intensive terraced gardens on a slope with characteristic retaining stone walls, allotment cottages, greenhouses, and fruit trees

found as a disconnected ring around the historic city center or as part of urban green corridors (Tóth and Timpe 2017, 208–10). Allotments were located in areas that were unsuitable for other forms of urban land use, especially housing, for example along heavy traffic roads or railways (Drescher et al. 2006, 8), as well as along urban rivers, where there was a long-term flood risk (Tóth et al. 2018, 173). Allotment gardens have a characteristic compositional configuration and layout within the urban fabric (Costa et al. 2016). They are spatially highly articulated, certain in shapes and division, and highly variable in visual features of allotment parcels. Allotments represent (peri-)urban vernacular landscapes that can be well recognized and perceived when entering a town or a city both on railroad and road. Setting this spatial and visual manifestation into a wider urban planning context as described in the previous section, allotments can be perceived as unique physical and visual evidence of urban development, especially throughout the twentieth century. Allotment sites from the nineteenth and early twentieth centuries are usually not at the urban fringe anymore, as the city has grown around them. Such preserved open land fragments, with characteristic inner spatial organization, can be understood as a testimony to the local site-specific history.

2. At the allotment colony scale, typical features include a planned road/path network; an overall landscape pattern, unified size of parcels and plots, and orientation of parcels toward the path/road, as well as a distinct building line of cottages that is characteristic especially in centrally planned allotment colonies with standardized layout. The heritage character consists in the overall spatial organization and systematic distribution of repeating physical features—including both built structures (traditional cottage architecture, crafted fences of unified height, etc.) and vegetation structures (traditional tree, shrub, and perennial species, annual crops, and flowers, etc.). Allotment sites are unique local landscapes with well-articulated spatial patterns and a well-balanced combination of uniformity and diversity.

3. At the allotment parcel scale, the tangible heritage of allotments consists in their overall spatial layout and division, the architecture of small buildings on the parcels, and the plants cultivated. Allotment parcels usually have a regular and geometrically organized inner layout divided into smaller parts and plots. Allotments located on slopes are characteristic with retaining walls built by allotment users themselves or within cooperative voluntary brigades **[Fig. 5]**. Architectural elements in the parcels include cottages that can be highly variable in their visual features, ranging from rather informal vernacular forms to centrally planned and regulated unified cottages of the same size, shape, and type, as well as garden sheds and greenhouses. Characteristic plants cultivated in the parcels are fruit trees (solitary trees, groups of trees, alleys, shaped and pruned fruit trees growing on espaliers/cordons), crops and vegetables cultivated on arable plots, and vines cultivated on pergolas and other constructions. Plant species grown in allotments include traditional and heirloom local varieties and represent an important genetic heritage (Supuka et al. 2013; Gilbert 2013) continuously transmitted by allotment gardeners throughout time. Also, the multifunctionality of allotments can be perceived as a heritage feature, since allotments from the very beginning combined several functions, especially growing food with recreation, which is physically manifested on a diverse mosaic of different land uses within the parcel.

An allotment garden as a physical space consists of the abovementioned physical components and tangible heritage features. These are strongly interlinked with intangible heritage of allotment gardens that consists in local stories, memories, the social dimension of collective gardening, sharing and processing common goods, and organization into and by associations. The practices, experiences, and social interactions accommodated by an allotment garden, as well as meanings and memories attached to it, significantly contribute to its character as a lived space and accordingly to the local identity of its physical context. Urban allotment gardens are living heritage sites as gardening practices are still in place, although to a smaller extent than before. Their evolution is still in progress. While there was a decline of the food-growing function of allotments at the end of the twentieth and beginning of the twenty-first centuries, in light of contemporary urban society with a growing awareness of food self-sufficiency and healthy nutrition, the food-growing function of allotments has seemed to gain in popularity once again. Outdoor recreation in urban allotments strongly linked with growing food for self-consumption has become the lifestyle of a significant community. Allotments remain important social hubs, where urban residents spend time with their families and friends and interact with their neighbors. Thanks to a high plant species diversity, allotments have gained additional significance from the perspective of supporting pollinators, enhancing urban biodiversity, and contributing to urban green infrastructure (Borysiak et al. 2017).

In addition to the new interest in food production, allotment gardens in Western Europe also function as places of integration for migrants, who culturally enrich the colonies and find a way into local social life through their participation in allotment gardening (Maćkiewicz et al. 2021). This builds upon the important social role of allotments, which historically helped establish new urban communities.

Allotments should be recognized for their historical significance, heritage values, and multifunctional land use, and should be preserved for future urban generations as a historical legacy of urban food growing, recreation, community life, and urban development in Europe. ■

Russian Dachas: A Popular Urban Agricultural Heritage

Johanna Altendorf, Jay Heydecke, Katharina Christenn, and Axel Timpe

Dachas are pieces of land with a small house used for growing vegetables and fruit by private citizens. They are organized in gardening cooperatives or associations and located on the outskirts of almost all Russian cities [Fig. 1]. The word *dacha* is the colloquial umbrella term for different structures of urban gardening plots [Fig. 4], varying according to their level of agricultural and recreational functions.

A spatial analysis of St. Petersburg and its surroundings [Fig. 2] can help estimate their significance for the urban population. Dachas are usually located beyond walking distance from residential areas, so owners have to rely on cars or trains to reach them. Those located up to 50 kilometers from the city center and within a one-hour drive enable frequent visits and maintenance. The more distant plots located up to 120 kilometers and two and a half hours from the city are mainly used on weekends, those even further away only during holidays.

Based on geoinformation extracted from OpenStreetMap, the total area of gardening cooperatives and associations within a 120-kilometer radius around St. Petersburg comprises 830 square kilometers. Dividing this by a standard allotment size of 600 square meters, we can calculate around 1.3 million plots. In correlation to the roughly 7 million inhabitants within the radius and an average household size of 2.6 persons (Statista 2019), it can be estimated that half of the urban population has direct access to gardening plots. Confirmed by other research studies (Semyonov 2017), this demonstrates the general popularity of dachas.

Historical Development

The history of the dacha (from Russian verb *dat'*, "to give") starts in the early eighteenth century, when Tsar Peter the Great built his summer palace outside of St. Petersburg and granted large estates to his closest aristocratic courtiers to enjoy the garden as a place for arts and beauty, but also for agricultural research and innovation [Fig. 3]. Industrialization toward the end of the nineteenth century then led to the first dacha boom: new gardens were organized as allotments and distributed to the bourgeoisie such as industrialists and storekeepers as a way to ensure their loyalty toward the tsar and control the political power (Rumjanzewa 2015,10–12).

Fig. 1 Gardening cooperative "Chimic-1," Pereslavsky District, Yaroslavl Oblast

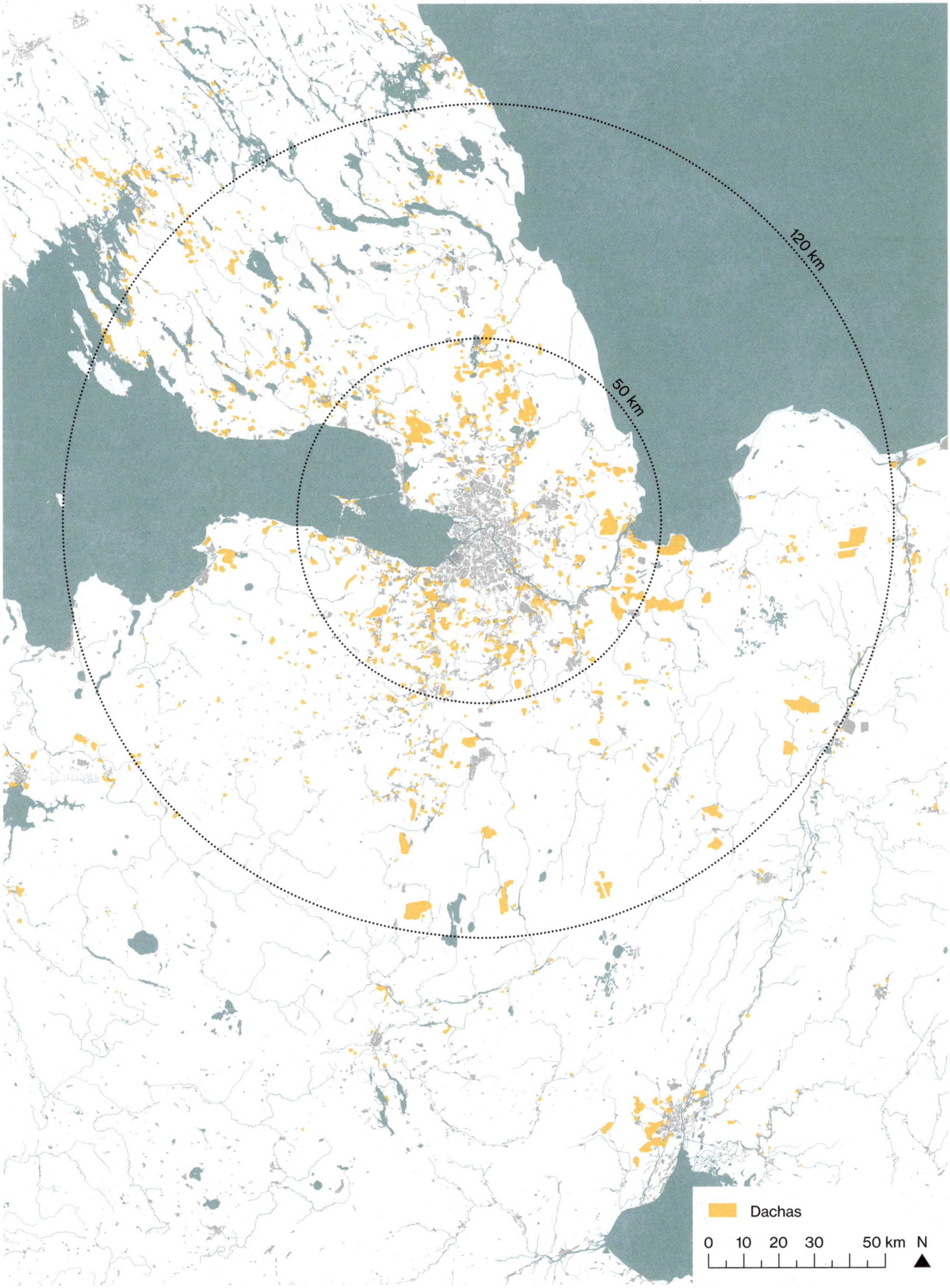

Fig. 2 St. Petersburg and surroundings divided into distances from city center to dacha

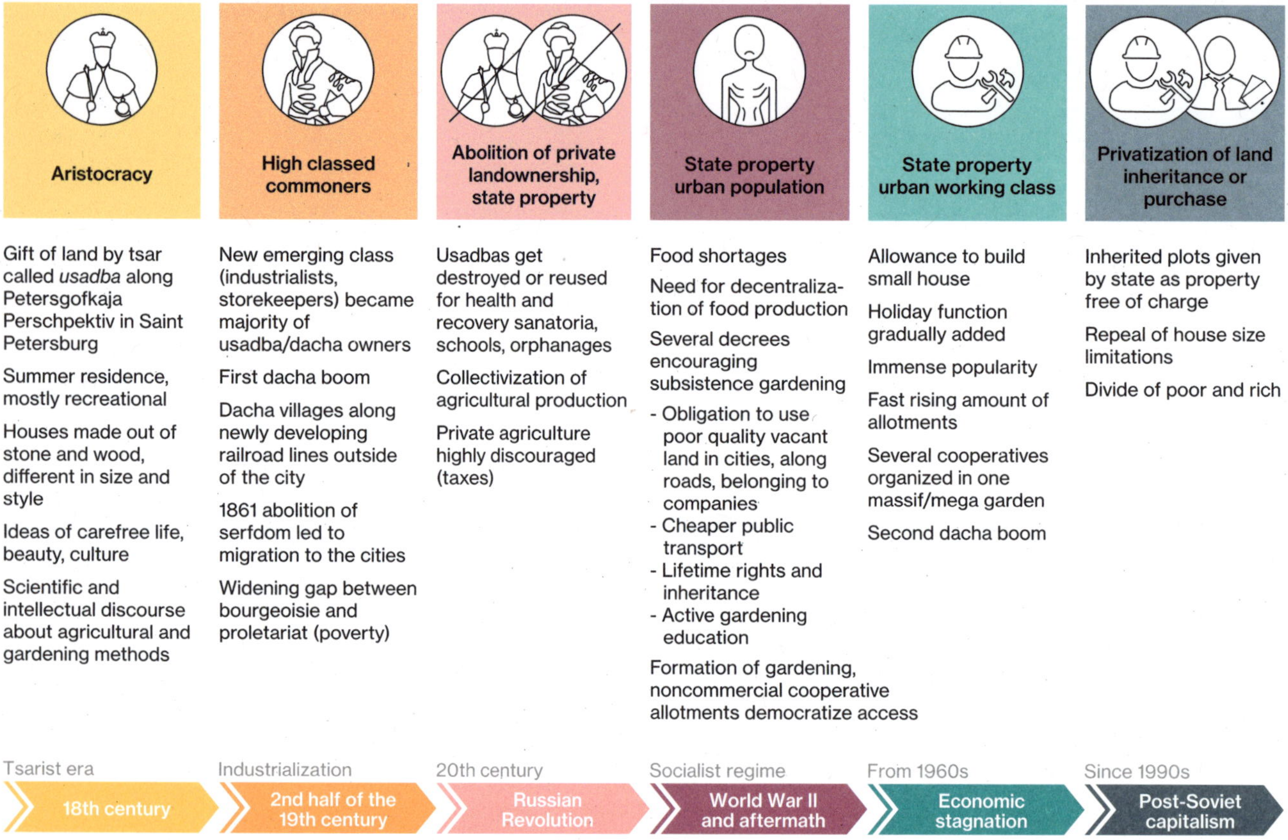

Fig. 3 Historical development of the Russian dacha

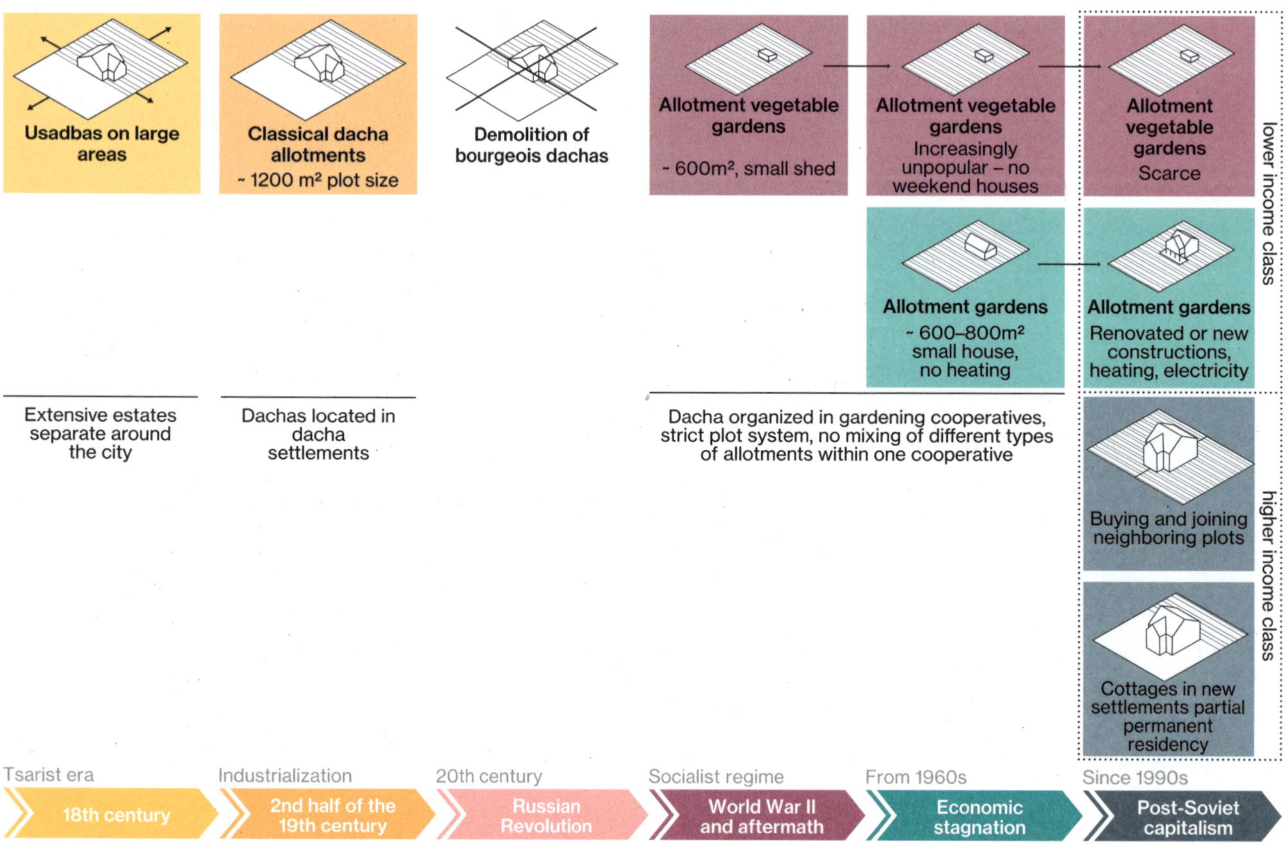

Fig. 4 Development of dacha plots

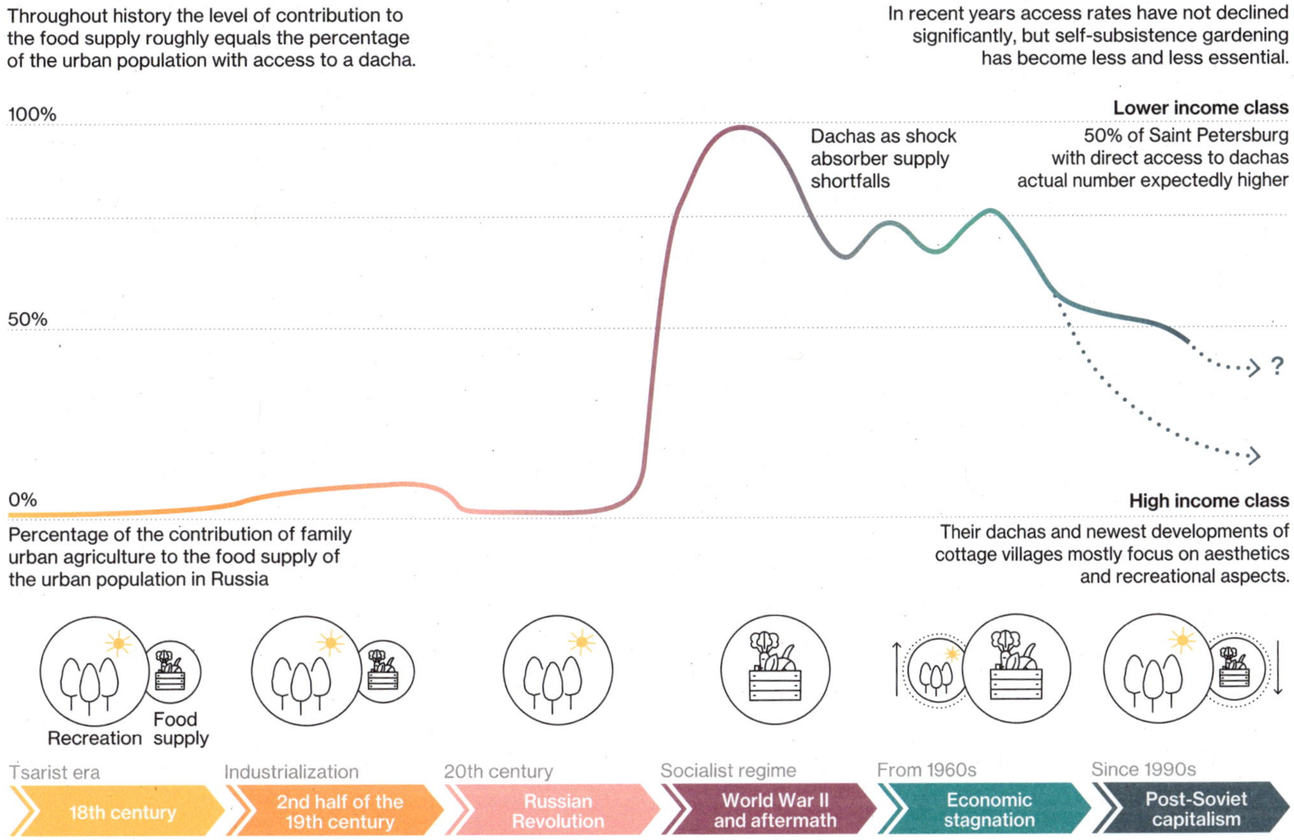

Fig. 5 The contribution of dachas to the food supply over time

Subsequently, when the Russian Revolution in 1917 abolished private landownership, many of the noble estates and allotments were destroyed, neglected, or transformed into orphanages, schools, or sanatoria. (Boukharaeva and Marloie 2015, 32ff). The Socialist idea of supplying food for the population by means of collectivization and large agricultural cooperatives caused the regime to impose taxes on private cultivation and thus discouraged urban gardening (42).

World War II and its famines, combined with the failing collectivized production system, prompted the Soviet regime to reevaluate dachas as a necessity for food production. Allotment vegetable gardens **[Fig. 4]** were formed on a large scale, focusing on agricultural productivity while suppressing recreational functions and housebuilding. During the economic stagnation between the 1950s and 1990s, allotment gardens were made easily accessible and affordable. Plots of 600–800 square meters and a small house without heating were assigned as a lease by factories or the state to workers and their families. Strict rules within the cooperatives dictated the specific land use or kinds of crops to cultivate, and prohibited permanent residence (Dornblüth 2018). Private urban gardening offset the loss of productivity of the planned-economy agriculture and provided the major proportion of food for the urban population **[Fig. 5]**. Because of an increasing social pressure and longing for green getaways from the city, the government became more tolerant of recreational use in the 1960s (Boukharaeva et al. 2015, 70–71). Because of the growth of St. Petersburg, dacha settlements were absorbed into the city's fabric.

Since the end of the Soviet Union, most of the allotment gardens have been privatized and renovated. Many garden houses were newly constructed with heating and electricity. It is now possible for *dachniki* (owners of dachas) to buy the neighboring plot in order to create bigger allotment gardens. In some newer settlements, dachas became plots with villa-like detached houses where the owners partially live (83–84). While the need for self-sufficient food production has decreased, the demand for recreational functions continues to rise. The idea of a second home in a natural setting outside the city prevails and explains the lasting popularity of dachas within the Russian population.

Heritage Characteristics and Potential

Based on their historical development, the Russian dacha culture can be considered an intangible rather than a tangible urban agricultural heritage. Dachas are a widespread phenomenon in constant transformation. The individual plot or house is not an object of protection or conservation. Instead, dachas within their associations and cooperatives have to be considered as a whole, providing the agricultural, sociocultural, and ecological benefits to the Russian society which are listed in **[Fig. 6]**.

History has proven the adaptability of dachas to new needs. In contrast to allotment gardens in Western Europe, Russian dachas are not only associated with self-subsistence farming, but rather provide flexible usability ranging from food supply, recreational functions, meet-up space for families and friends, to a second home outside the inner city **[Fig. 7]**. Their multifunctionality grants resilience, that is why the idea of dachas stayed attractive throughout their history and withstood regime changes as well as different economic situations. Nowadays, they are still perceived as a potential "shock absorber" (193) for future crises. During the COVID-19 pandemic, an increased usage of dachas as places for self-isolation away from the crowded city was reported (Nikolaeva and Rusanov 2020). Because dachas reduce dependence on the social welfare system, they offer an approach to prevent and fight poverty. Having access to a piece of land is the most decentralized form of empowerment for individuals as well as communities. Gardening cooperatives have the potential to provide an exchange platform for different social groups.

The resilience of dachas contributed to their establishment as part of the Russian culture. Throughout their development from prestigious summer residences of the political elite to allotments for everybody, the original idea of a getaway with the family to a second home outside the city center prevailed. Visiting the dacha after work, on weekends, or on holidays became an inherent element of Russian popular culture; it is seen as a tradition and thus passed on to the next generation (Ortar 2005, 182). The atmosphere of intimacy, seclusion, and one's own creative scope creates a sense of belonging and home, strengthening family ties and friendships **[Fig. 8]**. One proposal to assure the continuation of family urban agriculture would be to include gardening in the school curriculum again.

The dacha should be treated as part of an "integral human habitat" (Boukharaeva et al. 2015, 129), which considers having access to a garden plot as a civic right. City dwellers should be able to extend their limited living space in a city apartment to fulfill their need for an active relationship with nature as well as the opportunity to produce their own food.

Problems arise from the resulting consequence for urban planning, since the required area to fulfill this right can't be met within the city boundaries. A proposal to relieve the congested road system is to develop and strengthen the local public transportation as well as promoting carpooling to the cooperatives.

Agricultural	Ecological	Sociocultural
Informal economy, non-professional family urban agriculture	Biodiversity, big variety of crops and animals/insects	Large-scale phenomenon concerns up to 60% of the urban population
Challenges the concept of city dwellers as simple consumers	Cultivation of wasteland, green islands within cityscape	Established as part of the Russian culture, using the dacha as tradition
Contribution to food supply and supporting subsistence	Improvement of soil quality within city unsealed sites	Part of the integral human habitat/ civil right, need of active relationship with nature
Multifunctionality – resilience, adaptable use according to current need	Local food production, reduction and recycling of household waste	Development of self-reliance, strengthens family ties, DIY, and sharing culture

Fig. 6 Particular aspects of Russian dachas indicating the need for an urban agricultural heritage status

Current Threats and Challenges

The persistent popularity of the dacha among all social groups and its integration into Russian culture, private family life, and education allows the conclusion that the common interest in them will not decrease. The demand for a plot of land is not declining. Russia aligns itself more and more to the Western system of social strata, and the gap between rich and poor is increasing significantly. A low standard of living prevails for the majority of the population. The low average income level and a weak social insurance and pension system animates Russians to continue gardening as part of self-subsistence (Grimonpont 2019).

Families with a higher income can afford to give up self-subsistence gardening, though they mostly keep the gardening tradition alive in a small area. The global trend of urbanization triggers real estate investors to transform allotments into suburbs (Boukharaeva et al. 2015, 83). "Allotment plots officially remained property of the state until 2006. They have since been transferred into private hands at a rapid rate. The increase in the standard of living and the loosening of rules have also meant that there is a higher number of permanent structures within certain communities. This change is often accompanied by merging the plots to make them bigger, installing gas and electricity, and strengthening access roads. The community gardens are therefore moving significantly toward the model of European housing estates" (Grimonpont 2019). More and more people are deciding to permanently live on their dachas (Boukharaeva et al. 2015, 83).

Fig. 7 Vegetables and people (Овощи и люди)

Fig. 8 The family of Boleslav Telichan, worker at a chemical plant in St. Petersburg, at their dacha, 1981

In general, due to an absence of clear and nationally recognized standards on how to deal with dachas, municipalities and politicians are often divided by the conflict of protecting cultural and gardening traditions on the one hand and focusing on financial benefits from real estate investments on the other.

Because the administration is decentralized and situations are locally different, city administrations have to take on the leading role in preserving dachas. Therefore, local authorities and municipalities need to work out guidelines on the sale, building permits, area usage, community involvement, and organization for cooperatives in accordance with national guidelines.

The government of the Russian Federation has finally recognized the problems and started to set out a legal framework for gardening communities (Russian Federation 2017). By prohibiting merging neighboring plots or the registration of the dacha as a main residence, the misuse of land and property speculation could be restrained on a national scale.

To conclude, even though dachas are a phenomenon specific to Russian history and culture, they offer inspiration and serve as a model for gardens as part of human habitat. They are a positive example of an active involvement of citizens in shaping their living space. Dachas as an adaptable land use concept can continue to provide resilience in future humanitarian emergencies. ■

General remark: Authors' own translations from Russian to English and from German to English.

Resilient Cities with Urban Agricultural Heritage: Tokyo

Giles B. Sioen and Makoto Yokohari

City planners in the twentieth century adapted zoning policies in which they separated urban and rural land uses. This resulted in a removal of farmlands that were within or considered too close to a city. The separation by location was widely adapted around the world, yet exceptions remain. In Japan, farmlands were classified by ownership, even if located within the city boundaries. This classification ensured that urban agriculture followed the jurisdiction of agricultural policies, resulting in the preservation of urban agricultural heritage. Agricultural lands in Japan, however, have been protected so strictly that they are now in decline, threatening the valuable services urban agricultural heritage provides to cities. The history and policies that have led to the present situation in Tokyo provide insights into the modern-day applications of heritage, ensuring accessible and livable urban agricultural heritage in cities.

The Reasons for the Presence of Urban Agricultural Heritage

Tokyo was established during the seventeenth century, then called Edo, and by the mid-twentieth century grew into the largest metropolitan area in the world. The modernization of Tokyo happened during the Meiji Restoration period (1868–1912), when the city adapted modern infrastructure such as railroads (Okata and Murayama 2011). Although Japan took on many urban planning policies from Western countries, some domestic policies, such as the one that connects farming households with their land, have shaped the city to date.

Urban agriculture has been a harmonious part of Tokyo's urban fabric since the Edo period (1603–1868). Tokyo flourished during this period, where social elements are known to have a strong connection with the environment (Yokohari and Amati 2005) **[Fig. 1]**. As part of a circular economy, farmers collected human feces from households and used it as fertilizer. Interestingly, farmers even paid a higher price for the feces of high-ranking residents (such as upper-class warriors), who were known to have more nutritious diets. This small-scaled recycling system made the farmlands an integral and functional part of the urban fabric (Hirohara et al. 2002). It also showed how connected the urban population was with urban agriculture, a phenomenon that is—although to a lesser extent—still visible today.

Urban Agriculture and Sustainability in Cities

The increased interest in urban agriculture comes during a time when the majority of the global population lives in cities and there are grave concerns regarding climate change, food safety, and food security. Urban agricultural heritage in Tokyo provides open space to compensate for the small living spaces of apartments and even serves as a supplementary source of dietary nutrition during the COVID-19 pandemic (Sardeshpande et al. 2020).

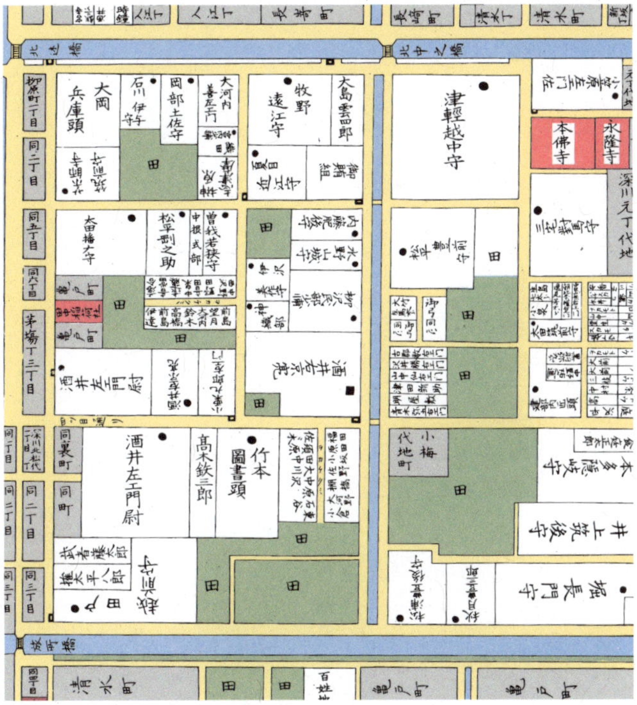

Fig. 1 Segmented urban agriculture (in green) in a residential neighborhood of Tokyo. The scene is from the Honjo-Fukagawa district during the Edo period (1863), two kilometers east of the Edo Castle.

Benefits provided by urban agriculture worldwide vary depending on context and have often been forgotten in modern planning concepts. Increasing environmental awareness resulted in greater appreciation of urban agriculture for its ecosystem services (Elmqvist et al. 2015; Langemeyer et al. 2016; Lin et al. 2015; La Rosa et al. 2014). A study analyzing the urban heat island effect in a small district of Tokyo indicated that a paddy field land coverage of more than 30 percent reduces the temperature in the study area by two degrees Celsius (Yokohari et al. 1997). As a dense city with 6,169 people per square kilometer (Statistics Bureau of Japan 2016), Tokyo contains a mere three square meters of green space per capita (7,600 hectares in 2010). This number does not include urban agriculture (7,900 hectares in 2010), which in Tokyo comprises a greater area than that of parks (Tokyo Metropolitan Government 2016) and provides ecosystem services that have been linked to healthy lifestyles. Ensuring accessibility to these productive green spaces could allow urban agriculture to be counted in the per capita green space indicator.

Studies have also found that urban agriculture can provide dietary nutrition to the population. In Tokyo's Nerima ward, urban agriculture can provide an annual vegetable self-sufficiency of 5.24 percent, with availability depending on the season (Sioen et al. 2017). Some studies have shown that residents engaging in urban agriculture have increased their intake of fresh, local, and seasonal fruit and vegetables, which has been linked with the prevention of cardiovascular diseases, cancer, and other dietary-related health problems (Slavin and Lloyd 2012; Wilkins et al. 2015).

Another positive contribution to sustainability is by physically engaging in urban agriculture, whether by supporting a professional farmer or renting an allotment plot to grow fruit and vegetables. The increase in physical activity results in health benefits across ages with the greatest overall benefits being found in older participants (Van den Berg et al. 2010). For Japan, a country with an aging population, these benefits are welcome.

Concerning social benefits, urban agriculture also functions as a platform for residents to engage and connect within the community **[Fig. 2]**, which improves their overall physical and mental health status. Such motivations have previously been documented as the reasons for residents to engage in urban agricultural activities (Armstrong 2000).

If policymakers wish to preserve this nonexhaustive list of benefits, then urban land use policies need to consider urban agricultural heritage, fight the decline of the number of farmers, and discourage land abandonment. Various stakeholders in Japan, including farmers, local city governments, residents, and academics have been promoting the benefits of urban agricultural heritage as a motivation for its preservation. Preservation is also sought to ensure that the farmers can remain on plots where they are accessible, and provide services in line with modern-day needs (Yokohari et al. 2011).

Contextual Characteristics of Urban Agriculture in Japan and Its Contributions to Resilience

Urban agriculture in Japan is characterized by several contextual phenomena that may not be present in other places around the world. Four descriptions below will elaborate on the most distinct characteristics that call for a unique urban agricultural integration.

Fig. 2 A temporary farm called Oak Village in Kashiwa-no-ha, Chiba. A private company leased the land to cultivate it as an experience farm until it was developed with buildings and parking spaces.

First, 93 percent of the population in Japan live in cities (The World Bank 2016, data from 2015), which makes these important centers to focus on. Simultaneously, Japan is located at the triple junction of the Pacific, Philippine, and Eurasian plates, resulting in high levels of seismic activity, which makes Disaster Risk Reduction (DRR) crucial in land use planning. Although a considerable number of households prepare for disasters and secure rations, there is more needed than food alone to overcome a disaster situation (Nakazawa and Beppu 2012). In response, the Tokyo Metropolitan Government has created a system of various services, such as evacuation spaces, dietary nutrition, and fresh water to be used in times of disasters, as well as drills for people to be better prepared for disaster situations (Sioen et al. 2017). School grounds have conventionally been the go-to place in case of a disaster, both as shelter and as an open space for evacuation. With the aim of improving safety, local administrations are experimenting with urban agriculture for disaster preparedness. For example, local administrations developed the Disaster Prevention Cooperation Farmlands (Tokyo Metropolitan Government, 2015), a voluntary system that provides a framework for urban agricultural lands to be transformed into evacuation spaces when a disaster situation occurs **[Fig. 3]**. This system increases the total evacuation space and ensures that a greater number of locations are available within proximity. Another example is that local governments, if the farmers agree, can build temporary shelters on urban agricultural lands when houses have been damaged or destroyed. This flexibility improves the resilience of the community. The combination of adaptation systems is challenging and a trade-off must be made (either politically or quantitatively) between whether to choose food production, short-term evacuation spaces, or spaces for temporary shelters.

Second, international competition in the agricultural sector has globally led to increases in cropland sizes. While this is also true for Japan (9.7 percent annual growth from 2005 to 2010), the average cropland size of a farming business remains small (2.2 hectares) compared with that of Canada (493.1 hectares), the United States (89.0 hectares), or France (84.9 hectares) in 2010 (OECD 2016, 62). As an island of which only 12.4 percent (2010) of the total land surface can serve agricultural purposes (Statistics Bureau of Japan 2016b), land use efficiency was deemed important and led to the preservation of small-scale urban agriculture, which can be easily managed by one farmer and is located in proximity to consumers.

Third, the country has the highest proportion of seniors (65 years or older) in the world. Of farmers too, 60 percent were more than 65 years old in the year 2010, with concerns that they cannot continue to perform the necessary manual labor required in the long term. This "super-aging society" (Muramatsu and Akiymama 2011) has resulted in the emergence of new urban agricultural business models that better consider the associated costs of the demographic shift and land abandonment. At the same time, growing one's own food has become a popular hobby among retirees, which can help achieve successful aging (Rowe and Kahn 1987 and 1997). The trend is also catching on with an increasing number of young families, who value urban agriculture as an educational platform for their children.

Fig. 3 Conventional urban agriculture farm in Kokubunji, Tokyo, with a sign indicating that this land serves as Disaster Prevention Cooperation Farmland

Fourth, farmlands are not exempt from high tax rates. Farm households have subdivided and sold portions of farmlands because of the high inheritance tax (55 percent). Furthermore, high land taxes have pushed innovation (higher quality and diversity in crops) instead of conventional upscaling and mechanizing strategies, resulting in 10 percent more revenue per square meter for urban farms compared with their rural counterparts (Ministry of Agriculture, Forestry and Fisheries of Japan 2011).

The four contextual phenomena described above indicate that urban agriculture in Japan is generally small-scaled, mixed within high-density urban areas, and owned by an aging farming population; but it is increasingly recognized for providing resilience for natural disasters, green spaces for neighboring residents, and high-quality fruit and vegetables for dietary nutrition. By studying the contextual situation of the urban agricultural heritage of Japan, preservation can help meet modern-day societal needs, increase resilience, and provide cobenefits to the city.

Land Use Policies and Their Effects

Agricultural lands in Japan used to be based on the landlord-tenant system (Minami et al. 1999). Most tenant farmer households endured hard labor with meager incomes. After World War II, the system was abolished. The government forcibly bought the lands at a cheap price and sold them to the former tenants. Since then, policies have protected farmers from the risk of becoming poor tenants again by prohibiting major capital (such as businesses or wealthy individuals) from purchasing agricultural land and dominating the sector with scale advantages. Other protection mechanisms were developed as well. For example, you can only purchase or lease agricultural land if you are a registered farmer. To become registered, there are three options to choose from. You either

1. Get an agricultural college degree (duration: two to three years);
2. Take an arranged apprenticeship in the area where you wish to become a farmer (duration may vary depending on the area); or
3. Marry into a farmer's family.

These protection mechanisms have caused a gradual decline in the number of farmers (M. Shiraishi 2001, 18–27), threatening the existence of agriculture (OECD 2016) and thus also Japan's urban agricultural heritage.

Although the protection mechanisms have served their purpose, new households struggle to join the agricultural sector. The number of agricultural households was some 5.0 million in 1975, but fell to 2.5 million (5 percent of total households) in 2010 and has continued to decrease (Statistics Bureau of Japan 2016). The situation is even more severe with urban agriculture. Tokyo had 32,000 urban agricultural households in 1975, but merely 13,000 in 2010. Although the decrease of urban agricultural households in Tokyo is no longer as rapid, the majority of farmers remaining are above retirement age (65 in Japan) and lack successors. The only way to protect these lands is by making the urban agriculture sector attractive for newcomers.

Present urban land use policies came into existence under the City Planning Law (1968), which divided lands into "urbanization promotion areas" (UPA) and "urbanization control areas" (UCA) (Okata and Murayama 2011). This policy came into existence toward the end of the rapid growth of the city in the 1960s and early '70s. Designated UPA were to be developed within ten years; after this period they would be taxed under the higher urban taxation rates. Yet many lands remained agricultural because the growth of the city did not continue. This required a shift in priorities. To ensure farmers would not get into tax debts, the Productive Green Land Act (1974) was developed and lowered property taxes on the remaining agricultural lands. The condition was that farm households would then continue their agricultural activity for the next thirty years. Land that was designated UCA already benefitted from lower tax rates than that designated UPA and was prohibited from urban development (excepting farmhouses, retail, and public facilities). In effect, the creation of the Productive Green Land Act in UPA, together with the UCA designation, enabled urban agricultural lands to persist in Japan's cities.

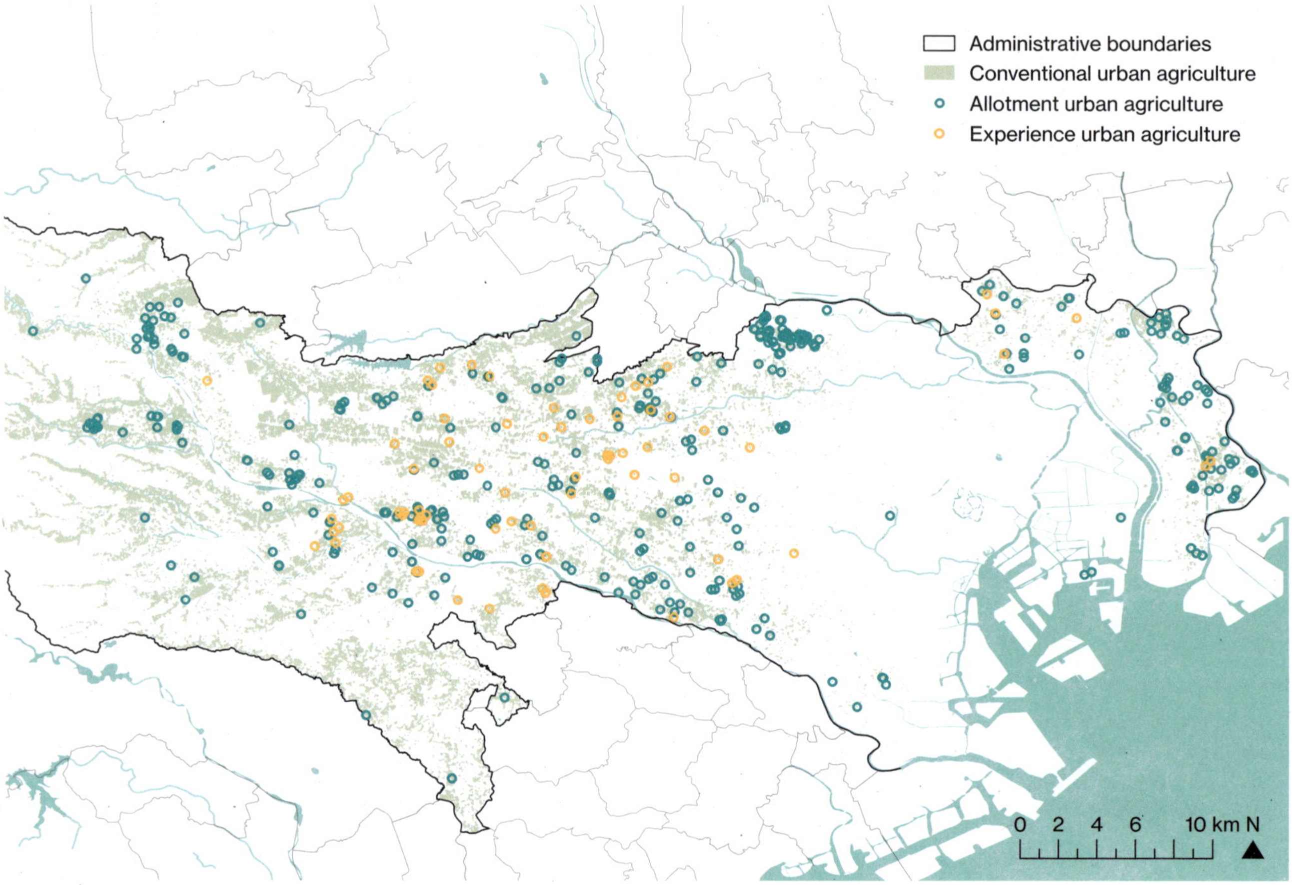

Fig. 4 Locations of urban agriculture according to type in the 23 special wards of Tokyo

Fig. 5 Conventional urban agriculture farm in Nerima ward, Tokyo

Fig. 6 Allotment urban agriculture farm in Nerima ward, Tokyo

Urban Agriculture in Different Forms

Previous studies have observed three distinct types of urban agriculture in Tokyo (Sioen et al. 2017; Sioen et al. 2018) **[Fig. 4]**:

1. Conventional urban agriculture, followed by two forms that can be categorized as hobby farming, called
2. Allotment urban agriculture, and
3. Experience urban agriculture.

The first and most prevalent type is that of conventional urban agriculture. These farms have a production method similar to that of their rural counterparts but are located within the city **[Fig. 5]**.

The second type, allotment urban agriculture, is much like its European or North American counterparts **[Fig. 6]**. These farms can be owned by government, private owners, or farmers. The landowner rents out all or a portion of the plot to hobby farmers. The engagement between landowner and hobby user is limited to the contractual agreement without further interaction.

Experience urban agriculture was created by conventional urban agriculture farmers, local governments, and entrepreneurial businesses working together **[Fig. 7]**. Although similar forms exist in countries around the world, in Japan they emerged in response to specific challenges: small-scale plots, aging farmers in an aging society, and land abandonment. Experience urban agriculture can be defined as a mix of conventional and allotment urban agriculture, where a professional farmer owns the land and provides experiences to hobby farmers, renting out land and teaching them about cultivation processes according to a designed planting, growing, and harvesting plan (Sioen et al. 2016; Tahara et al. 2011). Experience urban agriculture has the added benefits of maintaining farmland that might have been abandoned due to the lack of successors in the agricultural sector, and also connecting farms to the community, optimizing land uses. The first experience urban agriculture farm was developed by urban farmer Yoshitaka Shiraishi, from Nerima ward (Y. Shiraishi 2001). He developed the model when he found himself challenged to cultivate the land he had inherited and realized that nearby residents were interested in experiencing farming. He has written about it in his book, *Tokai no hyakushōdesu. Yoroshiku* (I am an urban farmer. Nice to meet you). This led to other farmers adopting the model, but also sparked a demand from Tokyo's residents. The disadvantage of a location that did not allow for upscaling in size turned into an advantage when surrounding residents were invited to farms. Retirees who during their working life had commuted to the business district and were disengaged from their local community could now enjoy neighborly interactions through the planting and harvesting activities.

Fig. 7 Yoshitaka Shiraishi's experience urban agriculture farm in Nerima ward, Tokyo

Various other forms are emerging in the meantime. See, for example, the case of Nerima ward's annual radish harvesting rally **[Fig. 8]**, where the community can engage in harvesting through competition. The event is a collaboration between the local Nerima government urban agriculture section, a local farmer, community leaders, the Japan Agricultural Cooperatives, and residents.

In Tokyo there are 75 experience urban agriculture farms, totaling 151,054 square kilometers. A study showed that experience farms in Tokyo provide an average potential vegetable self-sufficiency of 5.86 percent for residents living within 300 meters of the farmland (Sioen et al. 2016). In contrast to conventional community and allotment gardening found in Europe and North America, urban agricultural farmers in Japan keep their commercial/professional activity and provide experiences to urbanites to diversify their income. Experience urban agriculture farms even produce higher crop yields (average: 8.45 kilograms per square meter) than allotment (average: 4.16 kilograms per square meter) and conventional urban agriculture farms (average: 6.24 kilograms per square meter) (Tahara et al. 2011). Reasons may vary, but because professional farmers are involved, there is an increased chance of a successful harvest, and produce can exceed market standard sizes.

Conclusion

Distinct types of urban agriculture can be found in Tokyo because of its specific history, geography, and set of policies. Urban agriculture in Japan, especially in Tokyo, remains dependent on manual labor because of the small plot sizes that do not easily allow mechanization. In response, urban agriculture provides cobenefits that go beyond mere food production. They contribute to resilience by providing evacuation spaces and diverse food supply in case of disaster, provide ecosystem services, are a tool to tackle a super-aging society, and function as a social platform where the population learns about and can experience Japan's urban agricultural heritage. An increasing number of countries around the world face this demographic shift, making urban agriculture and its heritage a component that may have the potential to tackle some of the social and environmental challenges for future cities (Jarzebski et al. 2021). To avoid a further decline in the number of urban agriculture heritage sites, the urban agricultural sector should adapt a cobenefits approach and provide services that in addition to productivity meet other modern-day needs such as experiences and green space. Simultaneously, policies need to be modified to allow for the protection of the urban agricultural heritage, both in its tangible forms and spaces and in its intangible traditions inside the city. Only then will the farming sector be able to flourish and contribute to the sustainability and resilience of the city with its full potential. ▪

Fig. 8 Radish harvesting as a community event on professional farmlands in Nerima ward, Tokyo

Linking Urban Agricultural Heritage to the Concept of Cultural Memory and Practice

Belgrade's Garden Colonies: Where Memory, Nature, and People Meet

Slavica Čepić, Dragana Ćorović, and Jelena Tomićević-Dubljević

As a form of urban agriculture, urban gardening has always been part of everyday life in cities in Serbia. Belgrade brimmed with private urban gardens during the Ottoman Empire's reign until the end of the nineteenth century (Vuksanović-Macura and Ćorović 2016). With the withdrawal of the Ottoman Empire from Serbia in the late nineteenth century, and Turkish families forced to leave the city, the network of gardens, which for centuries had contributed to the city's structure and character, fell into disrepair (Vuksanović-Macura and Ćorović 2013). The pro-European urban development of Belgrade at the turn of the twentieth century also had an impact, increasing the value of the land in the city, inducing a higher degree of lot coverage (Vuksanović-Macura and Ćorović 2016) and pushing gardens toward the urban fringe.

With the urbanization of Belgrade, sanitary conditions in the central parts of the city started to worsen. The concept of allotment gardens or *baštenske kolonije* (garden colonies) was mentioned for the first time in this context. In an article published in 1932 in the Belgrade municipal paper *Beogradske opštinske novine*, the head of the Department for Parks and Reforestation, Aleksandar Krstić, proposed the establishment of garden colonies in Belgrade, similar to cities in England, Denmark, Germany, and other European countries. He presented garden colonies as a reaction to the poor conditions of life in the overpopulated central parts of the city where inhabitants "had no or at most insufficient contact with nature" (Krstić 1932, 206). Hereby, the importance of contact with nature was recognized, stressing that "the population from big cities should never lose it completely, since most noble human characteristics come from it" (206). It took another three decades for the first garden colonies to appear, unregistered and invisible to official town planning.

Historical Development of Garden Colonies and Their Status Today

The period after World War II was a time of rapid industrialization in Yugoslavia, followed by a massive migration of people from rural areas into cities, and the large-scale development of collective housing. Beside the significant positive impacts of the new settlements on the quality of life in the city, small living spaces, unused open spaces, the scarcity of public and commercial services, and a lack of architectural identity of apartment blocks were less favorable characteristics of these new neighborhoods.

The transition from rural to urban life in Belgrade was abrupt. For most of the inhabitants, the material conditions in new residential blocks were far above the level of their housing in rural areas (Stojanović 1975), and living in collective residential buildings meant a massive change in their habits and the way of life. In such circumstances, in the 1960s and 1970s, the first garden colonies started to emerge. The process was spontaneous and informal. Driven by old habits of land cultivation and a desire to be in contact with nature (Djokić et al. 2018), new residents claimed vacant public land in the

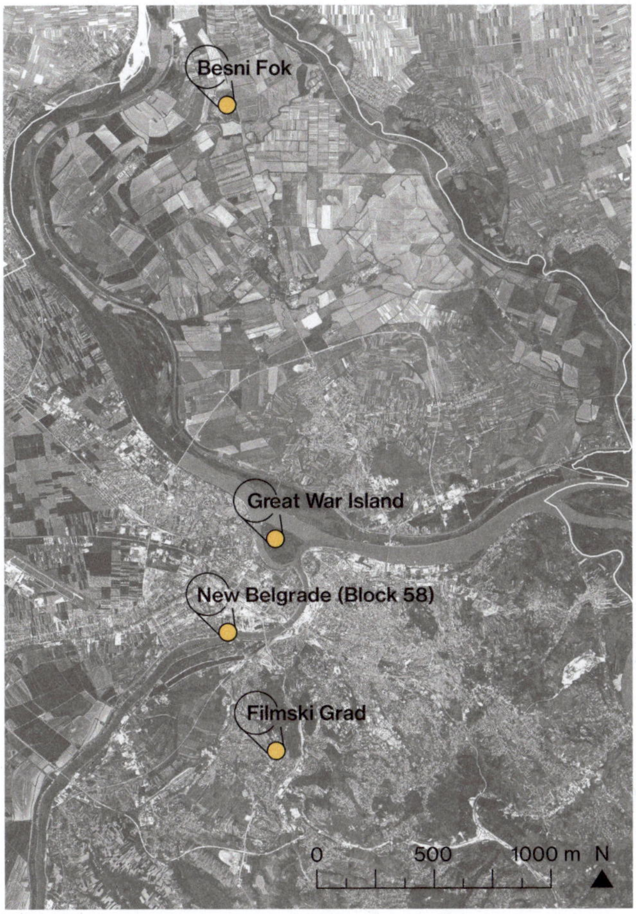

Fig. 1 Locations of the studied garden colonies

proximity of their apartment blocks, divided it into plots, and transformed it into gardens. Gardeners tended their plots individually and used them as their private gardens despite the mainstream ideology of the time that advocated communal property. In that period, a similar phenomenon was also taking place in other large cities in Yugoslavia, such as Zagreb (Gulin Zrnić and Rubić 2018; Slavuj Borčić et al. 2016).

The history of garden colonies in Belgrade is poorly documented. This can be attributed to their informal (or illegal) character and the lack of plans that would explain their development. The first official record of garden colonies inside the boundaries of the Master Plan of Belgrade was in 2007 when they were recognized and mapped as a biotope type (Urban Planning Institute of Belgrade 2007). The first planning document offering recommendations for the development of garden colonies was adopted in 2019 (Urban Planning Institute of Belgrade 2019). However, these documents did not consider the social and historical importance of the existing garden colonies, and they failed to offer specific and implementable measures for the gardens' protection and integration into the urban green infrastructure.

Study Areas

The content of this paper is based on studies conducted in four garden colonies located in different urban zones, from suburban to central, in geographically distinct parts within the administrative boundary of the city of Belgrade **[Fig. 1]**. The studies were done within the framework of the dissertation of Slavica Čepić on the socioeconomic benefits of urban gardens and opportunities for their integration into the green infrastructure of the City of Belgrade. During the studies, elements such as boundaries, paths, and places of assembly, as well as the structures, materials, and plants within the garden colonies, were identified and recorded and the overall accessibility and social use of the studied spaces were observed and documented. Furthermore, eight semistructured in-depth interviews with the gardeners were conducted in April and May 2019, focusing on the garden colonies' history, the motivations for gardening, and gardening practices.

The garden colonies in the municipal district of New Belgrade and the neighborhood of Filmski Grad are located in highly urbanized areas. They

Fig. 2 Aerial view of the garden colony in New Belgrade (Block 58)

are situated in blocks that are either undeveloped or partially developed, waiting to be transformed according to the land use predicted by the planning documents **[Fig. 2]**. New Belgrade is the largest collective housing settlement in Belgrade, whose construction began in 1948 (Blagojević 2005). Filmski Grad is at the edge of the forest park Košutnjak **[Fig. 3]**. The garden colony here is in the vicinity of the modern residential settlement Skojevsko, which was developed at the beginning of the 1980s (Tomić 1981). The high value of construction land in these areas combined with the pressure of developing residential and business complexes in these locations poses a real threat and puts the future of these two garden colonies at risk.

The garden colony on the Great War Island has a remarkable position—the island is the city's green heart and is under nature protection **[Fig. 4]**. On the other hand, the gardens here are characterized by the proximity to and good connection with the residential urban tissue, separated from it only by the river. Besni Fok is one of the settlements developed after World War II in the north peri-urban zone of Belgrade and was conceived for the employees of the Agricultural Combine. In the 1970s, modern buildings for individual and collective housing were constructed in the area (Mendelson 1975), and the gardens were formed in their surroundings **[Fig. 5]**.

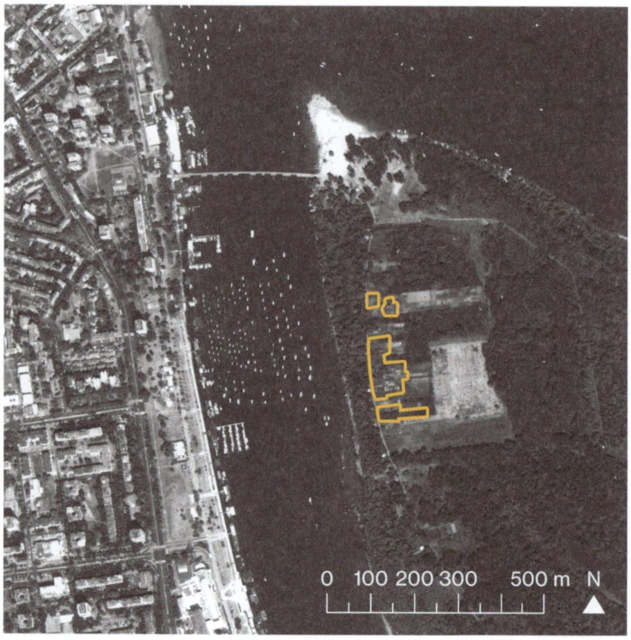

Fig. 4 Aerial view of the garden colony on the Great War Island

Fig. 3 Garden colony in Filmski Grad

Garden Colonies as Social and Cultural Arenas

Most of the interviewed gardeners belong to the second or third generation of plot holders. In most cases, they inherited the gardens from their cousins, neighbors, or friends who previously gardened the plots. The median age of respondents is seventy, and most have been gardening the plots for an average of twenty years, some as long as forty years. The majority of them moved from the countryside to the city at a young age and later worked in the industrial sector. They learned about gardening from their older and more experienced neighbors, who taught them how to cultivate the soil and to grow fruits and vegetables, passing on valuable knowledge of practices in the process. A gardener from Besni Fok who inherited the plot from his parents-in-law said: "Even today, my mother-in-law comes here with a walking cane and shows me at what distances to plant." This intergenerational transfer of knowledge and continuity in gardening practices suggests the existence of what Barthel et al. (2010) call social-ecological memory. Social-ecological memory is how "knowledge, experience and practice about how to manage a local ecosystem and its services is retained in a community, and modified, revived and transmitted through time" (256). This occurs through participation processes, such as sharing gardening advice, exchanging seeds and planting material, imitating

Fig. 5 Garden colony in Besni Fok

Fig. 6 Garden plot on the Great War Island

cultivation practices, and planning and tending the garden, including the physical elements that persist through time, such as trees and built structures like toolsheds and fences **[Fig. 6]**. These elements are "products of past participation," and they continue to influence "on-going practices and relations" (261). For instance, a gardener from New Belgrade showed us the nut trees that he planted twenty years ago at the edge of the garden right next to the sidewalk. Nowadays, these trees conveniently conceal the garden from the street, serving as a hedge and attracting passers-by, who stop and pick nuts. Furthermore, each garden plot usually has a gathering place—a table with benches and chairs where gardeners and their friends and families spend time together **[Fig. 7]**. An 89-year-old gardener from the colony on the Great War Island described the social life in the garden as follows: "When we have a bit of free time, we play a game of chess. We sit down, have a drink, coffee, hang out. It is nice."

Through gardening practices, some gardeners also revive the connection with their homeland. For instance, in a garden in New Belgrade, a gardener planted a fig tree "just like in Montenegro," where he was born. Another gardener grows a mixture of herbs on the Great War Island that is typical for the mountain area in Croatia where he was born, which he talks about emotionally and with pride. Connection with a place of origin, which is realized through gardening and contact with nature, reinforces the gardeners' sense of identity.

When asked to reflect on their motives to garden, the connection with nature appeared to be an underlying motivation for many. Being outside in the fresh air, working with soil and plants, and enjoying nature were common answers. The garden colonies provide an escape from the busy and frenetic life of the city. As Crouch noted, a garden is a place to escape from the family, a refuge "from the sounds and associations of home" (1989, 265), a sentiment echoed in the words of one of the gardeners: "I ran away from home, let me tell you. I leave the garden in the evening and I can't wait for the morning to come." Some gardeners described gardening also as a habit, an activity that the body longs for, that nurtures physical and mental health.

Fig. 7 Gathering place at an individual's plot on the Great War Island

Threats and Values

The garden colonies in Belgrade continue to exist today, although their number has reduced as a result of urban development (Adžić 2012). Despite the growing interest by citizens in collective urban gardening (Čepić et al. 2020), these activities are still not regulated. The lack of planning and institutional tools that would recognize and protect allotment gardens as a legitimate form of land use made garden colonies vulnerable to urban growth. Moreover, the insecure land tenure, the absence of garden associations, and the aging of the population of gardeners intensified the problem. As a consequence of this situation, the number of plots on the Great War Island has decreased from around 190 in the 1960s to 30–40 plots today, according to one of the oldest gardeners.

Against these challenges and threats, we argue that the preservation of the garden colonies is of great importance due to the following historical, spatial, social, and cultural values they incorporate:

1. Garden colonies testify to the development of the city and everyday life of the inhabitants of working-class neighborhoods built in the 1960s and 1970s in two ways: first through their spatial layout and physical elements, such as trees and built structures; and secondly through social-ecological memory and the intergenerational transfer of practice and knowledge.
2. Today garden colonies are a significant spatial resource for the collective housing settlements and their surroundings, where open green spaces disappear due to urban growth and construction. The gardens facilitate local food production, contact with nature, leisure and recreation, and socialization, especially for the elderly population. Furthermore, gardening is an important economic activity for some users.

A Way Forward

Based on all abovementioned, it is evident that perceiving garden colonies only as ecological elements of the biotope network, which is currently the case, is not sufficient. To integrate the historical, cultural, and social dimensions of these places into the reflections on the city's future development, the historic urban landscapes approach (UNESCO 2011) could be used as a framework. This holistic approach takes into consideration the goals of both urban heritage conservation and social and economic development. Through the lens of the historic urban landscape approach, it would be possible to explore the potential of garden colonies to be a source of local heritage—providing information on the history of the place as well as on the needs, social interactions, traditions, and agricultural practices of the people who established them and those who still use them today.

Further research is needed on:

1. The historical context of the development of garden colonies (political, social, cultural, and economic factors);
2. The physical layout and built elements of the garden colonies as expressions of needs, creativity, and skills of former and present gardeners;
3. The opportunities of intergenerational knowledge transfer—older and more experienced gardeners may pass on knowledge and skills to young people who could otherwise lose touch with the natural environment and food production practices;
4. The economic importance of the production of fruits, vegetables, and flowers, especially for vulnerable groups.

A broader view of garden colonies as part of the historic urban landscape and green infrastructure would create arguments for their integration into public policies and planning practices, which is a necessary condition for their preservation as a valuable resource for future generations. ■

Acknowledgments:
The dissertation of Slavica Čepić on the socioeconomic benefits of urban gardens and opportunities for their integration into the green infrastructure of the City of Belgrade was supported by the Ministry of Education, Science and Technological Development of the Republic of Serbia.

From Marshes to Market Gardens: Hortillonnages d'Amiens and Marais de Bourges

Leandra Brunet, Nicole Laufhütte, Axel Timpe, and Katharina Christenn

The Marais de Bourges and the Hortillonnages d'Amiens are two of the last few representatives of market garden swamps in France. They were an important part of life in both cities. For centuries, fruit and vegetables have been grown in the former swamps close to the city for commercial purposes and self-supply. Over the last century, these ecosystems have been threatened by various urban developments. Today the importance of this urban agricultural heritage is recognized and kept alive by various strategies in order to contribute to urban sustainability, resilience, and quality of life.

Location and Characteristics

The city of Amiens is located about 140 kilometers north of Paris, in the Hauts-de-France region. The Hortillonnages are situated east of the city center and extend along both banks of the river Somme. At the end of the twentieth century, they still covered an area of about 300 hectares (Morris 1999, 270) **[Fig. 1]**. The Marais de Bourges occupy an area of approximately 135 hectares northeast of the historical city center. Bourges is located in the geographical center of France, about 200 kilometers south of Paris, in the Centre-Val de Loire region. The Yèvre River **[Fig. 2]** divides the Marais into the Marais du haut and the Marais du bas (the Upper and the Lower Swamp), which are separated by a height difference of two meters (L'Association des Maraîchers de Bourges 2009a).

The Hortillonnages were created by the monks of nearby abbeys in the thirteenth century. The former landscape was part of the marshy river valley of the Somme, overflowing its banks and flooding the surrounding areas. The soils were characterized by peat and high moisture as well as by a high fertility due to large proportions of organic matter and therefore excellently suited as arable land (Musset 2003, 327; Limouzin 1994, 157). The monks reclaimed the land by draining the area and creating islands used as agricultural plots (Conan 1993, 20). The French name Hortillonnages comes from the Latin radical *hortus* (garden). The gardeners were and are still referred to as *Hortillons* (Morris 1999, 270).

The Marais were also founded by monks, but only in the seventeenth century. Before fruit and vegetable cultivation developed, the area was used for fishing and to run mills, and thus was already essential for supplying the urban population with food (Narboux 2010, 15–16). From the beginning, the gardeners were called *Maretiers* (L'Association des Maraîchers de Bourges 2009c).

The plots of the Hortillonnages and the Marais were leased to city dwellers for agricultural use. Until then, vegetables were scarce and of poor quality due to transportation from distant production sites and difficulties in preservation. Furthermore, urbanization caused an increasing demand. The availability of large amounts of water made the marshes of Amiens and Bourges an ideal location for cultivation (Morris 1999, 270; Narboux 2010, 15–16; Fleury 1998).

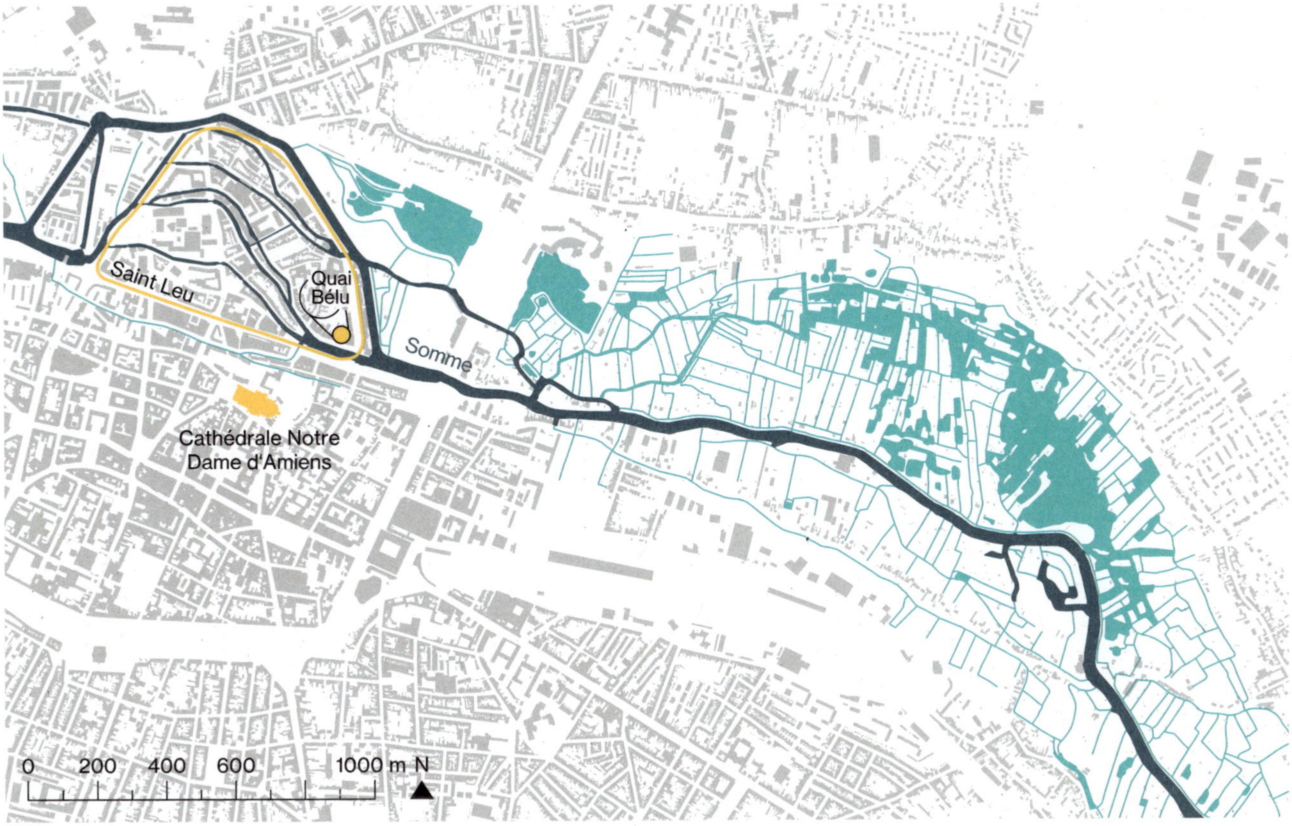

Fig. 1 The Hortillonnages d'Amiens, the gardeners' quarter Saint Leu, and the floating market on Quai Bélu in a figure-ground plan of the city

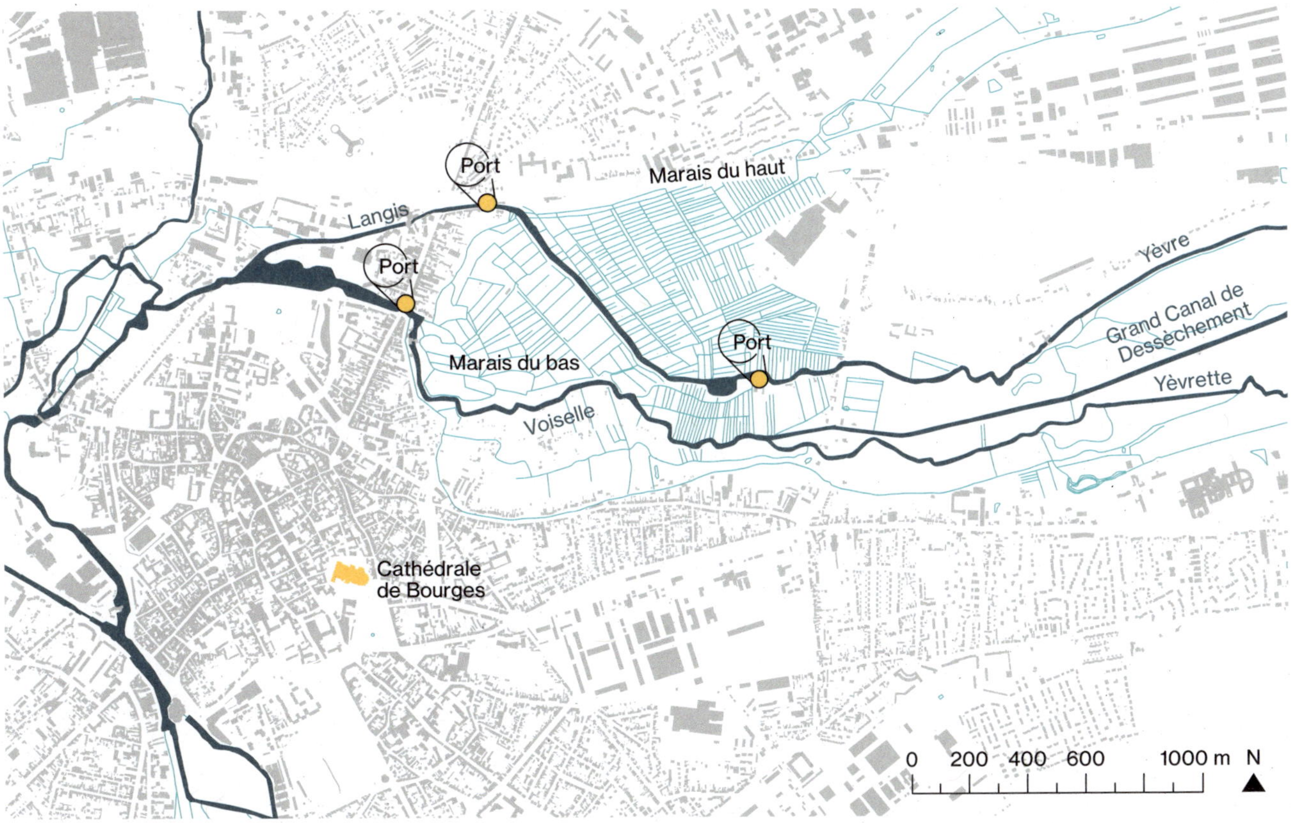

Fig. 2 The Marais de Bourges, its rivers, and its ports in a figure-ground plan of the city

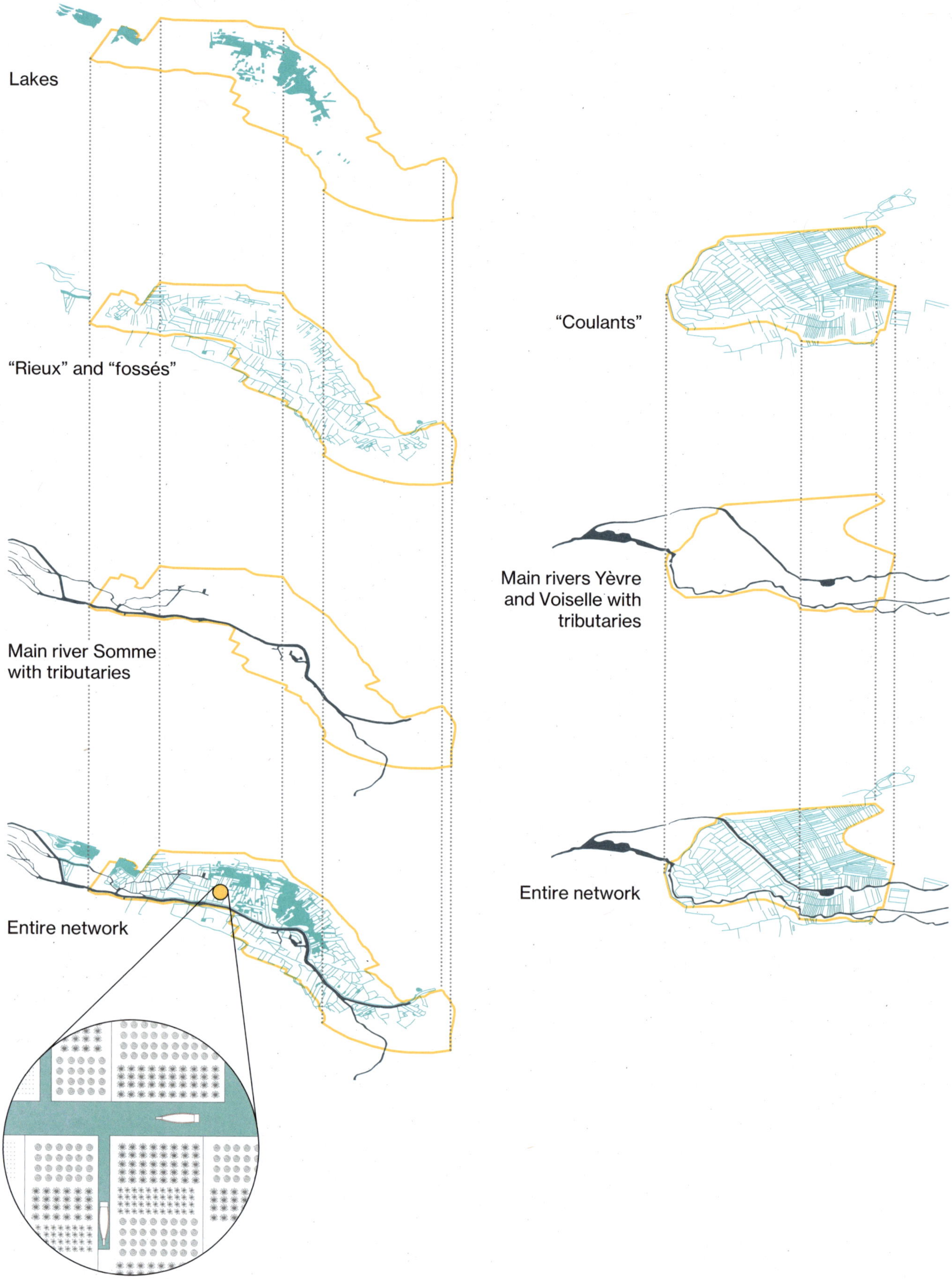

Fig. 3 Categorization of the water network in the Hortillonnages (left) and in the Marais (right)

Both areas are characterized by an artificially created, close-meshed canal network that has existed for centuries to drain the swamps but which has evolved and changed over the years. It bears witness to the living conditions of the inhabitants of Amiens and Bourges over time as well as to their way of adapting formerly unattractive areas to supply the urban population with fresh vegetables. The Marais and the Hortillonnages form almost unique river landscapes and are important features of both cities' identities. Channels are organized in a decided hierarchy, starting with the main rivers to the smaller, public *rieux* or *coulants* and ending with the private *fossés* (Clauzel 2008a, 54; Narboux 2010, 6). The canals surround the land parcels, border them, and form a mostly rectangular arrangement of islands, especially in the Marais. In addition to the canals, the area of Amiens is characterized by larger ponds resulting from peat extraction in past centuries (Limouzin 1994, 157) **[Fig. 3]**.

The waterways of the Hortillonnages and the Marais du haut serve to access the cultivated plots; special boats that have been adapted to the areas' conditions are used. In Amiens, they are called *barques à cornets* (horn boats), characterized by flat bottoms and high sides (Les Hortillonnages d'Amiens n.d. [b]), while in Bourges, the barges are known as *chalands* (Donadieu 1999, 3). They are usually the only way to reach the *aires* (garden plots) (Morris 1999, 270). In the Marais du haut, three large ports have been built as mooring facilities (Narboux 2010, 6–7) **[Fig. 2]**. By contrast, the Marais du bas must be reached on foot, as the canals and rivers, including the Voiselle and Yèvre, are no longer navigable (Fleury 1998).

Today, only a small part of the Hortillonnages is used for commercial vegetable cultivation. Most plots have been converted into leisure gardens with lawns and weekend houses **[Fig. 4]**. The Marais, in contrast, have been transformed from commercial to mostly private fruit and vegetable cultivation; only a few parcels are used as recreational areas. The changes of use have an impact on the market garden swamps' ecosystems and their visual appearance.

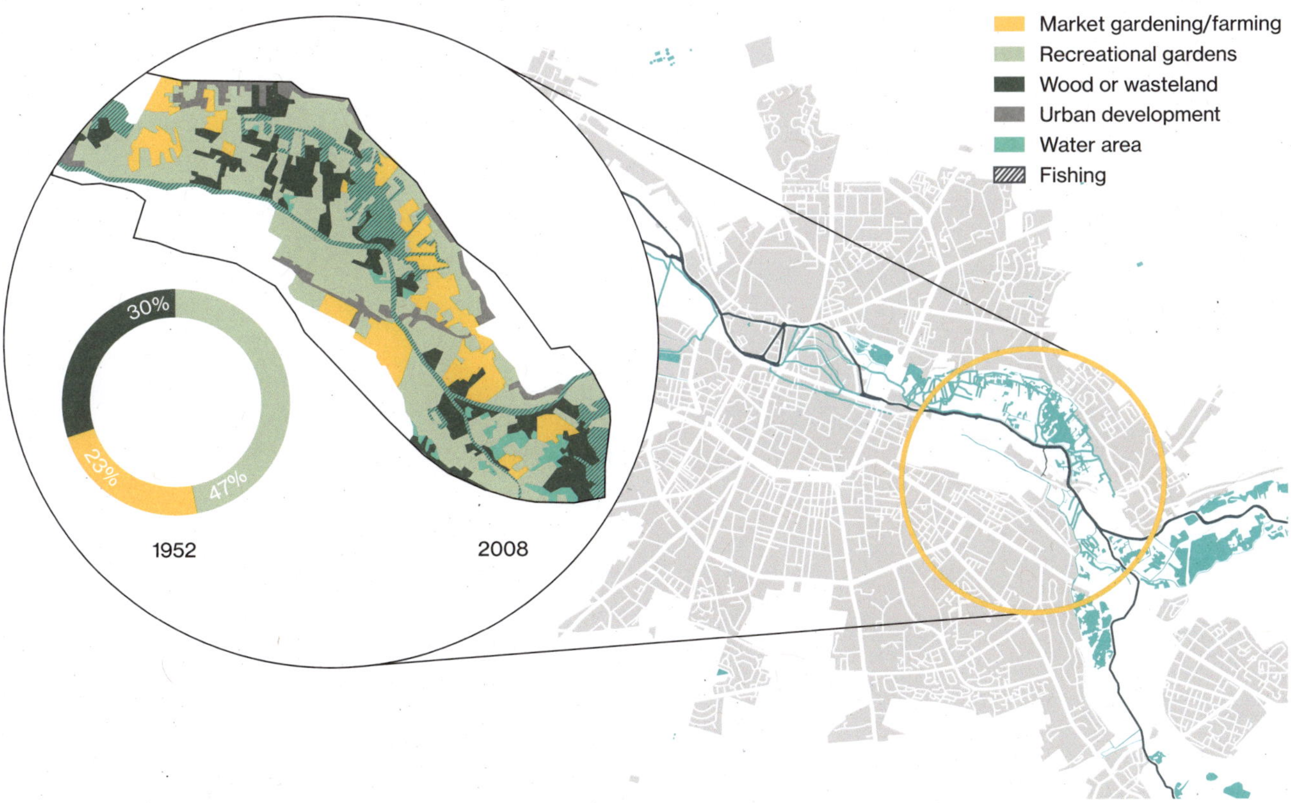

Fig. 4 Mapping of the different uses in the Hortillonnages 2008 and their extension 1952

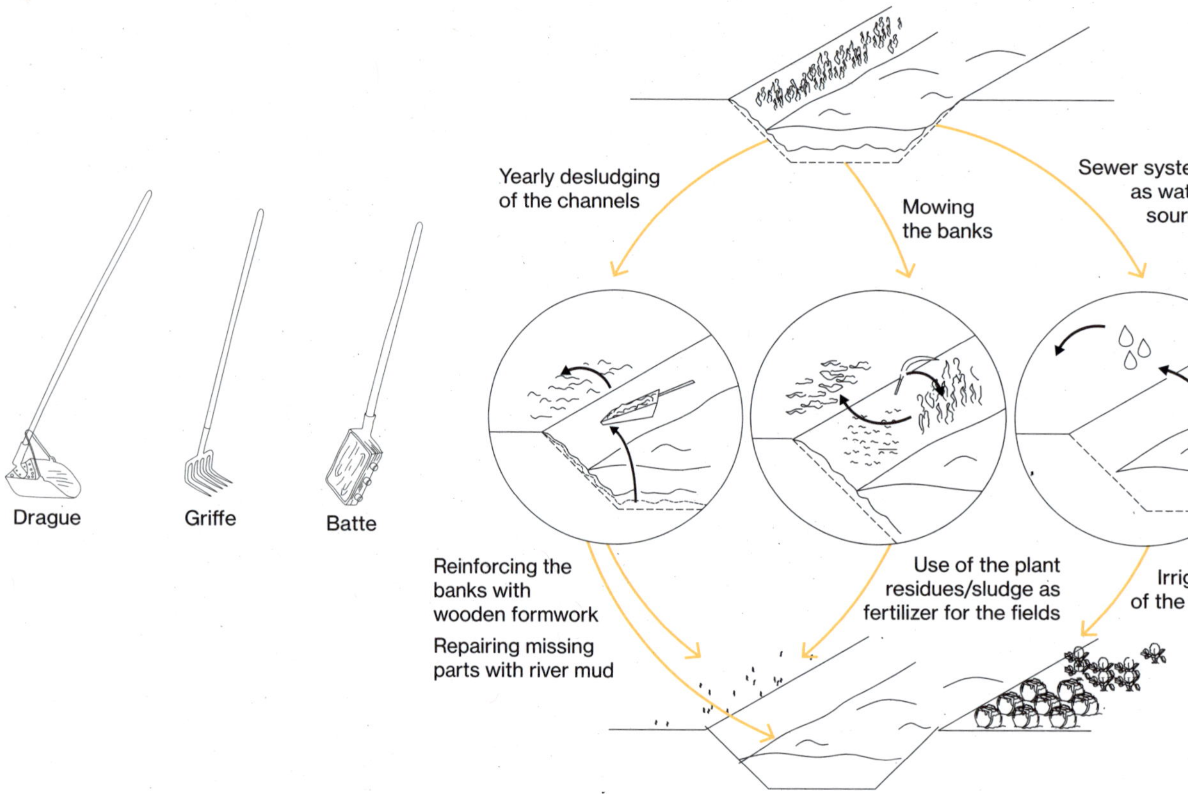

Fig. 5 Scheme for the maintenance of canals and cultivated areas and tools being used

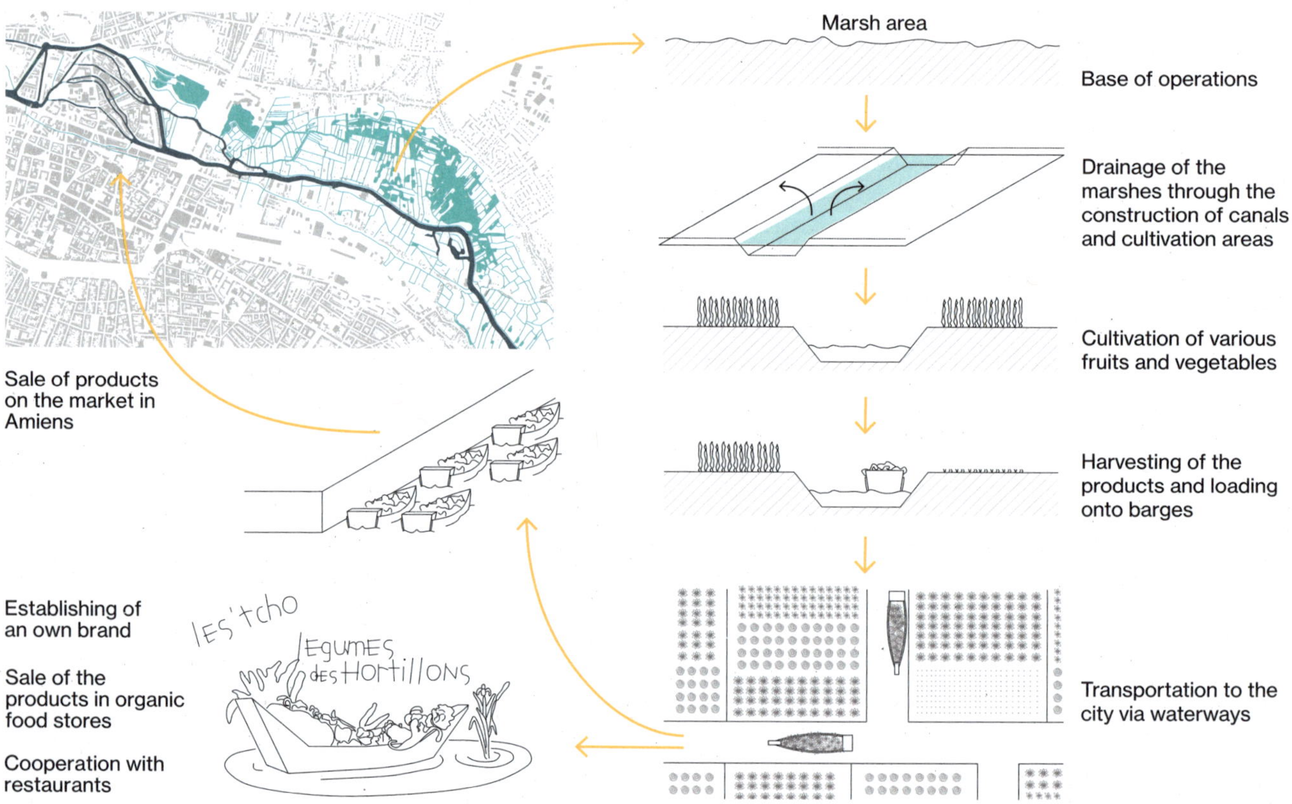

Fig. 6 Overall scheme for the cultivation of the Hortillonnages

Cultivation

The cultivation of the areas harnesses the environmental conditions of marshlands. The Hortillons and Maretiers transform the ecological conditions to take advantage of water and nutrient flows for their cultivation systems. Besides the process of preparing the soil, sowing, and harvesting, regular maintenance of the waterways and the plots is essential. In order to ensure a steady waterflow and to avoid a flooding of the plots, the banks are mown and the canals are desilted every year in spring, before the seeding season starts. The mud is used to mend the banks and rebuild the islands. Silt and plant residues are used as fertilizer in the fields (Musset 2003, 334; Clauzel 2008a, 21) **[Fig. 5]**.

The fields are harvested three times a year. In earlier years, in Amiens, produce was loaded onto barges. Via the rieux and the river Somme, fruits and vegetables were transported to the city center to be sold on the *marché sur l'eau* (floating market) (Morris 1999, 270). Today, the market still exists on Place Parmentier on Quai Bélu, and is used by the remaining Hortillons to sell their products (Les Hortillonnages d'Amiens n.d. [c]) **[Fig. 6]**.

By contrast, only one professional Maretier operates in the Marais, selling his products directly from a stand on his plot, offering them on the Internet, and supplying nearby restaurants (Lajoinie 2019). In the days of professional farming, there was a market hall in the center of Bourges where residents used to buy produce, but it was given up in the 1960s. Today the Marais are mainly cultivated for self-consumption (Fleury 1998) **[Fig. 7]**.

Heritage Values

Both areas have numerous aspects that today represent an important intangible and tangible (agri-)cultural heritage and should be preserved as such. Besides the man-made landscape of canals and islands, the tangible heritage includes tools, invented by the Maretiers and the Hortillons. For maintenance of the Marais, three special tools are used: the *griffe* (claw) to remove debris lying at the bottom of the canals, the *drague* (a kind of curved shovel) to dredge the mud and the *batte* (beater) to level the mud in the fields (Narboux 2010, 58) **[Fig. 5]**. In addition, the gardeners invented and built boats adapted to the marshes, as mentioned above.

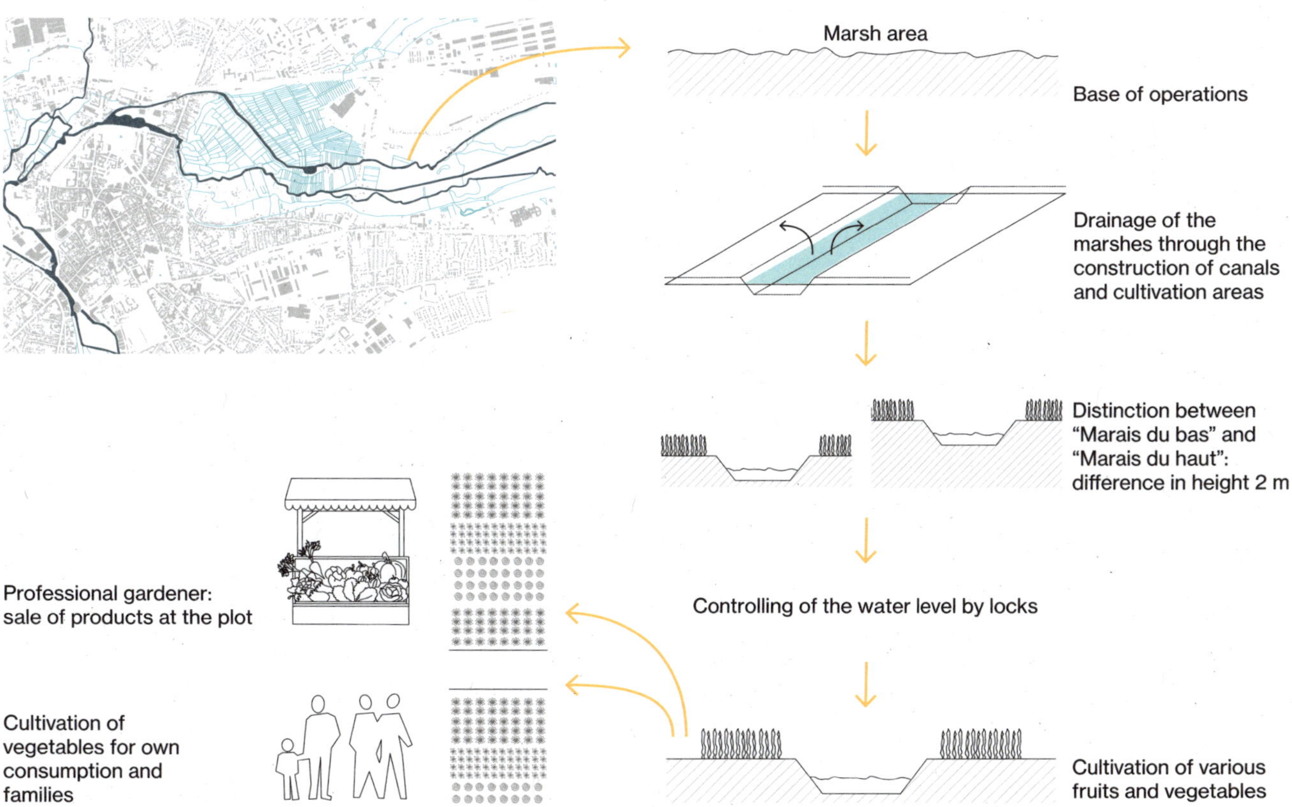

Fig. 7 Overall scheme for the cultivation of the Marais

Fig. 8 Satellite images of the Hortillonnages (left) and the Marais (right): recreational use (top) and cultivated plots (bottom) in comparison

The intangible heritage comprises the knowledge of the Maretiers and the Hortillons to manage the ecosystem. Cultural and social aspects include two gardeners' societies in which the profession was organized in the two cities. The plots have mostly been handed down from father to son, so that even in the twentieth century the same family names as in documents of the fifteenth century can be found among the landowners (Conan 1993, 43). Social life took place in a small environment with its own social hierarchy, dialects, and traditional costumes (Morris 1999, 271; Conan 1993, 43). Traditional festivals—the Fête de Saint Fiacre in Amiens and the Fête des Marais in Bourges—are organized every year in September to revive the traditions of the gardeners (Clauzel 2008b; Narboux 2010, 78).

Threats, Changes and Opportunities

A steady decline in gardeners, due to the nonprofitability of cultivation, is resulting in plots being sold to outsiders, becoming built-up areas, going wild, or being used as recreational gardens (Clauzel 2008a, 26; Clauzel 2008b; Limouzin 1994, 157) **[Fig. 4]**. The areas have shrunk, and the appearance of both sites, especially of the Hortillonnages, is changing: the formerly open areas are now increasingly closed by hedges and trees, more cottages and houses are being built in place of the former small sheds, and arable land is becoming grassland (Clauzel 2008b) **[Fig. 8]**. A part of the Hortillonnages was transformed into a park, and art exhibitions on the water are organized (Morris 1999, 272–73). The focus has changed from agriculture to culture and tourism. In the Marais, the original character of the agricultural land was partly preserved by the installation of allotment gardens, in which the owners continue to grow vegetables for their own use (L'Association des Maraîchers de Bourges 2009a).

A great interest in the preservation of both areas has arisen. In Bourges, two organizations, Patrimoine Marais and Association des Maraîchers de Bourges (short form: AMB) were founded, the first in 1977 (Patrimoine Marais n.d. [a]), the second in 1998. The AMB has 605 members (2012), consisting of private individuals and private vegetable gardeners (L'Association Maraîchers de Bourges 2009b). They aim to pass the heritage of the Marais to future generations and to support, encourage, and defend local gardeners as well as to combat the threats and risks of the area and promote the interest of the outside population in the Marais and its culture (L'Association des Maraîchers de Bourges 2009c). To this end they organize information days, look for new actors, and publish newsletters and brochures (L'Association des Maraîchers de Bourges 2009d). The second organization is committed to the regular maintenance of the Marais and organizes various events, including the Marais Festival (Patrimoine Marais n.d. [b]). In Amiens, the Association pour la Protection et la Sauvegarde des Hortillonnages (Association for the Protection and Safeguarding of Hortillonnages) works to protect the area. It was founded in 1975, when a bypass road was planned to run through the middle of the Hortillonnages. The project was prevented. Today, the organization takes care of the regular maintenance and offers tourist activities such as guided tours through the Hortillonnages (Les Hortillonnages d'Amiens n.d. [a]). In addition, the city of Amiens has developed a global plan, which includes the support of gardeners through the establishment of their own brand (Clauzel 2008b).

Conclusion

The Hortillonnages and the Marais are almost unique urban agricultural heritage sites with a centuries-old tradition. Out of the necessity to supply the cities with fruit and vegetables, these cultivation areas were constructed and have always been important for the identity of both cities. A consciousness for the preservation of the sites is present; both areas have a national status of protection, preventing them from being used as construction land. Furthermore, the city of Amiens has recognized the potential of the Hortillonnages by creating incentives for professional gardeners to avoid a complete loss of culture and heritage values. However, the valorization of the Hortillonnages is partly based on tourism, turning them into a kind of amusement park. The city of Bourges does not participate in the preservation of the Marais. Local organizations have developed their own strategies and focus on the aspect of traditional cultivation and the transmission of knowledge.

From being the basis of the fresh food supply for the urban population, both areas have transformed into a place of community or leisure and recreation. The Hortillonnages must be regarded more as a relict landscape that has lost most of its original productive function. They can be seen as a green space and ecological zone that must be preserved within the urban space of Amiens. In the Marais de Bourges, their productive function is still in evidence today. Although there are hardly any professional gardeners left, private, productive family gardens still form a large part of the heritage area. The original structures of the plots are thus still visible, as are the social structures and the community spirit of the people. ■

From Orchard to Wetland Park: Guangzhou's Approach to Transform Urban Agricultural Heritage

Mengyun Chen and Guangsi Lin

The urban population in Asia grows by more than 45 million per year on average, resulting in the loss of up to 10 square kilometers of farmland per day (Dahiya 2012), which has eliminated the open spaces of the rural-urban fringe to a large extent. This is especially true in China, where urbanization has transformed large tracts of farmland.

Wanmu Orchard is a typical example of a shrinking agricultural system in Asia. This ancient orchard in Guangzhou, the most dense urban area in China **[Figs. 1 and 2]**, was originally located in the suburbs, far from residential areas, but due to rapid urbanization it has been absorbed into and is now part of the city center. Using a top-down planning approach, China's state forestry administration declared the Wanmu Orchard as the Haizhu National Wetland Park in 2015, and it has been transformed since then. Though this designation preserved the green space, the already accomplished changes and ongoing renovations have destroyed a large portion of its historical spatial and social structures.

This case study aims to explain the effects of the top-down planning approach, reflecting on how this approach endangers the heritage and drawing lessons from the process.

Outstanding Characteristics of Wanmu Orchard

Wanmu Orchard is an ancient agricultural system whose history can be traced back two thousand years, when fruit trees were first planted on the riverbanks. It is located in the Guangzhou city center in the Guangdong Province in South China, and although much diminished in size today, its 11 square kilometers is three times larger than Central Park in New York City. The orchard consists of lakes, rivers, and subtropical fruit forests and is organized by a dike-pond system, which was first adopted in the seventeenth century. The dike-pond system allowed low-lying areas that had not been usable farmland to be planted with trees and other crops, greatly expanding the orchard planting area and drawing on the local wisdom of how to live with water and nourish the local population in the Pearl River Delta **[Fig. 3]**.

As the most distinctive feature of Wanmu Orchard, the dike-pond system is an ancient, naturally balanced system used in the riverine plains and estuaries of East and South China, which integrates agriculture and aquaculture (Astudillo et al. 2015). In this system, different species, organized in layers, form a working ecosystem: fruit trees (such as lychee, longan, and orange) and crops (such as taro, elephant grass, and flowers), planted under the trees, on the dikes; and fish, birds, aquatic plants, plankton, microorganisms, etc., in the ponds **[Fig. 4]**.

The dike-pond system is formed by digging the low-lying land into ponds to farm fish, and using the excavated soil to raise the surrounding land and to create the dikes, which are used for planting. This construction protects fruit trees from flooding during the monsoon season by draining surplus water, and also builds a productive closed loop for the transfer of energy and exchange of matter.

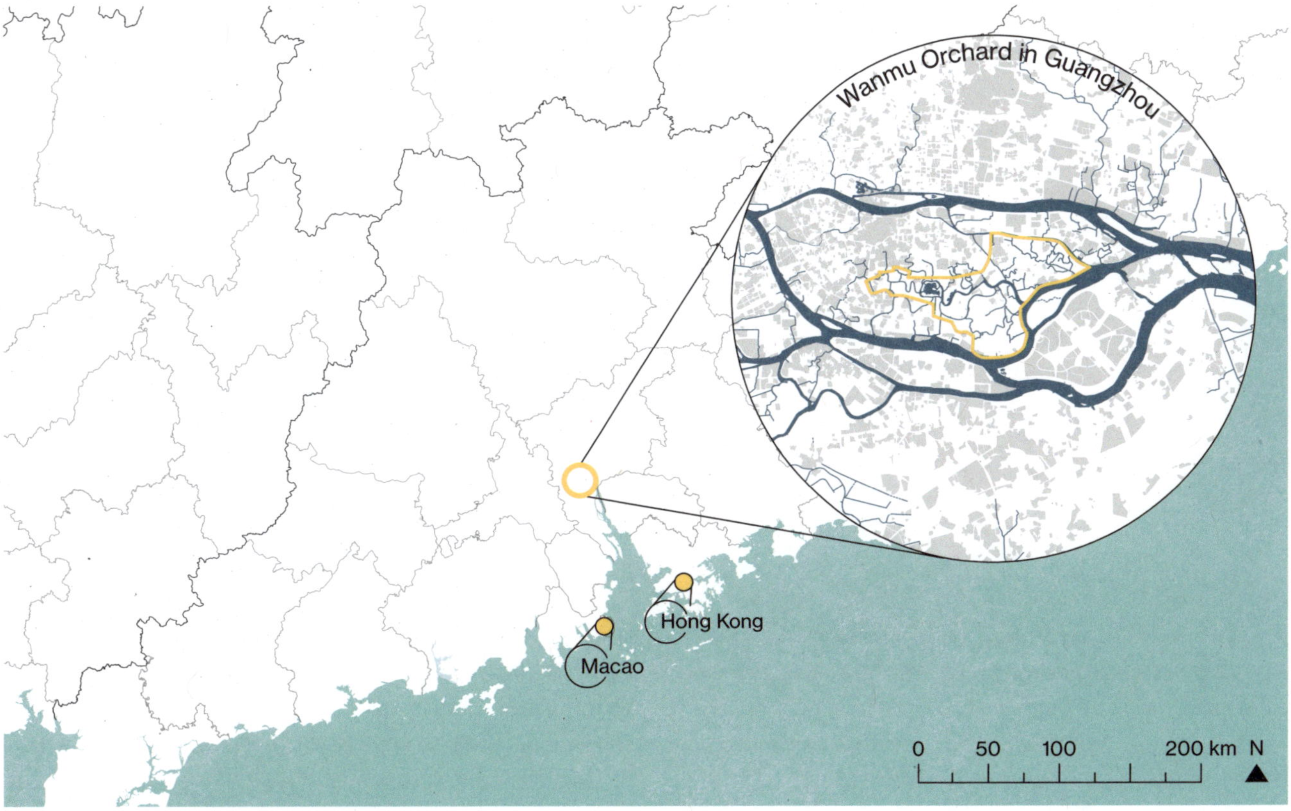

Fig. 1 Location of Wanmu Orchard

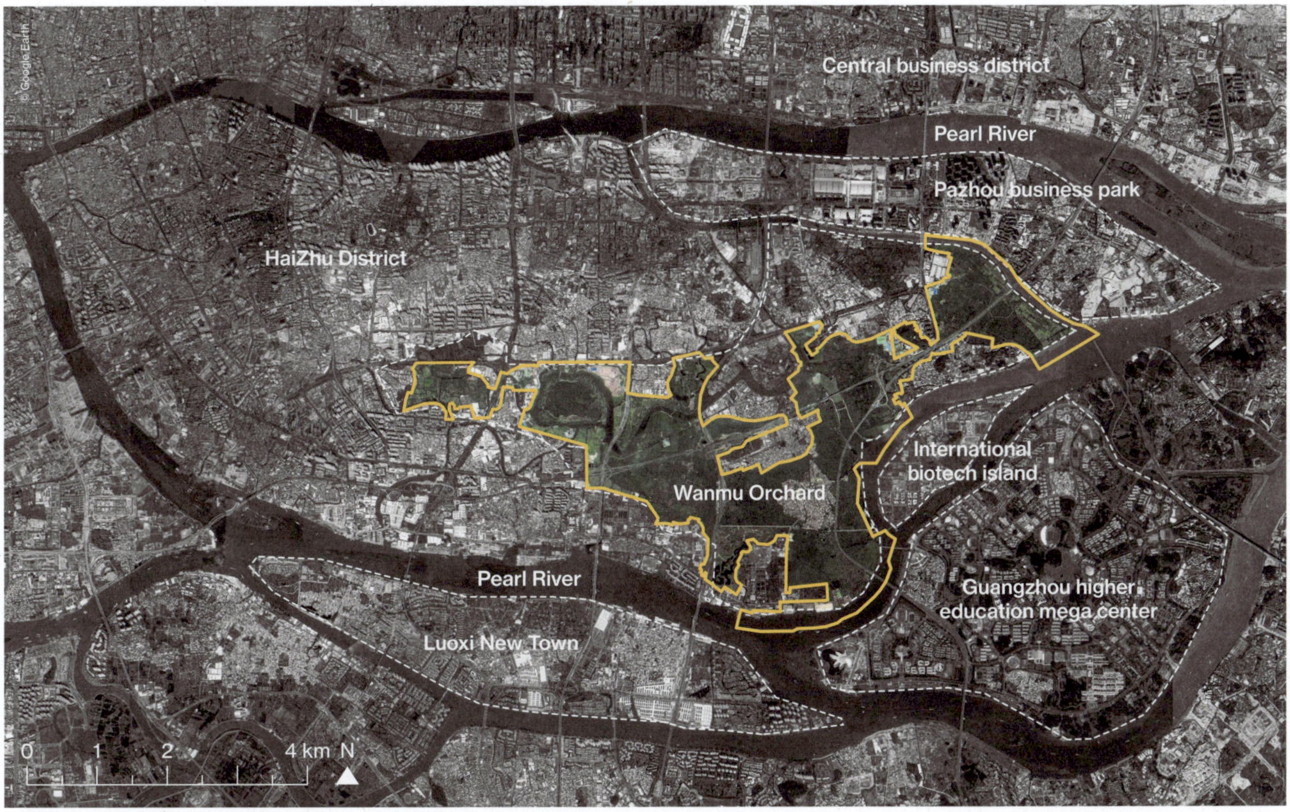

Fig. 2 Wanmu Orchard surrounded by dense urban fabric

However, not all dikes and ponds are the same size; they vary according to the quantity and species of fish and fruit trees. In Wanmu Orchard, it can be roughly divided into three categories depending on the width of the pond: 0.5–1 m, 1–2 m, and 3–5 m **[Fig. 5]**.

The ponds of the dike-pond system are connected to the Pearl River; thus, an automatic irrigation and drainage system is formed. When water is needed, the rising tide is used to divert water into the pond; when water is not needed, the low tide is used to drain the pond. The fish ponds play a role in water retention during the rainy season, and maintain moisture in the soil, providing water to the crops on the dikes through soil capillary action, especially important during the drought season.

In the circle of the system, the fruit tree is the first trophic level. Its leaves are eaten by wild birds and fish. The aquatic organisms in the pond work as reduction agents, breaking down the organic matter in the ponds such as fish excreta and algae, and producing nitrogen, phosphorus, and potassium in return. These elements are then returned to the dike when pond mud is used as fertilizer (Gongfu 1982) **[Fig. 6]**.

In order to make this system work successfully, it relies not only on each family in the community, which is responsible for their own land cultivation and daily maintenance, but also on the cooperative, a nongovernmental, village-based collective economic organization, to carry out product sales and benefit distribution.

The Effects of Rapid Urbanization on Wanmu Orchard

Due to the rapid expansion of the city center since the 1980s, Wanmu Orchard has undergone many changes affecting its size, functions, and landscape patterns. Urbanization has transformed Wanmu Orchard from a traditional agricultural system **[Fig. 7]** first into an urban agricultural park and then into a national wetland park. The orchard has decreased in size massively from 40 square kilometers in the 1980s to 11 square kilometers left today **[Fig. 8]** (Shidong and Qifeng 2017).

Since Guangzhou's city center crossed the Pearl River and expanded into the southern region in the late 1990s, the location of Wanmu Orchard has gradually transformed from a remote area into a peri-urban fringe zone. The agricultural land's relatively low price led to an increase in the construction of small factories in the orchards, followed by some illegally built residential buildings. House rentals gradually replaced agricultural production as an economic pillar for the villagers. Thus large parts of the original fertile and productive landscape gradually disappeared and were replaced by polluted rivers, the continued rapid growth of buildings, and the construction of several municipal roads through Wanmu Orchard.

All these changes reduced the quantity and quality of fruit production. According to the *Statistical Communiqué of the Haizhu District on the 1996 National Economic and Social Development*, the total output of Wanmu Orchard sank to 6,400 tons of fruit per year, a steep decline from the 20,000 tons that had been produced there in the early 1990s. This decrease aroused the government's concern and raised awareness of the need to protect the remaining orchard. From 1997 to 2008, the Guangzhou government rented 3.64 square kilometers of the orchard's land to build a series of agricultural parks for ecotourism, in order to prevent Wanmu Orchard from shrinking. Although this curbed the reduction of the cultivated land, a large number of fruit trees were felled, and the orchard's function as an urban food producer was gradually weakened.

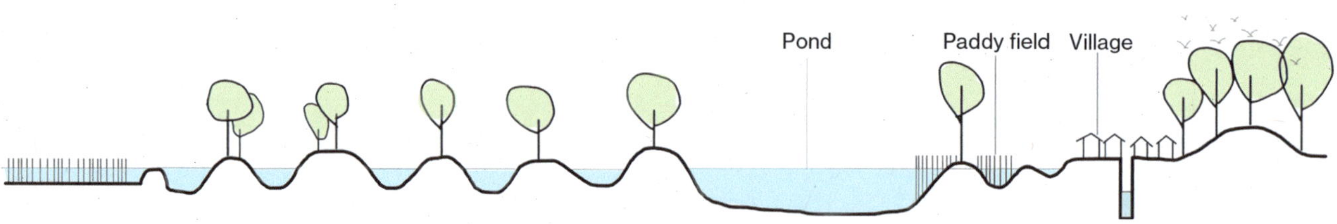

Fig. 3 The dike-pond landscape pattern of Wanmu Orchard

Fig. 4 Illustration of the dike-pond system's layers

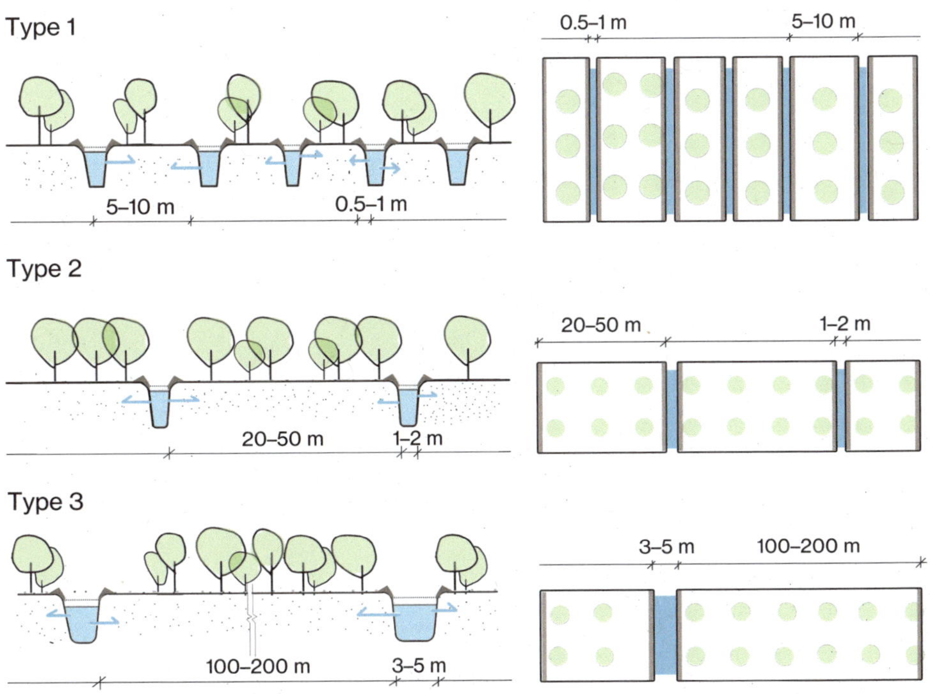

Fig. 5 Different sizes of dikes and ponds in the orchard

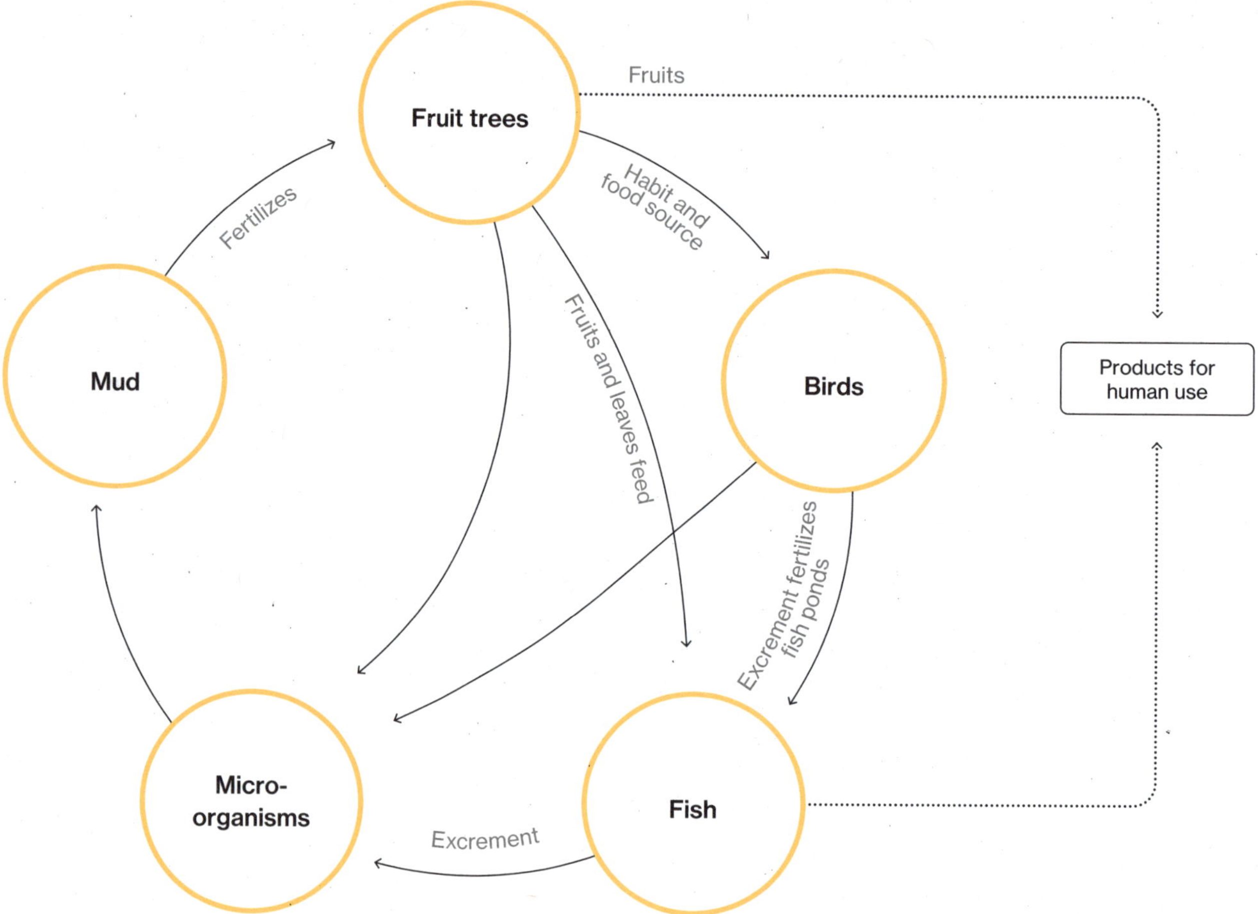

Fig. 6 Closed loop of the dike-pond system in the orchard

Fig. 7 Production landscape of Wanmu Orchard in the 1970s

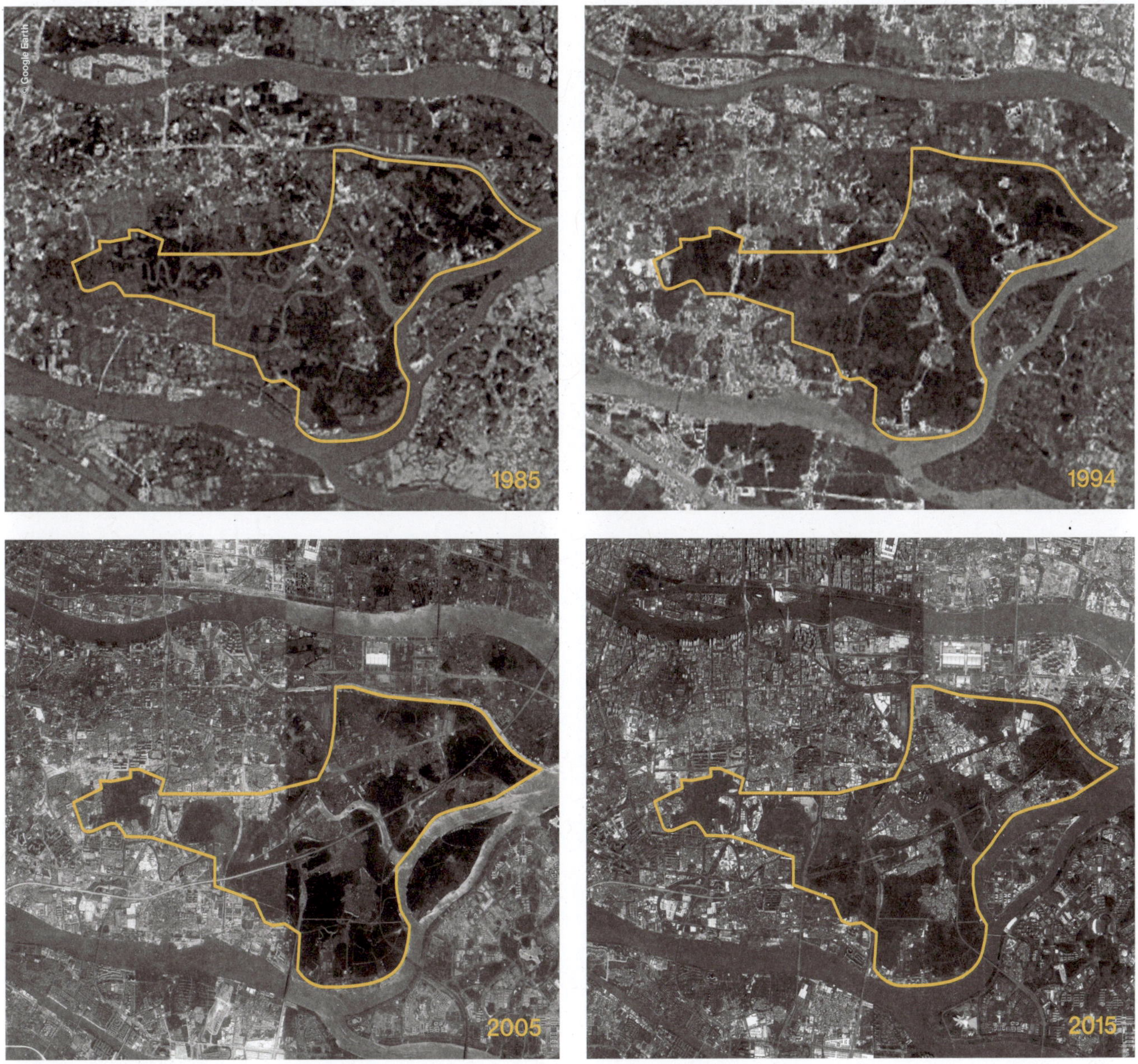

Figs. 8a–d The orchard area shrank with the expansion of urban construction from 1985 to 2015

Today, Wanmu Orchard is no longer an important source for providing fruit to Guangzhou's inhabitants.

In order to further maintain this green space in Guangzhou's high-density urban environment, since 2012 the local government has taken custody of the orchard's remaining areas of about eight square kilometers by expropriating the owners—mainly farmers. Although there was a statement of intent not to change the nature of the agricultural land, large parts of the traditional agricultural structure were transformed when the orchard became a national wetland park in 2015. During this transition, most of the dike-pond systems were destroyed; some were replaced by artificial wetland park elements, such as a lotus pool, rockery, and pavilions. The remaining fruit trees lost their closed-loop ecosystem **[Fig. 6]**. Moreover, the set of ecosystem services that are provided by the area has decreased, because Wanmu Orchard lost both its productive and inherited cultural services and today is oriented only toward water purification and leisure functions for urban residents. Today, Wanmu Orchard is known as the "Green Heart" of the city. Although it is zoned as agricultural land in the land utilization plan, it has actually assumed the function of an urban public green space.

Lessons from Guangzhou's Approach

As this case study illustrates, the government played a dominant role in the protection of the orchard. The question remains whether the top-down approach was the best choice.

It is obvious that government intervention can benefit an area by halting the decrease in surface area due to development. It delimited the protected area and took the land, which had been previously jointly owned and cultivated by the local community, into state control. Local farmers are now employed by the government to do some fruit tree planting and maintenance as well as fish and poultry farming and, thus, to maintain the landscape. In addition, a governmental wetland protection and management office replaced the local cooperative in carrying out daily management tasks such as water-quality restoration and fruit tree pest control. After the change of the orchard into a wetland park, the ecological problems originally caused by sloppy management, such as damage to the quality of the water and soil, have improved.

Despite these positives, the government's top-down approach has exerted a negative effect on the orchard's agricultural heritage. While a number of open-water areas still exist in the former orchard, its transformation into a wetland park has deeply modified the local ecosystem, for example through the replacement of ancient fruit forests by artificial lakes, which has broken the energy and nutrient cycles. Furthermore, most of the local inhabitants who used to own and farm in the orchard are now excluded from it. Only a few people are employed to take care of the remaining trees on a daily basis. Wanmu Orchard's dike-pond system, which was well adapted to the local ecological conditions of the Pearl River Delta and was maintained based on local knowledge, has become an ordinary artificial wetland no different from any other in a built-up urban area **[Fig. 9]**. The interventions of the first phase of construction from 2012 to 2015 destroyed the site's existing routine and erased its historical texture. It not only separated the geographical connection and memory from the people who have lived on this land cultivated by their ancestors, but also caused many of them to lose their incomes from fruit production, as well as traditional cultural knowledge.

There may be better approaches to urban agricultural heritage systems like Wanmu Orchard, approaches that balance agricultural production and ecological needs, in which the government can support farmers by adapting their practices to the site's ecological necessities and still meet city dwellers' demands to spend their leisure time in the area. Today, it would not be feasible to restore Wanmu Orchard to its original structure. With land prices so high in the city center, it is a luxury to continue traditional farming, which is not profitable, especially compared with other industries. Moreover, since other industries are much more attractive than agriculture, few farmers want to go back to farming. Finally, there is a vast ecological need for flood regulation and water purification in the city. However, the erasure of this historical agricultural system and its multiple heritage values and the area's transformation into an urban park was too rash. When we discuss the protection of urban agricultural heritage in rapid urbanization processes, we should neither fall into the trap of static protection nor blindly cater to the city by radically altering agricultural systems through beautification. Instead, the land should be protected taking into account its innate and historical functions.

It may be a good choice to combine the historic urban landscape approach established by the United Nations Educational, Scientific and Cultural Organization in 2011 with the approach taken in Guangzhou (UNESCO 2011). First, it is necessary to analyze the historical evolution process of the agricultural systems and to understand the mechanism of their formation in different periods in order to assess the overall heritage value and social meaning. We should also analyze the vulnerability of heritage to socioeconomic pressures and the impacts of climate change to determine which positive effects the heritage can contribute to the city's social, ecological, and economical resilience and future. Finally, heritage values and their vulnerability status should be integrated into the wider framework of city development. By delimiting the protected area based on such an assessment, governments can transfer ecosystem services provided by private agriculture into state-financed services of general interest. In this way, we could integrate the core values and ecosystem services of urban agricultural heritage into future urban development. ■

Fig. 9 Current situation of Wanmu Orchard as a wetland park

Urban Agricultural Heritage of Lisbon: From the Past to the Future?

Mariana Sanchez Salvador

Cities face pressing challenges regarding food security and sustainable development, aggravated by fast urbanization and globalized, industrial food systems. Urban agriculture has been pointed to as an innovative approach to overcome the current urban-rural divide (FAO 2019) and achieve urban sustainability. Yet agriculture has always been part of cities, and its heritage stretches far beyond land use. Its recognition and promotion could mitigate those challenges, but also revive sites, socioeconomic functions, and cultural connections, turning urban agricultural heritage into a valuable tool for sustainable urban planning.

Lisbon's Agricultural Past

Lisbon, Portugal's capital city, has a long tradition of urban agriculture, due to its natural topography and orography. Located by the Tagus River, on the Atlantic shore, the region possesses basaltic soils suited to grain cultivation, while the Miocene soils were suited to vineyards, olive groves, pastures, and vegetable gardens (Gaspar 1994, 83). Thus, since prehistoric times, and then with the Romans and Moors, the valleys and slopes have long been cultivated.

The medieval land uses showcased an organization similar to von Thünen's model: a ring of fruit and vegetable production was located around the city center (on average 1.8 kilometers from it), followed by a ring of vineyards with olive trees (on average 5 kilometers) and a third for grain cultivation and livestock (Trindade and Gaspar 1973, 5–7). Historically, the fertile outskirts stretched for 30 kilometers around the city. The Saloia Region spreads to the north and west, while the Outra Banda is located across the river [Fig. 1]. Despite subregional differences, both have supplied abundant vegetables, fruits, grain, dairy cattle, and sheep [Fig. 2]. The Mediterranean trinity—bread, wine, and olive oil—held a particular economic role (Brito 1976, 168). Although the Saloia Region yielded an impressive 360,000 réis per hectare in 1887, even higher yields were attained within the city, reaching 500,000 réis (Pereira 1971, 181).

For centuries, numerous *hortas* (vegetable gardens) intertwined with Lisbon's built fabric [Figs. 3 and 10, p. 95], especially in the extremely fertile valleys of Valverde and Arroios (toward the city center), of Alcântara in the west [Fig. 4], and of Chelas in the east. Also, until the mid-twentieth century, the northern highlands of Campo Grande [Figs. 5 and 6] displayed an especially high concentration of hortas in the city, as well as Campo Pequeno and Campolide (*campo* meaning "field"). Traditionally, hortas were small (less than one hectare) and highly productive, with up to five or six crops a year (180). In the early twentieth century, at least 40 percent of the municipal territory was still cultivated (Marat-Mendes, Bento d'Almeida and Mourão 2015, 280), with hortas, vineyards, and olive groves predominating in the east, and ploughed lands for grain and potatoes in the west (Niza et al. 2014, 8).

This productive character is further attested by the cartographic survey of 1904–11 [Fig. 7], where 529 *quintas* (farms) and 52 *casais* (smaller agricultural

Fig. 1 The land surrounding Lisbon, 1856–66. Map showing the outskirts of Lisbon, spreading to the Saloia Region in the north (yellow outline), and Outra Banda in the south (red outline)

Marat-Mendes, Bento d'Almeida and Mourão (2015) which enabled the mapping of cultivated areas. The identification of hortas was clear **[Fig. 8]** amounting to 751 hectares (8.56 percent of the municipal area)—enough to feed a tenth of its population—as well as of vineyards, occupying 606 hectares (6.91 percent). The built area remained at 530 hectares. Less conclusively, according to the provided legend, olive groves could reach 22.7 percent of the municipal area, and ploughed lands up to 28.5 percent, summing up a considerable cultivated area. Lisbon and its region were one of the greatest productive areas in the country.

Urban agriculture was thus an important activity, as an extensive land use with constant presence over time, providing livelihoods, income (high yields and exports), and intensive labor, particularly required by hortas and vineyards, and one reason why they were located close to the houses. Food production is embedded in the city's memory, evident in many place names—streets, alleys, and entire neighborhoods, such as *Laranjeiras* (orange trees) or *Olivais* (olive groves) **[Fig. 9]**—and even Lisboners' was a popular Sunday activity in Lisbon, especially for the lower classes, a practice known across Portugal and that became part of the city's identity. Plus, the hortas' beauty and fertility had been praised by writers and travelers for centuries. Lisbon's urban agricultural heritage thus consists of a material dimension related to land use, and an immaterial one, connected to daily labor, weekly leisure, everyday comings and goings, literature, and long history, becoming part of its cultural character.

However, despite its exceptional productivity, the capital, which hosts the country's largest population, has never been self-sufficient. Each year, it produced 172,735 kilograms of potatoes, which represented merely 0.95 percent of its consumption; 228,570 kilograms of fruits (1.59 percent of consumption); and 1,033,565 kilograms of wine (2.20 percent of consumption), among others (Marat-Mendes et al. 2014, 8). Thus, Lisbon has always imported food from the rest of Portugal and even overseas using both land routes and the river.

As demographic and economic transitions occurred, the perception of urban agriculture declined. Across

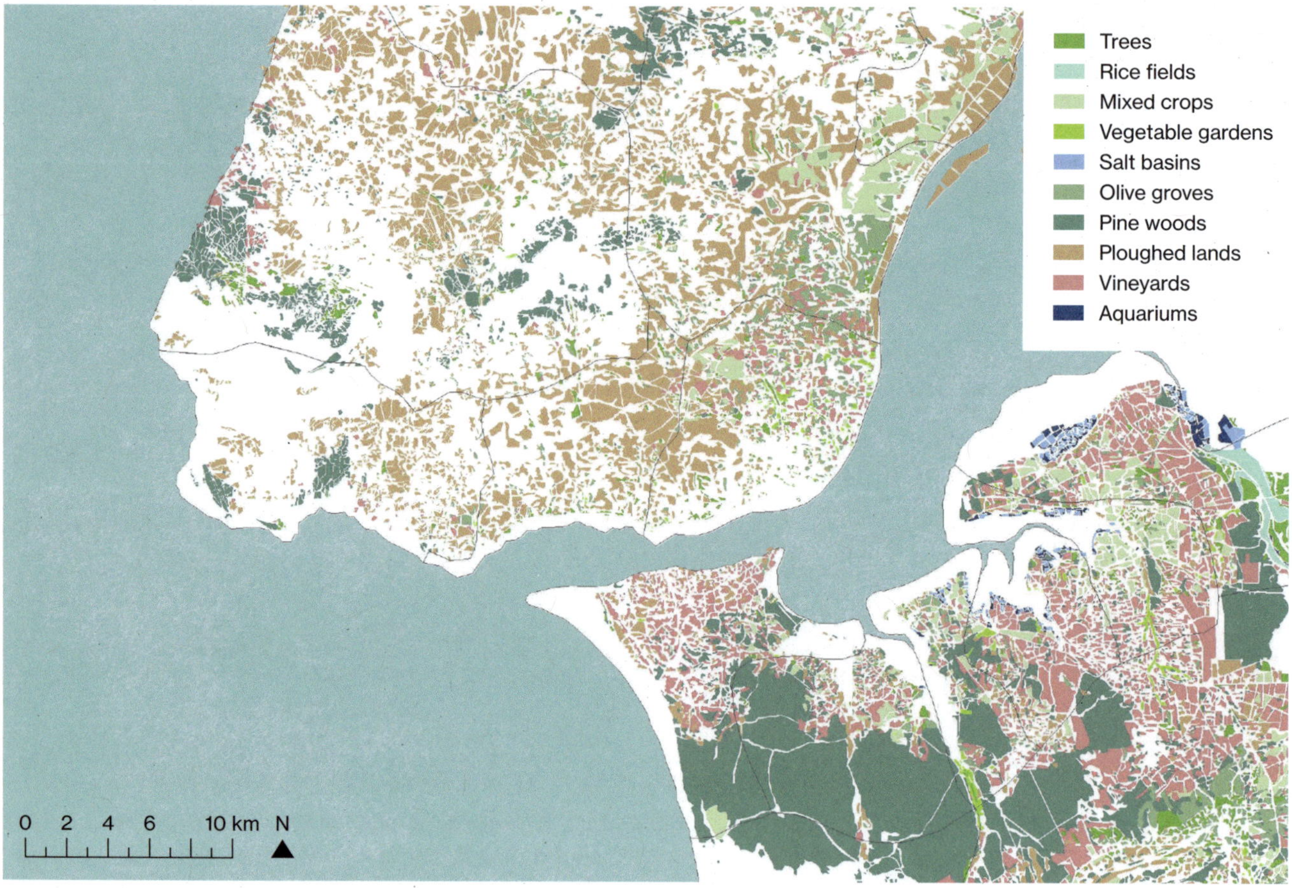

Fig. 2 Crops in and around Lisbon, in 1900

the city, many agricultural sites were progressively lost to systematic urbanization and to an ideal of modernity, where urban hygienist conceptions prevailed. Agriculture was generally seen as a backward, rustic, and dirty activity by early twentieth-century society, and modernizing the city became a priority for the city council (Barata 2010; Henriques da Silva 1994). The cultivated areas of quintas (hortas, orchards, fields) were built over, while buildings and ornamental gardens were kept (Ribeiro 1992). From the mid-twentieth century on, and particularly since the 1970s, hortas were found mainly among illegal housing neighborhoods (CML 2015, 45).

Lisbon's Agricultural Present

Recently, urban agriculture has (re)gained a positive connotation within urban planning. The Municipal Master Plan, Lisbon's main planning instrument (CML 2012), sets the goal for a "multifunctional green infrastructure," where integrating urban agriculture is taken as a possible strategy, among others. For this purpose, the Plan thus classifies areas of "green and productive spaces" (94–95).

In an interview, Rita Folgosa (2020), coordinator of the municipal Working Group for the Development and Promotion of Urban Agriculture in Lisbon, stated that urban agriculture is integrated into green spaces for environmental and aesthetic purposes to attract people and increase biodiversity, besides all the recognized benefits of urban agriculture, such as social cohesion, migrant integration, and food resources for families and individuals in need.

Therefore, a number of municipal horticultural parks were created, where farmers pay low rents for plots equipped with paths, fences, sheds, composters, and water supply. The city council commits to the structures' maintenance, monitoring, and farmers' training, while farmers must cultivate the soil, practice organic agriculture, keep hygienic standards, ensure that plots look aesthetically pleasant, and restrain from building constructions unrelated to agriculture (CML 2018). Plus, the parks carry economic benefits, since the

Fig. 3 Panoramic view from Parada do Alto de São João over Graça and Penha da França street, 1941. In this historical neighborhood it was still possible to identify, in mid-twentieth century, patches of hortas and olive trees.

Fig. 4 Alcântara Valley, ca. 1930. This was for centuries one of the most cultivated valleys of Lisbon, until its occupation by road infrastructure.

Fig. 5 Aerial view over Campo Grande, ca. 1934. Having a leisure park in the center, its edges were mainly occupied by vegetable gardens, being one of the biggest concentrations of vegetable gardens in the city in the early twentieth century.

Fig. 6 Campo Grande, 1945. This area was still intensively cultivated in the 1940s, reaching some of the highest yields in the city.

City gets rents and saves in maintenance. There are now 20 parks, from 430 to 32,600 square meters **[Fig. 11]**, with 771 plots cultivated by 732 individuals and 19 institutions (Folgosa 2020).

Since the horticultural parks are placed on municipal property and already defined as "green and productive spaces" (CML 2012, 94–95), they face minimum pressure by urbanization. The main challenges relate to management, resistance by farmers to adopt new practices, cultural challenges with communities, or negotiations with other institutions regarding the type of green space to be implemented.

Although some are located near previously farmed areas, the parks do not adapt to old structures or work with heritage values. In fact, despite the rich agricultural history, Folgosa (2020) admits that creating new parks is a decision mainly connected to land availability and perceived demand in a neighborhood. The six members of the Working Group for the Development and Promotion of Urban Agriculture believe the municipality probably possesses sufficient information regarding previous quintas and farmed areas, so if that route were chosen, a lack of information would likely not be an obstacle. However, Folgosa states that using this data to plan the new parks is not a priority at the moment due to lack of resources and people to organize and analyze it.

Besides municipal top-down strategies, private hortas subside within the built-up fabric, in an informal (at times illegal) way. Their numbers and areas are, however, difficult to assess due to insufficient data. There are also educational hortas at universities and schools; but no organized bottom-up agricultural projects are known at the moment. Thus, although urban agriculture is recognized as an economic activity, a tool for greening the city, and for its social role, its heritage value remains unstated, as it has not yet been addressed by Lisbon's urban policy.

One dimension of urban agricultural heritage that has been recognized, however, is agricultural biodiversity (Folgosa 2020). In fact, an impressive

Fig. 7 Cartographic survey of Lisbon by Silva Pinto, commissioned by Lisbon's City Council, 1904–11. This survey was the first to portray the final municipal area of Lisbon, defined after a number of transformations occurred during the nineteenth century; the perimeter is similar to the present-day one. At the time, buildings (in black, excluding sheds and warehouses) occupied a minimal surface (6.05 percent), in an area dominated by agriculture.

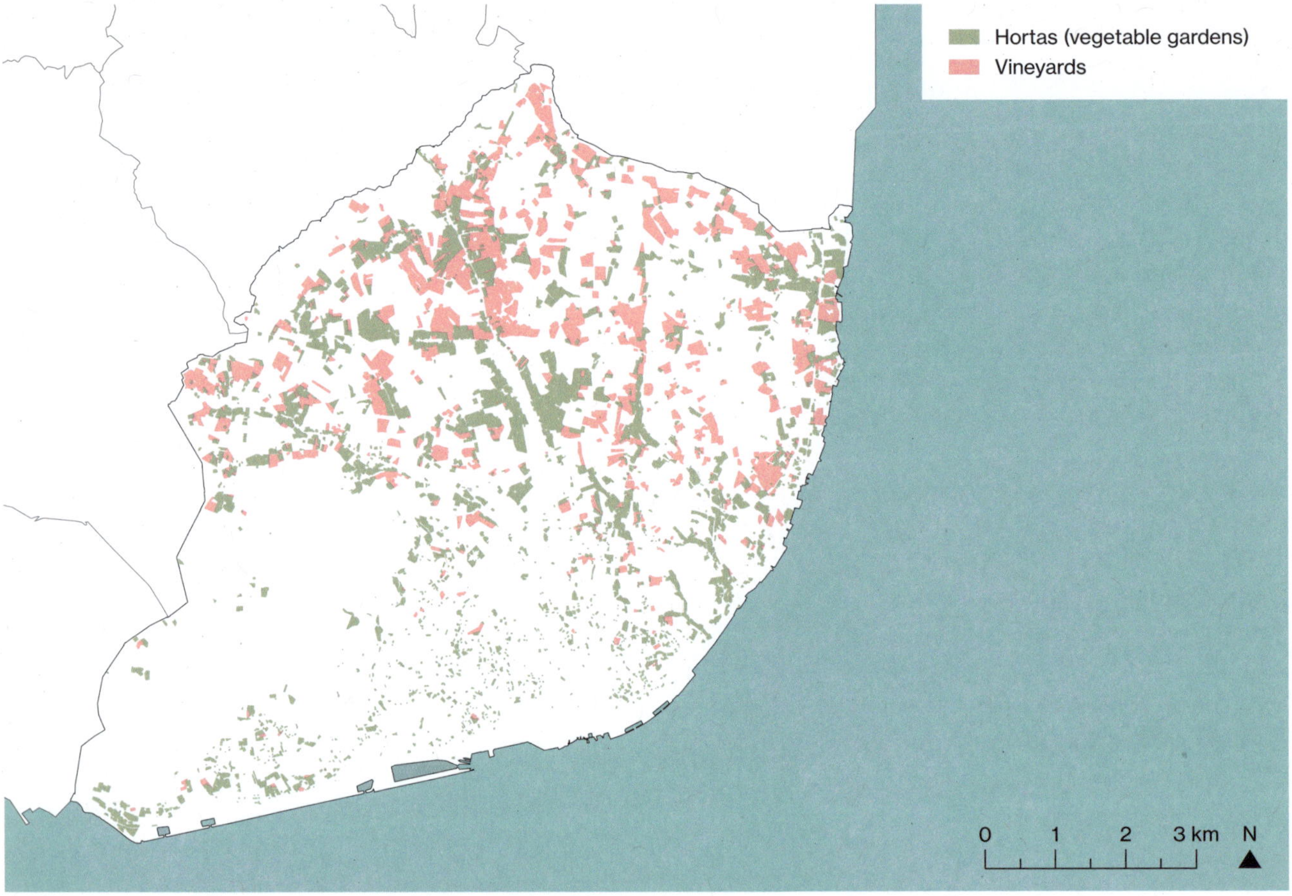

Fig. 8 Hortas and vineyards in Lisbon. These crops occupied around 15 percent of the city's area in 1904–11.

Fig. 9 View of Olivais, 1940. This photograph attests to the existence of centenary olive trees at Olivais, whose constant presence the neighborhood owes its name to.

Fig. 10 Horta in Lisbon, ca. 1900. Vegetable gardens existed around and within the built fabric, being part of the city's everyday life and landscape.

variety of vegetables, fruits, and pulses was identified during a survey in seven parks: some native, some—for residents who were not born in Lisbon or who are second-generation—from the farmers' homelands. A book on this seed survey was published to raise awareness, and it is a key feature in a current Lisbon European Green Capital 2020 exhibition. Fur-ther, Lisbon's seed heritage is actively preserved by cooperatives and by the farmers themselves.

Lisbon's Agricultural Future: Steps toward Recognition and Promotion of Its Heritage

Lisbon is a city proud of its material and immaterial heritage—monuments, food (Mediterranean diet), even *fado* (traditional songs classified by UNESCO). However, despite its important role in the city's history, urban agriculture is not acknowledged as heritage, neither by its citizens nor its politicians, at least not yet; hortas' sites and land uses are not preserved, and farming practices, knowledge, and traditions are not recognized or promoted as heritage, nor as assets for the city. There are also no current educational or awareness-raising actions in progress to address them as such.

Possibly, this might be due to ignorance about the potential of urban agricultural heritage on the urban environmental, social, and economic balance, and even tourism. In this sense, contact with cities where this recognition is in progress could be key in revealing this potential to stakeholders and politicians, providing a framework and reference models, and clarifying the specificities of Lisbon's case.

Comprehensive organized data and overall education on the subject are lacking, both in academia and society, to inform actions and policies. Much in the same way that active steps are taken for the recognition of seed heritage, the same should be done for urban agricultural heritage as a whole: surveying, compilation, disclosure (publications, documentaries, exhibitions, etc.), promotion (activities, workshops), and eventually policies regarding its different dimensions. Possibly existing conflicts, priorities, and challenges should be assessed through interviews with stakeholders. A comprehensive survey on informal urban agriculture—including location, area, crops cultivated, practices, farmers' profiles, etc.—could also be a valuable contribution for an in-depth overview of the city's current agricultural situation, and possibly uncover surviving elements of its past.

Gathering all this information may hold tremendous potential for Lisbon, both culturally and environmentally. Reactivating hortas may promote circular metabolism and the local economy, but also bring a sense of historical identity to newer neighborhoods (some built over previous hortas themselves) and strengthen social interactions among neighbors. Bottom-up projects could be initialized to create additional spaces for cultivation (the City recognizes that long waiting lists exist for all horticultural parks), and to educate residents on the benefits, history, and potential of urban agricultural heritage.

However, unveiling Lisbon's urban agricultural heritage is not a matter of recreating what went before. Most sites farmed a century ago have disappeared; the farmer's profile has changed; and contexts and values have been transformed. It needs to be reframed to accommodate updated knowledge, new farming techniques, and acknowledge its wider role on urban sustainability and social cohesion. Some historical systems and values—proximity to food sources, food security, circular flows, sense of community, a better built-to-green space balance—can, however, be revived. Finally, this awareness could ripple on more active and protective policies, shifting from tourism and foreign investment toward urban agriculture, not only as a land use to be integrated in its green infrastructure, but as an urban agricultural heritage to be valued in the city's dynamics, life, and overall landscape.

To sum up, awareness, education, data, and reference models are required to emphasize urban agricultural heritage's true potential and its specific relevance in the case of Lisbon, which may bring historical solutions to life and inform actions for a sustainable city, so that urban agriculture can not only be part of Lisbon's past, but also be part of its future. ■

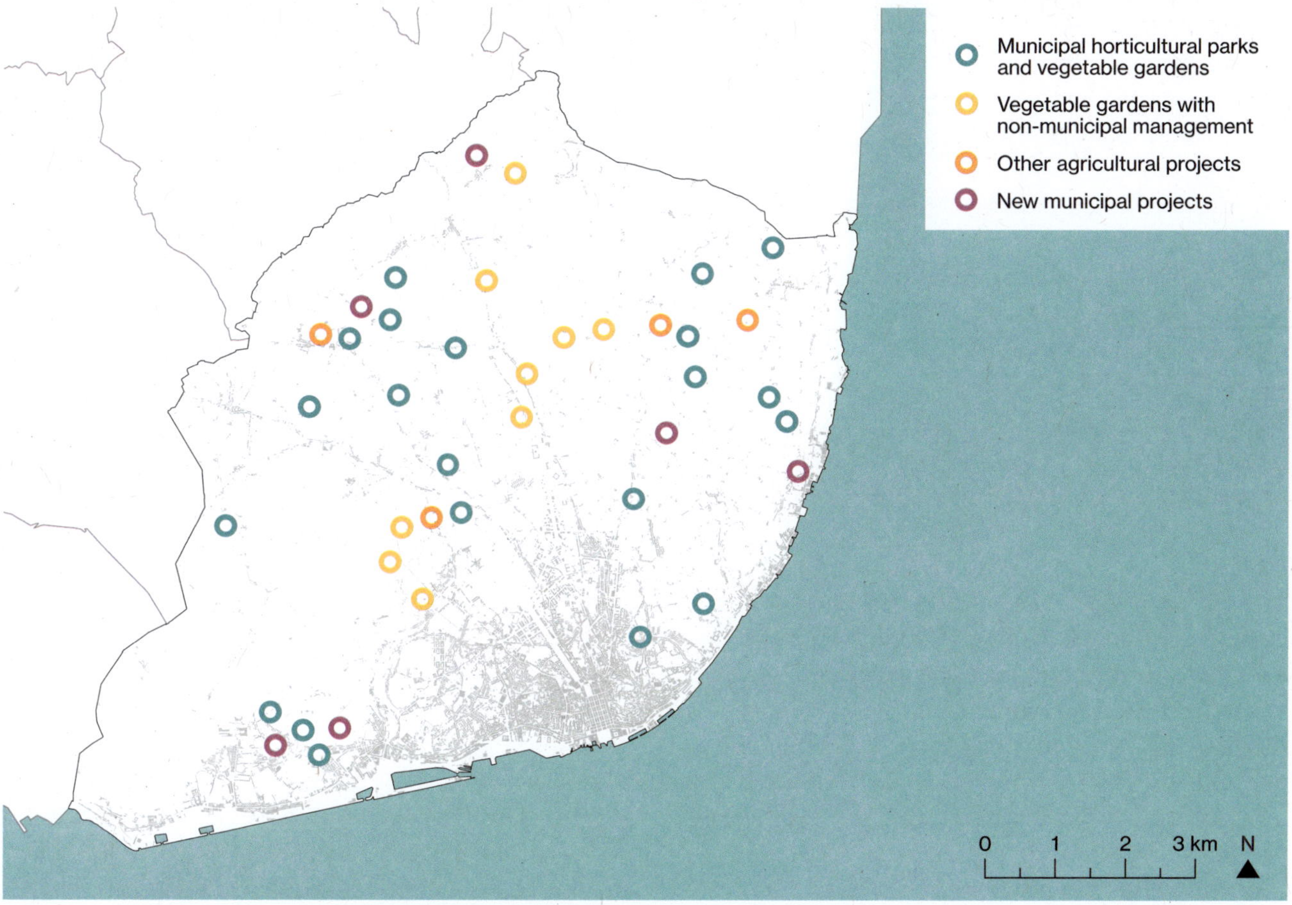

Fig. 11 Location of municipal horticultural parks and other agricultural projects in the city, 2020. If compared with the second image, it's noticeable how some of these parks are located in areas that were farmed a century ago, although they do not adapt to old structures or work that heritage values.

Urban Agricultural Heritage in Benin: The Role of Traditional Coconut-Cattle Systems in Cotonou

Bossima I. Koura, Eric Boenecke, Frank Lohrberg, and Luc H. Dossa

Given the challenges of rapid urbanization, population growth, and food security, urban agriculture has gained much importance in African cities within the last decade (FAO 2012). Seen for a long time as an issue linked to poverty and uncontrolled urban growth, local governments now turn to systematically support urban agriculture not only to secure food provision, but also to create jobs and informal income opportunities, especially for women. Initiatives focus very much on smallholder businesses producing vegetables and fruits for urban markets. However, a systematic stocktaking of urban agricultural types is exceptional; mainly, a focus on their history and traditions is missing.

Facing this knowledge gap, we present a case from Cotonou, the Republic of Benin **[Fig. 1]**, focusing on the interaction of coconut cultivation and cattle breeding. We address this as the "Coconut-Lagune system" with reference to a special cattle breed called Lagune Shorthorn, which is traditionally kept in Benin and other Western African countries. We will point out that the Coconut-Lagune system has its roots some hundred years ago when coconut plantations became a prominent land use in coastal areas, not least promoted by integrating cattle breeding. Today this traditional form of food production is vanishing due to the loss of land and increased professionalization in agriculture, especially in milk production. However, we provide evidence that the Coconut-Lagune system is worth being acknowledged and safeguarded as an outstanding example of a traditional form of land use that holds plenty of lessons to be learned for the future of urban agriculture.

The Coconut-Lagune System

In Benin, coconut production is mainly located along the coastline because of the climate and environmental conditions **[Fig. 2]**. Coconut trees, originally native to Southeast Asia, grew well on the sandy soils and under conditions of high humidity. Railliet and Petit (1912) indicate their existence for more than a hundred years.

As coconuts are easy to transport, they were exported to regional and foreign markets—that's why the production system could be turned from a few trees shading enclosed habitations to larger plantations covering up to more than eight hectares with about 1,500 coconut trees. It is known that coconuts were exported from Benin already before 1895 (Albéca 1895). Today, most of Benin's coconut production is exported to Nigeria, Benin's neighbor to the east, to be used in the cosmetics and food industries.

The liaison of coconut production with the Lagune cattle breed is also recorded first by Railliet and Petit (1912), underpinning the assumption of the Coconut-Lagune system as a traditional land use activity **[Fig. 3]**. Others have also reported a symbiotic relationship between coconut cultivation and Lagune cattle breeding (Childs and Groom 1964, Cornevin 1970, Adeniji 1985). Floquet and Nansi (2005) have identified remnants of pure Lagune farms under palm or coconut plantations around all West African coastal cities from Benin to Togo, Ghana and the Ivory Coast.

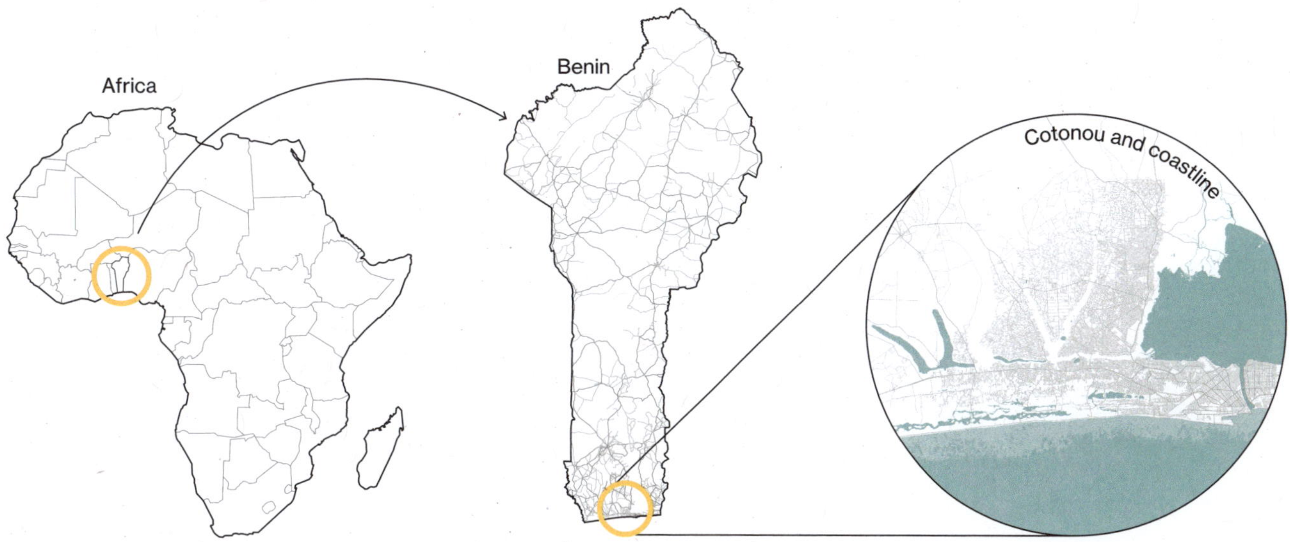

Fig. 1 Cotonou, seat of government of the Republic of Benin, located on the West African coast

Like other Shorthorn cattle breeds, Lagune cattle are described as hardy, trypanotolerant, and adapted to the hot and humid tropical conditions (FAO 1994). They therefore need little veterinary care in the coastal belt (Rege et al. 1994). For this reason, in Southern Benin, the Lagune is "the" traditional breed. Cattle are kept and graze freely on natural pastures, on fallows with no supplementation, and—as focused here—under coconut plantation trees, in a sedentary system.

The traditional sedentary practice was to hold small herds of three to six animals (Rege et al. 1994), each animal of the herd attached to a coconut palm (Cornevin 1970). After some days, an ox was moved under another coconut tree. Traditionally, the people who owned the plantation also owned and managed the cattle. Kept under coconut trees, the livestock was mainly used to enhance soil fertility with manure (Childs and Groom 1964). Aboh et al. (2001) argue that while the trees do benefit from the animals' organic manure, the cattle also benefit from the available grasses and the shelter beneath the plantation trees. Koura (2011) reports that the production of coconuts is ten times higher when cattle are kept under the trees. Other sources state an increase in income by 60 percent for coconuts and milk production (Childs and Groom 1964). In addition the cattle help maintain the plantation by eating competing herbs (Koura 2011). Hence, combining fruit and animal production within the Coconut-Lagune system can be called a symbiotic arrangement with a fine-tuned balance of coconut trees and livestock at a given site (Msellati et al. 1993). The system can be called a low-input system, as no external manure or fertilizer is used.

However, the Coconut-Lagune system is not only of economic and ecological value, but is to be seen also through its sociocultural dimension. As mentioned above, local residents have a strong relation to Lagune cattle, which have accompanied their daily lives for centuries. The robust Lagune breed was affordable for smallholders and widespread also in (sub)urban areas. It is mandatory for many cultural events like weddings and other festivities. The cow's urine is used in traditional medicine, and there are even special rituals, called *Fâssoun*, linked to its breeding. According to Ahozonlin and Dossa (2020), the Lagune is essential for the sustainability of agricultural production systems in the coastal areas of Benin, as cattle serves as a guarantee for borrowing money from traditional informal moneylenders.

Challenges for the Coconut-Lagune System

The rapid growth of cities in South Benin, especially in terms of demography (per INSAE 2012, 4.7 percent per year), has much impacted Cotonou's agricultural situation. Aside from the loss of land, the intensification of land use that characterizes this process threatens traditional forms of urban agriculture such as the Coconut-Lagune system **[Fig. 4]**. In this respect, consider the continuous reduction of grazing areas: in 25 years (1990–2015), there has been a 34.7 percent decrease in green-covered land due to replacement by habitations, urban infrastructure, or crop fields (ECARESE 2019).

Also, with urban sprawl and city growth, the demand for milk and milk products has increased. Cattle production has become more market-oriented, shifting the production system from subsistence agriculture by indigenous smallholders breeding the Lagune to high-production systems making use of other cattle breeds that deliver greater yields of either milk or meat (Herrero et al. 2009; Koura et al. 2015; Sandrine et al. 2019; Ahozonlin and Dossa 2020). The Lagune as "local all-rounders" are being replaced by more milk-producing breeds (White Fulani, Gudali, Girolando), breeds which require supplements but also offer more manure **[Fig. 5]**.

In addition, cattle no longer belong to the owner of the coconut plantations but to herders who make maintenance and manure contracts with the plantations and also with crop farmers (Floquet and Nansi 2005). Consequently, cattle herds are no longer kept within the coconut plantations but move around searching for forage and water (Koura et al. 2015). However, as grazing areas have declined, this practice has caused conflicts—for example, with crop farmers—which calls for new sedentary production strategies.

Heritage Approach

The decline of the Coconut-Lagune system is challenging sustainable development. Rediscovering this traditional form of land use as heritage could raise awareness of its neglected values, which can be distinguished threefold:

1. In general, combining different land uses on the same plot is regarded as an efficient strategy to serve human needs under conditions of land scarcity, as is the situation in urban areas. The Coconut-Lagune system has proved that coconuts, cattle, and often crops can be produced simultaneously at the same place for decades. By having survived this "test of time" (Koohafkan and Altieri 2011), this system's inherent agroecological knowledge might

Fig. 2 Typical arrangement of grazed coconut plantations along the Benin coast

Fig. 3 The liaison of coconut production and cattle breeding has survived mainly along the coastline – however, herds are larger, include crossbreeds, and move around to neighboring sites like the Lagune swamps.

also be adapted to new forms of silvopastoral land use. In particular, its knowledge might lead the way to define an equilibrium balancing the numbers of animals to be kept with the corresponding space available.

2. The Lagune cattle, a robust, indigenous breed, is under threat. Once widespread—Cornevin (1970) reports of 190,000 head in Benin—it has declined dramatically, as shown by the last monitoring in 2004 (MAEP-CNN 2004), which counted 27,000 head. There are no farms with purebred Lagune in the Cotonou region, only a mix of different breeds and crossbreeds, such as Lagune x Zebu or Borgou **[Fig. 6]**. As a robust land race, the Lagune breed is to be considered a highly valuable genetic resource, allowing cattle breeding in West Africa to adapt to future needs caused by climate change or more carbon-sensitive forms of production. Still today, compared with other breeds (Borgou, Azawak, Gudali), the Lagune breed is tolerant to trypanosome, thereby reducing chemical animal healthcare (pesticides and drugs) with its adverse impacts on cattle and humans.

3. As pointed out, the Lagune cattle—as *the* smallholders' cattle—is linked diversely to the people's lives. Keeping this breed is to be seen as preserving essential parts of collective memory and allowing traditional living forms to persist.

Operating a heritage approach, one must be aware of the galloping urbanization, which has led to less space for livestock in and around the city. Therefore, animals will be confined in one place, such as a coconut plantation, which is also a chance to restore the Coconut-Lagune system. This implies participatory actions between the plantations' and animals' owners and the herders, and improving their knowledge and skills in breed selection and heritage preservation. As the size of the coconut plantation area is also declining (Koura 2011), it is necessary to progressively reconstitute this habitat to its original agroecological system. The Programme Gouvernemental de Plantation Cocotiers Long and Côte Atlantique, a governmental initiative to restore coconut plantations along the Atlantic coast, has begun (RB-MAEP 2021) and offers the opportunity to revive and sustain the Coconut-Lagune system.

For underpinning this heritage-oriented approach, we propose to better mainstream the benefits of the traditional Coconut-Lagune system. In particular, Lagune's nonmarket traits have to be identified and better promoted. To this end, we also propose establishing some heritage farms showing the Coconut-Lagune system in its traditional form and constituting part of a breeding program to keep alive the genetic attributes of the Lagune cattle. These farms would have educational and recreational functions and also a touristic value. By doing so, the traditional Coconut-Lagune system could serve as an essential part of Cotonou's future in urban agriculture. ■

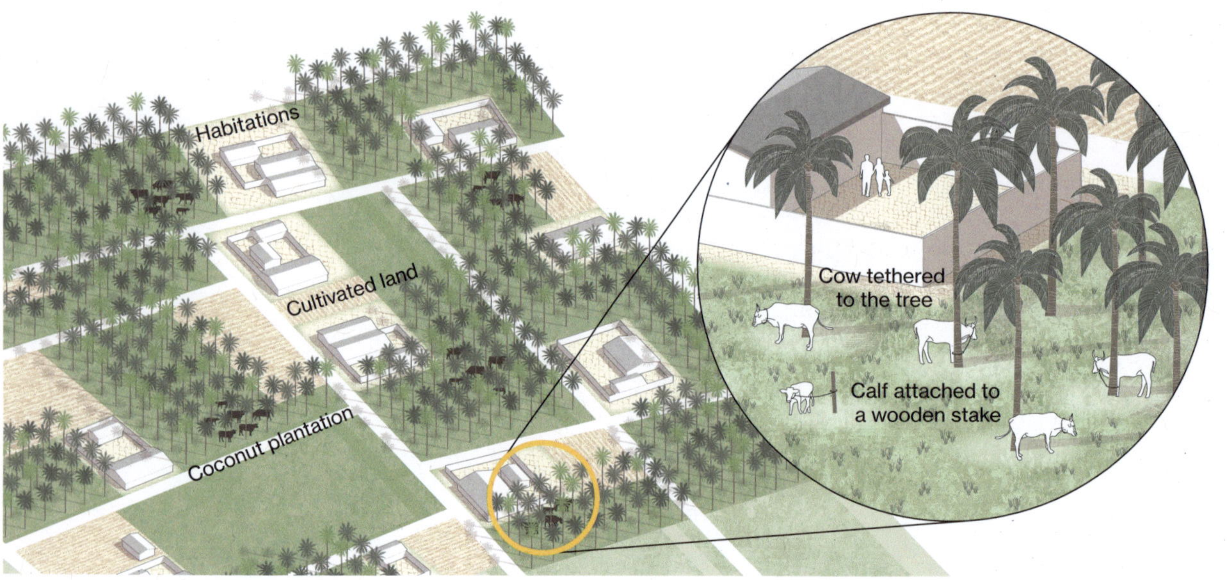

Fig. 4 Typical suburban area in the western part of Cotonou. Today's housing areas are still marked by coconut groves, but meanwhile Lagune cattle breeding is the exception rather than the rule.

Fig. 5 Lagune cattle tethered under coconut trees—a typical traditional smallholders' practice

Fig. 6 Lagune and its crossbreed with Zebu cattle kept in herds in the suburban area of Cotonou

Linking Urban Agricultural Heritage to the Concept of Cultural Landscape

La Vega de Granada: A Cultural Landscape Built Around Irrigation

Anna Kerfers, Ardiana Rahimi, Axel Timpe, and Katharina Christenn

The city of Granada is best known for its medieval monuments. Architecture such as the Alhambra bears witness to the rich history of the former Nasrid dominion. But outside the gates of Granada extends a landscape that is just as complex and historically significant: For centuries, the Vega de Granada (floodplain of Granada) has been a continuously anthropized agrarian space, a breadbasket for the city and its surrounding villages. It is one of three main Andalusian basins. Surrounded by calcareous mountains in the shape of a horseshoe **[Fig. 1]**, it opens up to the west through the narrow course of the river Genil (Zurita Povedano 2015, 166). The climate in this area is dry and continental, since the surrounding mountains serve as a barrier to humid Atlantic winds and Mediterranean breezes. Therefore, there is very little rainfall throughout the year, concentrated mainly in the winter season (24–33).

These conditions are difficult for farming and require optimal use of the available water resources. Prosperous agriculture is made possible in the Vega by a complex irrigation system, which covers approximately 15,500 hectares (Castillo Ruiz 2010, 21). This system was developed over centuries to ensure a widespread and fair distribution of water in the plain. Its preservation depends on a rich cultural knowledge that has been passed down over generations and is still in use today. However, urban development and vanishing cultural practices threaten the existence of the Vega's urban agricultural heritage.

Reshaping the Vega for Agriculture

Agriculture in the Vega dates back to the Roman Empire, when it consisted mainly of the "Mediterranean triad": olive trees, grapevines, and wheat—plants suited for dry soils and hot summers. Due to their cycles, they were harvested either in spring or autumn, while summer was a period of agricultural inactivity (Trillo San José, 2005, 168). This changed with the Muslim conquest in the eighth century, when tropical and subtropical plants such as aubergine, cumin, and mulberry were introduced to the Iberian Peninsula **[Fig. 2]**. In order to grow them, a constant water supply is needed. The development of an extensive irrigation system allowed higher yields per hectare and an extension of the growing season into summer. One of the oldest documents explaining the irrigation system dates back to 1219 (Zurita Povedano 2015, 142). It shows how the areas around Granada were divided between family clans, with *alquerías* (a small group of dwellings) in their center, which later grew into villages (132). However, water canals not only supplied the agricultural plots but also the city of Granada. For this purpose, water from the Genil was diverted and carried toward the city by a canal (151). Due to the combined use by the rural and urban population, a clear organization in the distribution of water was essential to avoid conflicts. During the day, water was used for the fields; at night it filled up communal water reservoirs in the city (Trillo San José, 2005, 177). The distribution followed Muslim prayer times, dividing

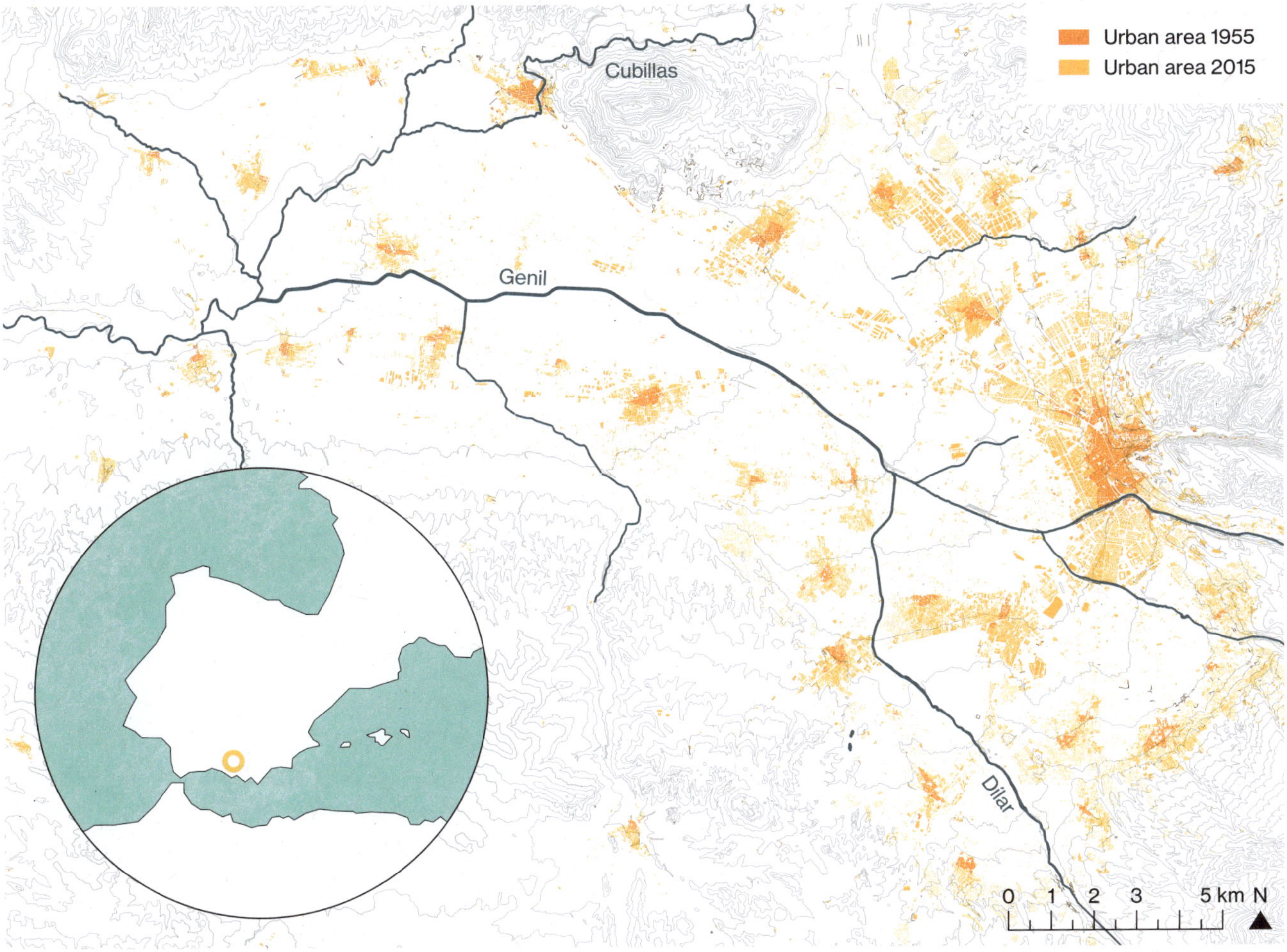

Fig. 1 Map of the Vega de Granada with its topography and urban development between 1955 and 2015

the day into five time slots—irrigation and daily life were closely linked (178).

The Muslim kingdom resisted the Castilian forces for about 300 years but eventually, at the end of the fifteenth century, the Christians conquered Granada. With the expulsion of the Muslim population, agricultural activity decreased and changed. While the cultivation of certain crops—for example mulberry—disappeared altogether, the new Christian inhabitants imported methods like crop rotation and adapted them to the existing irrigation system. Wheat, grapevines, beans, and later corn became the main products grown in the Vega **[Fig. 2]**.

The Irrigation Network and Its Hierarchy

While inhabitants and farming techniques changed, the irrigation system has hardly been altered because of its efficiency. Its backbone is formed by the rivers Genil, Dílar, and Monachil. Together with smaller tributaries, they are the natural water suppliers of the plain **[Fig. 3]**. Throughout the Vega, the alquerías were turned into official irrigation communities, which branch off water from a riverbed or spring and conduct the water to *pagos* ("payments," meaning subareas of an irrigation community). An irrigation network is composed of the *acequias* (canals) for water transport and volume-dividing objects like gates, loops, or dividers. The acequias form a hierarchy **[Fig. 3]**: The entire community depends on the *acequia madre* (mother canal). It feeds the smaller *acequias secondarios* (secondary canals) which then branch off into *tertiarias* (tertiary canals). As the water advances, the canals decrease in category and size, finally turning into simple ditches. While some ditches end on a plot, others return surplus water to the river or feed the next irrigation community downstream (Junta de Andalucia 2017, 91). Farmers use simple blocking mechanisms to direct the water from the ditches onto plots and over a relief of ridges and slopes. Depending on water availability, ground inclination, and soil, the field is modeled in certain ways, directing water faster or slower over its surface **[Fig. 4]** (Gimeno García et al. 2006, 5).

How to Share and Distribute Water

The organization of the water supply is essential for the functioning of the Vega and depends on elaborate social arrangements, from the communal level down to individual farmers. In most cases a volumetric and a chronological division are combined **[Fig. 5]**. The volumetric division is carried out through channels, controlled by their width and depth (García Leal 2014, 10). To ensure that the water volumes comply with the established regulations, the *acequieros* (farmers chosen to be in charge of distributing and dividing water according to customs) regularly check the water level in the canals (11). The chronological division is conducted by water gates, which are opened or closed at certain times. The complex space-time organization in the distribution allows for an efficient and precise use of water, but any alteration at one point of the grid can affect the whole unit.

An example of such a complex system is the river Dílar and the six villages that draw their water from it **[Fig. 6]**. There, the arrangements for water supply between the villages have not changed for centuries, with records dating back to the 1570s (8). Metal frames with identical proportions divide the river water into six portions, which are then distributed. Consequently, there are villages whose acequia madre is one metal frame wide, and villages with a higher water demand whose acequia madre is two frames wide. In addition to this volumetric split, there is a distinction between day and night usage **[Fig. 7, right side]**. While some villages draw water continuously, the village Las Gabias draws its water only at night, using acequias from three neighboring villages **[Fig. 7, left side]** (13). In this process, water is led to a watermill which, in addition to its grinding operation, also functions as a water distributor

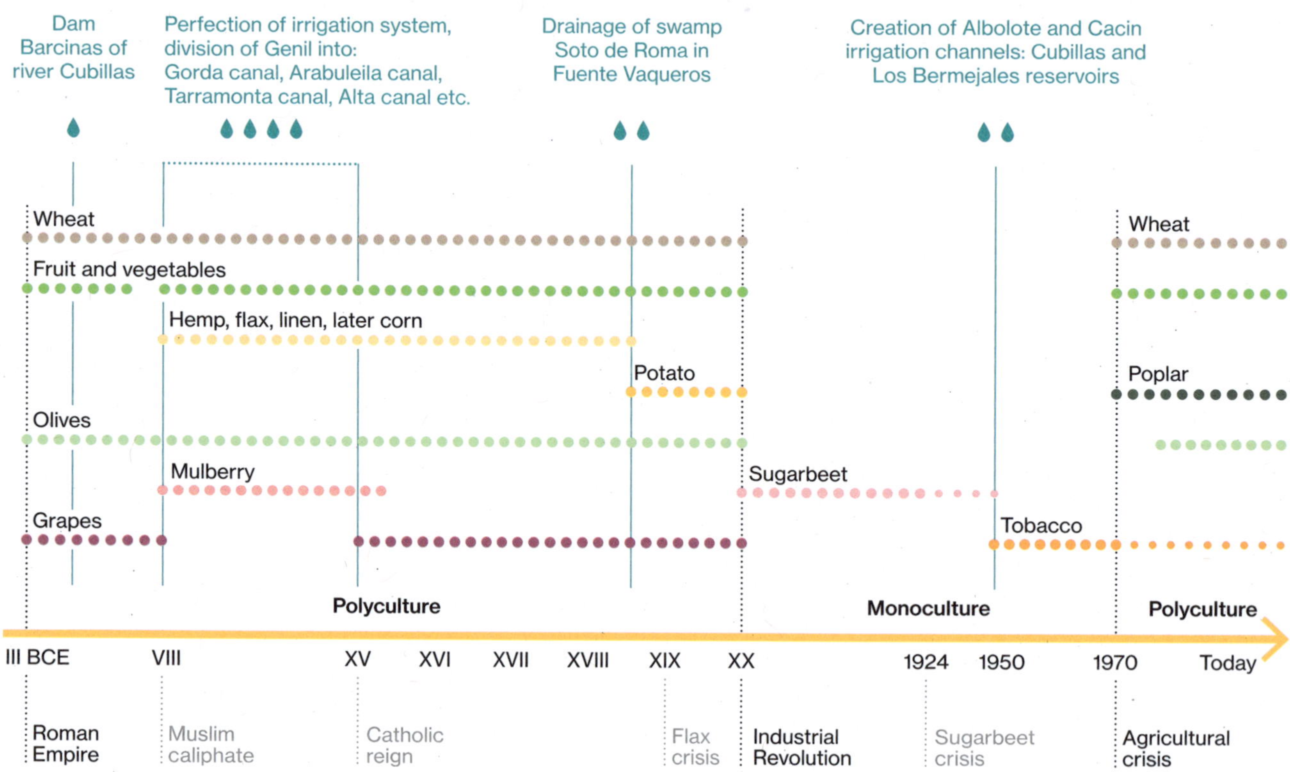

Fig. 2 Timeline of main irrigation developments, agricultural products, and cultural contexts in the Vega de Granada from 300 BCE

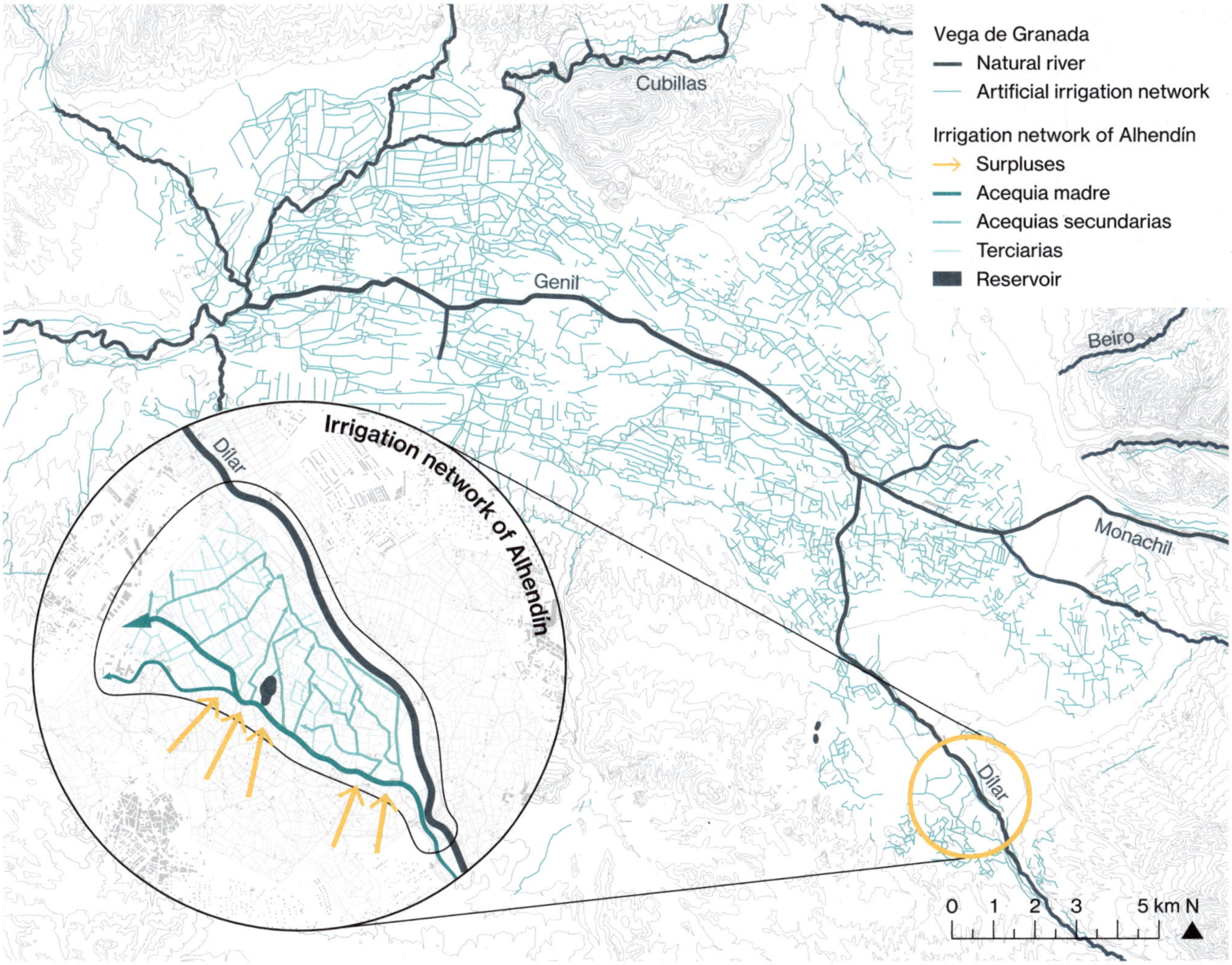

Fig. 3 Map of the Vega de Granada with its natural rivers and main irrigation elements; bubble: map of the irrigation network of the village Alhendín with its different elements

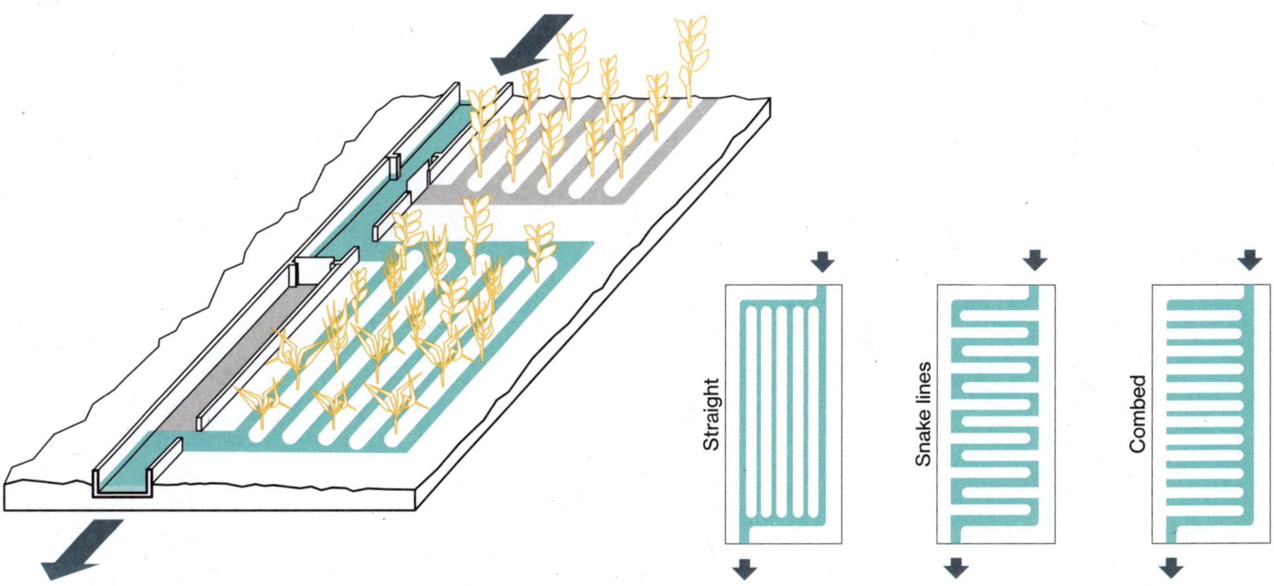

Fig. 4 Axonometric projection of an irrigated field section with ridges and slopes

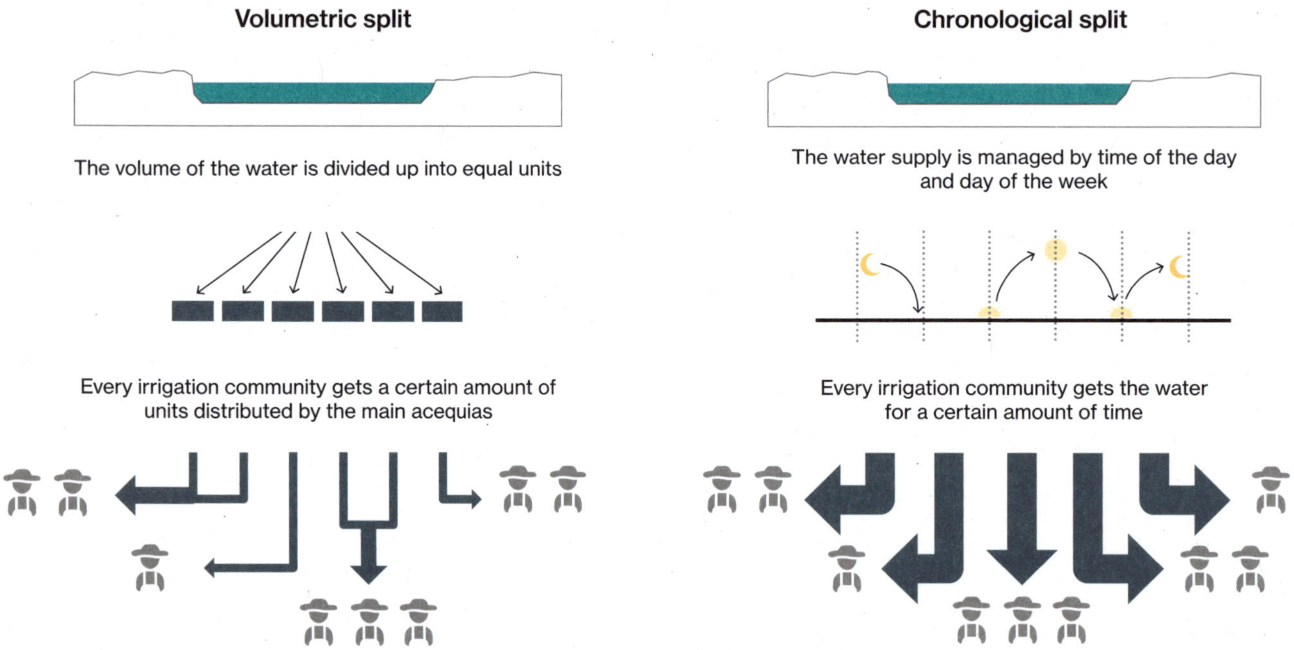

Fig. 5 Main organization principles for water distribution in the Vega de Granada

between the villages through built-in gates. This example shows how parties are closely interrelated through their shared use of infrastructure and the transfer of surpluses. In the Vega, tangible and intangible elements of water distribution are inseparably linked, forming an entire cultural landscape **[see Figs. 5–7]**.

Threats Leaving Their Mark on the Vega

Since the twentieth century, the Vega has been facing two extensive transformation pressures: the industrialization of agriculture; and urbanization with its modern infrastructure. Agriculture evolved from polyculture to industrial monoculture **[Fig. 2]**, and new irrigated areas were created with the construction of reservoirs and canals (García Leal 2014, 3). Cash crops such as sugar beet and tobacco consecutively replaced traditional crops and varieties (Puente Asuero 2013, 197). Polyculture has survived only in smaller orchards dedicated to self-sufficiency. Today the Vega as a whole is returning to a larger crop variety (197).

While the preservation of agricultural plots and the irrigation and road network had been given considerable attention since the Muslim era, urban transformation endangers the integrity of the heritage. As a metropolitan region with 450,000 inhabitants, the demand for new housing and industrial facilities **[Fig. 1]** consumes the agricultural land of the plain. Traffic infrastructure cuts through the

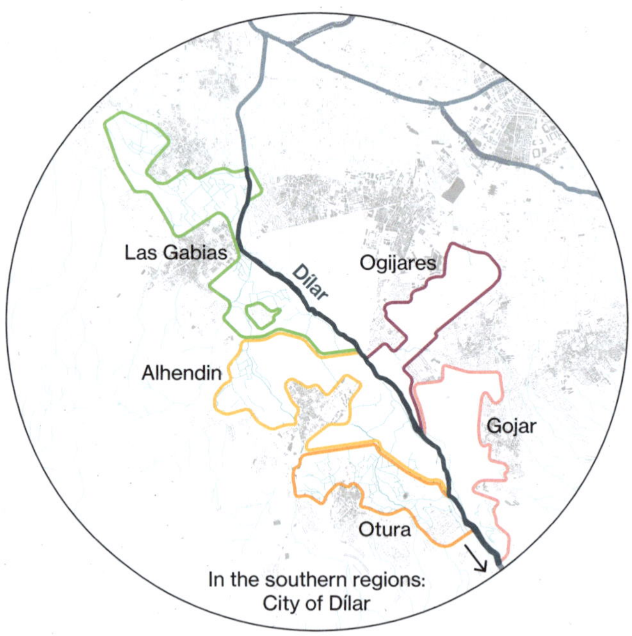

Fig. 6 Map of the Dílar river and the villages that draw their water from it

finely ramified networks of irrigation and agricultural roads and not only endangers their functionality but eliminates the visual connection between the agricultural landscape and the city.

Preservation as Urban Agricultural Heritage

At present, activists on the local level are advocating for declaring the Vega de Granada a Heritage Area. These efforts have emerged from grassroot movements and are not exclusively academic or institutionally motivated. The association Salvemos la Vega (Save the Vega) is the backbone of these attempts. Existing laws and regulations in Spain could only be used to preserve certain tangible aspects of the Vega, such as industrial sugar factories, archaeological sites, or historical urban structures. This leaves large parts of the cultural landscape unprotected—in particular the agrarian space and the activity surrounding all these tangible objects (Castillo Ruiz and Matarán Ruiz 2020, 225). Therefore current endeavors are aimed at declaring the Vega a BIC-Heritage Area (*Bien de Interés Cultural*, meaning "asset of cultural interest"), basing the argumentation on the concept of agrarian heritage, which is not yet anchored in international heritage law. The concept is based on the demand for a specific focus and validation of agricultural goods, techniques, and landscapes as valuable elements of local culture. It focuses on the omnipresent dependence of society as a whole on agriculture. The aspired declaration of the Vega as a BIC-Heritage Area aims at the preservation of its natural and cultural, tangible and intangible values as heritage assets created by agrarian activity throughout history, with the irrigation system being the most important element, enabling agricultural practices and defining the Vega as a living heritage area (226–32). To reinstall the Vega as the breadbasket of Granada and the region, as was the case in the past, its agricultural practices should be recognized and embraced as an important part of the city's identity (Cáceres 2013). In order to gain recognition for the Vega's heritage value, action in other areas, such as education, training, and social awareness, has to rise as well. Current efforts are aimed at restoring a general understanding of the agricultural practices in the Vega as part of Granada's identity, including not only local farmers or interested consumers but also retailers, logistic companies, and marketing strategists as well as political and administrative decision-makers. ■

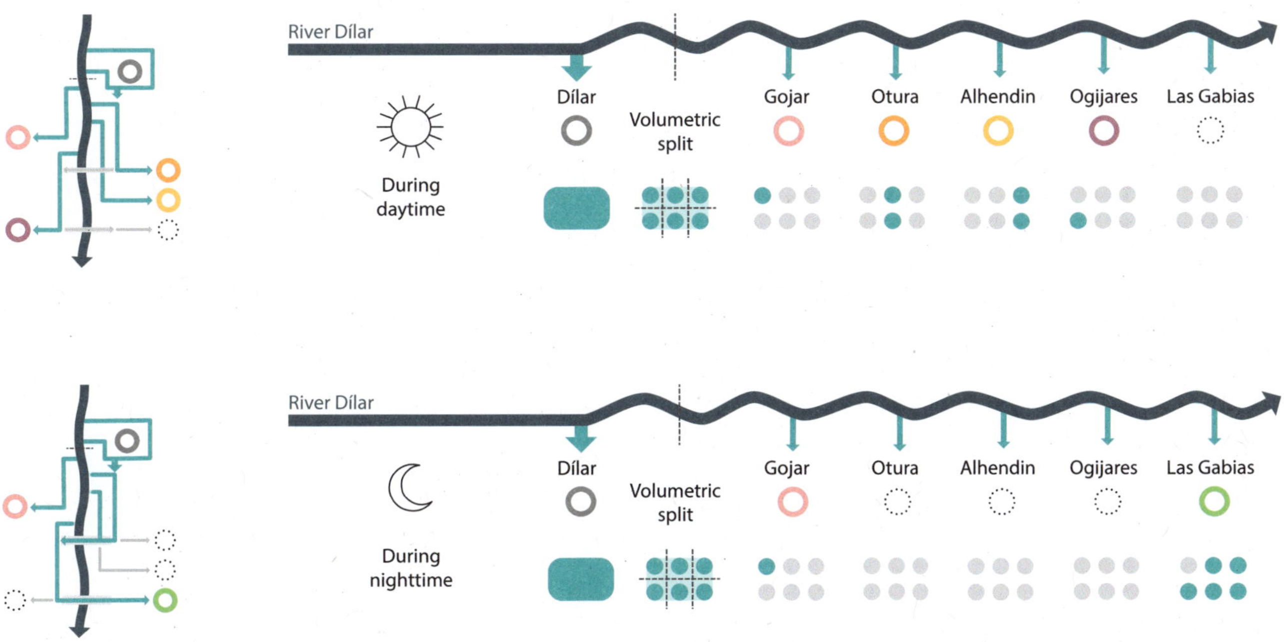

Fig. 7 Left: water transportation at the Dílar river during day- and nighttime; right: volumetric water distribution at the Dílar river during day- and nighttime

Hidden Urban Agricultural Heritage at the Manzanares River: Toward an Agroecological Wedge in the Southeast of Madrid City

Nerea Morán and Marian Simón Rojo

The Last Agricultural Wedge in Madrid City

Sometimes, against the odds, agriculture survives in hostile environments. That is the case in Madrid, at its southern limits along the Manzanares River, where urban agriculture, encroached on by urban extensions and infrastructures, waits for a better future that now seems closer. The Manzanares River crosses Madrid from northwest to southeast **[Fig. 1]** and is the central axis of a green infrastructure that comprises three interlinked parks: the Madrid Rio Park and the northern and southern sections of the Manzanares Linear Park. Joined together, these green areas cross the entire city from north to south, linking two different landscapes included in two protected natural areas: the Mediterranean forest of the Pardo Hill located at the north of the city, and the agricultural landscape of the Southeast Regional Park. The latter is home to ecosystems linked to the Jarama River and its tributaries—Manzanares, Henares, and Tajuña—comprising steppes, dryland cereal crops, riparian vegetation, cliffs, and lagoons.

The banks of the river have undergone a profound transformation in recent years. From 2004 to 2007, a section of Madrid's inner ring road (M-30), which runs parallel to the riverbed, was relocated to an underground tunnel system. In the same period, two interlinked linear parks that house sports fields and recreational facilities were created: the Madrid Río Park was built over the relocated ring road, and the northern section of the Manzanares Linear Park was built to its south. The southern section of the Manzanares Linear Park, however, has not yet been developed. Remarkably, this area comprises agricultural fields which have persisted despite fragmentation, degradation, and lack of attention to agricultural activity. The agricultural wedge shows a surprising image of grain fields and orchards located at the foot of Mercamadrid, one of the largest wholesale markets in Europe, surrounded and crossed over by railroads and motorways, as well as by energy and sewage-treatment plants. With an area of 250 hectares, the wedge offers a unique opportunity to revitalize a historical agrarian space embedded in the city.

This paper proposes key ideas for the revitalization of the southern section of the Manzanares Linear Park, based on the authors' studies of the agricultural heritage of the park, its history, and land use changes, as well as planning documents, municipal plans, and social claims. The proposals are, furthermore, based on the authors' work within social and agroecological initiatives providing technical assistance to the municipal government in the development of food policies related to the Milan Urban Food Policy Pact as well as their advisory work for the Federation of Madrid's Neighborhood Associations in defining proposals for the Linear Park.

Agricultural History and Heritage Elements

The Manzanares River was an essential source for provisioning the medieval city, and the cultivation of its banks has been documented since the Muslim

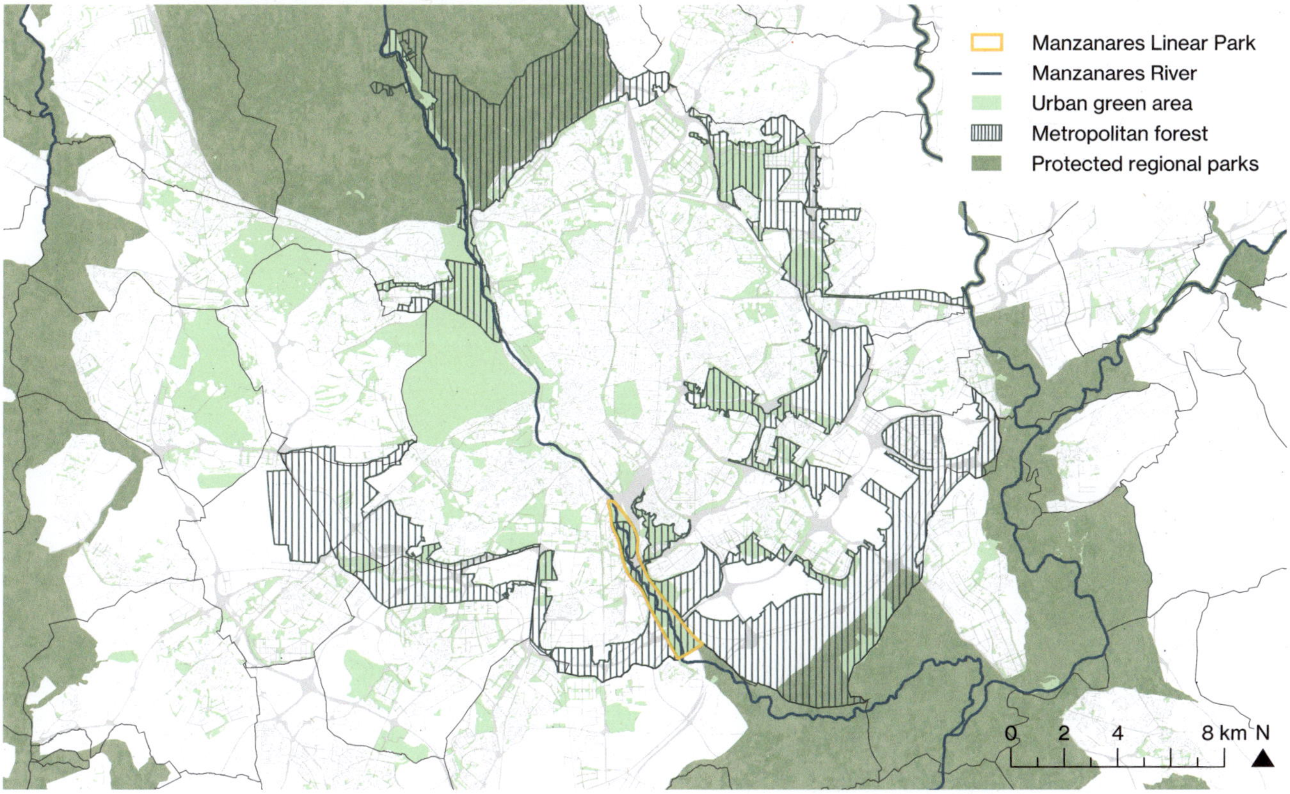

Fig. 1 Location map showing the green infrastructure of the city, its connection with protected natural areas, and the Manzanares Linear Park

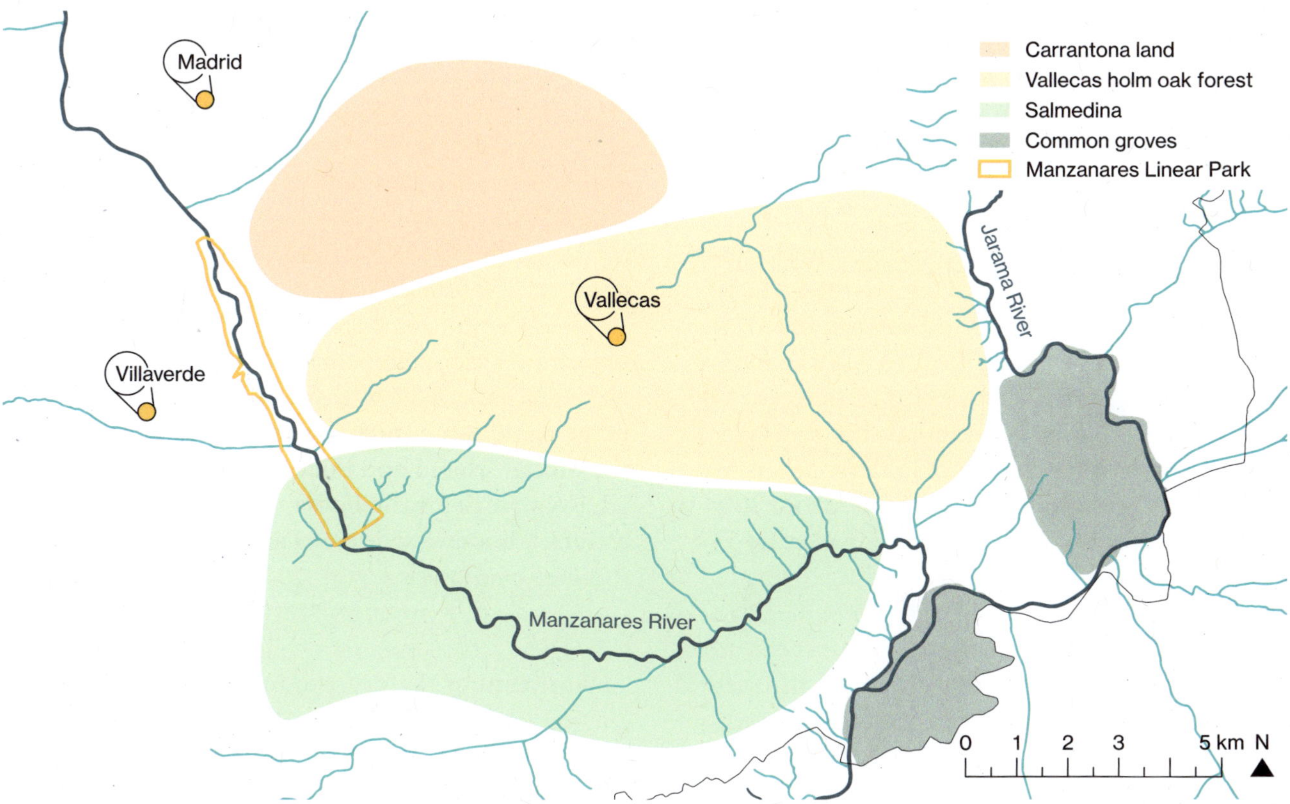

Fig. 2 Medieval land divisions, Field of the City, XIII century

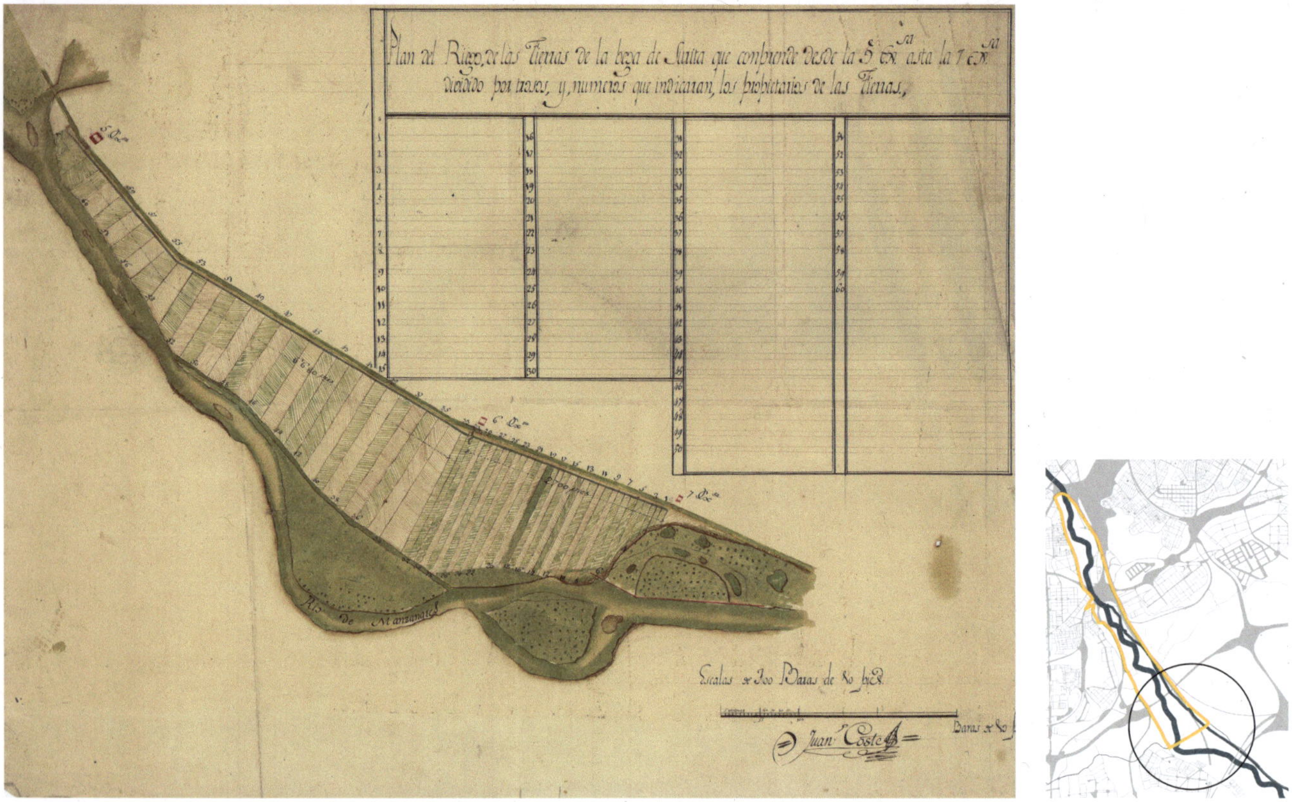

Fig. 3 Watering plan from the 5th to the 7th lock of the Royal Channel of the Manzanares, created between 1830 and 1860

times. The banks were covered by private fields as well as by the common good, called *fahs al-Madina* (Field of the City—this term is a direct translation, as the area was named in the Muslim times). The banks at the lower basin of the Manzanares River and at its tributary streams Gavia, Culebro, and Migueles comprised groves, pastures, and orchards. On the hills to the east of the river, grain fields, vineyards, olive groves, and holm oak forests were located. After the Christian conquest in 1162, the king fragmented the Field of the City and donated part of the land to religious orders and knights. The code of municipal laws from the thirteenth century defined the rules for the land that continued to be a common good of the citizens—the Salmedina pastures and troughs—as well as the rules for the land owned by the city council, the Vallecas holm oak forest, where pastures, acorns for feeding pigs, and wood and charcoal could be obtained **[Fig. 2]**.

The main tangible heritage element in the area is the Royal Channel of the Manzanares, a hydraulic infrastructure that was intended to create a navigable connection with Lisbon as well as to provide irrigation. The construction of the channel began in 1770; however, by 1830 only a section of the channel was completed. With the inauguration of the Aranjuez railroad line in 1851, the channel project became outdated. During its short life—1830 to 1860—the channel was used for watering crops, pastures, and mulberry trees to raise silkworms, as well as for mills and gypsum manufacturing. The plots between the channel and the river were designed in a way that they were watered by gravity **[Fig. 3]**. In 1860 the channel and its locks were abandoned, and the adjacent constructions sold (López García et al. 2008).

Today, in the southern section of the Manzanares Linear Park some remains of the Royal Channel can be found, namely the section from the third lock to the sixth lock as well as the fourth lockhouse, the latter declared an asset of cultural interest **[Fig. 4]**. The original channel bed is occupied by orchards or buried under soil, but a narrow stream of water still flows.

In the area, pastoral and agricultural uses have persisted, and the municipality has rented the public land to shepherds until recent times, especially for grazing. The topographic cartography of 1875 depicts an extensive area of crops—arable land, irrigated orchards, and pastures—linked to the Manzanares River and its tributary streams **[Fig. 5]**.

An Agrarian Riverside Encroached by Infrastructures

The southern section of the Manzanares Linear Park is a naturally narrow riverside, limited by gypsum escarpments in the east. In the second half of the twentieth century, it has progressively shrunk, fragmented by roads, highways, and railroad lines **[Fig. 6]**. The motorway of the South (A4), built in the 1960s and passing along the western bank of the river, reduced the dry land for cereal cultivation. Two ring roads—the M-40 in the north and the M-45 in the south of the area—cross the riverbed at elevated passes **[Fig. 6]**. During the 1950s and 1960s, industrial estates and railroad facilities were located on the western bank of the river, in the district named Villaverde, and largely transformed into residential areas as the city grew. On the eastern bank of the river, in the district named Villa de Vallecas, construction of the wholesale market Mercamadrid began in the 1970s.

Further infrastructures and urban services have been located in the area: an electrical substation, constructed during the 1970s and scheduled to be dismantled, and three sewage treatment plants, inaugurated respectively in 1950, 1983, and 2005.

Vegetable cultivation in the area has almost disappeared: the irrigated fields are now covered by cereal crops, and abandoned pastures have reverted to scrubland. The agricultural activity that persists in the area is marginal and disconnected from the local food chain. Some of the plots are squatter gardens for self-consumption, leftovers from the precarious agriculture phenomenon of the 1980s. During the economic crisis that Spain experienced 40 years ago, up to 1,300 informal vegetable gardens were identified on the periphery of Madrid. Indeed, the closest neighborhoods to the Linear Park have a history of informal settlements and precarious urban agriculture, and nowadays comprise some vegetable gardens as well as croplands of larger extension.

The northern section of the Linear Park has been designed and completely developed, evicting any sign of agriculture but for a plot with an olive tree. In the southern section of the Manzanares Linear Park, however, squatter gardens and croplands are still operating. They are located on publicly owned land which is designated as green space in the city's master plan. This condition of public land for public use is an opportunity to develop public policies that would enhance multifunctional urban farming linked to the area's agrarian heritage.

Fig. 4 The fourth lockhouse

Bottom-Up and Top-Down: Heritage-Based Initiatives for the Manzanares Linear Park

The Master Plan of Madrid (1998) is a mandatory urban planning instrument that sets the uses for every plot in the municipality. It designated the Manzanares Linear Park as a public green space. With the exception of the strategic plan of the southern section of the Manzanares Linear Park—a non-mandatory planning instrument from 2008—neither the master plan nor any of the sectorial or spatial plans have ever mentioned agriculture. The development guidelines defined in the strategic plan gave priority to renaturalization; cultivation was considered mainly in aesthetic terms, designating crops to be grown in delimited areas, according to their color qualities (Gómez Orea 2008). Under such an approach, with heritage elements converted into ornaments and renaturalization dominating urban agriculture, the area risks losing its farming character. The potential of establishing a dialogue between renaturalization and cultivation through agroecology remains a missed opportunity.

Fortunately, urban agriculture and sustainable food systems have entered the scene in the last decade, both on the political and on the social agendas.

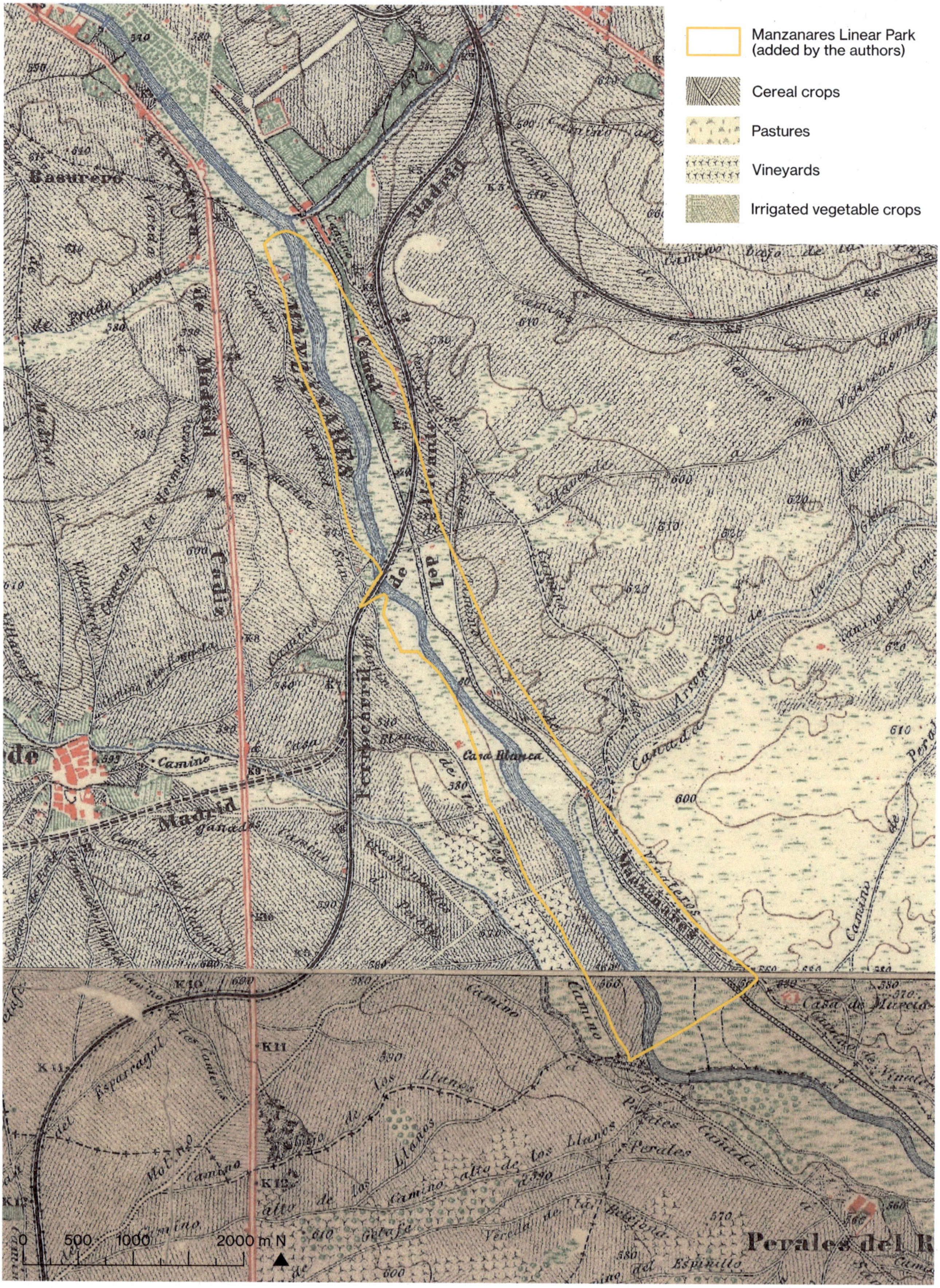

Fig. 5 Topographic map (1875)

Nowadays there are favorable conditions to—at least partially—recover the agricultural character of the area, levering preserved historical elements. In 2019 the Biodiversity and Green Infrastructure Plan was established (Ayuntamiento de Madrid 2019, 30). A year prior to this, the Madrid-Regenera Plan was developed, aiming for the renaturalization of the city and proposing the development of a metropolitan forest as the flagship of green municipal policies for the period of 2018–22. This second plan envisions a large natural recreation area with a few vegetable gardens as a tool for raising environmental awareness.

Several social movements have made proposals for the Linear Park. Madrid Agroecológico emerged in 2015 as a civic platform aimed at driving the agroecological transition in Madrid's bioregion. It stands up for the coproduction of public policies that boost agroecology and proposes access to land, training, and support, mainly for unemployed people who want to become farmers but have no professional or family background in farming. Additionally, neighborhood, heritage, and environmental associations offer plans for the recovery of the Linear Park through the development of public facilities, such as vegetable gardens, a traditional trades and agriculture school, an environmental interpretation center, and a heritage museum. There are also proposals for the improvement of a pedestrian path parallel to the Gavia stream, which connects the western district with the river. The Southern and Eastern Neighborhoods Assembly and the Neighborhood Association Federation co-developed these proposals with a panel of experts for urban planning, heritage conservation, and agroecology.

At the institutional level, Madrid is a signatory of the Milan Urban Food Policy Pact and in 2018 approved its Healthy and Sustainable Food Strategy, which includes an agroecology training school that would be located in the southern section of the Manzanares Linear Park (Ayuntamiento de Madrid 2018, 94). The strategy is closely related to Productive Neighborhoods, another ongoing municipal plan that aims to promote urban agricultural entrepreneurship projects. Finally, in July 2020 an international contest for designing the metropolitan forest as a green belt around the city was launched. The contest brief indicated that along the Manzanares Riverside agrarian land has been maintained and "could be part of an agrarian park" (Ayuntamiento de Madrid 2020) in the future. Taking into account all these municipal initiatives, there is an opportunity for a public-social partnership for rebuilding local food chains in this area.

Using Agroecology and Social Economy to Create a Green Edible Corridor

The tangible and intangible heritage elements of the southern section of the Manzanares Linear Park and their values offer great potential for the revitalization of the area:

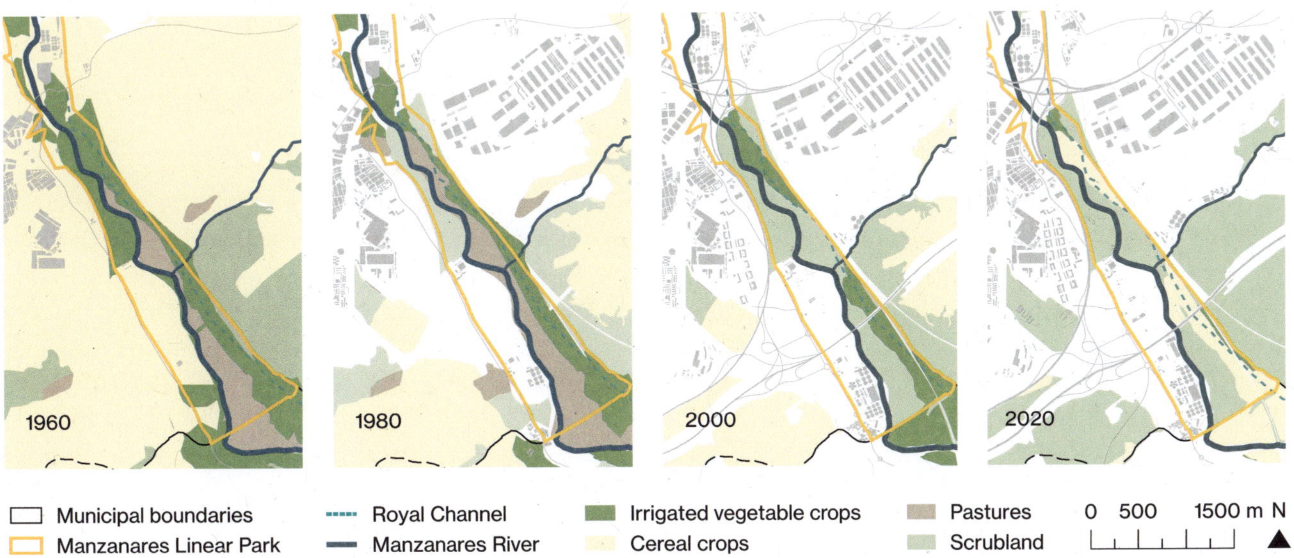

Figs. 6a–d Land cover changes in the southern section of the Manzanares Linear Park: 1960, 1980, 2000, 2020

1. Articulating element of the urban-territorial structure: The persistence of the agricultural character of this area reminds citizens of the agricultural origin of some contemporary green areas in and around Madrid, which were ancient orchards and common pastures (Móran 2018). The southern section of the Manzanares Linear Park could restore the role of urban agriculture to the urbanization patterns by becoming a green edible corridor or agroecological wedge in the urban area, and as the gateway into the Southeast Regional Park.
2. Multifunctional agricultural area: The historical coexistence of different agricultural uses can inform the planning and regulation of contemporary uses and activities. In order to respond to the contemporary urban challenges, forms of traditional farming in the area—orchards, grain fields, and pastures—can be adapted, facilitating the enhancement of biodiversity, water management, and local food provisioning.
3. Neighbors' common: The stewardship conducted by citizens throughout history—first in the Field of the City and afterward through the rental of public land—is another key heritage element that can inspire and inform future development. It can be linked to the contemporary concepts of urban green commons (Colding and Barthel 2013) and public-social comanagement of public goods.
4. Hydraulic infrastructure and watering system: The remains of the Royal Channel of the Manzanares give the opportunity to build a watering infrastructure following the old channel layout. This irrigation system could guide the reparceling of the collective garden plots and the commercial crop fields for a better use of water.
5. Memory of the territory: Finally, the fourth lockhouse as a historic building constitutes a suitable space for indoor facilities associated with the revitalization of the area. To make visible the heritage value of urban agriculture in the area and to explore its role in the contemporary city, a small museum could be located in the fourth lockhouse, containing spaces for exhibitions, workshops, and lectures.

The southern section of the Manzanares River has the potential to be a hotspot as a living urban lab linked to food and agriculture, with transversal connections to the surrounding neighborhoods and following local demands. To this end, we propose the implementation of the following uses and

Fig. 7 Informal gardens and precarious bridges over the Royal Channel of the Manzanares

activities—based on the study of the area, which we have conducted for writing this chapter, and based on the results of discussions and proposal processes by the Madrid Agroecologico Platform and Madrid's Neighborhood Associations Federation.

The green edible corridor is proposed to unfold into two subareas: urban gardening in the north, with a more social character, and urban farming in the south, with projects based in social and solidarity-based economy and taking advantage of the proximity to the city (Simon-Rojo et al. 2016). In both cases environmental values and closing nutrient cycles through composting are to be boosted and water quality improved.

In the first stretch, we suggest revisiting the squatter gardens **[Fig. 7]**, paying attention to their governance but also to the quality of their enclosures to guarantee adequate landscape integration. This area would be redesigned to contain community, educational, and allotment gardens oriented toward educational and cultural activities with the community **[Fig. 8a]**.

The second stretch was assessed as suitable for reviving urban farming, recovering land for cultivation. When the railroad was built in the nineteenth century, the orchards allocated between the channel and the Gavia stream disappeared. This proposal brings them back, with renewed functions (social gardening and experimental farming), allocating them to the west of the Channel and providing a continuous stretch of orchards. The fourth lockhouse is proposed to house an urban agriculture museum **[Fig. 8b]**. A city farm oriented toward education, recreation, and therapy would be located in the historic pastures **[Fig 8c]**, and in its north, agroecological and diversified orchards would be developed **[Fig 8d]**.

Altogether, appreciating this space as a valuable and recoverable heritage landscape can generate ecosocial, urban, and economic innovation. The area has the potential, through community-supported agriculture, to host economic activity linked to farming and short supply chains, reinforcing local identity, and dignifying part of the history of the neighborhoods. In this scenario, food becomes an ally to unveil agricultural heritage and its values. Agroecology serves as a fundamental strategy for making urban agriculture compatible with the ecological and social functions assigned by the local government to the Linear Park (biodiversity, water management, pedestrian connection, recreation ...). To achieve this, we conclude that the planning and design of the southern section of the Manzanares Linear Park should be based on the following principles:

1. Preservation of the agrarian landscape with trails and permeable sidewalks while using local materials for enclosures and new constructions.
2. Diversification and adaptation of crops—cereal, vegetables, fruits, and grazing—according to the local conditions.
3. Promoting collective management, working hand in hand with gardeners and urban farmers, and recovering the historical origins of the area as a common good of the citizens. ■

A

B

C

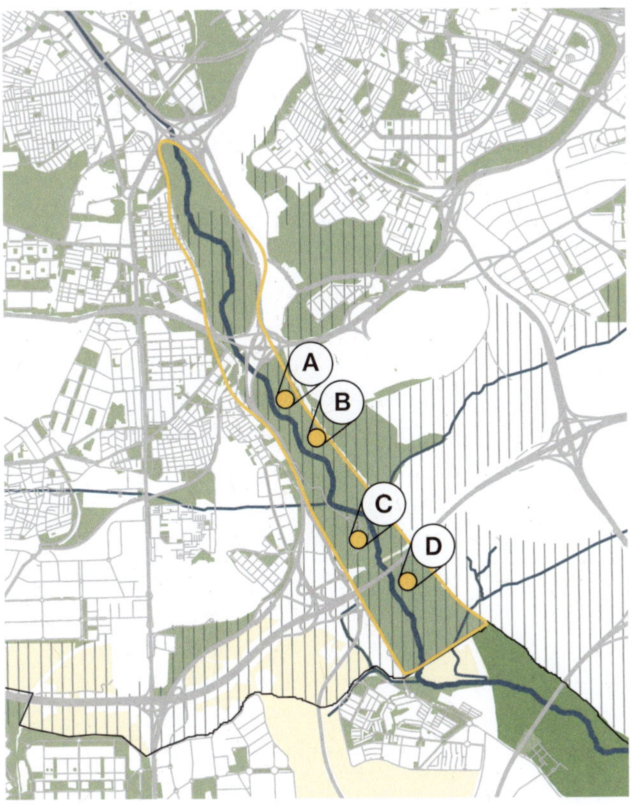

D

Figs. 8a–d Areas of interest with specific design opportunities

Protection and Values of the Cultural Heritage of the Campagna Romana between Public Policies and Movements from Below

Anna Lei

The Cultural Value of Urban Agricultural Landscapes

In 1963, Emilio Sereni defined the agricultural landscape as "the shape that men, throughout and for the purposes of their agricultural production activities, consciously and systematically imprint on the natural landscape" (Sereni 2008, 29). The cultural value of this particular interaction between man and nature was initially only attributed to valuable historical rural landscapes, but since 2005 it has been conferred by UNESCO to some metropolitan areas as well. These agricultural landscapes, although often residual, are considered highly symbolic and representative of a past virtuous economic, social, and environmental balance between the city and its countryside. Therefore: "Urban agriculture today [...] continues to play a dual role as a supplier of tangible and intangible goods, products and culture: its visible manifestation is the landscape, place of life of local communities and bearer of the tangible and intangible traces of agricultural history. It is therefore also a cultural heritage" (Branduini et al. 2016, 55).

Landscapes of the Campagna Romana

In Rome, the city-countryside relationship is historically paramount. The Campagna Romana is an illustrious example of "territory as palimpsest," a product of the incessant stratification and continuous reuse of the traces of the past (Corboz 1983, 34–35). In the context of this "long-lasting relationship" (Braudel 1987), agriculture, understood as the first form of territorial colonization, seems to have had the role of anticipating the expansion of the city, delineating its territorial development (Arena 1983, 12). The way in which Rome spreads across its surrounding territory has always determined a very jagged physical limit between city and countryside. Already in his *Map of Rome* (1748), Gian Battista Nolli—the first cartographer to raise the countryside from the role of "approximate and generic outline" of the city (Insolera 1980, 308) through an equally accurate description—testifies how "the passage from the built city to the green belt is far from clear. Villas and vineyards enter the town; the districts fray between gardens and vegetable gardens" (316) **[Fig 1]**.

This same lack of regularity characterizes contemporary Rome, where the boundary between city and countryside sometimes seems to even dissolve: "The countryside around Rome is a belt of land that embraces the city, wraps it in the cardinal points and sometimes penetrates the inhabited area. It is not just a frame [...] it is instead a context that gives the city a 'more' of meanings. Up to the point that Rome would not be fully recognizable without the constant interaction between the built and the unbuilt" (Erbani 2013, 56) **[Fig 2]**.

From the years of the "Great Expansion" (1945–1960s) (Insolera 1971, 192–208) to the first decade of the twenty-first century, Rome has dispersed into the settlement forms of sprawl (Secchi 2005, 13–40). But in the meantime, the Campagna Romana has a

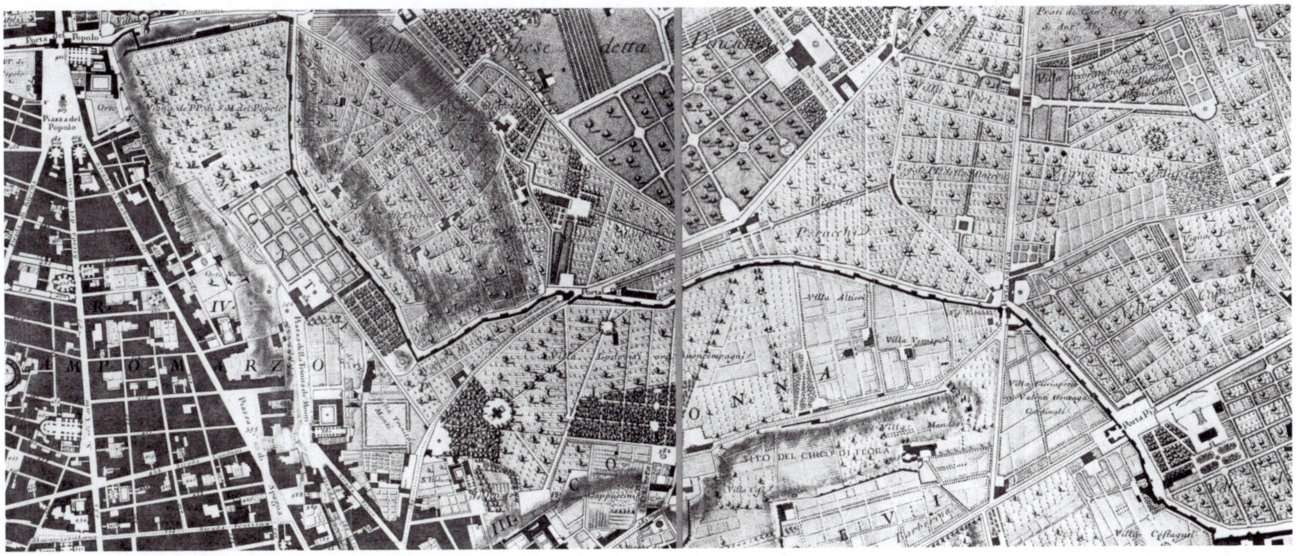

Fig. 1 Rome map. Gian Battista Nolli (1748). Detail of the Aurelian Walls between Porta del Popolo and Porta Salaria

large (spatial) extension: cultivated lands and woods represent more than 90 percent of the unbuilt land in Rome's territory (Istat 2011). It has maintained an extraordinary ecological, environmental, historical, and archaeological value thanks to a complex system of protective measures. Despite one of the highest indices of settlement dispersion among European capitals (ISPRA 2017, 33), Rome's metropolitan area counts 144,550 hectares of protected natural areas (21 percent of Italy's protected natural areas), 50,933 hectares of archaeological parks and sites, 16,164 hectares of urban parks, and 34 wetlands hosting 162 rare species, 167 nesting bird species, and 13 rare amphibian species.

Fig. 2 Acilia Madonnetta (Southern Rome) (2012)

The ensemble of such ecological, historical, and cultural values has for a long time been traced back to established imaginaries and images that have stood over time: the descriptions of the Campagna Romana by the seventeenth-century Grand Tourists correspond exactly to the views painted by the XXV of the Campagna Romana, a large group of landscape painters from the early twentieth century (Formica 2009, 89–104) **[Fig 3]**.

Only at the end of the twentieth century did Vittoria Calzolari, one of more important architects, university professors, and activists of landscape research and design of the 1900s in Italy, analyze the cultural values of this great imaginary by looking at their actual consistency: she identified seven "historical landscapes[,]" the result of interweaving relationships between the physical-naturalistic characteristics and the historical features of a specific territory (Calzolari 1999, 135–96).

This operation, defined as the "construction of the historical territory" of the Roman area, was guided by the "critical judgment on the degree of permanence and significance not of 'isolated objects' but of 'historical systems' still recognizable" (137). Following this interpretation, which today still represents a reference for those engaged in the study and design of the Roman area, we can recognize: the landscape of swampland reclamation, with farmhouses and pine trees on the hills; the landscape of the nineteenth century coastal

Fig. 3 Filippo Anivitti, "Appia Antica" (1926) (watercolors; detail). The ruins and the boundless meadows for free-range grazing are symbolic elements of the Campagna Romana.

reclamation around the mouth of the Tiber; the landscape of the fort belt around the city; the landscape of the urban and suburban villas of the sixteenth to the eighteenth centuries; the landscape of the vineyards, along the slopes of the Tuscolane villas; the landscapes of fortresses, towers, and castles, in strategic position for controlling roads, hills, canals, and viewpoints; and the landscapes of great monuments and archaeological complexes **[Fig 4]**.

The assemblage of these landscapes still characterizes the territories of Rome's settlement diffusion today. They are complex realities in continuous movement—unlike the previous imaginaries—contemporary (actual or potential) places of life, in which the degree of vitality of agriculture contributes to determining the conservation and recognition of the historical and cultural heritage.

Reviving Urban Agricultural Heritage for Landscape Protection: Top-Down Policies and Bottom-Up Actions

In Rome, ongoing and recent policies and projects for agricultural landscapes show a double dynamic: on the one hand, the general failure of more traditional instruments promoted from above (such as town plans); on the other, the success of initiatives promoted from below, in which agriculture changes from "suburban" to "urban" (Fleury and Donadieu 1997, 45) thanks to its role as an ecological and social reactivation device for the contemporary city (Lei 2019, 95–139).

Over the past twenty years, the municipal governments have given various conflicting messages about protecting the agricultural landscape. Following Vittoria Calzolari's interpretive work, Rome's town plan, adopted in 2003, introduced a new form of protection for the Campagna Romana aimed specifically at its landscape aspects and values. By designing two traditional tools (a map and a guideline), the types of agricultural landscape have been reinterpreted in a "Guide to Planning in Landscapes," an operational tool for landscape enhancement and transformation (Municipality of Rome 2003). Regrettably, these two tools never became prescriptive and had no follow-up in the finalization of the town plan, ratified in 2008 (Municipality of Rome 2008) **[Figs. 5 and 6]**.

Also attributable to the 2003 version of the town plan is the Agricultural Park, defined as an instrument of management, enhancement, and protection of agricultural space through a more sustainable agriculture, the promotion of short supply chains, and the "creation of a system of public uses, through the creation of naturalistic itineraries with cycle and pedestrian routes, the strengthening of receptive, recreational, sports and service uses" (Municipality of Rome 2008, "Technical Standards," art. 70). Three agricultural parks are planned in Rome's metropolitan area, recognized as strategic for their accessibility and potential multifunctionality and to provide ecosystem services, from food production to landscape conservation (Costanza et al. 1997, Millennium Ecosystem Assessment 2005, 40; European Commission 2006, 1). The complicated mechanism of establishment and management required by the Town Plan has, however, decreed the failure of the Agricultural Park, so that the most successful experiences of multifunctional urban agriculture in progress find their driving force in bottom-up initiatives such as squatting and citizen ecological movements. This is the case with Casal del Marmo, where for almost forty years the Co.Bra.Gor agricultural cooperative has occupied and cultivated 60 hectares of public land illegally. Here, the promotion of the landscape

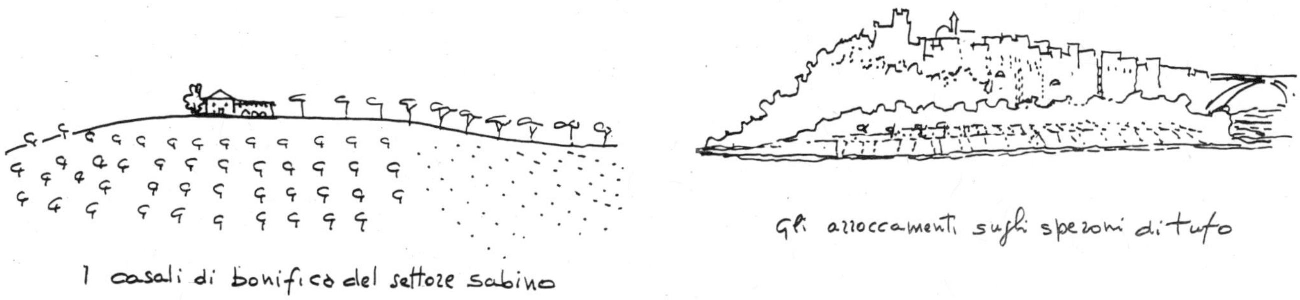

Fig. 4 Profiles of the Campagna Romana: on the left, a typological section of the landscape of swamp lands reclamation, with farmhouses and pine trees on the hills. This sketch shows the farmhouses and olive groves of the Sabina countryside, north of Rome. On the right, a typological section of the landscapes of fortresses, towers, and castles, in strategic position for surveilling roads, hills, canals, and viewpoints. The sketch shows the settlements perched on tuff spurs and the cultivation along the valley floor.

Fig. 5 Historical landscapes of the Roman area identified by Vittoria Calzolari

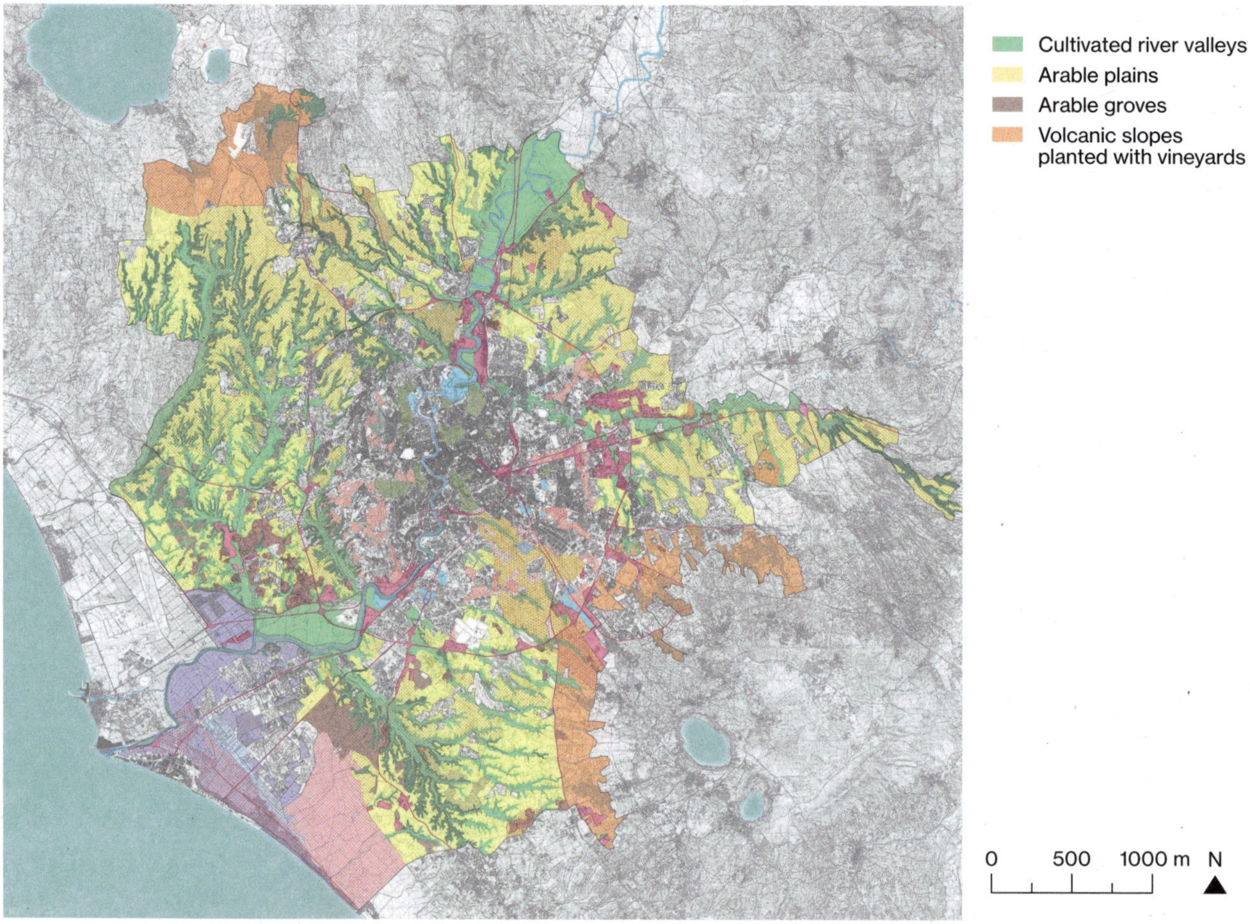

Fig. 6 Landscape system, Rome Town Plan 2003. The map investigates the structure of the territory by identifying a geography of the landscapes of Rome. The main focus of the analysis is the Campagna Romana shaped, in particular, by: the areas of the cultivated river valleys (in light green); areas of arable plains and groves (in yellow and light brown); and areas of the volcanic slopes planted with vineyards (in orange).

is made by organic growing of local cultivars, the maintenance of paths and fields left freely accessible. Farmhouses built in the early nineteenth century have been recently renovated and now host community activities: transformation and direct sale of farm products, farm receptions, environmental education, and food services. The combination of all these activities generates growing and heterogeneous flows of people, revitalizing the imagination of the Campagna Romana.

The "public lands for young farmers" movement takes further the Co.Bra.Gor experience and, in particular, the history of recovery and promotion of the Borghetto San Carlo Estate: 22 hectares of land inside Vejo Park—one of the 19 regional protected natural areas inside Rome's metropolitan area—and its early nineteenth-century farmhouses (for about 1,400 square meters) have been returned to life after a long process of restoring agricultural productivity. After more than fifty years of abandonment, a group of young farmers gave birth to a multifunctional agricultural metropolitan park, designed for the reception and involvement of citizens through the offer of numerous socio-environmental services: an educational farm and training courses for adults; summer camps and environmental education for schools; playgrounds and workshops; and social agriculture; all while enhancing local biodiversity.

And again: the cultural heritage of another 75 hectares of the Campagna Romana, first saved from private construction and then abandoned, has been recovered and "put back into circulation" thanks to the creation of the Tenuta della Mistica Park. Here the Agricoltura Capodarco Cooperative manages a social farm promoting highly innovative and effective support services for social fragilities **[Fig 7]**.

Conclusions

In this Rome of suburban dispersion where city and countryside are blended, the risk of cancellation of the historical agricultural landscapes is great. Here urban agriculture, through the direct and active involvement of local communities, has triggered forms of lasting protection and development aimed not only at the tangible heritage (land, farmhouses, landscape shapes) but also at the intangible one (imaginaries, uses, traditions). The dynamics of the "rediscovery of the neighborhood" (Nicolin 2012, 42), indissolubly linked to agricultural practice, generate a process of physical protection and collective regeneration of this precious heritage.

To put it in Donadieu's words, citizen participation transforms the Campagna Romana from a "paysage" to a "milieu commun" (Donadieu 2016, 4–9), that is, from simple scenery to a place of life and action where people are not spectators but actors, growth and planning factors, mediators between ecological knowledge and sense of memory. In fact, practicing urban agriculture makes it possible to share spaces that were previously abandoned or inaccessible, to experiment with new collective values of social inclusion and the spread of new, more sustainable, fairer, and healthier lifestyles. Urban agriculture not only makes spaces more resistant to the dynamics of abandonment, but is also capable of revitalizing traditional cultural values by building new representative imaginaries (Donadieu 2013, 59–70) **[Fig 8]**.

Fig. 7 Tenuta della Mistica Park, Campagna Romana (2017). The little farmhouse has been restored and used as a store of organic products and bio-fastfood. The outdoor area, used daily for social activities, is designed to accommodate customers of all ages and with limited mobility.

Fig. 8 Community garden 'People's Vegetable Gardens' Campagna Romana (Tor Tre Teste) (2017). The 'people's gardens' illegally occupied 150 hectares of land owned by the Vatican. Although urban agriculture curbed building speculation, and the educational farm soon became a reference place for the inhabitants of the suburb, in 2017 the community garden was dissolved by the municipal administration.

In Rome, the protection of agricultural heritage is implemented by civil society first. The case studies highlight, on the one hand, the success of highly innovative and participatory, place-based multifunctional agriculture projects directly promoted from below (citizens and farmers). On the other hand, they show a general difficulty of public administrations in shifting their strategies regardless of the lessons taught by the numerous successful experiences in progress. Local administrations are unsuccessful both in updating their implementation tools and in developing a rigorous unitary agricultural landscape strategy based on an open dialogue between public policies and local communities.

In the frame of the consolidated antinomies between city and countryside (Lei 2019, 30–46), the contemporary landscape project, understood as an open process, acts as an agile device for recomposing the distance between public control and social participation (Hirsch 2012; Corner 2001; AAA architects 2012), state and civil society (Ostrom 1996), and "strategy" and "tactics" (De Certeau 1980), supporting urban agriculture and the active protection of agricultural heritage for the regeneration of vast metropolitan territories. ■

Urban Gardening as a Practice to Safeguard Historical Agricultural Sites in Can Cabanyes and Torre Codina (Badalona, Catalonia)

Xavier Recasens, Dolors Nieto, Clara Forn, and Oscar Alfranca

In developed countries, where urban agriculture does not have an essential role in feeding people, the practice can fulfill objectives that go beyond food production. These objectives can be diverse, including biodiversity (Egerer et al. 2017), the maintenance of soil fertility (Camps-Calvet et al. 2016), leisure (Schram-Bijkerk et al. 2018), physical well-being (Park et al. 2015), and public education (Guitart et al. 2014). Moreover, urban agriculture can be an important agent to preserve cultural heritage (Camps-Calvet et al.), namely landscapes (De Silva 2019), historical buildings (Čibik et al. 2019), crop techniques, agricultural infrastructures, and even land races (Timpanaro et al. 2018). The city of Badalona in Spain includes two cases—Can Cabanyes and Torre Codina—in which the strengths and weaknesses of the heritage-supporting function of urban agriculture can be identified.

The Loss of the Historical Landscape

Badalona is located in the northeast of the Iberian Peninsula, ten kilometers north of Barcelona **[Fig. 1]**. The city is part of the metropolitan region of Barcelona. The settlement of its territory goes back more than 5,000 years. Its good climate and soil conditions as well as strategic location on the coast enabled a constant occupation. For many centuries, farming was an integral part of the city. Nearby small and medium-sized farms grew produce destined for self-consumption but also to supply the city's markets, providing Badalona mainly with food and wine, but also with secondary products such as hemp for its string industry (Villarroya i Font 1999).

From the 1850s to the present, the population of Badalona and its surrounding cities has increased exponentially due to several social and economic changes such as industrialization and the migration from rural regions. This transformed the landscape, reducing the importance of agriculture and the area of farmed land dramatically **[Fig. 2]**.

As a consequence, a large part of the agricultural heritage—including the patchwork of fields, tracks, paths, ponds, etc.—has disappeared, leaving isolated farm buildings that once represented the core of the agricultural units. Most of these buildings were abandoned or turned into (second) residences. Only a few farmhouses have retained part of their orchards and gardens. However, these remains offer a valuable resource to recover agriculture within the city.

Reintroducing Urban Agriculture for Noncommercial Purposes

In 2007 Badalona's city council decided to offer spaces for urban gardening to retired citizens. These gardens are concentrated around two historic buildings, Torre Codina and Can Cabanyes. The products grown in these allotment gardens are for self-consumption. Sales are not permitted, since the gardeners are not professional farmers. With the project Horts urbans, the city council created a legal framework to define the administrative

Fig. 1 Location of Can Cabanyes and Torre Codina

Year	1854	1937	1968	2009
Inhabitants	6,150	47,929	162,888	219,547
Farmland (ha)	1,554.9	1,291,2	990	53
% of vineyards	70	72	–	28

Fig. 2 Population and farmland evolution of Badalona from 1854 to 2009

Fig. 3 Torre Codina allotment gardens, 2018

Fig. 4 Map of Torre Codina

Fig. 5 Orthophoto of Torre Codina and its surroundings, 1965

procedures for awarding allotments and maintenance (Ajuntament de Badalona 2009). Each allotment has 25 square meters of surface and one tap for irrigation **[Figs. 4 and 7]**. It is only permitted to grow vegetables, herbs, and flowers, and crops must be produced according to the standards of organic farming.

The allotment gardens are opened to users Monday to Friday, 08:00–14:00, all year long. In order to avoid robberies, only the users are allowed to enter the allotment sites.

According to information provided by the city council, 58 plots were awarded by 2020—which accounts for one plot for every 715 inhabitants older than 65, or 0.7 percent of the population older than 65. Most of the plot holders are male; only five are female.

Torre Codina, where the first set of allotments was established, is located in the district of Canyet, Badalona **[Fig. 5]**. This district is one of the oldest settlements outside the city center, as well as one of its most fertile areas.

Torre Codina is a fortified, square building with two floors, a garret, and a hip roof **[Fig. 3]**. In one of its wings, it has a five-story tower with a hip roof and machicolation for its defense. The earliest catalogued information on the building dates back to the thirteenth century, when the owners were the Pedrós family. Over the years, ownership has changed several times and passed to the hands of nonresident owners in Badalona. In the seventeenth century, a two-story rectangular addition was built; at the rear, a large wine cellar was created—which bears witness to the importance of cultivation and the exploitation of vineyards in the farm holding.

At the beginning of the twentieth century, the property comprised only three hectares; it was divided into plots and sold for investment. In 2003, the building and a small plot of land was bought by the city council of Badalona. In addition to the historical building, the site of Torre Codina retains its traditional irrigation system using mine water and an irrigation pond **[Fig. 4]**.

Can Cabanyes, where the second set of allotment gardens is located, is an old farmhouse. Unlike Torre Codina, Can Cabanyes is in the middle of the urban area and surrounded by residential buildings and the motorway **[Fig. 8]**. The orchards of the farmhouse, 0.53 hectares in size, were transformed into allotment gardens and opened in 2010.

Can Cabanyes does not have a clear origin, and its architecture has been transformed over time. The last modifications, carried out during the nineteenth century, gave the building a colonial or manor appearance. It is known that the property was in the hands of a local landowner until the early nineteenth century and was inherited by

Fig. 6 Can Cabanyes allotment gardens, 2018

Fig. 7 Map of Can Cabanyes

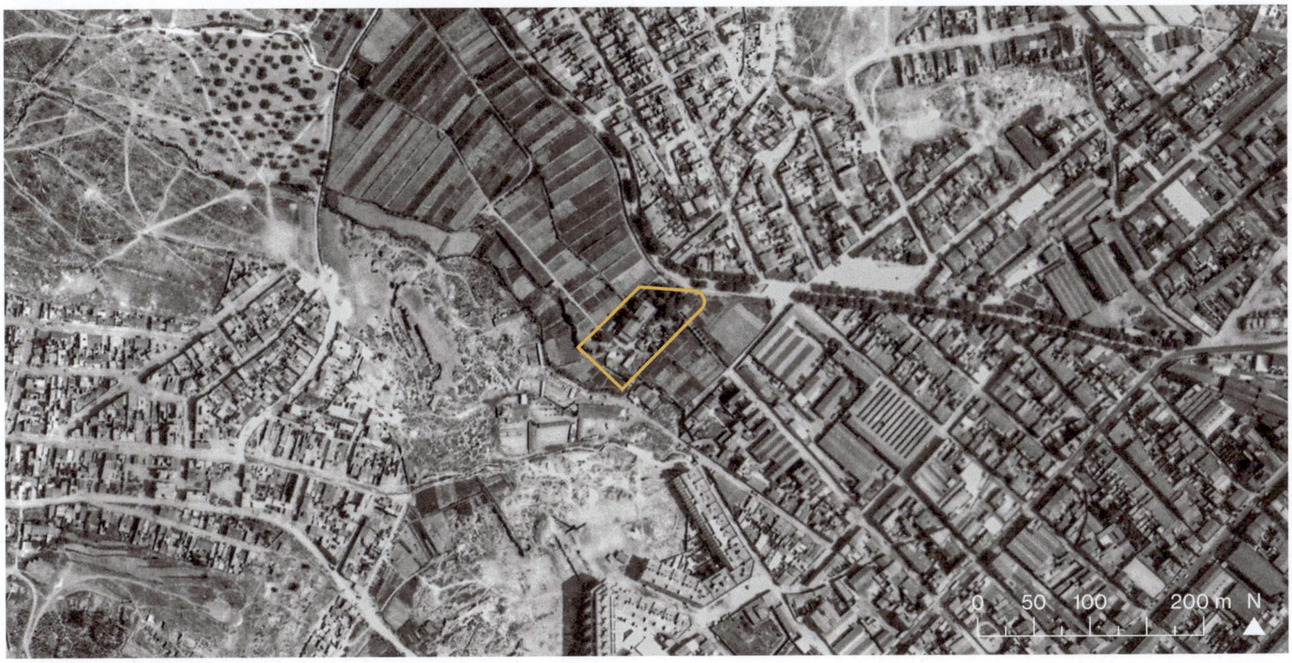

Fig. 8 Orthophoto of Can Cabanyes and its surroundings, 1965

his heirs, who lived in Barcelona. The property changed hands several times, during which the plots and the house were nothing more than possessions from which to obtain an economic return. In 1962, a regional plan changed the use of the lands from farmland to residential. The former farmland was sold to householders, and the manor house was abandoned. When the city council acquired the house in 1980, an important intervention was undertaken in order to consolidate and restore the property, maintaining its characteristics, and to adapt it to community use. The old orchards of Can Cabanyes were transformed into allotment gardens **[Fig. 6]**. Like Torre Codina, Can Cabanyes retains its original irrigation infrastructure: a water well and pond **[Fig. 7]**. The underground water is pumped to the pond.

Both Torre Codina and Can Cabanyes are well connected with the city by car, public transportation, walking and bicycling. The allotment gardens at Can Cabanyes can be seen by local citizens, since the gardens are surrounded by residential streets. In the case of Torre Codina, on the other hand, the main building is currently vacant, and the property is closed to the public. Only the gardeners have access to the allotment gardens.

Conclusion

The transformation of the orchards of historical farmhouses into allotment gardens is a valuable practice, since it retains soil fertility and revitalizes the agricultural heritage of historical irrigation infrastructures that had been abandoned. Urban agriculture also helps to recover a piece of the cultural landscape of the farmhouses, revealing their historical character and providing them with a territorial base. Urban agriculture furthermore enables a more harmonious relationship between the farmhouses and their surroundings by generating a space of transition between the historical buildings and the urban environment. Thus the historical buildings and their orchards—transformed into urban gardens—are brought closer to residents, raising awareness of both the cultural and the agricultural heritage of the city. ■

Acknowledgments:
Information for which no publication is referenced is based on the knowledge and expertise of Dolors Nieto and Clara Forn, who work as historians at the Museu de Badalona.

Showcasing and Reflecting Active Heritage Approaches

Intangible Agricultural Heritage as a Resource for Sustainable Contemporary Cities

Paola Branduini

The statement in the title sounds like an oxymoron, an unsolvable contrast. How can the contemporary city, so much projected toward the future and technology, look at its agricultural past and implement a strategy for the protection and enhancement of its heritage? By recognizing the consistent presence of heritage in our society and the benefits it brings to the contemporary age, the oxymoron can be reconciled. This makes us look at sustainable development with different eyes.

The sustainable development goals (SDGs) and the Paris Agreement recognize that cultural heritage can inform human action in supporting resilience and sustainability. The United Nations 2030 Agenda for Sustainable Development (United Nations 2015) defines 17 SDGs and offers an evidence-based framework for promoting a systemic understanding of the synergies and dynamics between the economic, social, and environmental dimensions of sustainability. In this regard, nature and culture connect the various SDGs to one another. Their integration often finds form in the rich biocultural diversity of the world's heritage, defining our spiritual and physical relationship with the planet in harmonious ways (ICOMOS 2019, 9).

Key to understanding this potential is an appreciation of the breadth of the concept of cultural heritage. Over time, the meaning of cultural heritage in professional practice has expanded from single monuments and sites identified as objects of art to cultural landscapes, historical cities, and serial properties. Contemporary practice further extends the concept beyond tangible heritage to the intangible dimensions of heritage.

In contemporary cities, although tangible agricultural heritage (such as farmsteads) has been consistently cancelled and the intangible heritage (such as farmers with their knowledge) has moved to rural areas, agricultural heritage is still present in urban and peri-urban areas, where it needs to be recognized, preserved, kept alive, and transmitted to future generations. This paper focuses on intangible agricultural heritage, which is mostly neglected in contemporary cities and less developed by scholars, as well as on the actions to enhance it for sustainable development. First, attention is focused on the bond between the two heritages. Second, an interpretive approach to assess the degree of permanence of agricultural heritage in the city is developed. Third, the different roles of the actors in the transmission of intangible heritage are clarified. Finally, the benefits to a sustainable city are outlined and suggestions to implement them are provided. The considerations stem from different studies done by the author and other scholars on London (Laviscio 2020), Seville (Prados and Santiago-Ramos 2020), Granada (Castillo Ruiz and Matarán 2020), Mexico City (Alcántara Onofre 2020), and Australia (Lennon 2020). The examples to support the theory are taken from the agrourban landscape of Milan.

Tangible and Intangible Heritage: A Tight Bond

Intangible heritage includes traditions or living expressions inherited from our ancestors and passed on to our descendants, such as oral traditions, the performing arts, social practices, rituals, festive events, and knowledge and practices concerning nature and the universe (UNESCO 2003). Among these, agricultural intangible heritage comprises the techniques and skills to produce food for human consumption and to construct agricultural buildings and tools; in addition, it includes local dialects, music, and oral literature that have emerged from nonwritten traditions (CEMAT 2003).

Agricultural intangible heritage is strictly related to the tangible one and, despite many radical transformations, is still perceivable in many cities. Today's landscape of the Milan plain, the division of the agricultural land, fields flanked by roads, canals, tree rows, and hedges, is based on the medieval land reclamation technique developed by Cistercian monks. It was continuously modified by small and precise changes over the centuries in order to increase arable land and improve its efficiency. It is the result of techniques that exploited the abundance of water and allowed the cultivation of the land that otherwise was not productive. This land division is still perceivable also in the peri-urban areas, where residential and industrial uses are mixed, but where tiny plots of agricultural land persist. The small roads of the neighborhoods often follow the former agricultural layout and its names. Open canals flanked by hedgerows still exist in the urban and peri-urban parks. Courtyard spaces of urban farms of the local four-sided farmstead typology *cascina*, delimited by specialized agricultural buildings (residence, stables for horses and dairy cows, hay barn, milk factory, granary), convey inclusion and separation from traffic, as well as acoustic and visual insulation from city noise. They frequently host celebrations, poetry and song performances in dialect. Moreover, in every agricultural farm in Milan, the ancient rite of the blessing of the animals by Saint Anthony and the construction of a bonfire to drive away the cold of winter are celebrated annually. These events gather hundreds of citizens from the neighborhoods Traditional Milanese dishes are highly sought after in agrotourism farmhouses, and Michelin star-rated restaurants go to the farms to find traditional recipes, prepare dishes with local agricultural products, and offer them under their names in dialect.

In these examples the tangible heritage reveals the intangible, and the intangible brings the tangible to life. The visible parts of the agricultural techniques that shaped the landscape and the agricultural building typologies provide evidence of agricultural specialization and offer places where traditions can be perpetuated. Agricultural variety can be tasted in the local food. The intangible heritage is the seed of contemporary culture and depends on the communities that reproduce it (UNESCO 2003), thus, we are going to focus on it.

Permanence of Intangible Agricultural Heritage

As mentioned in the introduction, the intangible heritage of agriculture is threatened by the expansion and densification of the city, by changes in the economy, and by new needs of society. If we recognize intangible agricultural heritage as an asset for urban communities, how can we identify it and evaluate its integrity and its benefits for society? The criteria of authenticity and integrity adopted by UNESCO for assessing the outstanding universal value of sites can help the investigation: in the Operational Guidelines for the Implementation of the World Heritage Convention, *integrity* is defined as "the measures of wholeness and intactness of the natural and/or cultural heritage and its attributes."

Fig. 1 High permanence of heritage and its transmission: traditional water meadows are explained by the farmer to the public at Tavernasco farm.

These attributes, which are "form and design, material and substance, location and settings, traditions, techniques, management system, language, spirit, and feeling," are used to define *authenticity* (UNESCO 2019, 27, arts. 82 and 88). The degree of permanence is given by the coexistence of many of these attributes. The following examples illustrate different degrees (high, medium, and low) of the permanence of intangible agricultural heritage in relation to the tangible one.

1. As a high degree of permanence we could consider a mixed Milanese farm (dairy and cereals), composed of agricultural buildings and the fields around them, whose position and dimensions have remained practically unchanged for centuries (location, form, and design). It maintains the long-standing proportion between arable land and meadows. The farmer cultivates the land with traditional techniques adapted to the region, like *marcita* (water submersion for meadows) and rice, and uses old seed varieties (tradition and techniques), creating a green landscape in winter and a water landscape in spring (feeling). The products are sold on the farmstead or at farmers' markets (management system) or used for catering by preparing recipes handed down within the family (other forms of intangible heritage: recipes) **[Fig. 1]**. Educational workshops and tours to the fields explaining the cultivation and transformation of agricultural products take place on the farm, valorizing unused building parts. Former employee dwellings may be transformed into flats for agrotourism. Old traditions like the blessing of animals are kept alive, inviting citizens to participate (spirit).

In this case there is a high integrity in the permanence of both tangible and intangible heritage. The visual evidence of tangible heritage strengthens the perception of intangible heritage and keeps both alive (Branduini and Carnelli 2021). They are transmitted to the next generation, and the valorization in agrotourism allows the maintenance of traditional cultivation and its products (Branduini et al. 2020; Scazzosi 2020). The proximity of the city has been turned into an opportunity: innovation enhances permanence instead of erasing it (Scazzosi 2018).

2. A medium permanence of agricultural heritage would be a farm where water meadows were turned into cornfields to avoid the manual labor of preparing the soil's slope (use); flooded paddy fields were turned to dry fields in order to limit the number of mosquitoes close to the city (practice) and to improve relations with the neighborhood; or cornfields were transformed into wheatfields due to water availability limited by the city (use) **[Figs. 2a–b]**. The intensive crop production changes the field division and dimension, cancels the finely ramified irrigation network, and eliminates hedgerows (form and design), but generally maintains the long-term structures (location and setting), such as terracing, the primary water system, trees, and hedgerows along canals (Scazzosi 2018).

Similarly, when farmhouses are restored and converted into a residential buildings, the historical matter is conserved and can be read (material and substance), but the new functions cancel the readability of the reasons the buildings were made **[Fig. 3]**. These become a container of new functions, bereft of the purpose that made them necessary (use and function). Nevertheless, the material and spatial characters provided by buildings can contribute to new contemporary sociability, to convivial or entertainment events; the setting provided by the agricultural fields, usually managed by a new farmer, last.

In both examples, the physical part of the heritage (fields, trees, canals, buildings) is permanent but the historical relationships that tied it have changed. The beneficial effects of the landscape are reduced: The transmission of a historical and consolidated (intangible) agricultural technique that has contributed to forging the landscape, to maintaining the vitality of the soil and which has characterized it for centuries has been partially modified.

3. Finally, a low permanence is detectable in a new urban neighborhood built in a previously agricultural area. The contemporary city destroys the tangible agricultural heritage but consciously or unconsciously keeps the intangible: the irrigation canals have been buried, the historical buildings demolished, but the streets follow the former subdivision of agricultural land, and toponyms recall. New roads destroy hydraulic structures and canals (material and substance) and interrupt the ancient structure (form and design, use and function). But the memory of the demolished farmhouses remains in the toponyms and metro stops of the district; the street names recall personalities of local agrarian history (language) **[Figs. 4 a–c]**. New Restaurants and taverns offer traditional dishes with dialect names,

Figs. 2a–b Changes in practice form new landscapes: Rice seeding with water (traditional technique) and without water at Battivacco farm

Fig. 3 Permanence of tangible heritage and loss of intangible heritage: Cuccagna farm in Milan

Figs. 4a–c
Agronomist Domenico Berra's house, the effigy, and street dedicated to him: in 1811 he wrote 'Dei prati del Basso milanese detti a marcita,' the handbook for implementing the agrarian technic of water meadows, a successful practice all over Europe at that time. He experimented on the meadows around his house, where there are no longer any agricultural fields. Only intangible signs recall the memory of his role in the implementation of Milan agriculture.

using local products from urban gardens and local farmers. The horticultural practice and knowledge exchange among gardeners can give new life to former agricultural and now abandoned areas (brownfields) (Branduini 2016) **[Fig. 5]**. The property of the intangible heritage of being movable and replicable allows it to be repeated by new and different actors. The permanency analysis confirms the strong bond between tangible and intangible heritage. Clear evidence of their role is provided when there is a high permanence degree of both. Intangible heritage is sometimes less evident but still present. Finally, in the medium degree of permanence, when tangible heritage seems persistent, we should pay attention to the intangible heritage and improve the awareness of actors in transmitting it.

Intangible Heritage's Actors

Actors are the communities that reproduce the practices "in response to their environment, their interaction with nature and their history" (UNESCO 2003, art. 2). We can distinguish the bearers of agricultural traditions (role models), those who attend and benefit from them (spectators), and those who try to reproduce them (replicators).

Role models are the generations of farmers who keep alive the agricultural practices handed down to them. They follow good agricultural practices, repeat traditional techniques and gestures, follow the saints' calendar to drown water meadows, call agricultural tools and fields by their local names, sing folk songs in dialect, and thank saints for cattle health and good harvest.

Spectators are inhabitants or occasional visitors who watch and attend to those practices with enthusiasm and awe. Farmers teach horticultural practices to new gardeners and perpetuate the religious or heathen rites. Groups of citizens take over the practices and aspire to become replicators. Sometimes religious celebrations such as the blessing of the animals or the bonfires mentioned above are organized by the citizens without a farmer. The celebration of agricultural rites strengthens the sense of community and fosters cohesion to the point that the presence of the role model and of the object and men of celebration is not necessary anymore (Branduini 2020).

New generations of farmers yearn to become new role models: they take up the baton from their parents or aged friends and reapply the practice with the enthusiasm and creativity typical of new generations. They understand the contemporary needs of urban society and are adaptive or proactive in offering new services and products to their fellow citizens. From mere replicators of agricultural traditions they become conscious role models of new integrated approaches between agricultural heritage and the urban community's social demands. These are the new farmers flourishing in the context of urban agriculture, who can perform the fundamental role of both heritage spokesmen and modernizers for the next generation.

Fig. 5 New urban vegetable gardens (left) keep the name of the former farm (right), now residence. Vegetable gardens of former Albana farm

Intangible Agricultural Heritage for Sustainable Cities: Actions to Enhance It

Agricultural intangible heritage, as demonstrated, is still present in contemporary cities even if it is at risk. It can reinforce the social, economic, and environmental dimension of sustainability, as the actions of identification, transmission, and maintenance can strengthen and enhance its potential. Heritage components, risks, and actions are listed in the table **[Fig. 6]**.

Agricultural intangible heritage can strongly contribute to social cohesion and enhance the sense of identity, stimulating local communities and young people. It can be a driver in using innovative adaptive (re)development solutions when restoring built heritage, reducing carbon emissions, and introducing environmentally friendly solutions. It can stimulate jobs based on culinary tradition, spread local recipes and fruit and vegetable varieties, and improve nutrition knowledge (Jelinčić and Glivetić 2020, 9). On a global level, heritage conservation practice is increasingly endorsing innovative tools that promote adaptive and systemic approaches to better manage climate change (ICOMOS 2019, 9).

To keep intangible assets alive and reinforce sustainable opportunities, citizens should strengthen and create heritage communities under the stimulus of the Faro Convention (Council of Europe 2005). They can evolve from spectators to replicators of agricultural practices; young farmers can progress from replicators to new agrourban role models. This can be fostered by enhancing people's involvement in heritage recognition, understanding, and care, in school education at all levels (practical activities, interviews and dialogue with older people, and historical memory of the places), in leisure time activities (gardening, cooking classes), and in professional training and job creation (courses in good agricultural practice, agroecology, organic horticulture, management of irrigation systems, etc.).

Thanks to the implementation of such initiatives, the contemporary city can transform its agricultural past into a valuable resource for empowering its population. This propels passive strategies of heritage protection toward an active heritage community engagement. ■

Dimensions of sustainability	Heritage	
	Intangible heritage	Tangible heritage components
Social	• Languages • Dialects • Idioms, common sayings	Roads, places, tools
	Traditional music and dance	• Musical instruments • Places where dancing occurs, e.g., in the courtyards, or in open spaces close to farmsteads
	Events to celebrate or propitiate a good harvest	• Fields • Courtyards
Economical	Skills in repairing artifacts	Hydraulic artifacts: terraces, canals, slopes, furniture
	Traditional recipes	Food production (cereals, legumes, sausages, cheeses)
Environmental	• Seeds variety of vegetables and flowers, both heirloom and local varieties • Local animal breeds for food production (e.g., poultry, pigs) • Agro-biodiversity	Garden vegetables, fields and garden hedgerows, tree lines
	Knowledge of natural resource (water, soil, trees, crops) management	• Natural resources (water, soil) and tools • Hydraulic artifacts
	• Technical cultivation skills as intercropping between tree and herbal plants (coltura promiscua) • Tying vine to tree (married vine) • Overseeding a legume on a cereal	• Tree alignments interchange with herbal crops (Coltura promiscua) • Vine ties to trees (married vine)

Fig. 6 Enhancing intangible heritage through actions in urban agriculture. The table illustrates intangible and tangible components of the heritage according to the dimensions of sustainability, the risks it is exposed to, the possible actions to preserve it, transmit it in the short term, and maintain it in the long term.

Threats – risks	Actions		
	Identify, collect, census	Transmit, involve	Take care, maintain
Loss of people able to speak a dialect or language	• Search archives for the histories of old names • Make video-record interviews (to collect dialect sound, gestures and expressions) • Make audio-record language exchanges between speakers • Gather/create a dictionary and grammar of the dialect from remaining speakers	• Add old toponyms (collect from interview and from old maps) to places on site and on maps (add old one to current one) • Organize spectacles or readings in dialect	Educate children to old language with immersion language programs
• Loss of dancing and playing skills • No intra- and intergenerational transmission	• Search archives for information and recorded performances of traditional music and dance • Interview older people • Solicit and collect recordings, photos, costumes, etc., from locals	• Dance, sing, and play music • Record performances on video • Offer compact courses for dance and play • Encourage events, promotion by citizens' association with farmers • Communicate events via social networks, local digital and print newspapers	• Organize festivals • Stage small events throughout the year in urban courtyards or in the middle of the fields
• Loss of farmers to continue traditions • Loss of intergenerational knowledge transmission	• Interview local farmers • Make video record on ceremony re-enactments • Collect artifacts dedicated to celebration	• Reviving ceremonies by citizens' association involving farmers in repeating traditional events • Organize events through social neighborhood networks • Organize common lunch during/ after the celebration • Communicate events via social networks, local digital and print newspapers	• Compile an events calendar • Clean and repair the tools employed • Consolidate gestures and rites
• Loss of handcraft technique • Loss of intergenerational knowledge transmission	• Interview old local farmers • Document and illustrate the techniques (how to do...)	• Create dedicated courses for job regeneration (for those unemployed or with mental health issues) • Teach techniques in professional schools • Create hobby courses for those unemployed • Organize common lunch during/ after the celebration	• Create learning-by-practice days to involve citizens (theory and practice) • Plan a volunteer activities' calendar
Loss of knowledge, ingredients, and culinary skills	• Interview agricultural families' women • Launch recipes collection on social networks • Search for particular processing techniques/recipes in older books or diaries	• Create and offer short culinary courses in urban farmsteads • Produce online or printed recipe book • Add the provenance of ingredients to restaurant menus • Teach dish preparation in professional schools • Teach processing cheese/sausages/ poultry preparation following traditional techniques	• Connect food production to recipes • Connect restaurants with the local farmsteads' production • Agro-tourism • Encourage farmers to sell products with recipes • Encourage farmers to process cheese/sausages/poultry following traditional techniques
Loss of biodiversity, local vegetable species' varieties and animal breeds	• Create a seed bank • Interview horticulturists or nursery-men for knowing traditional tech-niques useful today (intercropping, local variety, etc.)	• Develop and offer courses for recognizing heirloom varieties; learning multiplication and intercropping techniques; feeding animals with fresh grass (instead of corn silage) • Develop professional or technical courses for local farmers or interested non-farmers • Develop courses for gardeners to expand interest in local or heirloom varieties • Involve experienced farmers to explain practically traditional techniques during the courses	Encourage farmers to produce and sell local and heirloom varieties and races at farmers' markets and explain their qualities to the public
• Loss of good balance in natural resources exploitation • Loss of natural resources • Canalization abandonment and degradation • Abandon of manual/gravity irrigation techniques (without external energy input)	Interview local farmers practicing traditional irrigation techniques	Develop courses (as above) regarding traditional water management and cultivation techniques	Recover canals and encourage research to match traditional skills with new technologies
• Monocolture • Crop simplification • Loss in biodiversity and landscape variety	• Interview local farmers that are still using traditional techniques of mixing crops (coltura promiscua, married vine, overseeding ...) • Identify and map relict landscapes • Search for plants associations (trees + bushes + herbs) fighting against parasites and invasive insects	• Develop courses (as above) to explain the environmental and landscape benefits of mixing crops • Add signals/panels/explanation on the cultural and ecological values of relict landscapes	• Encourage organic farmers to use these techniques • Develop and sell products that enhance the mixture of seeds (mixed cereals flour and bread)

Bamberg Market Gardeners' District—A Living Cultural Heritage for Centuries: Solutions for Dealing with Tangible and Intangible Heritage

Diana Büttner

Since the Middle Ages, urban market gardening has been practiced in Bamberg, a city whose core area was inscribed on the UNESCO World Heritage List in 1993. Together with the *Bergstadt* (City on the Hills) and the *Inselstadt* (Island District), the *Gärtnerstadt* (Market Gardeners' District) is an integral part of the World Heritage Site **[Fig. 1]**. These late medieval structures of gardening, originally farmsteads, then adjacent acreage, and now in the center of Bamberg, have been exceptionally preserved to this day. The Gärtnerstadt is characterized by wide, open spaces within a perimeter block development **[Fig. 2]** (Gunzelmann 2019, 2–3). It is located not only in the World Heritage Site but also in its buffer zone, and not only characterizes Bamberg's townscape but also forms an important contrast to the densely constructed town of Bamberg.

Bamberg is one of the few cities, if not the only city, where urban horticulture has been able to preserve its traditional forms of cultivation authentically over such a long period. Thus, not only tangible but also intangible cultural heritage assets exist. These include the forms of building and living of the gardeners as well as horticultural traditions, including their religious dimension, clothing, and language, and furthermore the knowledge about seed production and processing techniques of the gardeners. In 2016, this gardening tradition was added to the German National Inventory of Intangible Cultural Heritage in order to preserve, maintain, and promote it as a living cultural heritage (Baier et al. 2018, 19), and also to further emphasize and raise awareness of its meaning and thus demonstrate the great importance of Bamberg's urban horticulture on a national and international level.

Defined by a Unique Spatial Structure ...

In order to gain a deeper understanding of the district's characteristics, it is important to understand its history and structures. A look at the oldest city map of Bamberg from 1602 is helpful and shows plenty of market gardens space, but also illustrates a decline in the intensity of land use and building density from the center moving outwards **[Fig. 3]**. Typical market gardeners' homes are single-story houses with high-pitched roofs, small windows, and large wooden gates. Not only was the exterior arranged in a special way; the interior layout of the houses is also arranged in a multifunctional manner. For example, a passageway connecting the street to the courtyard and house garden is a key element of a market gardener's house: It offers a roofed, weatherproof work area and also serves as a place to offer goods for sale. Another much-needed element was the black kitchen (a type of smoke kitchen), where there was cooking over an open fire. The fireplace provided dry air in the attic, where seeds and herbs were stored. The map also shows that the gardeners' houses follow an arrangement of their own, a perimeter block development. Another special aspect of the urban development is that the cultivation areas are almost exclusively accessed through the houses. Today, there is no direct

Fig. 1 The three parts of the UNESCO World Heritage Site 'Town of Bamberg' in one picture: Inside the Market Gardeners' District, in the background the City on the Hills and the Island District

Fig. 2 Aerial view of parts of the Market Gardeners' District: The perimeter block development encloses the gardeners' inner cultivation areas.

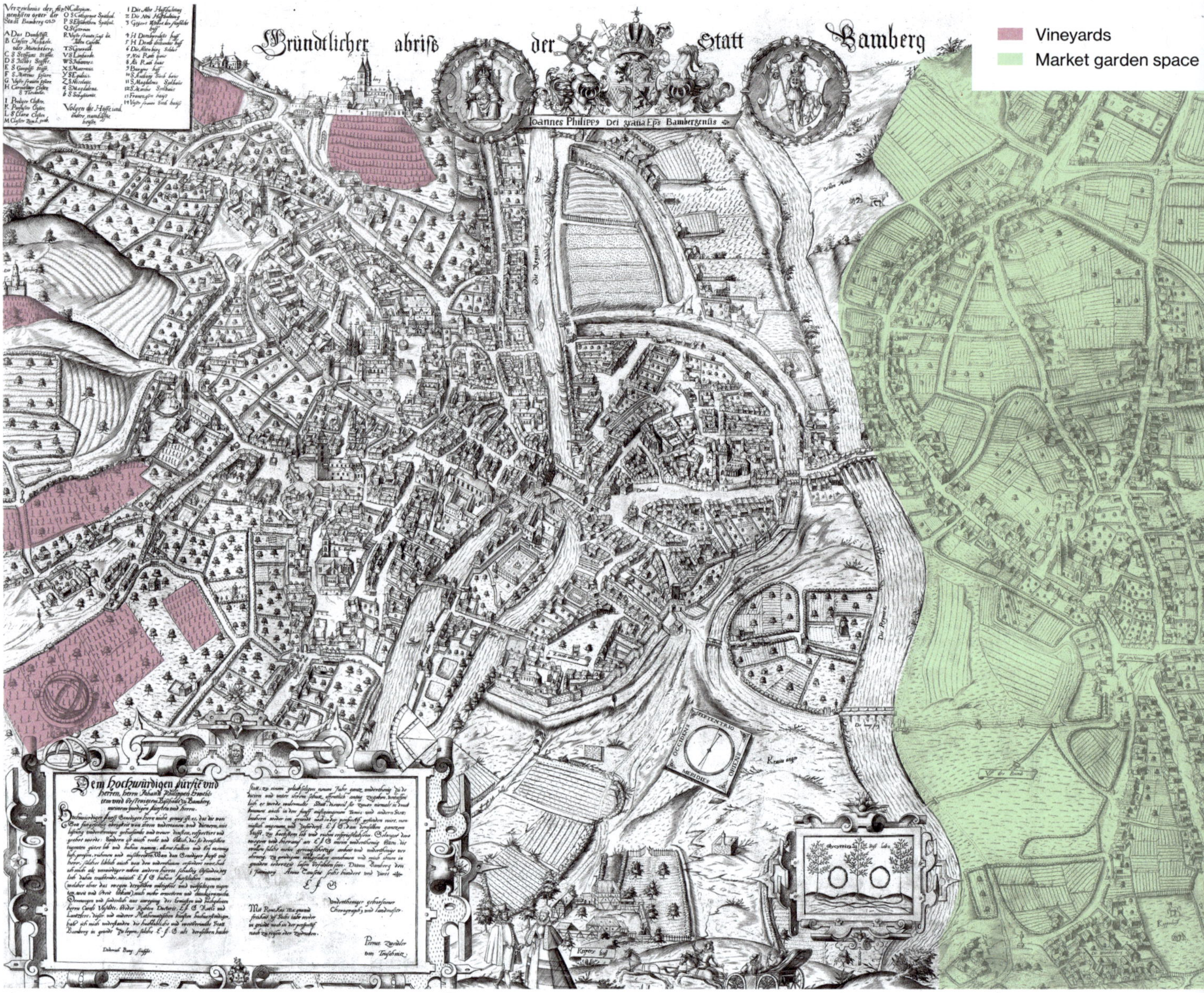

Fig. 3 The oldest city map of Bamberg from 1602 by Petrus Zweidler illustrating the overcoming structure of the town of Bamberg and especially of the Market Gardeners' District to the right

access to these areas from the street (Kloos 2018, 212) **[Fig. 4]**. At first glance, the streets lined with the original homes of the market gardeners seem ordinary (Wilhelm 2019, 29). Whenever a gate opens, however, passers-by can gain a glimpse of the courtyards and backstreet fields. Behind the houses—away from the street—is a series of outbuildings: a shed, a barn, and a well, for example. Due to the division of an estate, the latter was often on the property boundary for two parties to use. The thread is taken up by the wide, open spaces of the market-garden fields. At the parcel boundaries, gardeners erected field walls made of sandstone, which created a special microclimate for the cultivation of plants. Today, the Bayerisches Denkmalschutzgesetz (Bavarian Law for Protection and Preservation) protects these walls and most of the buildings in the area (Büttner 2013, 18–19). The legal protection is essential because these historical structures, which combine living with working—in this case, urban market gardening—are important historical monuments that need preserving for future generations. This is particularly important, as both the World Heritage status and Intangible Cultural Heritage status are moral and not legally bound protections and are not automatically linked to financial support from UNESCO or the Federal Republic of Germany. However, this special status is often a great advantage when it comes to acquiring funding. In addition, it gives international visibility and is of course a great privilege.

Fig. 4 A typical gardener's house. Today, this building houses the Bamberg Gardeners' and Vintners' Museum.

... as Well as by a Specific Social System, Local Knowledge, and Traditions

The Gärtnerstadt's great peculiarity is that in this district, it is not only the structure that is unique, but also the people who built the area, then worked and lived in it. The gardeners were *Ackerbürger* (farming townspeople), who ran smallholdings by growing vegetables and selling seeds. They built their international reputation on the quality of the produce they sold across Europe. This extensive trade in seeds and licorice root once formed a significant part of the local economy. The gardeners also played a major role in feeding the city's population, which was an enormous locational advantage for Bamberg, not only during wartime.

Until the mid-nineteenth century, the number of gardening businesses increased in line with the population. The spread of industrialization, the railroads from 1844, and the introduction of freedom of industry led to stronger competition both within and from outside the town. Consequently, the number of businesses reduced drastically, which still affects the situation today (Baier et al. 2018, 27–29). With the passing of time, globalization, and the move toward mass production, the traditions and with them the historical use of the fields and the cultivation of vegetables threaten to disappear. Furthermore, some locals would like to use the fields as building sites. Others have simply stopped cultivating the land. Out of 500 gardeners in the past, fewer than 30 businesses have survived until today (Alberth 2018, 215). At the same time, the urban structure of the Gärtnerstadt, as well as the horticultural knowledge of sowing, plant cultivation, and soil management, in conjunction with the city's religious tradition, are unique in Germany, even in Europe, and must be preserved **[Fig. 5]**.

The Initial Situation at a Glance

Since the World Heritage recognition of Bamberg was mostly focused on its architectural values, the urban gardens that are hidden behind private houses were often overlooked. The Market Gardeners' District is not a self-explanatory destination. The heterogeneous ownership structure of the area limits the municipality's influence on its development.

Commercial gardening activities face spatial restrictions, which preclude the use of machinery. High costs for essential resources, such as water, pose another obstacle. At the same time, increasing development pressure led to some gardening lands being lost to construction projects, with an accompanying loss of biodiversity and traditional local knowledge.

Protection Strategies

Therefore, the municipal administration aims to safeguard both the historical spatial structures as an integral part of the World Heritage Site, and also the knowledge and the traditions which form part of the intangible cultural heritage. In order to fulfill this task, it was almost a stroke of fortune that the municipality was supported by the Investitionsprogramm Nationale UNESCO-Welterbestätten (National UNESCO World Heritage Sites Investment Programme) in 2009, which was the first federal government program established exclusively for World Heritage Sites. It was only through the program's fundings that the project Urbaner Gartenbau (Urban Gardening) could be implemented in the first place: through this being financially able to develop.

The project's objective is to keep alive the typical Bamberg gardeners' culture and preserve the unique inner-city gardening lands as part of the World Heritage. It is a model project with many actors and stakeholders, and consists of three main fields of action: marketing, education, and land use. It includes aspects of urban planning, monument protection, tourism, and commercial horticulture. In addition, it serves to preserve and further develop gardening operations and phenomena as defining urban structural elements.

Integrated Actions on Different Levels

Important for today's success of the project were an awareness-raising campaign, consisting of various events, including a series of lectures targeting both locals and visitors, the promotion of local produce with several series in the local daily newspaper, and the protection of gardening lands by recultivation (UNESCO 2019, 59).

Fig. 5 Religious traditions: Gardeners carrying statues of saints during the Catholic Corpus Christi procession in Bamberg

A walking route through the Market Gardeners' District was created, which offers insight into the gardeners' cultural, religious, and economic lives. As the cultivation areas are not visible to the public, visitors now have the opportunity to enjoy the view over the market garden lands from the panorama platform installed inside the fields. Moreover, within the scope of this initiative, the Gärtner- und Häckermuseum (Gardeners' and Vintners' Museum) was reorganized and redesigned in close collaboration with the gardeners and winegrowers themselves. The new permanent exhibition informs visitors about Bamberg's gardening tradition, its religious aspects as well as the gardeners' and winegrowers' everyday lives **[Fig. 6]**.

Revitalization of Historical Cultivated Areas

Fig. 7 Bamberg licorice as a *Jungpflanze* (nursery plant) and as tea with souvenir cup

The urban gardening fields must be permanently preserved, cultivated, and developed to keep this part of the World Heritage alive and sustainable. Numerous measures were implemented – involving the gardeners, the neighborhood, and the interested local public (Eyink and Heck 2017, 33). Accordingly, the Bamberger Sortengarten (Bamberg Heritage Variety Garden) was established, which conserves and presents Bamberg's traditional vegetable varieties, including potatoes, radishes, savoy cabbages, and onions **[Fig. 9]**. The *Bamberger birnförmige Zwiebel* (Bamberg pear-shaped onion) was saved from extinction by the project, and its flower now features in the logo of the Bamberger Sortengarten. The garden itself contributes to biodiversity as well as to historical and environmental education. It enables people to get in contact with their food again, to experience the great variety of vegetables and especially their use in the kitchen. Since 2013, the *Bamberger Hörnla* (Bamberg cone-shaped potato) has been a *geschützte geographische Angabe* (protected geographical indication) and thus is already specially protected; unfortunately, not all other varieties are protected (yet).

As previously mentioned, licorice root was an important economic factor in Bamberg and had been planted since the sixteenth century. It was of great importance both as a medicinal remedy and as a sweetener. With the introduction of raw sugar and the progress of medicine, licorice was forced off the market. For display purposes only, a licorice field was kept in the Gärtner- und Häckermuseum. Through the project, licorice cultivation in Bamberg was revived on a small scale by the Bamberger Süßholz-Gesellschaft (Bamberg Licorice Society) (Daftary-Steel et al. 2017, 148). Its production is no longer competitive on the world market, but in Bamberg, various licorice products sell well as souvenirs among the citizens and, of course, among the many tourists **[Fig. 7]**.

Fig. 6 Inside the newly designed Gardeners' and Vintners' Museum – Winegrowers' showroom

Enabling Self-Empowerment

In order to better market their produce, it was possible through the project to establish an association of Bamberg's gardeners, through which they can now follow a shared sales strategy. The Interessengruppe Bamberger Gärtner (Bamberg Gardeners' Interest Group), an alliance of individual businesses, coordinates and implements communication and sales activities such as the annual Tag der offenen Gärtnereien (Market Gardens' Open Day) **[Fig. 8]**. These gardeners cultivate the historical fields in the urban area and pass on their knowledge to following generations. With the established brand Gutes aus der Gärtnerstadt (Good Products from the Market Gardeners' District), they sell their goods not only at the town market but also deliver directly to residents' houses, and have become a real tourist magnet. Furthermore, these recent developments show quite clearly how lively the gardening tradition in Bamberg is again. Another specialty of the

Fig. 8 Bamberg Gardeners' Interest Group: The Bamberg gardeners have joined forces in an interest group and work together to boost their marketing.

Bamberg gardeners is that in addition to selling their vegetables and flowers, they also offer services. They pick up and deliver plants, and they take care of private gardens and also graves. Through the marketing activities of the Interessengruppe Bamberger Gärtner, this service is brought closer to customers, and it is shown what variety the gardeners actually offer. Today, the Bamberg gardener families see themselves not only as the guardians of their traditional cultural heritage as producers of agricultural goods, but also as modern service providers (Daftary-Steel et al. 2017: 100–1). In this way, tradition and progress go hand in hand, and the living gardening tradition contributes to the protection of this World Heritage Site.

Challenges, Milestones, and Keys to Success

The City of Bamberg demonstrates a variety of possibilities for preserving and developing the tangible and intangible heritage of its Gärtnerstadt. This shows that preservation can be rather dynamic and can even lead to further development through customized solutions. Although the biggest steps are already taken, social and economic factors hamper the conservation of Bamberg's historical urban gardens. In the long term, financial and infrastructural support will be required to keep Bamberg's gardening tradition alive, to recultivate more areas, to further promote the marketing of the gardeners, and to further raise awareness of the importance of local food.

In summary, the following success indicators can be used for a general approach to the conservation and development of Bamberg's urban agricultural heritage. Due to the heterogeneous ownership structure in the Gärtnerstadt, establishing partnerships for the implementation of measures was indeed time-consuming, but it was the key element in the cooperation. Another important step was to bring to the table representatives from the municipality and its subsidiaries together with gardeners, landowners, associations (such as the Verein Bamberger Sortengarten – Grünes Erbe Bamberg e.V. and the Bamberger Süßholz-Gesellschaft), and garden lovers in order to implement measures successfully and sustainably. Residents' privacy concerns had to be carefully addressed while at the same time finding suitable uses for uncultivated land. Overall, the most important point and the key for a successful implementation is the personal contact that made measures possible in the first place and which will make them possible in the future. ■

Fig. 9 Growing traditional vegetables in the Bamberger Sortengarten

Strategies to Reanimate the Urban and Agricultural Heritage of Oasis Settlements in Oman: The Case of Al Hamra

Alexander Kader

For hundreds of years in Oman, cities and agriculture were in a symbiotic relationship, its inhabitants sustained by a sophisticated food cultivation system irrigated by a refined network of water channels called *falaj* (plural form, *aflaj*) **[Fig. 1]**. Settlements were built using local construction materials and techniques. However, the advent of the oil industry in the 1970s saw the disruption of this symbiotic coexistence of agricultural and urban environments. Rapid population growth and unsustainable urban development in previously uninhabited spaces have led to what we now call urban sprawl. Even though the falaj irrigation systems have been registered as a UNESCO World Heritage Site since 2006, the historical urban and agricultural spaces of nearly all of the centuries-old oasis settlements in Oman are endangered and in severe decay.

Al Hamra

Perched on the lower slopes of the Al Hajar mountain ranges, the 400-year-old town of Al Hamra is a former agricultural center containing mud-brick mansions of two to three stories. Local materials, mainly earth, stone, and wood from date palms, form the built structures of the compact agglomeration of houses, while the course of the aflaj determined the positioning of every feature of the settlement, including the grain and vegetable fields, the palm gardens in the west, and the layout of the plots of land (Gangler 2003) **[Fig. 2]**. The scarce water had been harnessed by farmers for hundreds of years by canalizing surface runoff, tapping springs, or filtering subsoil water. The water of Al Hamra's falaj system originates from the nearby Wadi Ghul and the Jebel Shams mountain range. It arrives at the westernmost part of the agricultural plantation area, where it splits to irrigate the agricultural area as well as the settlement. Once made accessible, the water is channeled through small irrigation canals to the fields, operating on gravitational flow, without external energy inputs (Luedeling 2007). Aligned with such a viable system of water flow is a stratification of cultivation in three tiers to make effective use of the limited water supply: the lowest tier includes vegetables and grain such as wheat and sugarcane; the middle tier has small fruit trees such as banana, mango, pomegranate, citrus, apricot, and peach; while the uppermost tier consists of a roof of date palm crowns, the leaves of which provide shade for the tiers below **[Fig. 3]**.

In a setting like Oman, where water is scarce, the formation of the falaj system to channel groundwater from sources like wells and wadis was a gamechanger. A strong interdependence was established between available water, agricultural plots, crop cultivation, and the inhabitants. The amount of available water determined the quantity of food that could be produced and thus also determined the size of the settlements and so the number of inhabitants who could be supported. Apart from nourishing individual families and trading the surplus in *souqs* (markets), harvests were also used to feed livestock. The need for imported food was minimal. Thus, like other traditional centuries-old

Fig. 1 Refined falaj system operating on gravitational flow to irrigate agricultural fields

Fig. 2 Compact agglomeration of houses representing the vernacular architectural heritage of Al Hamra with the agricultural land in the background

Fig. 3 Three-tiered agricultural system characteristic of Al Hamra, irrigated by the water from the falaj system

mountain settlements in Oman, Al Hamra developed autonomously and flourished with its sophisticated agroecosystem.

Strong social structures were reinforced for the construction and maintenance of the aflaj systems, with sets of rules, roles, and institutions relying on the bidirectional interdependence between community and agriculture. The importance of the aflaj systems to communities is also reflected in the numerous watchtowers built along these waterways to guard them. The inhabitants of the settlements formed social structures that regulated and built houses, urban structures, and agricultural systems (Nagieb et al. 2004). The fair and effective management and sharing of water in villages and towns were—and remain to this day in some cases—underpinned by mutual dependence and communal values, and guided by astronomical observation (Chakraborty 2019). **Fig. 4** illustrates this interrelationship between key players of the closed system within the settlement.

With the advent of the oil industry in Oman during the 1970s, the interdependent relationship between falaj, agriculture, and built structures was destroyed. Prosperity led to rapid population growth. While old centers and plantations were abandoned in large parts, resulting in historical buildings falling to ruins, newly generated income from the discovery of oil provided families with the means to build and settle in larger houses outside the old towns, spreading into the surrounding barren lands and previously uninhabited spaces **[Figs. 5 and 6]**. Unsustainable construction grew rapidly.

As a result, significant vernacular and agricultural heritage are in danger of dying out. Numerous cities in Oman testify to this unfortunate course of development. Inhabitants' sustenance shifted from locally produced agriculture and livestock to less healthy, cheaper, and more readily available supermarket food, which is mainly imported.

These developments evoked unprecedented changes to the agricultural systems of the oases, and the implications of these changes altered the settlements from a set of autonomous systems into one that is linear, unsustainable, and greatly reliant on external income and imported food. The complex social structures that maintained and regulated the aflaj systems have almost entirely dissolved in most settlements, leading to only a very few active aflaj side branches being maintained by individual families for their agricultural lands. As a result, there is a significant reduction in the cultivation

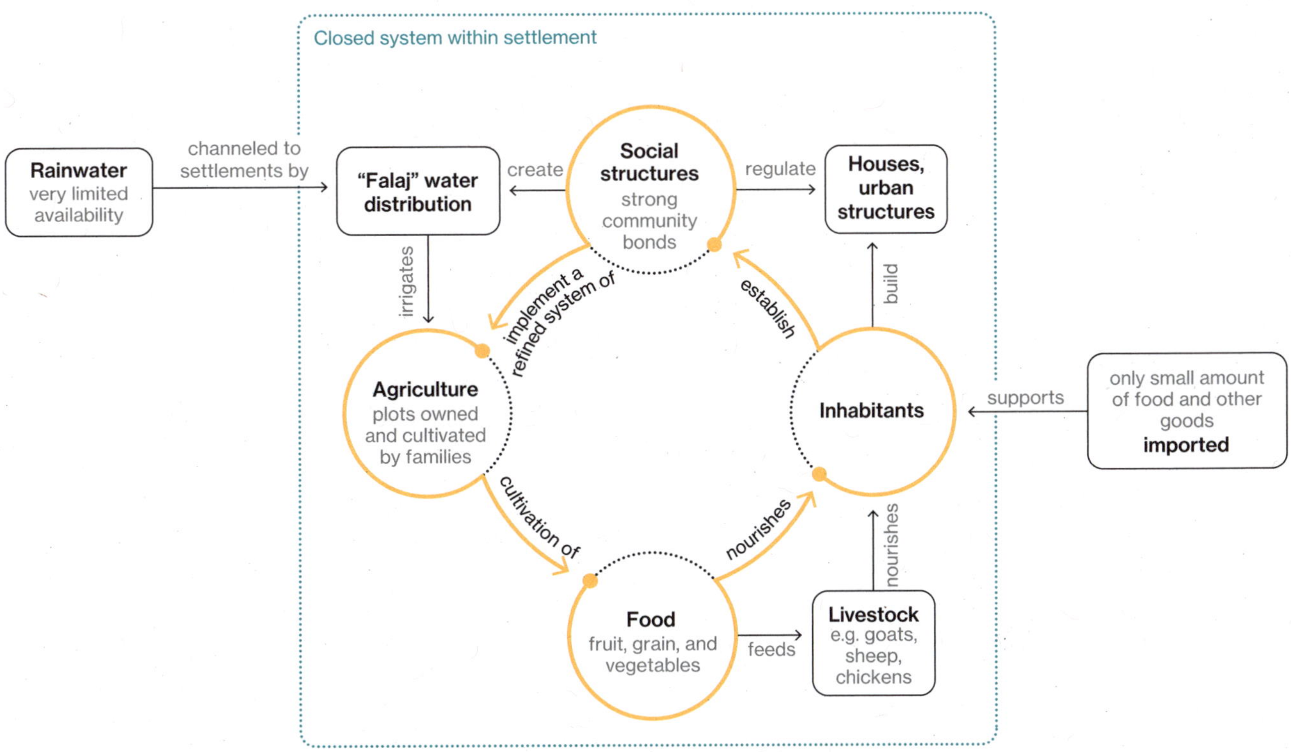

Fig. 4 Traditional, centuries-old mountain oases of Oman

Fig. 5 Overview of the lush agricultural fields of Al Hamra, which are closely connected to the compact old town with mud-brick houses (to the far right of the image), in contrast to the sparsely placed newer parts of the town (as shown at the outskirts of the agricultural fields), which represent urban sprawl

of food and maintenance of livestock. Due to the heavy reliance on imported foods and goods, the once pivotal aflaj structures are now neglected in large parts along with the abandonment of agricultural plantations across vast areas. While the main water channels remain active to this day in many cases, the side branches have been subjected to severe decay or have decomposed entirely. Most restoration efforts for the main aflaj channels make use of unsustainable materials like concrete instead of the vernacular construction materials available in abundance. This new settlement pattern on the rise since the 1970s has been illustrated in **Fig. 7**.

Today, with depleting oil resources it would be worthwhile to restore and revisit these traditional construction and cultivation techniques to identify the potential for them to become a living heritage, one that prevails, is constantly enhanced, and supports the local demand for healthy and organic food in a beneficial way.

Potential Approaches to Reanimate Al Hamra's Agricultural Land with Organic Food Cultivation and Integrated Sustainable Tourism

In order to address the aforementioned challenges common to many historical settlements and their agricultural spaces in Oman, Al Hamra has been selected to serve as an exemplar. Raising awareness about the need for organic foods and healthy nutrition within the local community as well as among tourists could lead to an increase in demand. Thus the market for fruit, grain, and vegetables grown without fertilizers, and meat without antibiotics—bottom line, any food produced through ecological farming practices—could be strongly increased. Given the current lack of local organic food in the region, harvests from Al Hamra could be sold as a more healthy alternative to the imported supermarket food. The three-tier cultivation could be repurposed for organic food production. The diversity of crops cultivated on three tiers using the same historical principles would mean that a polyculture production system is ensured, leading to increased biodiversity and appropriate soil quality. Ownership of plots could be remodeled from family-owned to the following: Small plots could be rented under a tenancy agreement, allowing tenants to use these plots not only for organic food production but also for other activities. Educational gardens could be established to become teaching sites for the production, processing, and consumption of food, thus raising public awareness and ensuring that centuries-old agricultural knowledge would be passed on to a new generation. Agricultural lands could also be recognized as therapeutic gardens, where the healing effects of farming and building a close relationship with nature could be demonstrated and utilized, emphasizing the symbiotic relationship of man and nature. Lastly, community gardens would serve a bottom-up initiative of engaging the local and universal tourism-based community—where these agricultural lands could be tended to collectively, resulting in growing social networks and a restored sense of community (Vejre et al. 2016). The custom of organic food production would reanimate vital public spaces such as the souq, which could bustle once again with trade, culture, and heritage, generating employment opportunities and the conception of a circular economy within the settlements. Besides local souqs, organic food produced could also be sold nationally, catering to the increased demand for nutritious foods created amid the population.

In conjunction with organic food production, agriculture, and its various applications, Al Hamra could become a tourist center, highlighting its local identity based on urban agriculture. Tourism could be explored through several means—for example, by instilling a culture of "self cultivation" during a visitor's stay, where one could hand-pick organically grown fruits for breakfast, cook their own meals, and live in vernacular houses. While this would contribute significantly to the local economy, it would also create opportunities to

Fig. 6 Plan of Al Hamra illustrating the layout of the agricultural area in relation to the old town (houses highlighted in white) and the new parts (houses highlighted in gray). A schematic representation of the falaj irrigation system is shown with blue lines.

amplify the outreach of these special agricultural practices. As agricultural practitioners, the local community would be a vital player in sustaining the system, relying heavily on human labor, local expertise, and local farmers' creativity. These critical elements would ensure that tourism development would be well informed and locally oriented (Su et al. 2018). The sustainable development of the local community would be critical to sustaining these important agricultural systems and ensuring that the organic food industry established in Al Hamra could work independently from the tourism industry.

In an idealistic scenario such as that presented in **Fig. 8**, a restored falaj system and its underlying social structures could once again become pivotal to the functioning of future mountain oases. In parallel to this, the social structures would also be tasked with the restoration, renovation, and modification of the traditional houses and urban structures so they can fulfill new functions, making them useful to inhabitants and tourists alike. The organic food produced by the ecological agricultural plantations would nourish inhabitants and tourists as well as feed free-range livestock for organic meat, poultry, eggs, and dairy products. Increased income generated by the surplus production of organic foods and livestock would facilitate an improved local economy while also securing capital to import food and other goods when necessary. Thus the sophisticated settlement structure with its balanced interdependence between agroecosystem and agrotourism could be reinstated.

Applying the Principles of Circular Agrosystems and Agrotourism to Other Traditional Settlements in Oman

While we, as a community of researchers, recognize the necessity to preserve the intricate human-nature relationship within these oasis settlements, several initiatives could be taken on a national scale. Local communities should be recognized as key stakeholders in tourism development and heritage conservation, especially since their livelihoods would inevitably be impacted by conservation efforts made nationally or internationally. This could even result in the reformation of complex social structures, enabling communities to have a greater say in any decisions being made with regard to the agricultural plots or the aflaj systems. Special incentives could be provided by the government to communities and families who work toward preserving their local heritage. This would be key to raising awareness of the importance of ecological living on a national level.

While Al Hamra would be a starting point, the culture of organic, healthy food production in combination with integrated sustainable tourism should be viewed as a tool to reanimate decaying agricultural spaces in other oasis settlements of Oman and elsewhere. The designation, conservation, and touristic development of these assets could become an essential strategy for an effective reanimation and sustainable redevelopment of the largely abandoned urban agricultural heritage of Oman, including the UNESCO sites, as a means to preserve and revive the otherwise rapidly decaying cultivars and agricultural practices. ■

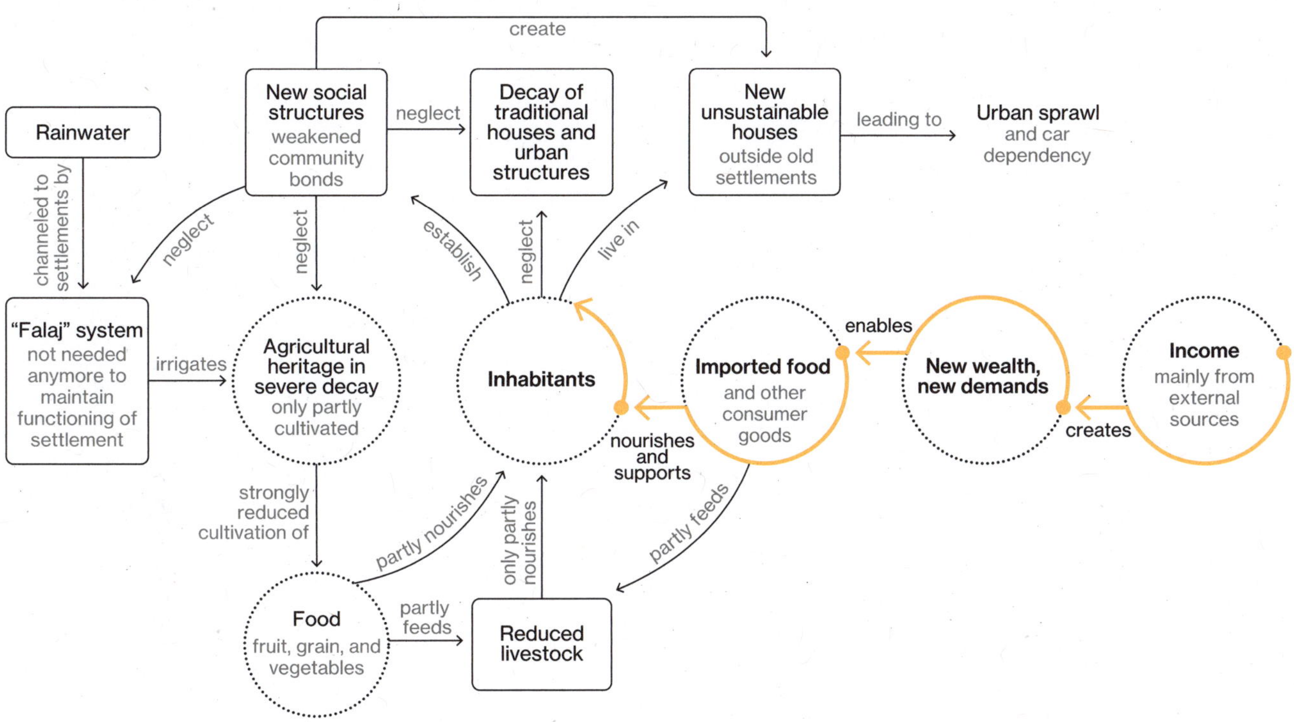

Fig. 7 Ongoing transformations of the mountain oases of Oman since the 1970s

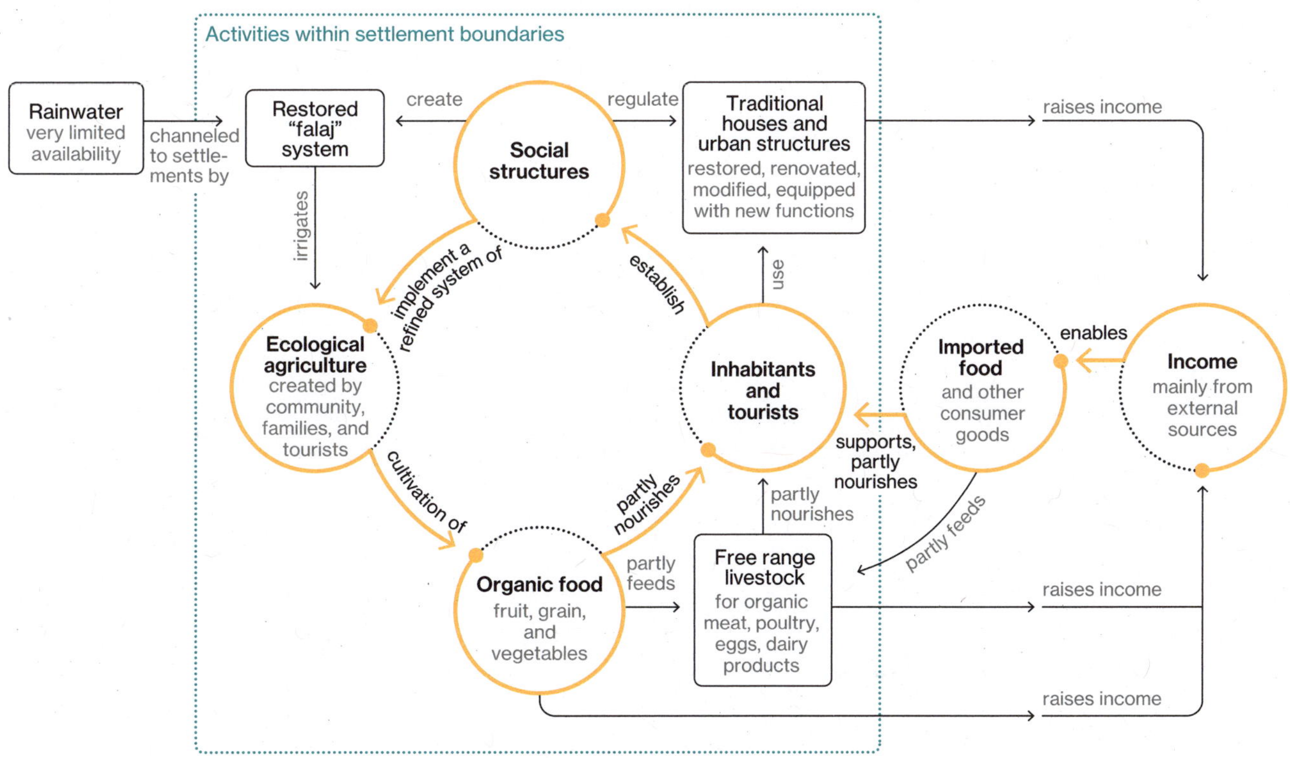

Fig. 8 Proposal for future development of the mountain oases of Oman

Chinampas of Xochimilco: Urban Agriculture from the Ancient Americas Until Today

Laura Camacho Latz, Sophie Laukemper, Katharina Christenn, and Axel Timpe

Historical and Geographical Origins: The Challenge of Nourishing the Aztec Capital on a Lacustrine Area

Since the Aztec period, the *chinampas* of Xochimilco have served as an agricultural supplier for Mexico City, then called Tenochtitlan. Chinampas, which are manmade islands on a freshwater lake, experienced a great expansion during the fourteenth and fifteenth centuries. Their agricultural landscape, which still exists in part, is characterized by an extensive canal system and fertile rectangular fields.

Xochimilco, a former independent village in the south of Mexico City, is located in the Valley of Mexico at an altitude of over 2,200 meters. During the Aztec reign, that area in the basin was dominated by a large lacustrine area **[Figs. 1a–d]**. A dam constructed by the Mexica, a Nahua tribe that would form part of the Aztec empire, separated the lakes. While the northern lacustrine area had saline water, the southern freshwater lakes, especially Lake Xochimilco and Lake Chalco, could be used for chinampa agriculture (Government of Mexico City 2017, 108).

As this lacustrine area was originally an unfavorable environment for agricultural production, the unique system of the chinampa was established in the valley. An exact time of construction of the first chinampas cannot be defined. Between the ninth and the thirteenth centuries, the Valley of Mexico was populated by different Nahua tribes, who readopted the already existing chinampa tradition (González Pozo 2016, 41). The Mexica were the last tribe to arrive at the basin. When they founded their capital Tenochtitlan in 1325, the Mexica expanded the chinampas in order to provide for their growing population. Therefore, Xochimilco became one of the main food suppliers for Tenochtitlan (Government of Mexico City 2017, 110–11). During the 200-year Aztec reign **[Fig. 2]**, the non-noble *mācēhualtin* formed the majority of the population. Initially they were working mainly as farmers, but as their farming system became more efficient, the occupations shifted to merchants and craftsmen (Aztec History n.d.).

Constructing Arable Land by the Bank of a Lake

The construction of a chinampa is a very traditional process. It dates back to pre-Hispanic times and continues to be used today. Different layers of reeds, soil, and mud are stacked on the banks of the lake **[Fig. 3]**. Thus a system of canals and artificial islands is created. For this process, the farmers—*chinamperos*—use the mud from the lake by desludging the bottom of the canal and spreading it on their fields to create a nutrient-rich soil (Government of Mexico City 2017, 42–47). In the middle of these fertile fields, with an average area of about 1,500 square meters, a variety of crops is cultivated.

In order to prevent the layers, especially the mud, from falling back into the lake, the *ahuejote*, a native willow tree, is planted to stabilize the borders of the fields. As its strong roots are water-resistant, it is traditionally the only tree used

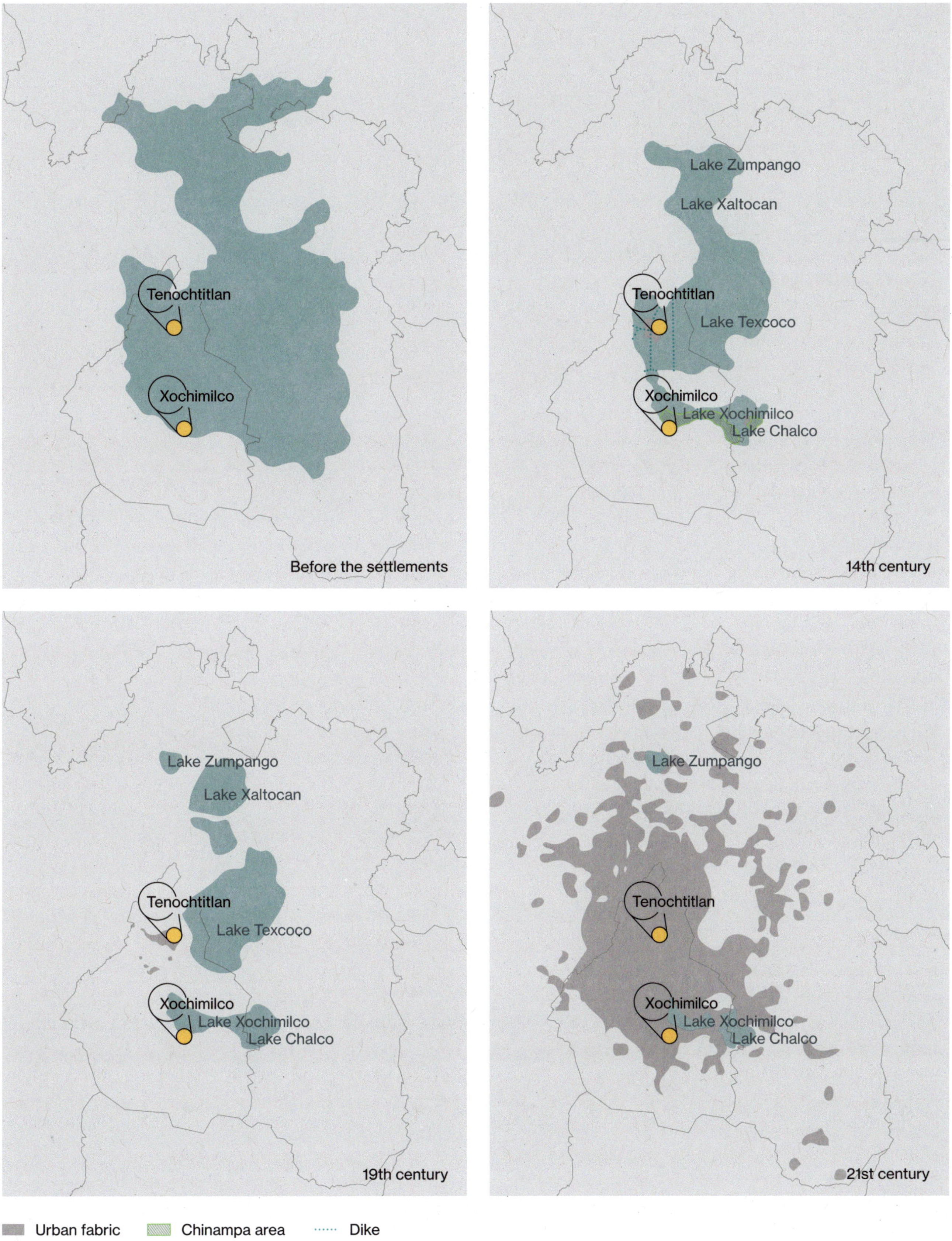

Figs. 1a–d Schematic development of the urban and lacustrine area in the Valle de México

for the water-based construction (128). Thus, besides the channels and the fields, the ahuejotes are distinctive for the chinampa landscape.

Permanent Wetlands and a Two-Part Irrigation System

Over the years, a complex system of channels and fields has developed, which at its peak covered three-quarters of the lakes of Xochimilco and Chalco. The canal network is particularly important because, first, it serves as a water filter for the plants in the rhizosphere and, second, the fine-grained, clay-like sediments at the bottom of the canal prevent water loss. Due to these characteristics, the agricultural landscape of the chinampas is a permanent wetland, and the constant availability of water makes chinampa agriculture independent of rainfall (Government of Mexico City 2017, 128–30).

For the canal system, a combination of wider main canals and smaller canals, named *acalotes* and *apantles*, is characteristic. While the main channels are used to transport the harvest from the chinampas to the city and nowadays are also used by tourists, the smaller ones are used to access the fields and for agricultural activities (176). Since chinampas are built as narrow but elongated rectangles, farmers can irrigate any part of the chinampa from the channels without leaving the canoe (43–44).

Nevertheless, a two-part irrigation system is typical for chinampa agriculture. While the active irrigation from the channels is additional, the most important part is the subirrigation system. Chinampas must have a specific height so that the plants' roots have enough scope to spread downwards but still reach the water, and the soil must consist of rough silt and fine sand to form a capillary rim. In addition, the capillary rim must be at least 30 centimeters underneath the surface, and the roots must be less than 85 centimeters above groundwater, while they should not extend too deep in the capillary rim (Crossley 2004, 192).

Desludging the Channels: Virtuous Cycle of Biodiversity, Fertility, and Cultivation

The process of desludging the channels has a strong interconnection to the subirrigation system and contributes both to the biodiversity within the channels and to the fertility of the chinampas (Robles et al. 2018, 6) **[Fig. 4]**. Due to this process a unique ecosystem has developed, which hosts a great biodiversity. The channel system accommodates threatened species, such as the *axolotl*, a native amphibian endemic to Xochimilco, which plays an important role in Aztec mythology.

Furthermore, the sludge removed from the canals fertilizes the cultivation areas in addition to the

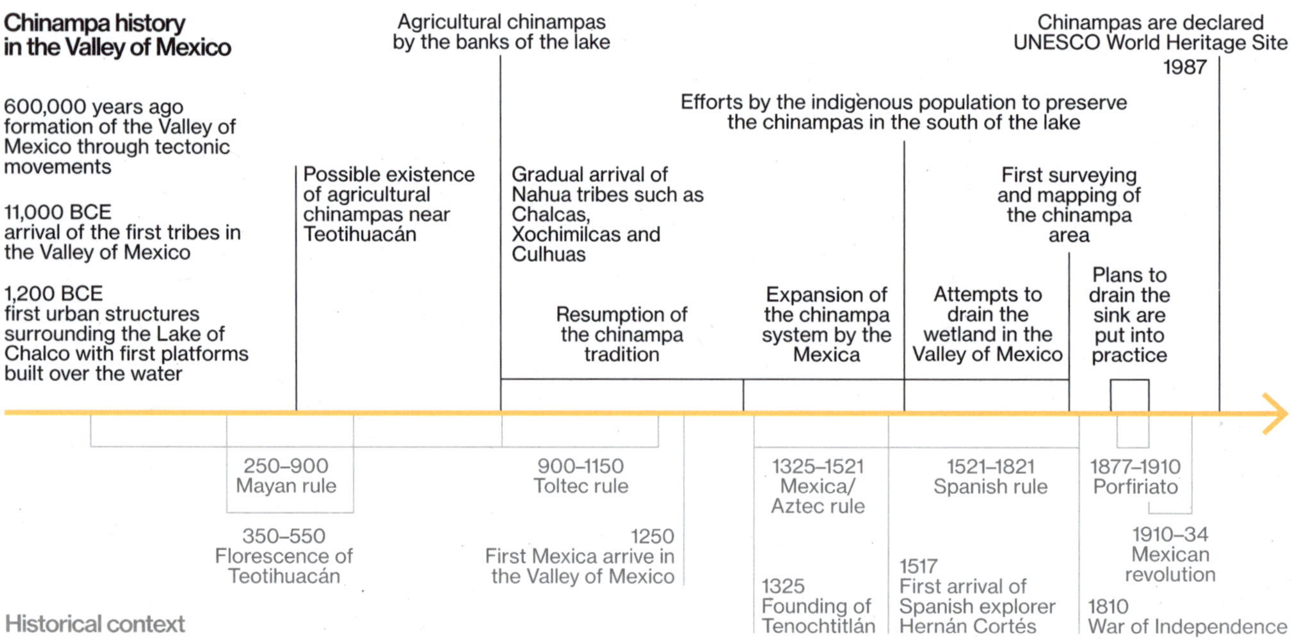

Fig. 2 Timeline of the chinampa history in the Valley of Mexico, with historical context

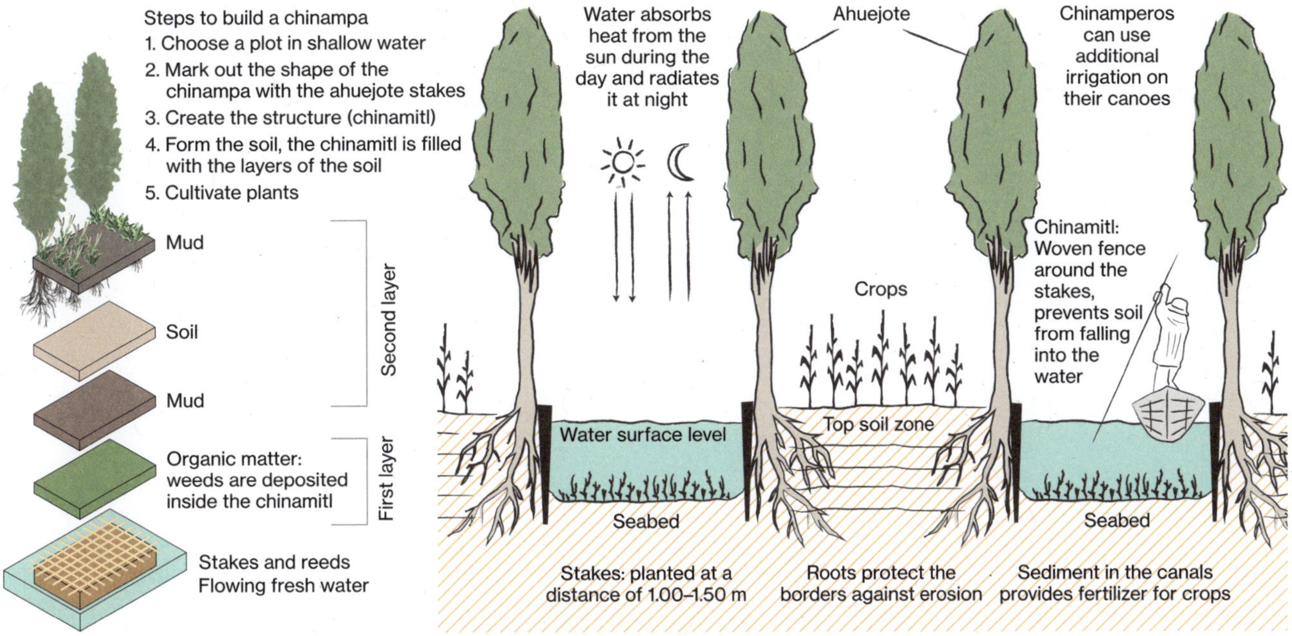

Fig. 3 Construction of a chinampa and a schematic vertical section of the chinampas and canals

effective irrigation. The best-known crops cultivated at the chinampas are the "three sisters," which include corn, beans, and squash (Salem Media 2020). Nevertheless, a great variety of vegetables such as the chilacayote, amaranth, tomatoes, radishes, and beetroot are also grown (Government of Mexico City 2017, 22–24, 28). Additionally, a great variety of ornamental plants, such as the *cempasúchil,* also known as the Aztec marigold, are cultivated.

Deserving Protection: From Construction and Cultivation Techniques to Ancient Rituals and Traditions

The value of this unique urban food production system was recognized when a large area of chinampas was declared a UNESCO World Heritage Site in 1987. Together with the well-known historical center of Mexico City, they form a composition that, as a whole, bears witness to the complexity of the Aztec urban system. The chinampas form a fundamental part of this system, as they supplied the urban Aztec population with food. In addition to Xochimilco, the World Heritage property includes the chinampa zones of Tláhuac, and the buffer zone extends to parts of Milpa Alta (González Pozo 2016, 22) **[Fig. 5]**.

While the physical appearance of the chinampas and channels is protected as tangible heritage, the traditional processes of constructing and cultivating a chinampa are important intangible values that need to be handed over to future generations in order to maintain the unique agriculture and ecosystem. In conjunction with the agriculture, a large variety of characteristic traditions and rituals have developed. Many chinampa traditions are characterized by a mixture of Indigenous religious practices combined with Catholic beliefs. These regional traditions evolved around the importance of agriculture: many of the festivities are celebrated to ask for or give thanks for a good harvest. An example would be the religious devotion of the Little Holy Cross, where a local chapel is decorated with a *tularco,* a flower arrangement, which represents a decorated chinampa **[Fig. 6]**. It is offered by the neighborhood with the wish for a good crop (Government of Mexico City 2017, 50). Furthermore, the traditional calendar continues to influence the agricultural production, as at solemnities, such as the Day of the Dead, the demand on flowers increases.

Drainage and Urbanization: Recession of the Chinampa Landscape

After the Spanish Conquest of Tenochtitlan in 1521, the chinampa area declined due to the reduction in the Indigenous population and several attempts

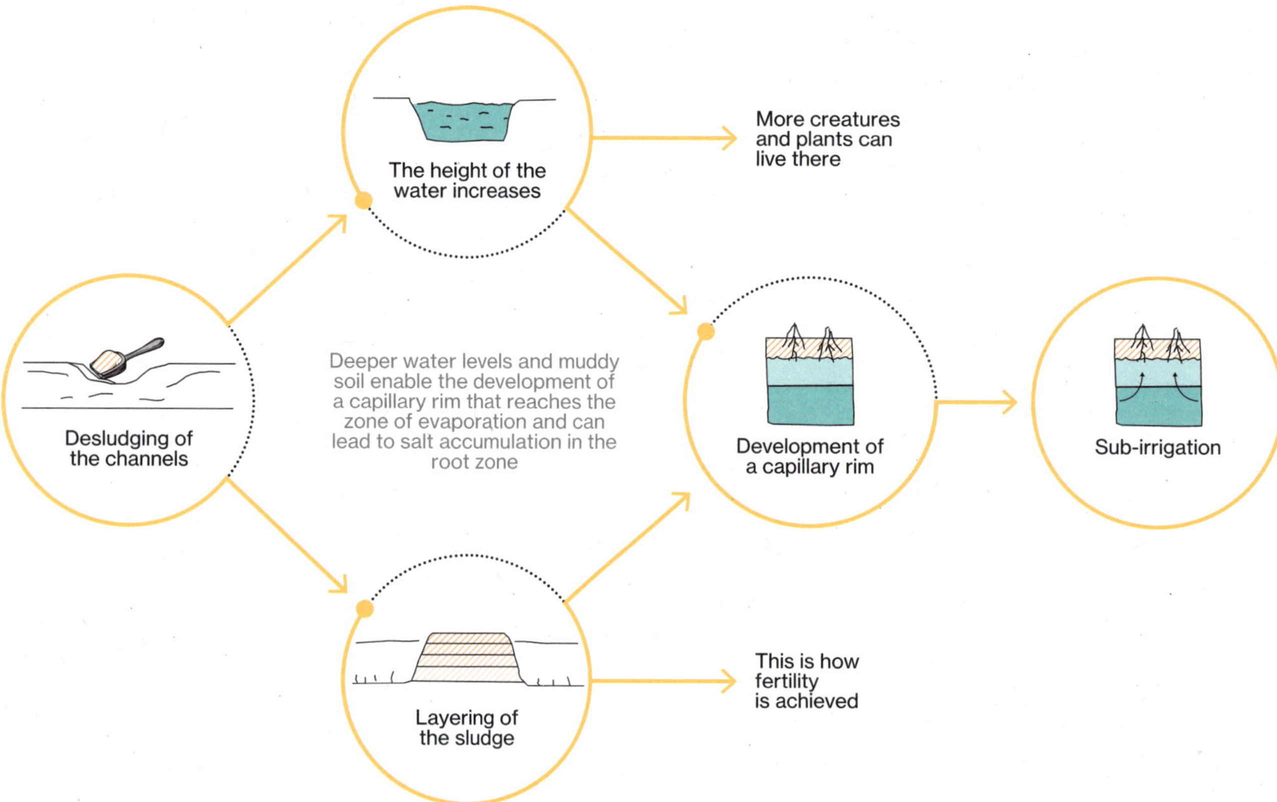

Fig. 4 Function of the agricultural system with the interdependence of the channels, fertility, and irrigation

to drain the valley (Government of Mexico City 2017, 121). As the lakes dried up, many chinampas could no longer be properly irrigated.

In addition, over the following centuries the population of Mexico City continued to grow, and the urbanized areas overran the agricultural chinampas. Xochimilco, which still has rather suburban characteristics, is no longer an independent village but one of the 16 municipalities of Mexico City.

Nowadays, only parts of the chinampas in Xochimilco remain. Many of the chinampas have been urbanized or drained **[Fig. 5]**. Five chinampa zones still exist, three of which are located in the municipality of Xochimilco and two in the contiguous municipality of Tláhuac (González Pozo 2016, 15). The chinampa zone of Xochimilco in the western part of the area attracts many tourists, while the neighboring zone of San Gregorio Atlapulco realizes most of the current agricultural production.

Agricultural Production: Current Potentials and Threats

When it comes to agricultural production, the chinampas remain the most important areas in Mexico City. Chinampas can be harvested up to five times a year, meaning that they could cover the vegetable diet of 400,000 inhabitants (Government of Mexico City 2017, 24). However, the main part of the former chinampa areas has been abandoned **[Fig. 7]**. If reactivated, these chinampas could feed another one million people (data calculated according to González Pozo [2016, 219] based on 1,099 hectares of potential chinampas and the proportions proposed in Government of Mexico City [2017, 24]). Additionally, based on estimates, a chinampa of one hectare can provide 15 to 20 people with an income (Hirst 2019).

In addition, due to Mexico City's continuous groundwater extraction, natural soil and water resources used in the agricultural production cycle

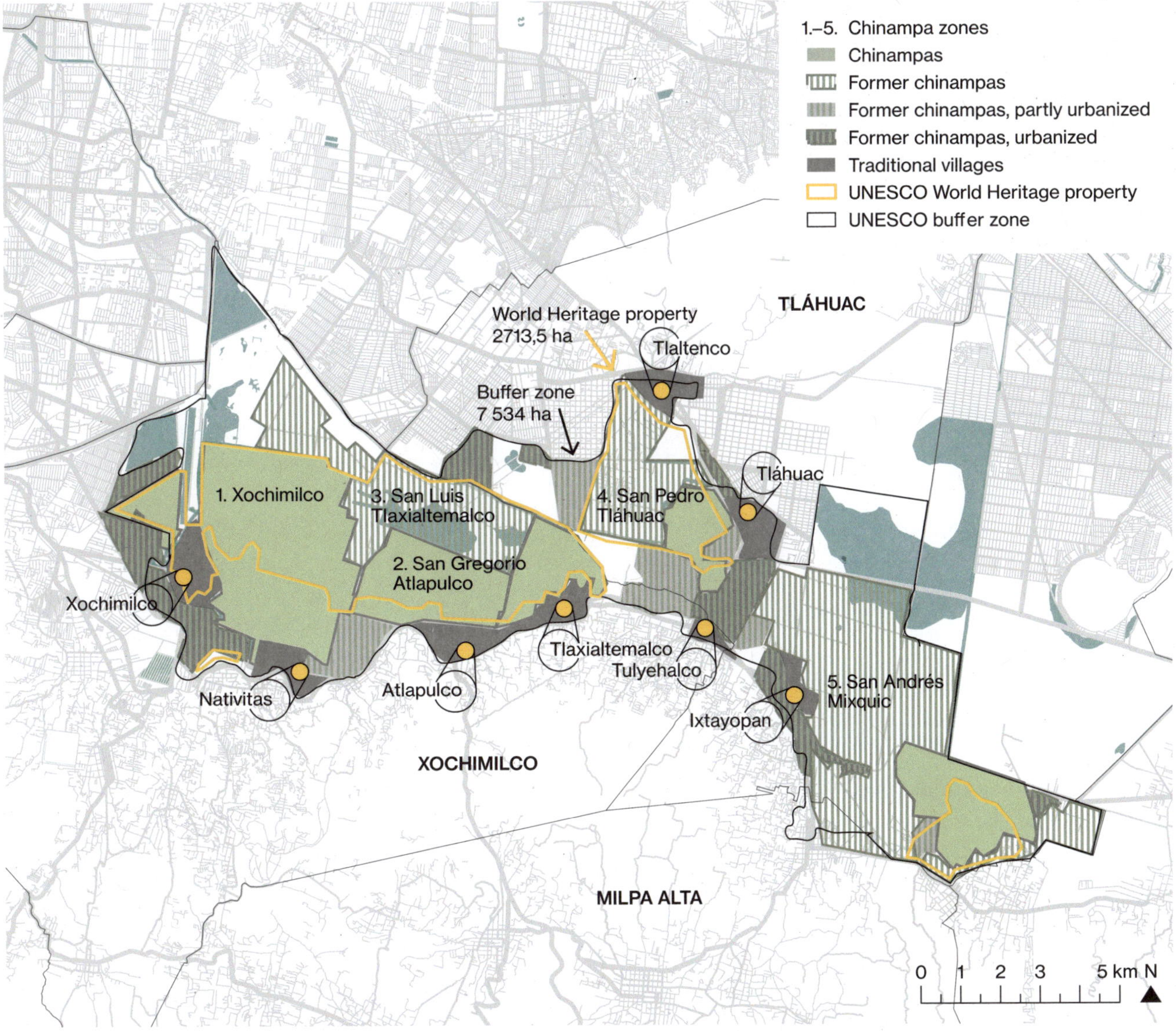

Fig. 5 Current usage and canals of Xochimilco, San Gregorio Atlapulco, and San Luis Tlaxialtemalco

Fig. 6 Left: trajineras; right: tularco; far right: cempasuchil flowers

are being destroyed. One result of the degradation of these resources is an increase in pests, which leads to lower yields. Therefore, production processes have had to adapt, and farmers now increasingly need to use chemical products and additional irrigation (Government of Mexico City 2017, 68–69).

In order to support the chinamperos, the government of Mexico City has established the Authority of the Natural and Cultural World Heritage Zone in Xochimilco, an organ that proposes actions to protect the chinampas and their biodiversity. A ten-point plan has been established to help preserve active chinampas and reactivate potential ones (81–83).

Tourism: Threat or Opportunity?

With its declaration as a UNESCO World Heritage Site, Xochimilco has become a very popular destination for local and international tourists. The most popular activity is a round trip on a *trajinera*, a colorful, decorated flat-bottomed boat **[Fig. 6]**. Some trajineras offer, as well as the trip through the canals, a traditional meal and Mariachi music **[Fig. 7]**. Even though this commercial form of tourism is important for the economy of Xochimilco, its noise and trash harm the ecosystem. In addition, many actual values of the chinampas are missed, as the typical round trips barely show the history or agricultural processes of the place. Instead, other activities such as Mariachi music—which originates from a different state of Mexico—were introduced to attract more tourists.

Facing the Challenges

Local initiatives are currently being formed with the goal of a more sustainable and conscious tourism, which focuses on the values of the agricultural traditions. Therefore, alternative round trips are supported, which should give visitors greater knowledge of the chinampas' history and processes (Government of Mexico City 2017, 92). This conscious form of tourism gives the chinamperos and their work more attention.

In addition, this form of tourism may help link farmers directly to potential customers and establish new marketing strategies. Also, networks such as Lum K'inal unite chinamperos, who are competing against industrial agricultural production, to distribute their products. During the COVID-19 pandemic in 2020, some local farmers were able to increase their sales by distributing goods directly to customers (AJ+ Español 2020).

This shows that the chinampa as a local food production system that has proven its functionality over hundreds of years can contribute to the future resilience of Mexico City. Protecting the local knowledge and practices in managing ecosystem conditions for food production can help the city withstand crises induced by climate change or restricted global exchange, as occurred during the pandemic. Combining top-down government action and bottom-up initiatives of chinamperos and other citizens will help to raise awareness and and protect the chinampa system by securing its values on three different levels: its functional role as a food production system, its material and immaterial heritage values, and its natural value as a unique ecosystem. ■

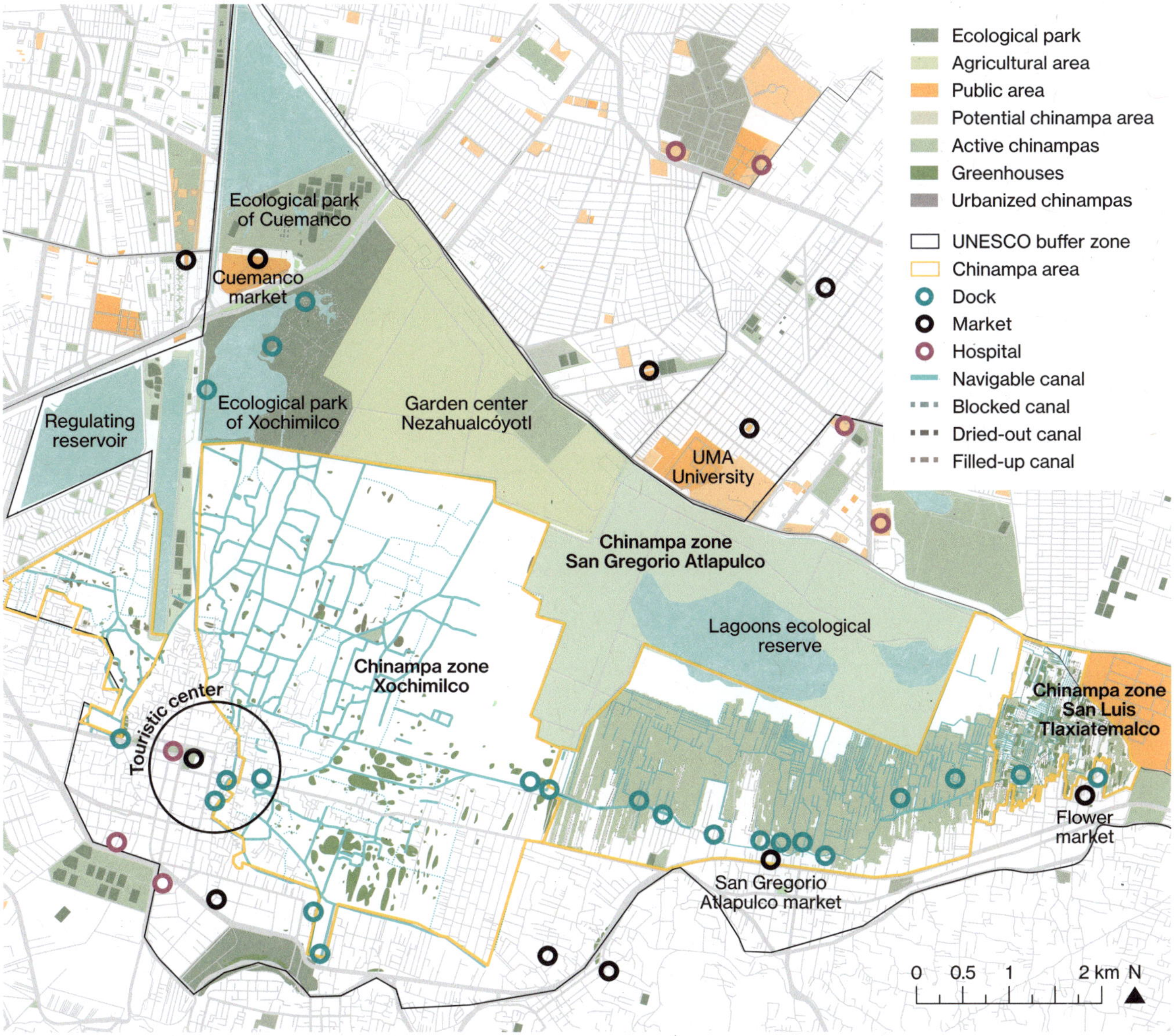

Fig. 7 Current usage and canals of Xochimilco, San Gregorio Atlapulco, and San Luis Tlaxiatemalco

Informal and Local Approaches to Urban Agricultural Heritage

Transformation of Everyday Landscapes into Heritage: A Driver for Territorialized Agro-Food Systems in the Peri-Urban Context of Madrid

Rafael Mata Olmo, Carolina Yacamán Ochoa, and Esther Sanz Sanz

Multifunctional urban agriculture provides a series of ecological services in addition to the supply of fresh and local quality food. Landscape services (Termorshuizen and Opdam, 2009; Bastian et al. 2014) are specifically acknowledged as being important for the strengthening of the territorial embeddedness of agro-food systems, going further than the functions of leisure and recreation. Quality landscapes increase the added value of local production and help farms become economically viable (Yacamán Ochoa et al. 2020). Furthermore, agrarian landscapes are the foundation for rethinking rural-urban relationships through the sharing of memories and the communication of knowledge (Sanz Sanz 2011, 134; Mata Olmo 2015).

This new focus has led us to propose a conceptual, methodological, and empirical approach to analyze an initiative of concerted, institutional, community-based enhancement of agricultural and peri-urban landscape heritage, the ordinary *huerta* (name of the historical irrigated agricultural landscapes owned by smallholders in the Mediterranean basin, usually close to cities and towns, cultivated with vegetable crops) of Fuenlabrada in the south of the metropolitan region of Madrid, Spain. This initiative is part of a set of wider overall strategies for the preservation and revitalization of extremely vulnerable agriculture in peri-urban contexts in Spain (Yacamán Ochoa et al. 2020). As will be shown, the landscape and its heritage features are highlighted as an objective and a strategy to bring about a change in the territorial model of congested urban and metropolitan regions and to improve their environmental and cultural quality. We present the process of the historical construction of peri-urban agricultural landscapes as cultural heritage. Our aim is to highlight that especially a bottom-up heritage creation can transform an everyday landscape into heritage. This involves the collective appropriation of mostly ordinary landscapes that apparently do not have an important heritage value but do show strong historical links between the agrarian landscapes and small-scale family businesses. We explain how local communities use urban agricultural heritage to create a nexus between local agricultural production and quality food, as well as a sense of place. This procedure contributes to healthy, well-managed, educational environments on the outskirts of urban settlements.

The loss of agrarian land brings risk to the outskirts of many Spanish cities, in particular to the south of the metropolitan area of Madrid, where the abandonment of a large number of farms, the low intensity of production, and the fragmentation of agrarian areas have caused the deterioration of the formal, functional, and aesthetic features of the inherited agrarian landscape. There has been a loss of memory: the history of the place and the know-how that agricultural landscapes hold and express is being forgotten. This material and symbolic loss of peri-urban agriculture in Madrid has led to an increasing invisibility of and lack of interest in local agriculture. Farming is disappearing from the collective urban consciousness, and so is the legitimacy of farmers themselves, who are increasingly ignored by the city.

From our heritage perspective, taking action in the context of an ordinary, degraded, and fragmented agrarian landscape does not mean making inventories and protecting historical remains, as so often happens. Based on our own experience, the most important, and probably the only viable, aspect of these degraded and pressured areas is to start a process of social reappropriation that moves away from traditional heritage approaches. In the end, this is about understanding the values of traditional agriculture and treating these as resources on which territorial sustainability can be built through the consideration of its three dimensions: economic, environmental, and social.

The Renewed Sense of Heritage and the Everyday Peri-Urban Agricultural Landscapes

The initiatives for creating heritage in agrarian spaces in crisis, as in the south of the urban region of Madrid, are based on the convergence of two strategic approaches: on the one hand, moving toward a more open and democratic approach to heritage and landscape, including the whole territory and its communities; and on the other hand, developing projects that defend and activate multifunctional and local scale agro-food systems, with different alliances between stakeholders. These projects, as expressions and experiences to boost the character of territories, find more than one solution for the protection of landscapes. They work to establish closer links between farmers producing quality food and urban residents as consumers.

Since the 1990s and based on the work of Guy Di Méo (1995), José Ortega Valcárcel (1998), and other geographers and professionals, the significance of diverse values of natural and cultural heritage and of landscapes has been increasingly recognized in academic and political fields. In recent years, the concept of heritage has developed a spatial dimension, thus widening the attribution of heritage-related meanings and values to territories. The semantic aperture and the "accumulative widening" (Castillo 2007, 4) of heritage has been reflected in both spatial and interpretive terms, as well as in the fields of government and territorial management (Mata Olmo 2010; Feria 2012; Manero Miguel 2017; Silva Pérez and Fernandez Salinas 2017). On the one hand, the number of heritage entities has increased, covering a trajectory from individual elements to historical settlements, and from historical settlements to territories as a whole. An important document for debate and exploration drawn up by the Council of Europe in 2002 (Council of Europe 2002) finally understands heritage as an expression of the character and diversity of places and communities, compared with the eminently symbolic and singular nature of the past. It is noteworthy that there is a conceptual proximity between this understanding of heritage and the modern idea of landscape as defined by the European Landscape Convention (Council of Europe 2000), which builds upon the character, perception, and representation of the territory.

However, it is important to highlight the fact that this bottom-up approach of opening up and renewed thinking is also present in the governance of heritage and in the conservation and management of cultural resources. This opens up a path that is different from the conventional heritage declaration, which is simply based on the imposition of authority, as criticized by the anthropologist Llorenç Prats (2004), and moving toward a participatory form of heritage creation. Kate Clark and Paul Drury have addressed this turn explicitly with the expression "from the monument to the citizen" (Clark and Drury 2002, 119–24). Therefore, the increasingly open conception of heritage can be interpreted, according to these two authors, as a form of democratic progress involving the local community in the enhancement of agrarian landscapes in territorial policies.

This open and democratic understanding of heritage is included in the Council of Europe's Framework Convention on the Value of Cultural Heritage for Society and in the European Landscape Convention. The former defines it as "a set of resources inherited from the past which are considered to be a reflection and expression of continually evolving values, beliefs, knowledge and traditions, going beyond the ownership of assets." In this way, the Council of Europe has made important advances in conceptualizing cultural heritage in recent years.

The European Landscape Convention, which is clearly linked to heritage, was the first international agreement to consider landscapes as being a quality belonging to a whole territory and to all types of territories. Therefore, the landscape study and management should not be limited to outstanding landscapes but cover all kinds of landscapes. This means also to include the commonplace landscapes—the rural, urban, and peri-urban ones in which people go about their daily lives (Dewarrat et al. 2003).

The Case Study of the Agrarian Park of Fuenlabrada: A Renewal Heritage Approach for the Activation of Peri-Urban Agricultural Landscapes

In line with this conceptual and strategic renewal of heritage thinking, a participative approach for the agrarian landscape of Fuenlabrada was set up to drive and innovate its peri-urban agro-food systems. The Fuenlabrada municipality, with barely 3,000 inhabitants in 1960, currently has a population of 200,000 and is the third-largest city of the urban region of Madrid. In spite of the drastic reduction of cultivated land due to urban expansion and road networks, Fuenlabrada still has 800 hectares of land for agrarian use, of which 220 hectares can potentially be irrigated **[Fig. 1]**. Its huerta and rainfed land covered with cereals make up a unique peri-urban agricultural landscape, as it is one of the few enclaves with professional agrarian activity in the metropolitan region of Madrid.

Fig. 1 View of the huerta of Fuenlabrada (Metropolitan region of Madrid). In the foreground, a farmer harvests chard, a traditional and high-quality crop in this city.

The huerta of Fuenlabrada still witness a practice that was common for many municipalities of the southern metropolitan area of Madrid until the beginning of the 1970s. Urban sprawl has now caused the loss of much of this fertile land. Despite urban pressures and the decline of production activities, the remaining agricultural land in Fuenlabrada still shows the structure, signs, and symbols of traditional small-scale family farming, mainly the patchwork of fields and an intricate network of rural paths and livestock routes. These elements have always been linked to the food supply of Fuenlabrada but also the capital city of Madrid.

Fig. 2 Working group for the creation of the territorial and action plan; a SWOT analysis was done to identify the strengths, weaknesses, opportunities, and threats with the participation of public administration technicians, policy makers, and representatives from the agricultural sector

In 2012, the City Council of Fuenlabrada decided to develop an agrarian park by using a multifunctional, agroecological, and participative approach. The aim was to preserve and strengthen professional agrarian activity and drive specific programs to allow the development of the economic, environmental, and landscape potential of the territory. Two years later, the Management and Development Plan of the Agrarian Park of Fuenlabrada was drafted **[Figs. 2]**. It was based on an exhaustive participative diagnostic document that identified the problems, needs, and demands of the local agrarian sector and the peri-urban space in general. The document revealed the strengths and opportunities to drive the local, quality agro-food system forward. It was agreed that one of the keys to strengthening the identity of local production should be adding value to the landscape, which presented a challenge, as this was not an exceptional location like the large huertas in Valencia, Murcia, and Aranjuez, but an ordinary everyday landscape, ignored by the urban citizens. Therefore, it was necessary to start a bottom-up process of a collective landscape appropriation and enhancement of the agrarian landscape with the participation of the different stakeholders, especially farmers, citizens, and policy makers.

The Participative Approach to Territorialize the Agro-Food Systems in Peri-Urban Contexts

The participative approach for the activation of the peri-urban agriculture was developed in the context of the "new ruralities" following the guidelines of the European Landscape Convention (2000). It was supported by public participation aimed at defining the character of the landscape and identifying the specificity of the traditional agrarian activity that has modeled it (that is, types of crops, irrigation systems, land ownership, size of the properties and plots, surnames of the landowners, productive organizational models, role of historical local agriculture, agricultural techniques and tools, places of residence of the land owners and peasants, and common property resources); other examples of this kind of approach can be consulted in Ambroise et al. (2000). This process was materialized through the historical reconstruction of the role that the huerta played in the local and regional food supply. Furthermore, this approach enabled an understanding of the importance of the past local agriculture in both the symbolic and collective memory of the city, which is still present in the know-how and life experiences of the older farmers. And it reconnected production with consumption by incorporating a territorial approach.

The process of valorization of agrarian heritage developed in the Agrarian Park of Fuenlabrada started with different phases aimed at the description of the territorial context and dynamics of peri-urban agriculture and the identification of the territorial instruments of protection and management of the fertile areas. Statistical analysis and spatial analysis of urban sprawl, farmland loss, and territorial fragmentation were carried out by experts from the agrarian park and researchers. This was the starting point for the real participative heritage creation process. The Agrarian Park became a living laboratory for designing and testing new heritage-based strategies for the conservation and valuation of multifunctional agrarian

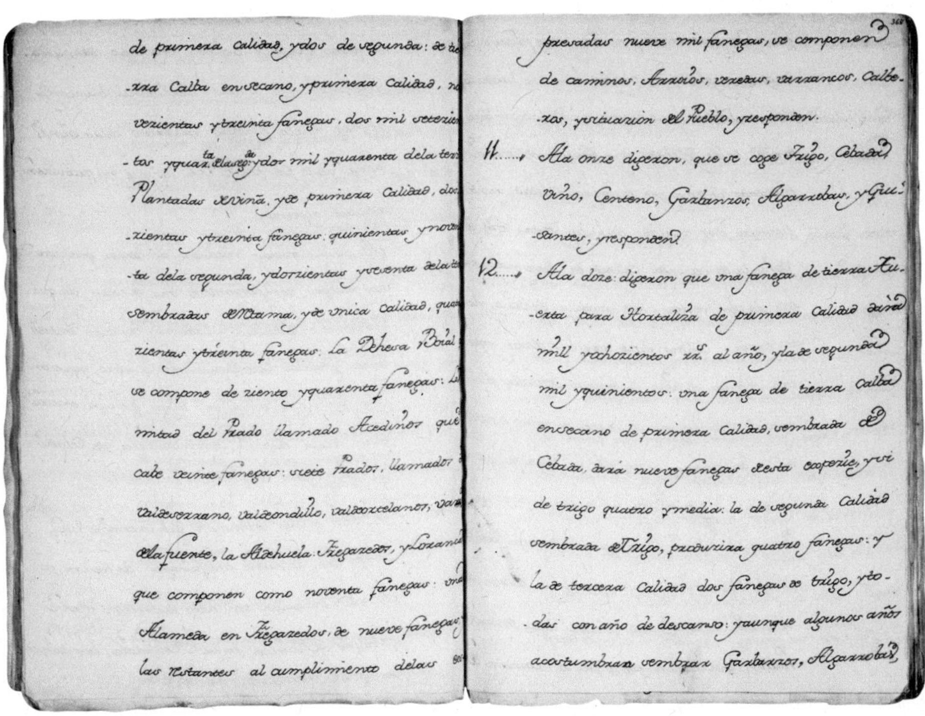

Fig. 3 Respuestas Generales del Interrogatorio del Castro de Ensenada (1749) (General Answers to the Interrogatory of the Cadastre of the Marquis de la Ensenada), containing questions on the names, limits, jurisdiction, and sources of wealth of neighbors, including plots, crops, and livestock, among other things, in the municipality of Fuenlabrada

Figs. 4a–i Traveling photographic exhibition on Fuenlabrada, with photographs provided by residents, farmers, and findings from the municipal archive

landscapes through the cooperation of several stakeholders. This type of geographic and historical studies concerning how cities organized their food supply in the past are extremely useful to understand the general logic, character, organization, and techniques of agriculture and related societies over the centuries (Scazzosi 2020, 19).

The Phases and Content of Participatory Heritage Creation Process

We will go on to summarize the participatory phases followed during the heritage creation process of the huerta within the framework of the Fuenlabrada Agrarian Park. The process consisted of combining different participative methods (workshops, perception surveys, semistructured interviews, and video interviews) with the support of historical and modern maps and photos on the social perception of the landscapes. The comprehensive research methods used in the first phase included an analysis of national and local historical archives of the eighteenth, nineteenth, and twentieth centuries, which contain historical cartography and land registry documents **[Fig. 3]**. The study allowed us to interpret the foundations and structures inherited from the agrarian landscape, in particular, those of the huerta, characterized by a series of major features. These are: the structure, morphology, and ownership of the land that was of a predominantly peasant nature, despite the presence of a small number of large properties belonging to the clergy, nobility, and bourgeoisie who resided in Madrid; the significant role of property and the management of communal assets used for farming through the annual distribution of land among the inhabitants who were most in need; and the historical influence of the proximity of the markets of Madrid and the Royal Court.

The second phase was crucial for combining expert knowledge with the accounts of the protagonists of the agrarian history of Fuenlabrada, the traditional family-owned farms. The in-depth interviews with different members of the family-owned farms were designed to identify the traditional farming know-how and the historical governance of the agrarian space (communal and private practices, estate-leasing systems, irrigation regulations, etc.). The accounts that came from the interviews were complemented with historical family photographs provided by the residents and farmers of Fuenlabrada related to the countryside and the agrarian activity. This information was used to gain a greater insight into the tangible and intangible heritage aspects of the agricultural activities and the landscape **[Figs. 4a–i]**. Finally, the rediscovery of stories and images of the actors themselves were complemented with the analysis of press releases and books on the historical cultural events related to agriculture. As a result, a documentary and a traveling photographic exhibition were made for schools and municipal buildings. Also, a book with the title *Huertas y campos de Fuenlabrada* (Yacamán Ochoa and Mata Olmo 2017) was published to recover the agrarian memory.

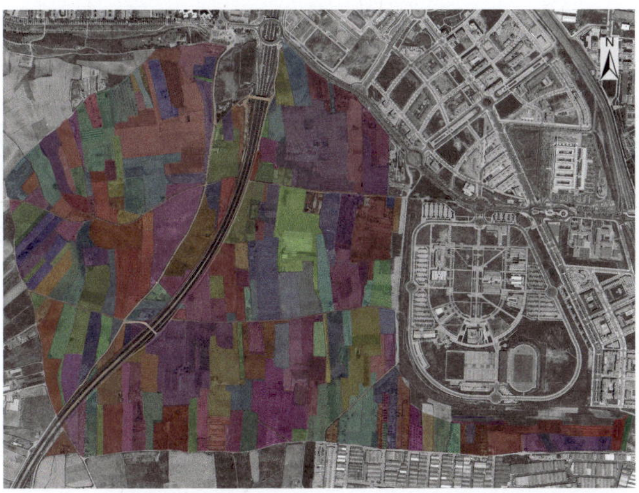

Fig. 5 Historical plots in the Fuenlabrada Agrarian Park. Each color represents the property of a different landowner.

These accounts and photographs provided by the inhabitants are excellent proof of the enjoyment of the landscape as a collective asset and are useful to create public awareness of the public goods and services provided by peri-urban irrigated landscapes.

The third phase of the process of heritage creation regarding the huerta of Fuenlabrada aimed to describe the recent transformation dynamics and define the landscape character based on shared heritage values related to agriculture. This process started with fieldwork conducted together with the farmers, which focused on visually identifying and characterizing the main landscape features and values:

1. The layout and tangible components of the landscape (agroclimatic, geomorphological, hydrological and soil conditions, and land use, including the crop mosaic);
2. The structure of properties and farms **[Fig. 5]**;
3. The dynamics and pressures of the territorial context; and finally,
4. The identification of the key elements of the landscape for later expert study and valorization.

Interviews were later carried out with urban residents in Fuenlabrada who are not involved in agriculture to discover their perception of the current landscape. Moreover, we conducted a workshop using participative techniques based on collective creation processes to map the relevant sociocultural information regarding the agrarian space that remains in the memory of the agrarian community and the local residents **[Fig. 6]**. During the workshop, people marked sites on the maps that were valuable in the past as they represent history, cultural identity, and places with values related to traditions. The aim was the identification of observation points and itineraries, making the most of the network of rural paths and livestock routes, and the inventory of the cultural and natural elements of major heritage interest (hydraulic infrastructure, plots, rural path network, other elements of ethnological interest, etc.). This information is useful for the valorization of the agrarian landscape to enable public use and enjoyment.

The objective of the last phase was to promote agreed-upon practices to boost the quality agro-food system and the enhancement of the living landscape between public and private bodies. Some of the most important strategies developed until now are:

1. Strengthening the relationships between farmers and urban residents through the promotion of short food supply chains;
2. Granting strategic value to food as a cultural asset, which recognizes the singularity and quality of local production with a historical background;
3. Improving the links between food production and the historical and cultural narrative from where the products originate to provide added value to local produce;
4. Creation of walking and bike paths to access the agrarian landscape and to enable public use and enjoyment. All these strategies also reinforce the objective of the Agrarian Park of Fuenlabrada, which focuses on developing measures aimed at ensuring the profitability of local production and the protection of the agrarian land.

Fig. 6 Workshop for the mapping of identity-forming elements associated with the cultural values of agriculture. The points mark features related to water, grazing, common pastures, public laundry areas, shrines, spiritual locations, and hills.

The methodology used for the transformation of everyday landscapes into heritage as a driver for territorialized agro-food systems in peri-urban contexts is described below **[Fig. 7]**. The main objectives and actions of the proposed methodology enhance the multiple values and functions of peri-urban landscapes through a strategy that involves local stakeholders using different participatory techniques.

Conclusion

The participatory and historical approach used in the case study seeks to identify the agricultural evolution of communities and their landscapes within the context of urban sprawl. Therefore, the methodology presented enables the characterization of peri-urban agricultural landscapes that integrate both tangible components (for example, plots of land, traditional paths, historical hydraulic infrastructure, and buildings of ethnographic interest) and intangible and symbolic aspects (such as know-how, community practices, narratives, images, meeting places and memory, needs and aspirations). Such landscape characterization should be developed within a participatory process of heritage creation that aims to strengthen the self-confidence and role of farmers in the current urban society through the recovery of memory and the enhancement of the landscape. Thus this process of cocreation can transform an apparently ordinary landscape, which has been ignored and become almost invisible, into a heritage landscape, with both tangible and intangible values that become evident in the process itself. Finally, this bottom-up process of the valorization of peri-urban agricultural landscapes can be used as a territorial resource to support strategies to improve the sustainability of the local agro-food systems, focusing on their multifunctionality and territoriality, strengthening the production and consumption of local high-quality food, and safeguarding the environment (Yacamán Ochoa et al. 2020). To sum up, the valorization of agricultural landscape values from a renewed heritage perspective should be seen as an opportunity for cities to address the challenge of sustainability. ■

Acknowledgments:
The authors will carry out further research on this topic within the recently granted project, Multifunctional and Territorialized Agro-Food Systems for the Development of Rural Spaces in Spain (SAMUTER)' PID2019-105711RB-C6.

Objectives	Actions
Define the steps, the objectives, and the method for the patrimonial activation process of the territorial and landscape agro-food systems	Establish the phases of the participatory process combining different methods (workshops, perception surveys, semistructured interviews and video interviews, discussion groups, etc.)
Describe the territorial context and identify existing tools and policy instruments for the protection and enhancement of the values of the agricultural landscape	• Classify and describe tangible and intangible characteristics of the landscape to improve knowledge recognized in official documents • Diagnose the dynamics and pressures of territorial phenomena due to anthropic actions using methods of SWOT analysis • Select the landscape and territorial planning instruments for the conservation of natural and cultural heritage elements at various scales (national, regional, and local) • Identify labels that indicate the quality of food products (for example, Protected Designation of Origin and Protected Geographical Indications)
Define the actual resources, actors, and policies to have a wider understanding on peri-urban agriculture for the activation process of heritage creation	Select active stakeholders and identify their relevant interests: farmers, experts, local authorities, members of the scientific community, representatives of associations and social organizations, etc.
Synthesize the noteworthy aspects and elements of the heritage creation process for the recovery of a co-evolutionary relations between urban and rural domains, especially around sustainable agro-food systems	Create an inventory and map the main cultural heritage elements linked with agriculture: hydraulic infrastructures, plots, rural path networks, and other elements of ethnologic interest that can be requalified
Develop policy and an action plan for a multifunctional peri-urban agriculture and its landscape	• Develop a territorial action plan with management guidelines to boost the quality of the agro-food system and the living landscape • Encourage local networks to promote farmers, citizens, and experts to work together to improve participation in the decision-making and action process • Make awareness-raising programs and campaigns to promote the consumption of local products • Promote local labels of fresh products to support local agriculture • Scale up short food-supply chains (farmers' markets, box schemes, farm sales, community-supported agriculture, food festivals, sales to school canteens, etc.) • Organize a traveling historical photographic exhibition in the city's districts and a documentary of the local agricultural history • Design a route with information panels going through the whole agrarian space with information on the landscape and agrarian history of the municipality • Start new programs for visiting educational centers

Fig. 7 Objectives and actions for the transformation of everyday landscapes into heritage as a driver for territorialized agro-food systems in peri-urban contexts

Murs à Pêches de Montreuil: Rediscovering Urban Agricultural Heritage

Ayda Hamid Kargari, Kevin C. Wehnert, Katharina Christenn, and Axel Timpe

The *Murs à Pêches* (peach walls) are located in the city of Montreuil, a municipality within the first ring of the *banlieue parisienne* east of Paris. Starting in the middle of the eighteenth century, they were a highly scientific, spatially unique cultivation environment for peach trees and other fruit plants **[Fig. 1]**. Today they are spread over an area of roughly 38 hectares, measuring a wall length of approximately 17 kilometers. Contrary interests in the site led to a complex social framework resulting in slow-moving preservation actions and thus the ongoing destruction of the remaining walls by weather and aging (Maison des Murs à Pêches 2016, 2, 5).

History of the Murs à Pêches

In the late seventeenth century, Réné-Claude Girardot (c. 1734), a musketeer who served under Louis XIV, started developing a special interest in arboriculture (Johanneau 1825, 3–5). On his property in Bagnolet, he planted peach trees alongside head-height walls that provided shelter against the weather and reflected the sun **[Fig. 2]**. This allowed the Mediterranean fruits to grow in a temperate climate. Selling his peaches, he earned 30,000 francs per annum (Johanneau 1825, 4). By comparison, a day laborer around 1750 earned a franc a day; meanwhile, a kilogram of wheat was worth nearly five francs (see Fourastié 1986, a; McCuscer 1974, 360, table 3).

Girardot taught his technique to the villagers of Montreuil (De Salaberry 1838, 401–3) and as their yields grew, the Murs à Pêches increasingly attracted more farmers. Internal competition fostered innovation and resulted in the development of new, more efficient cultivation techniques.

Until the start of industrialization during the 1870s, peaches from Montreuil were unique around Paris. The Murs à Pêches measured about 300 hectares with more than 600 kilometers of walls yielding up to 17,000,000 fruits annually (De Decker 2015). When railway transport was established, it became possible to import cheaper, less labor-intensive peaches from southern France, forcing the farmers of Montreuil to focus on fruits more typical for their climate, such as pears and apples (Deville and Brondeau 2017, 112).

Reacting to the international competition, they united and founded the Société régionale d'horticulture de Montreuil (Regional Horticultural Society of Montreuil) in 1878, hoping to achieve higher

Fig. 1 Peach wall compartments (stamp in use from 1907 to 1922)

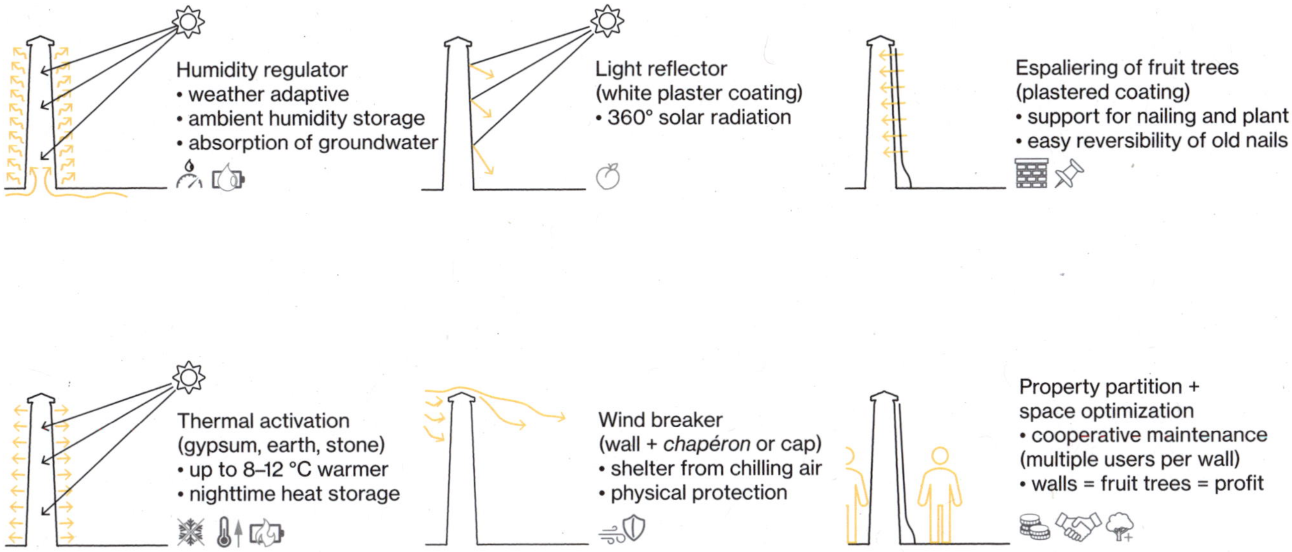

Fig. 2 Peach wall functions

returns by branding their fruits as high quality and using merchandising (such as vine-leaf packaging). These attempts failed, so that farmers were ruined by the cheaper competitors and started to leave the Murs à Pêches (Freidberg 2009, 148–54).

Until the period of deindustrialization starting in 1980, great parts of the walls were demolished, mainly to develop industrial areas. Postindustrial transformation in recent years has given way to new ideas to revive interest in the site (Deville and Brondeau 2017, 109–29).

Spatial Structure and Construction

A detailed map from 1773 allows us to analyze the Murs à Pêches spatial structure **[Fig. 4]**: Each garden compartment is usually bound by two short and two long walls. They are either oriented in a highly radiation intensive northwest direction or a less radiation-intensive northeast direction. Both provide two sunlit and two shaded wall surfaces (Fintelmann 1849, 307). The center of these compartments is planted with smaller plants such as berries or flowers. Hence, each compartment offers three different climate zones, allowing growth of a variety of plant species. The walls consist of small stones (flint, siliceous limestone), earth and gypsum found locally, and a plastered gypsum-charcoal coating **[Fig. 5]** (Maison des Murs à Pêches 2016, 4).

Cultivation Techniques

The Murs à Pêches area features a mixture of harder and softer soil. Soil conditions indicated whether to choose an almond or a plum tree for grafting a peach tree on top so that peaches could be cultivated in all soils (Eßlinger 1767, 100–5; Fintelmann 1849, 307–8).

The most common cultivation method of the eighteenth century focused on “quantitative cultivation” **[Fig. 6]**: As many trees as possible were planted close to one another, gaining a maximum count of fruits. The alternation of large, older trees covering the upper wall and small, younger trees covering the lower wall led to a “tree-continuum.” Old trees were cut down to make way for the young ones, while saplings were planted in between the trees again. This way, the Murs à Pêches were always covered in the leaves of three generations of trees (Eßlinger 1767, 20–28).

Starting in the 1820s two qualitative cultivation methods evolved, using just a small count of trees: The *L’arbre à l’etoile* (star-shaped tree) and the *L’arbre Baucer* (Baucer tree), which was invented by a farmer named Mr. Baucer **[Fig. 6]**.

Only new shoots produce fruits, so those were attached to the walls, while old shoots were cut. The juice pressure—another key factor—was manipulated by removing and bending parts of the tree in a symmetrical way, leading to stronger, more fruitful branches (Fintelmann 1849, 268–306).

Fig. 3 Farmers harvesting peaches, 1907

As the wall's heating effect was essential to achieve a large output of fruits, trees were grown broad and flat in order to widely cover the wall surface. This was performed by wrapping their branches with small pieces of cloth that were nailed into the plaster with flat, sharp iron nails.

The work in the Murs à Pêches was shared in the family: The men usually cared for the plants and the walls. The women harvested the fruits and took them to nearby markets to sell them **[Fig. 3]** (Mozard 1814, 84–91, 138–43). During the winter, families prepared cloth pieces for wrapping branches the next year. In the 1870s they also applied small paper bags—often made from old newspaper—to protect the fruits against the snout moth. They were removed two to three weeks before harvest, allowing the fruits to finish ripening in the sun. This resulted in bigger, juicier and more colorful peaches. By carving the bags with pictures or writing, it was possible to stencil the fruits with light, making them stand out on the market (Freidberg 2009, 148–52).

Heritage Specifics: Values and Potentials

The history and cultivation techniques of the Murs à Pêches demonstrate how exotic fruit can be cultivated in adverse climatic conditions to serve the urban market. The Murs à Pêches have seen a long period of neglect. The site was cut into two by the feeder road of the A186 highway. Former orchards were used for the construction of factories, and the remaining wall compartments have been occupied by travelers and illegal waste dumps. But today the site is regaining interest again. Its initial purpose of food production and the need of the densely urbanized Paris region for improved green infrastructure are the most important inspirations for a transformation that keeps the characteristic values of the site alive.

The Murs à Pêches are located within a dense and heterogeneous urban fabric **[Fig. 7]** and can be reactivated to serve environmental as well as social goals for and with the local people. After the site's importance had been rediscovered by citizen groups in the late 1990s, 8.5 hectares were protected in

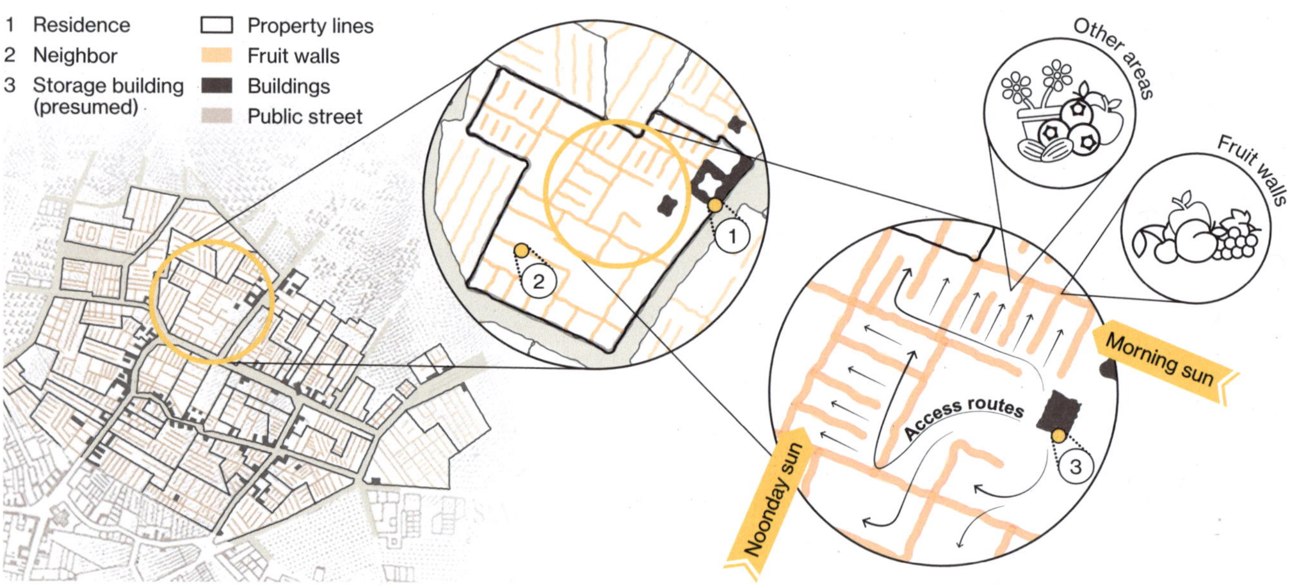

Fig. 4 Spatial analysis of the Murs à Pêches (map, 1773; analysis, 2021)

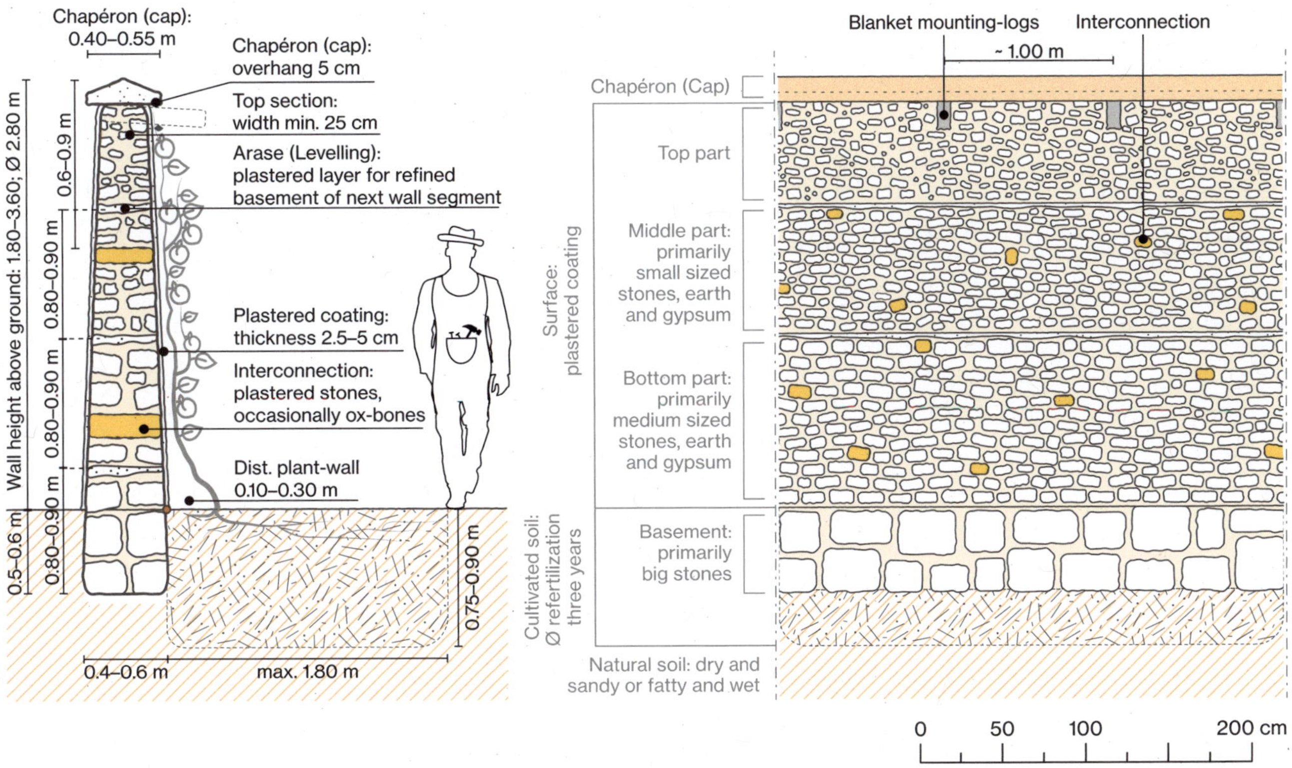

Fig. 5 Peach wall constructive details

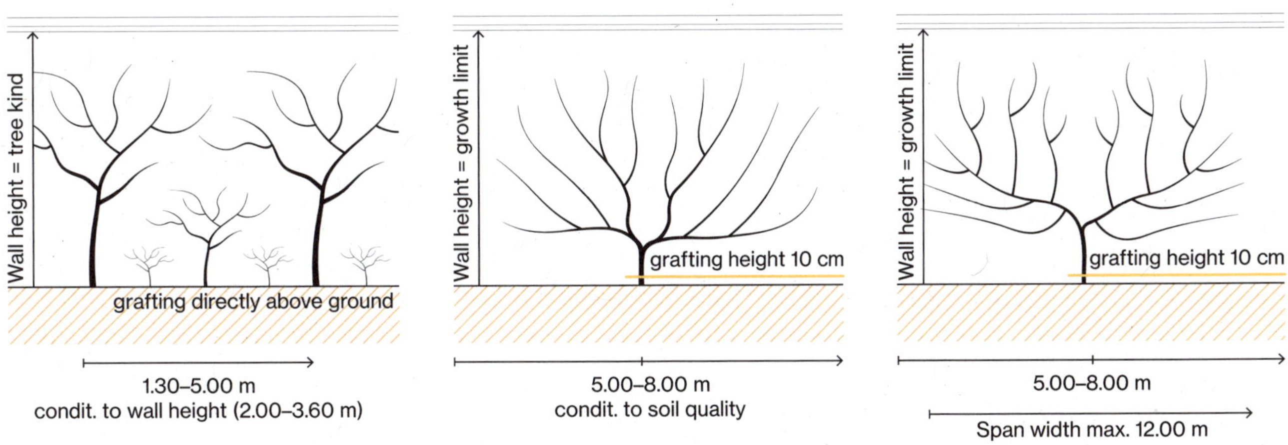

Tree continuum

+ different heights covered by multiple plants
o growing young trees replace old ones, new saplings are planted in between

L'arbre à l'étoile (star-shaped tree)

+ higher safety in case of damage
- difficulty in keeping middle part tidy

L'arbre Baucer (tree of Baucer)

+ better balance of juice – pressure
- higher impact of damage

Fig. 6 Peach wall cultivation techniques

2003 as a historic urban landscape but continued to degrade (Ville de Montreuil 2012).

The most valuable tangible aspects of the Murs à Pêches are the walls' substance, as witness to the historical craftsmanship, and the unique layout. Important intangible aspects are the cultivation techniques and the site's polyvalent development. Today, the city of Montreuil uses the site's unique character for a development strategy at different scales, combining top-down and bottom-up initiatives. The compartment structure can host different programs designed to fulfill the needs of different groups of people.

Current Initiatives, Actors, and Challenges

At the city scale, the Murs à Pêches are today recognized by the zoning plan. Instead of the housing or industry projects which had been conceived for the area and were part of the local urban plan until 2010, Montreuil now aims at preserving the walls, giving life to them, and opening the area to the public. Twenty-eight hectares are classified as the only protected agricultural zone in Montreuil (Est Ensemble Grand Paris 2020). Nearly 8 percent of the area will allow camps for travelers and the construction of micro-farms preserving the initial usage and character of the site (Ville de Montreuil and Est Ensemble Grand Paris 2018, 108). The classification as an agricultural zone rather than for nature protection or urban green space was a deliberate choice accompanied by the project to implement new urban agriculture. Nine micro-farms are envisaged in the area for growing fruit, vegetables, and flowers together with training, workshops, and public events. The City of Montreuil has used the instrument of calls for project to involve the local community. Ideas for the reuse of individual peach wall-compartments could be submitted by citizen groups and were selected for implementation. Two examples of the 15 initiatives working on the site are the Murs à Fleurs (flower walls) and the Fruits Défendus (forbidden fruits) gardens (Ville de Paris 2019; Eva G. 2019). Both preserve the walls and use them as a border for the cultivation of flowers and fruits, but add new functions like festivals and workshops. The Maison des Murs à Pêches (House of the Peach Walls) opened in 2016 and serves as a common infrastructure for the different initiatives, as a place for meetings and exhibitions, and as an access point to the site for visitors (Ville de Montreuil 2019, 6).

In these and other projects, production, social, cultural, and educational activities are key elements, enhancing the quality of the Murs à Pêches and making them a popular site. As shown in **Fig. 8**, some questions, especially the future development of the former industrial buildings on the fringe of the Murs à Pêches, are still being debated between the bottom-up initiatives and the municipality.

One of the challenges that appeared in almost all of the projects is the lack of financial support; but since 2015, 100,000 euros are earmarked for the area in the municipal budget every year. In addition, funding from private donations, lottery funds for cultural heritage, and EU funding of more than 1,000,000 euros have been acquired between 2018 and 2021 (Ville de Montreuil 2012).

Two main action methods can be concluded: Both aim at preserving the walls, but one focuses on agricultural use, fulfilling their original purpose, meanwhile the other aims at integrating new functions into the existing structure.

Conclusion

For the urban agricultural heritage of the Murs à Pêches, the City of Montreuil has opted for a living heritage approach. The authentic restoration of a peach wall costs up to 2,000 euros per running meter (Ville de Montreuil 2016, 7), so the alternative choice of reviving the area through a careful transformation managed by independent local community groups and maintaining the walls with low-impact measures appears to be the more promising approach to preserve the site **[Fig. 9]**. Not only is this less expensive, but also actions can be carried out more immediately. It may not preserve the historical substance identically, but invites us to remember it by giving the Murs à Pêches a new productive vocation and thus closes the gap between past and present. Within the living heritage area, the reconstructed portions give an example of how the whole site has been used in the past, making it unnecessary to reconstruct the entirety of the walls. ■

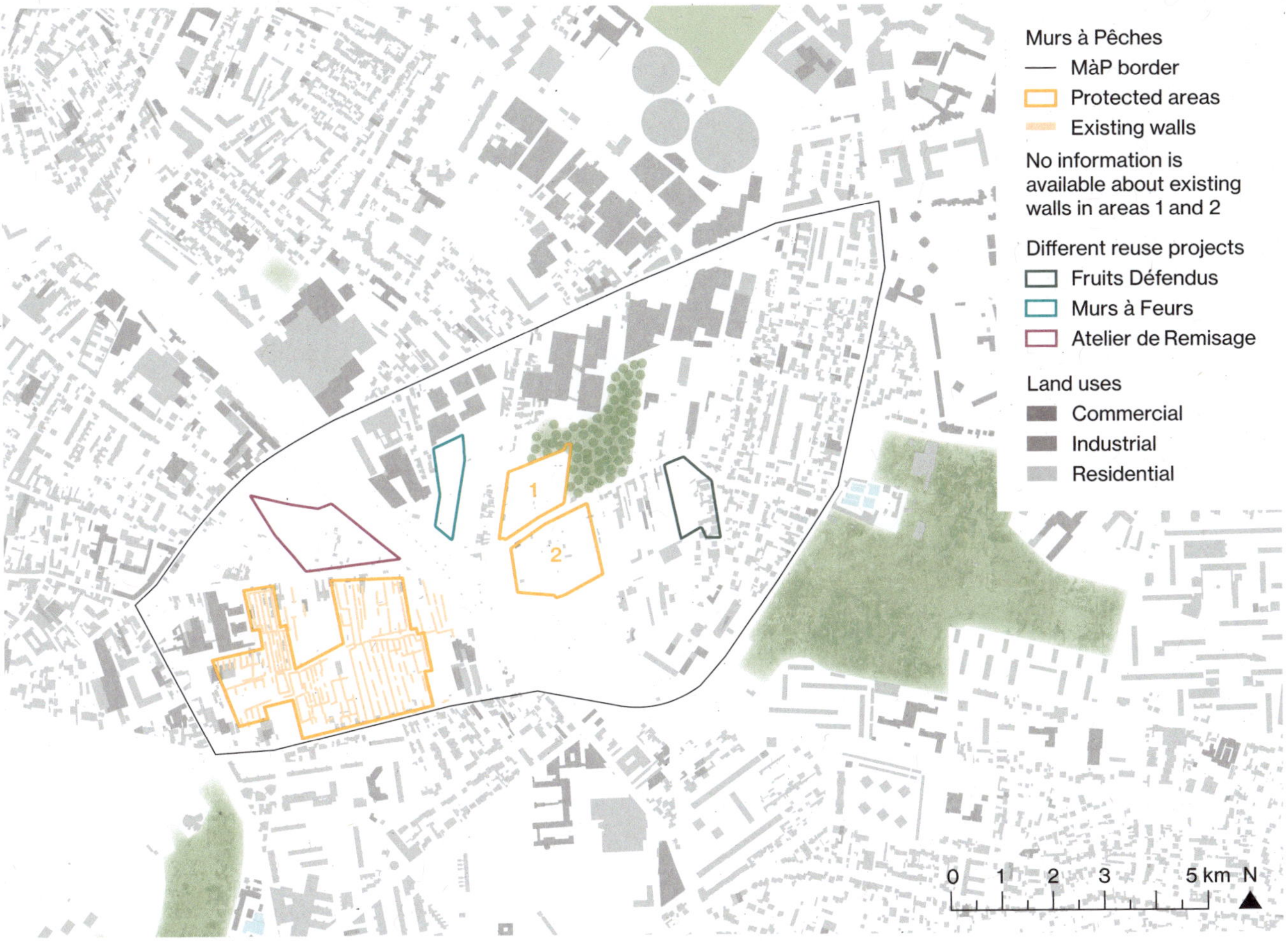

Fig. 7 Plan of the present contextual situation of the Murs à Pêches, 2021

Fig. 8 Pas à Vendre (not for sale) protest, 2020

Fig. 9 People visit a reconstructed compartment of the Murs à Pêches, 2019.

Reconnecting City and Countryside: Participatory Solutions for Hamburg

Ole Oßenbrink, Birte Mehrkens, Andreas Ulbrich, and Cord Petermann

Hamburg: Horticulture Shaping the Cultural Landscape around the City

In Hamburg, horticulture is concentrated in historically developed production areas in direct proximity to the urban space: in the southeast of Hamburg are the Vier- und Marschlande and in the west is the Alte Land (Old Country). Both areas have undergone contemporary intensifications and technical adaptations in their use; they are living cultural landscapes which still have a spatial impact today and can be described as historically persistent landscapes (Kleefeld et al. 2007, 8).

The Vier- und Marschlande is the largest vegetable and flower growing area in Germany. About 3,000 workers are employed on more than 600 farms, some of which are run by the eighth generation, in an area of almost 11,000 hectares. In the Alte Land, apples, pears, and cherries in particular are cultivated on an area of about 10,000 hectares. This makes the Alte Land one of the largest fruit-growing areas in Europe. Both areas extend close to the city center and have long been an important factor in providing food to the city of Hamburg.

Both growing areas are located in fertile alluvial land, the marsh. **Figure 1** shows the characteristic apple trees of the Alte Land next to the harbor. The geometry of their network of ditches for drainage, the resulting structuring of the floodplain, and the clarity of the lines remain characteristic of the landscape: dikes, drainage ditches, and small plots of land on which typical local crops (apple trees and vegetables) are still grown today (Stadtentwicklungsbehörde Hamburg 1994, 83).

In the past, the connection between city and countryside was mainly defined by agricultural products: Urban consumers used to buy the majority of goods directly from the producers. At the end of the eighteenth century, around 100 open-air *Gärtnerstellen* (gardener's market stands) served to sell horticultural products **[Fig. 2]**; these are the roots for today's wholesale market (Marktgemeinschaft Blumengroßmarkt Hamburg eG 2021).

City and Cultural Landscape: Fading Link

The location of the agricultural sector close to the city is an important factor for the development of cities. In almost all classical location structure theories, the proximity of agricultural production to city markets plays an essential role for the food supply (Farhauer and Kröll 2014). Thünen considered the optimal arrangement of the production of various goods around a city in his publication *The Isolated State in Relation to Agriculture and National Economy* and developed a theory of land use (Farhauer and Kröll, 30) which describes the proximity of fruit and vegetable production to the city as a critical factor. The interaction between the urban fabric and horticultural production areas in Hamburg was and is characteristic and of high testimonial value. However, the close economic interdependence, which is a basis for the develop-

Fig. 1 Altes Land: Characteristic apple tree culture in the direct vicinity of the harbor

ment and preservation of the cultural landscape, has been cracked in modern times by various factors. Today, horticultural companies in Hamburg are under great economic pressure. Annually, a significant number of them cease production (Altmann and Berndt 2016). For the horticultural areas, their proximity to the city is both an opportunity (sales market) and a threat (urban sprawl). The Wirtschaftsverband Gartenbau Norddeutschland (Northern German Horticultural Association) forecasts a considerable loss of agricultural land due to an increased need for compensation areas (Heyen 2018). Smaller farms in particular have given up in this situation, thus their number has decreased from 2006 to 2016 by almost 50 percent (Altmann and Berndt 2016, 12).

Fig. 2 Direct exchange of consumers and producers at a Gärtnerstelle at the Hopfenmarkt in 1906

But the cultural landscapes are not only a cultural historical document. Due to their proximity to the city, they are also part of the open space system, which is particularly worthy of protection in terms of its socioecological and aesthetic functions (Stadtentwicklungsbehörde Hamburg 1994, 106).

The historically shaped cultural landscapes as well as the industry-related competencies in the horticultural region are in danger of being lost piece by piece. In order to preserve and develop Hamburg's local food production systems and the historically grown landscape, it is important to strengthen and preserve the relationship between producer and consumer, to reinforce the horticultural companies' connections to local markets and thus enable farmers to continue their businesses.

Shift of Markets and the Potential for New Relationships

As in Hamburg, gardeners throughout Germany are facing major challenges, likely to intensify under the conditions of a globalized market. The gardener is no longer responsible for the supply of the nearby center. He produces for an anonymous national, even international market. His survival as a company is not dependent on local conditions but on national or European conditions, especially agricultural policy decisions (Vogelsang et al. 2018, 6). Within the industry, priority is given to the competitiveness of horticultural products, which is proving increasingly difficult due to the high market pressure and the associated low producer prices and sales difficulties. According to a study by the Thünen-Institute, this is caused in particular by the producers' pricing policies and lack of market power (Dirksmeyer et al. 2013). While in the past producers and consumers were linked (Vogelsang et al. 2018, 6), the industrialization of production as well as societal changes (such as the development of different lifestyles) have led to a split. This is also expressed in a 2018 survey (Agra Europe 2019), according to which 61 percent of the population living in cities of more than 500,000 inhabitants do not know a farmer, and 38 percent have never spoken to a farmer. However, only 7 percent of the respondents considered a possible conversation with a farmer as not interesting.

Altmann and Berndt (2016) found that the citizens of Hamburg would like to see more exchange with the horticultural businesses and that there is potential in the future to connect residents and producers in order to develop new regional food supply. This could be enabled by locally oriented production and consumption patterns involving large numbers of Hamburg's 1.8 million residents. A development toward this direction could be generated by many of the urban initiatives and associations that advocate for a more locally sourced diet and urban gardens in Hamburg (Altmann and Berndt 2016, 3), or that are active in the fields of climate change and local production. A link can be formed by connecting the numerous urban civic society groups involved in urban gardening, local production, and nutrition. An inventory has shown that there are about 60 groups with a potential "bridge function" in Hamburg. In recent years, however, no networking has taken place between these groups of actors and the local horticultural producers.

What they have in common is an interest in involving people who no longer want to be mere consumers, but demand participation and co-production, that is, producers and consumers producing together and creating a common understanding of cultivation and the cultural landscape it shapes. However, these groups, which are active in urban areas, are rarely connected to actors who are seen as shapers of the cultural landscape, that is, with the horticultural enterprises located in the surrounding areas of Hamburg.

Reinventing a Historically Grown Connection by Networking

The research and development project Urban Horticulture – Innovative Concepts as Impulses for a Future-Oriented Horticultural Production in the Hamburg Metropolitan Region, is the result of the idea to connect the inhabitants of Hamburg with the horticultural producers and develop new possibilities of exchange. The participatory process **[Fig. 3]** follows the logic of transformation research: At the beginning, the different stakeholders and their goals are exploratively identified. Access to the research field is gained through appearances at meetings of key organizations (1. System knowledge) in order to develop shared objectives (2. Target knowledge), which in turn leads to a transformation (3. Transformation knowledge) (Beecroft et al. 2018, 79).

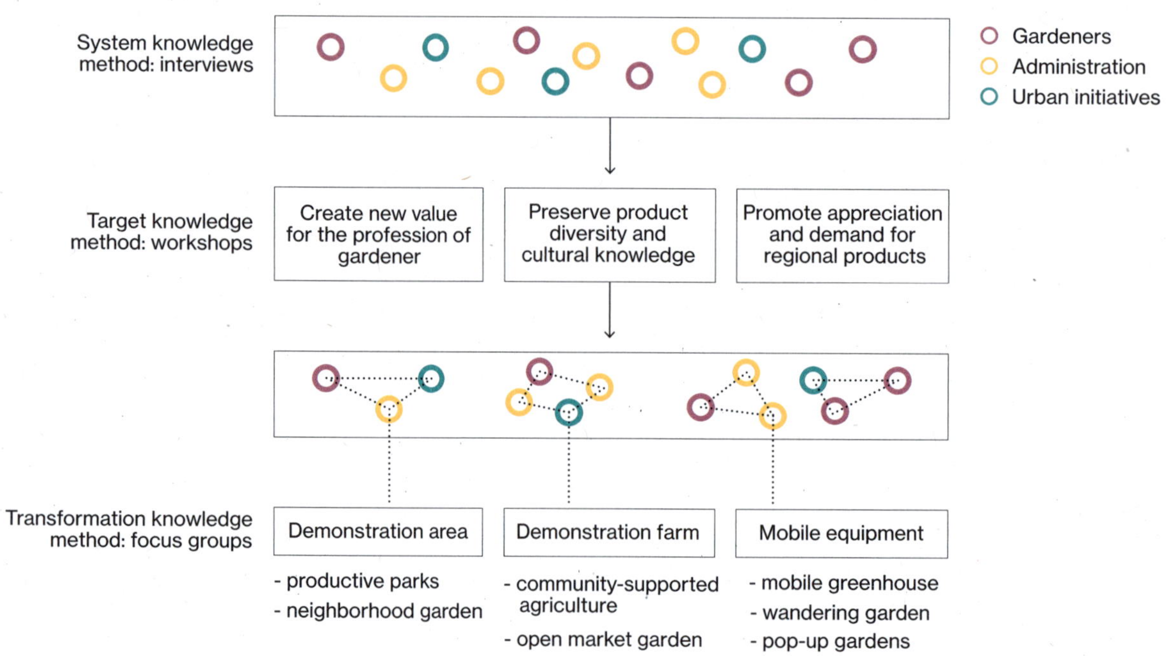

Fig. 3 Illustration of the participatory process

Fig. 4 Workshop to discuss the results with gardeners, urban initiatives, representatives of the city, and experts

To access the system knowledge in the first phase, more than 100 interviews were conducted and analyzed. Here it became clear that there was little to no exchange between the different actors, though they are sometimes pursuing the same goals. However, common goals could be defined from the interviews. These included: giving new value for the gardening profession; the preservation of product diversity and cultural knowledge; and the promotion of appreciation and demand for regional products. These goals were coordinated with the stakeholders and discussed in depth in a joint workshop. At the workshop, participants formed focus groups and developed different fields of action: demonstration area; demonstration farms; and mobile equipment. Within fields of action, the actors developed different space-related ideas. The concept for the Productive Park Finkenwerder is presented here as an example of such an idea and the process of communication behind it.

It became clear that shared processes of learning require places that allow the experience of different horticultural practices. A prototype of such a location was conceptualized by the actors in Hamburg Finkenwerder, with the goal of displaying the diversity of horticulture in all its dimensions (historically and in the future) and reinventing the once natural exchange processes between producers and consumers.

The idea of the actors was to create a place where different people come together, garden together, and share their cultural knowledge about their land, cultivation experiences, and knowledge about special local varieties (on the side of the gardeners), and about creativity, the high degree of networking, and experience in dealing with social media and public relations (on the side of the urban initiatives) through various events such as workshops and lectures. One of the last workshops discussed the idea of the Productive Park Finkenwerder with gardeners, urban initiatives, representatives of the city, and external experts **[Fig. 4]**. The group consisted of actors from administration, horticulture, the urban gardening scene, and the education sector.

The original idea is to create areas in the urban fabric where the range of horticultural production that takes place outside the city can be shown in the city and where information events and workshops can be held. People will come together to learn about the production that takes place outside the city of Hamburg and to exchange ideas about healthy food and sustainable production. The idea of pure demonstration gardening was expanded in the course of the project to focus not only on demonstration but also on active participation.

In particular, understanding production methods and the cultural landscape directly associated with them is a key issue to understand the historical cultural landscape and to protect it. However, it is important that the teaching is not only done through information and demonstration, but rather through one's own productive activity, exploration, and appropriation. This means applying the principle of co-production. In other words, the construct "cultural landscape" is reshaped, whereby it is not thematized as a museum artifact any longer but becomes recognizable in its dynamics—for example, through the integration of old varietals into new forms of cultivation or cultural techniques. The decoupled relationship between city and countryside is thus to be concretely reworked and made spatially and visually experienceable and discussable in an exemplary manner.

One hectare of land located at Finkenwerder's periphery was provided by an orchard business that had pursued the idea of opening its orchard to the public for some time **[Figs. 5 and 6]**. Through discussion with civic society actors, this approach was further developed jointly so that topics such as

Fig. 5 The productive Finkenwerder Park is located on the settlement edge of Hamburg in the direct transition from the city to the countryside and is to assume a bridging function between these in the future.

permaculture or old varietals and historical knowledge about production and cultural practices will find their way there. The area is to be made accessible to the public and will provide a meeting place for anyone interested in the subject of horticulture.

New Networks Create New Ideas

The result of the research and development pilot project is a written concept that includes both a schedule and financing plan, as well as the willingness of different actors to cooperate. Now the focus is on the question of how to support the new networking structures, how they can lead to increased exchange between producers and consumers, and to what extent the experience of the new spaces will lead to a further developed understanding of the cultural landscape.

Through an intensive communication process, knowledge and expectations of previously unconnected stakeholders were exchanged. This was the basis for developing common goals. The result is a new networking structure—a first step to strengthening the producer-consumer relationship in order to make more tangible the cultural landscapes around Hamburg that are close to the city. A network that—as a next step—will come up with practical and individually tailored ideas to reinvent the historically grown connection between the city and the Alte Land's horticulture businesses—keepers of the cultural landscape. ■

Fig. 6 Highlighted: the provided area on which apple trees still stand

Enhancing and Promoting Milan's Peri-Urban Agricultural Landscape as a Cultural Resource: The Case of MUSA

Andrea L'Erario, Paola Branduini, Raffaella Laviscio, G. Matteo Mai, Lionella Scazzosi, and Francesco C. Toso

Promising Trends in the Sociocultural Context of Southern Milan's Peri-Urban Agricultural Landscape

Southern Milan (Lombardy Region, Italy) has been a rich area for centuries, both from an agricultural and a cultural perspective. The area's agricultural landscape, which constitutes an enormous cultural heritage, can be summarized in one word: *cascina*, the typical farm of this region, often characterized by its central courtyard surrounded by the residences as well as the buildings related to production. Over the centuries, the evolution of the Milanese agrarian landscape and its cascinas has led to the development of the tangible heritage that we can see today and of the related intangible heritage made up of local knowledge, festivities, and traditions. This local heritage has reinforced the development of a strong local identity.

For centuries, the Milanese countryside had a solid relationship with the city of Milan. All the food produced in the peri-urban agricultural area and in the horticultural area within the ancient city walls—cereals, milk, vegetables, and fruits—was daily marketed in the city directly by the farmers from the countryside (Bisi 2012). However, during the twentieth century, the local identity of Milan's peri-urban agricultural area and the ancient commercial relationship between the city and the countryside surrounding it were partially lost due to several interrelated factors. Since the beginning of the twentieth century, the progressive development of industries in the city has attracted labor from the countryside. Factories guaranteed workers a wage and shorter working hours—albeit always exhausting—compared with those in the countryside. Simultaneously, technological developments in the agricultural sector led to a lower need for labor in the countryside. Therefore, this economic change favored a progressive detachment of local people from the farming activities, the countryside, and the ancient local knowledge and traditions. The intergenerational transmission of knowledge related to agricultural land management and local practices has gradually broken up. Furthermore, due to the development of food-processing industries and new ways of selling food, farmers no longer sold their agricultural products directly in the city. This phenomenon accelerated after World War II. Finally, the city's progressive spatial expansion also contributed to the cancelation of part of the tangible agricultural heritage made up of farms and agrarian landscape.

The economic, technological, spatial, and structural changes that Milan and its countryside experienced have led to social and cultural transformations as well as changes in the agricultural landscape surrounding the city. Farmers simplified the historical agrarian structure, for example eliminating numerous tree rows or changing historical land uses. For instance, the traditional agrarian use of winter meadows for fodder cultivation during the cold season, called *marcite* (water meadows), was mostly replaced by cereal production. Nowadays few people, mainly elders locally born, still bear the ancient memory, religious rituals, or technical skills: valuable knowledge which needs to be preserved.

Despite the described transformations in recent decades, agriculture still represents the economic base of the southern Milan area (Ferraresi 2009). Beside its economic importance, Milanese agriculture has a significant potential from a social and cultural point of view (Stroppa 1992). Municipalities, farmers, and citizens are gradually understanding the potential of Milan's agricultural landscape heritage by rediscovering it. In recent years, farmers and local municipalities have established measures for improving the undermined relationships between the city and the peri-urban countryside. Several farms opened to multifunctionality, and farmers—usually independently and in some cases assisted by the municipalities—inaugurated new services for citizens such as shops in the farmsteads, agritourism, and educational activities (Branduini et al. 2016; L'Erario 2019). Through these measures, residents are reconnecting with agriculture in a new and contemporary way (Cognetti and Conti 2014). In this context, the agricultural heritage is starting to play a crucial role in linking past and present values of agriculture and increasing awareness of the importance of preserving the historical landscapes.

The described process of reestablishing the relationship between the city and the peri-urban countryside was enforced by policies implemented at various scales—from regional to local—in recent years. The 2015 International EXPO, which took place in Milan with the title *Feeding the Planet: Energy for Life*, accelerated the establishment of new policies and tools targeted at agriculture and the agricultural landscape since the city's candidacy in 2007. Beginning that year, the Lombardy Region has been promoting the creation of agricultural districts, that is, networks of farming enterprises that support high-quality production and preserve the Lombard landscape identity as a food quality mark and a cultural resource (Lombard Regional Law 2007). Today there are 22 agricultural districts in Lombardy. Moreover, in 2013 the Lombardy Region started to promote a framework agreement for territorial development called Milan Rural Metropolis, signed by the Lombardy Region, the Province of Milan, the Municipality of Milan, and several agricultural districts. This agreement represents a governance model that pursues the integration of urban and rural development

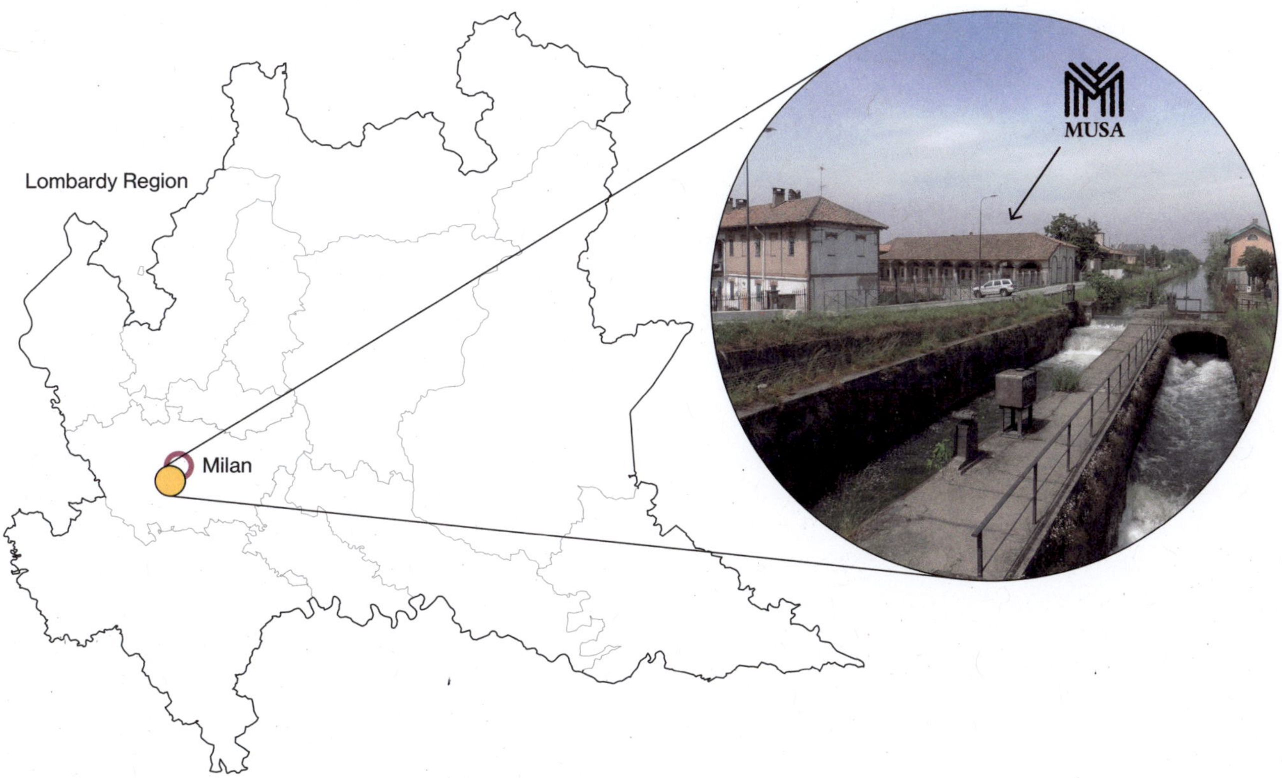

Fig. 1 MUSA is in the municipality of Zibido San Giacomo, located south of Milan in the Lombardy Region.

strategies by exploiting the agricultural heritage (Bocchi and Borasio 2013).

Through collaboration with universities and cultural institutions, local municipalities of the southern Milan area have acquired public and private funds to realize several projects. In the early 2000s, the project Camminando sull'acqua (Walking on water) was developed, aimed at promoting landscape heritage through the restoration of the historical roads connecting farms. These roads now serve as cycling routes that allow residents to reach farmsteads and directly experience the landscape. Ten municipalities of southern Milan started the project together, aware of the importance of joining forces to achieve longer-lasting goals concerning the preservation and enhancement of agricultural landscapes.

In addition to the measures described above, in 2012 the municipality of Milan launched a call for proposals for the refurbishment and enhancement of publicly owned farmsteads in the city, some of which were located in the urban context. The call aimed to preserve the Milanese agricultural heritage from decay and to answer residents' demands regarding the revitalization of several publicly owned agrarian buildings that were underused. The call was open both to farmers and nonagricultural residents.

What Is MUSA? Origin, Mission, and Related Cultural Projects

Born in the revitalized sociocultural context described above, MUSA—Salterio Museum: Taste and Landscape Workshop opened in 2015 as an initiative of the municipality of Zibido San Giacomo (Lombardy Region, Italy) **[Fig. 1]**. The museum is located within the boundaries of the South Milan Agricultural Park and settled in a refurbished nineteenth-century stable within the historical agricultural settlement of Cascina Salterio **[Fig. 2]**.

Despite its denomination, MUSA is not a traditional museum with a collection of tangible objects. It is meant to serve as a cultural hub and starting point for learning and experiencing the historical and contemporary values of the local peri-urban agriculture and landscape. Its aims are:

1. To educate citizens on the importance of preserving the agricultural landscape as cultural heritage;

Fig. 2 External view of MUSA in 2015: the refurbished historical stable

2. To educate citizens on food sustainability; and
3. To promote local agriculture and enhance farmers' roles in taking care of the countryside.

In the museum, people can experience and "taste" the landscape through cultural events and workshops. A large part of the peri-urban area of the South Milan Agricultural Park is connected to MUSA and the surrounding farms by cycling paths.

As an initiative of the municipality of Zibido San Giacomo, two different projects enabled the creation of MUSA. The first one was an EU project on the protection and enhancement of natural and cultural heritage. This project funded the refurbishment of the historical building in which MUSA is settled (European Regional Development Fund 2007–13). The second project, called MI-LAND Integrated Agri-Culture in Southern Milan, aimed to create a partnership among cultural and administrative institutions to link up different knowledge and expertise. This partnership was meant for the development of coordinated management actions to enhance and sustain local agricultural heritage, the conception of the museum's scientific program, and the joint realization of cultural activities. The municipality of Zibido San Giacomo created a partnership with other municipalities, the South Milan Agricultural Park, and cultural and educational institutions to recover funds for the launch of MUSA's cultural activities. Three universities contributed to the planning of the museum program according to their areas of expertise: landscape-based activities, activities on taste and food, and the development of a botanical garden.

After the conclusion of the MI-LAND project in 2016, new projects allowed the museum's activities and implementation of cultural and institutional partnerships to continue. These new projects, MU2 and Atlas of Memory, aimed at promoting the local food culture and landscape, and delivered larger-scale actions and activities that incorporated MUSA. As an action of these projects, a partnership between MUSA and several local farms was established through a memorandum of understanding (MoU). The purpose of the MoU was:

1. To strengthen the sense of local identity of citizens by promoting the agricultural landscape of the southern Milan area;
2. To help farms be in more direct contact with citizens, and vice versa;
3. To create awareness of the importance of preserving the landscape as a historical-cultural heritage and the culture of local agrofood products; and
4. To activate a time-lasting and robust collaboration among MUSA and farms to realize cultural events at the museum or in the farms by turning them into a sort of extension of the museum itself.

How Did MUSA Operate? The Museum Spaces and Activities

After refurbishing the historical stable (Laviscio 2019), the museum layout was designed according to the scientific program **[Fig. 3]**. The spaces and activities within this layout were intended to make the different facets of the agricultural heritage accessible to visitors. A thematic library on food and landscape was established as the core for a future documentation center. A kitchen equipped for professional use was set up to enable cooking classes and workshop activities such as food processing or pastry workshops, with local products provided by the partner farms **[Fig. 5]**. A multimedia exhibition was designed to help visitors discover and understand the historical evolution and the values of the

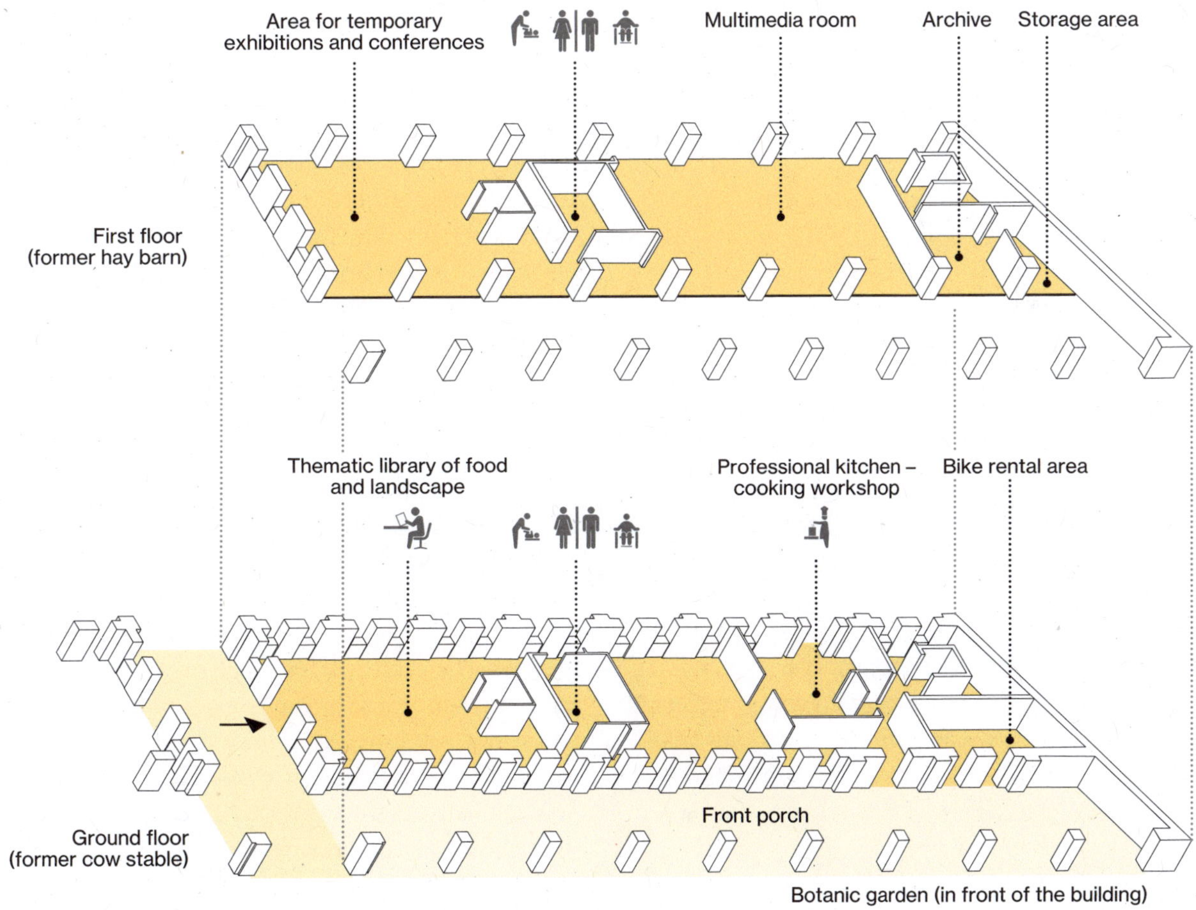

Fig. 3 Spatial layout of MUSA

local agricultural landscape system **[Fig. 4]** (Scazzosi 2015, 2018). A permanent digital exhibition was conceived to present informative content in an entertaining interactive way, communicating to visitors key concepts to interpret and better experience the surrounding agricultural landscape. Beside the permanent exhibition, several temporary exhibitions and conferences dedicated to specific topics were organized. In a botanical garden outside the museum building, both traditional historical food varieties and indigenous plant species of the Po Valley's agricultural landscape were collected **[Fig. 6]**. Local schools were invited to visit the museum and to discover its botanical garden and the agricultural landscape surrounding it.

Among its many landscape-oriented activities, the museum offered training courses for professionals on landscape conservation, dissemination activities such as lectures for adults, and workshops for schools on the historical reading of the landscape as well as research activities on landscape conservation and enhancement. A map presenting cycle paths along the surrounding agricultural landscape helped visitors deepen what they learned in the multimedia room directly in place **[Figs. 7 and 8]**. This map, which featured the museum's surroundings as a vast open-air exhibition, responded to one of MUSA's main objectives, namely not confining the landscape system's interpretation within the museum walls and encouraging the direct experience of the landscape (Colombo et al. 2017; Branduini et al. 2019).

With the described activities and spaces, between 2015 and 2017 MUSA was the core of a rich and structured cultural program led by the museum's partners. Furthermore, MUSA's cultural program contributed to the extensive cultural offer by the EXPO 2015 platform. By means of the aforementioned cultural projects that supported MUSA, targeted groups of citizens could be approached and become directly involved in specific actions, such as the collection of testimonies of older people on the agricultural traditions and knowledge of southern Milan, conducted by younger people.

Fig. 4 Discovering the agricultural landscape history of the Po Valley in MUSA's multimedia room

Fig. 5 MUSA's professional kitchen for cookery workshops

Conclusions: What about MUSA Some Years Later? Positive Outcomes, Shortcomings, and Lessons Learned

Several years after the museum's opening, it is possible to take stock of the MUSA experience. Various positive elements can be highlighted as well as some critical issues.

Some of the tools tested in MUSA have proved useful. People who visited MUSA and participated in the cultural activities showed a higher awareness of the importance of preserving the agricultural landscape as a cultural heritage, enhancing the local food system, and farmers' roles in the preservation process (L'Erario and Oppio 2020). Furthermore, the use of digital technology in explaining the agricultural landscape system, its history, and its values, made knowledge transfer easier, particularly to the youngest. Further short-term positive outcomes were the collaboration among institutions to

Fig. 6 Layout and view of the botanical garden

reach common purposes and the implementation of several cultural initiatives and projects, as described in the previous section.

An important lesson to learn from the MUSA experience is the need of a network for an effective heritage enhancement: The creation of MUSA was facilitated by the action framework and stakeholder network that were provided by preexisting initiatives, such as the aforementioned Camminando sull'acqua project. The protection and enhancement of the agricultural landscape—especially in urban or peri-urban contexts—require establishing partnerships among stakeholders and network management systems. These networks allow some outcomes that are difficult to achieve by a single actor, such as cost reduction, greater recognition of the individual initiatives, and the enhancement of the feasibility of complex actions. In these management systems, the landscape maintains its individuality as a project component. It becomes more robust and able to reconcile cultural and social needs with economic and entrepreneurial ones.

Another crucial aspect that the establishment process of MUSA highlights is the importance of the close link with local planning tools: The museum results from a long and gradual planning process at the local and metropolitan level using tools such as an urban plan, a refurbishment project, and several cultural projects implemented over time.

A further important aspect that MUSA sets an example for is the ability to respond to local needs for sociality, education, and identity formation. It utilizes the agricultural landscape's cultural dimension to develop activities that serve these needs.

Despite the described positive aspects, some critical issues prevented MUSA from achieving some of its longer-term objectives, namely the development of the museum into an "Agri-Cultural hub" and research center, the strengthening of the synergies with cultural institutions and local farms, and thereby the promotion of heritage conservation and improving the agricultural landscape quality. MUSA has partially failed in completing the heritagization of the agricultural landscape. Currently, most of the citizens of southern Milan—and in particular the inhabitants of Zibido San Giacomo—do not identify with the museum's purposes. This happened because the museum's objectives were defined in a top-down process led by the local municipality. The local administration decided not to involve the citizens of the southern Milan area in the decision-making process due to political reasons. The citizens, who did not codetermine the purposes and scientific program of the museum, only became the end-users of the proposed activities after its opening. This represents a critical factor that limited the long-term effectiveness of the museum's goals and the citizens' identification with these, leading to a decrease in their participation in museum activities over time. This confirms the central importance of a greater involvement of citizens in all phases in the design process (Council of Europe 2000, 2005), to reinforce both the project's role in the community and the link with the broader development of a local identity (Branduini 2020).

Another critical aspect has been the promotion of the cultural program of MUSA mainly to the closer local context, instead of strengthening MUSA's role as part of the more comprehensive peri-urban agricultural system and related cultural initiatives in southern Milan. This choice resulted in the gradual exclusion of MUSA from the broader cultural circuit and the loss of incipient collaboration with local farms. During the management phase, the municipality's ability to read and understand the systemic nature of the complex—the building and the agricultural landscape as a whole—was also lacking. Despite the memorandum of understanding with local farms, the municipality focused mainly on activities within the museum walls without seeking relationships with the outside agricultural area. The actions to enhance the historical agrarian system—made up of the farmsteads, the irrigation system, crops and minor artifacts—remained in the background.

Finally, the absence of political continuity (due to the municipal elections in 2018) and the new administration's choice not to continue with MUSA's original goals, led eventually to the dissolution of previous collaborations and the diminishment of its cultural offerings. After the expected conclusion in 2017 of all cultural projects mentioned in the previous sections of this paper (MI-LAND, MU2 and the Atlas of Memory), the lack of a political will led to the choice of the local administration not to continue with new related cultural projects and partnerships. As a tangible consequence of the described situation, the museum lost most of its visitors.

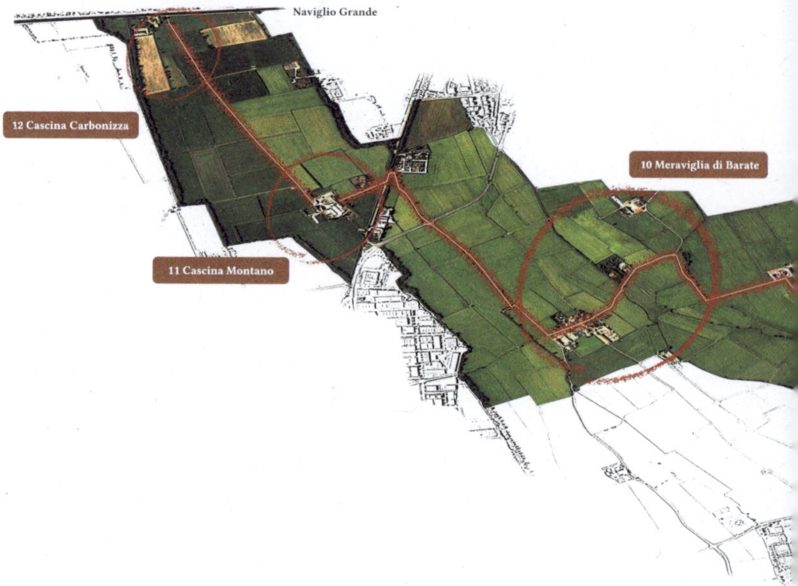

Fig. 7 MUSA as the starting point of discovering the heritage of the peri-urban agricultural landscape

Fig. 8 MUSA map, Agri-Cultural cycling routes

Its library was disassembled and its contents moved to the central library of Zibido San Giacomo.

However, MUSA remains a good example from which lessons can be drawn for the enhancement of urban and peri-urban agricultural landscapes. The MUSA experience confirms that a broad consensus among all local stakeholders, from the local administration to all political groups and citizens, and their active participation in all project phases—the definition of project objectives, implementation of the project, and management after the project realization—is crucial. Furthermore, it stresses the importance of going beyond local, municipal, and political limits: limiting the promotion of these kinds of experiences to small municipal areas (from an administrative point of view) or strongly linking these projects to the objectives of local political administrations (which in a democracy can change after a few years) can mean limiting opportunities and possibilities for the further development of these projects in the long term.

At the beginning of 2022, the Municipality of Zibido San Giacomo entrusted a recently formed private partnership with the management of the museum. The partnership comprises a local farmer and social associations engaged within artistic and food-related fields. The new initiative aims to valorize previous experience, thus trying to apply lessons learned to develop a more efficient and sustainable cultural program for the next five years. This new cultural program, which is currently being defined, will strengthen the innovative character of MUSA and its potential role as a cultural hub for landscape and food-related education. One of the first objectives will be to expand the network of collaborations and to find new opportunities for inter- and multidisciplinary co-operation (with universities and research institutes), in addition to sourcing external funding. After a few years of inactivity, a new life for MUSA is now envisaged. ■

Appendix

References

Urban Agriculture as Heritage
Frank Lohrberg

Barthel, Stephan, Carl Folke, and Johan Colding. 2010. "Social-ecological Memory in Urban Gardens – Retaining the Capacity for Management of Ecosystem Services." In *Global Environmental Change* 20, no. 2: 255–65.

Bernbeck, Reinhard. 2013. "Heritage Void and the Void as Heritage." In *Archaeologies* 9, no. 3: 526–45.

Bonta, Juan Pablo. 1975. *An Anatomy of Architectural Interpretation: A Semiotic Review of the Criticism of Mies Van Der Rohe's Barcelona Pavilion*. Barcelona: Gustavo Guilli.

Bonta, Juan Pablo. 1979. *Architecture and Its Interpretation: A Study of Expressive Systems in Architecture*. London: Lund Humphries.

Davallon, Jean. 2014. "À propos des regimes de patrimonialisation: enjeux et questions." In *Patrimonialização e sustentabilidade do património: reflexão e prospectiva, November 2014,* 27–29. Lisbon: IHC-NOVA FCSH, 2018.

Daviron, Benoit, Coline Perrin, and Christophe-Toussaint Soulard. 2019. "History of Urban Food Policy in Europe, from the Ancient City to the Industrial City." In *Designing Urban Food Policies*, edited by Caroline Brand, Nicolas Bricas, Damien Conaré, Benoit Daviron, Julie Debru, Laura Michel, and Christophe-Toussaint Soulard, 27–51. Cham: Springer.

FAO – Food and Agriculture Organization of the United Nations. 2010. "With Micro-Gardens, Urban Poor 'Grow Their Own.'" https://www.fao.org/ag/agp/greenercities/en/microgardens/index.html. Accessed November 29, 2021.

FAO – Food and Agriculture Organization of the United Nations. 2017. "Selection Criteria and Action Plan." http://www.fao.org/giahs/become-a-giahs/selection-criteria-and-action-plan/en/. Accessed November 26, 2021.

FAO – Food and Agriculture Organization of the United Nations. 2021. "Globally Important Agricultural Heritage Systems." https://www.fao.org/giahs/giahsaroundtheworld/en/. Accessed November 29, 2021.

ICOMOS. 1964. International Charter for the Conservation and Restoration of Monuments and Sites. Venice: ICOMOS.

Jiang, Yichen. 2021. "A Study of the Concept and Preservation Strategies for the Urban Agricultural Heritage: International Practices and Implications for China." PhD diss., RWTH Aachen University.

Kalakoski, Iida, Satu Huuhka, and Olli-Paavo Koponen. 2020. "From Obscurity to Heritage: Canonisation of the Nordic Wooden Town." In *International Journal of Heritage Studies* 26, no. 8: 790–805.

Koohafkan, Parviz. 2019. "Opportunities and Challenges of Dynamic Conservation of Agricultural Heritage Systems and Its Application to Urban Agricultural Heritage." Lecture given at the Herrenhausen Conference on Urban Agricultural Heritage and the Shaping of Future Cities, Hanover, May 6–8, 2019.

Koohafkan, Parviz, and Miguel A. Altieri. 2011. *Globally Important Agricultural Heritage Systems A Legacy for the Future*. Rome: Food and Agriculture Organization of the United Nations.

Landsteiner, Erich, and Tim Soens, eds. 2020. *Farming the City: The Resilience and Decline of Urban Agriculture in European History*. Vienna: StudienVerlag.

Lohrberg, Frank. 2001. "Stadtnahe Landwirtschaft in der Stadt- und Freiraumplanung." PhD diss., University of Stuttgart.

Misztal, Barbara A. 2003. *Theories of Social Remembering* (Berkshire, UK: Open University Press).

People's Government of Xuanhua District. 2013. "GIAHS Proposal Initiative: Xuanhua Traditional Vineyards System." http://www.fao.org/3/a-bp786e.pdf. Accessed January 2021.

Sánchez-Carretero, Cristina. 2015. "To Walk and to Be Walked ... at the End of the World." In *Heritage, Pilgrimage and the Camino to Finisterre*, edited by Cristina Sánchez-Carretero, 1–20. Amsterdam: Springer.

Sauer, Carl O. 1925. "The Morphology of Landscape." In *University of California Publications in Geography* 2, no. 2: 19–53.

Shackleton, Charles M., Margaret Pasquini, and Axel W. Drescher. 2009. *African Indigenous Vegetables in Urban Agriculture*. London: Routledge.

Shopov, Aleksandar. 2019. "Istanbul's Historic Produce Gardens and the Struggle for Their Preservation." Lecture at the Herrenhausen Conference on Urban Agricultural Heritage and the Shaping of Future Cities, Hanover, May 6–8, 2019.

Siebel, Walter. 2015. *Die Kultur der Stadt*. Berlin: Suhrkamp Verlag.

Smit, Jac, Joe Nasr, and Annu Ratta. 1996. *Urban Agriculture: Food, Jobs and Sustainable Cities*. New York: United Nations Development Programme.

Thebo, Anne L., Pay Drechsel, and Eric F. Lambin. 2014. "Global Assessment of Urban and Peri-Urban Agriculture: Irrigated and Rainfed Croplands." In *Environmental Research Letters* 9, no. 11: 1–9.

UNESCO. 2021. "Operational Guidelines for the Implementation of the World Heritage Convention." Paris: UNESCO World Heritage Centre.

Early Modern Urban and Peri-Urban Horticulture in German Territories
Ansgar Schanbacher

Abad, Reynald. 2002. *Le grand marché: L'approvisionnement alimentaire de Paris sous l'Ancien Régime*. Paris: Fayard.

Ahrens, G. 2008. "Von der Franzosenzeit bis zum Ersten Weltkrieg 1806–1914: Anpassungen an Forderungen der neuen Zeit." In *Lübeckische Geschichte*, edited by Antjekathrin Graßmann, 539–685. 4th ed. Lübeck: Schmidt Römhild.

Anon. 1799. *Die vollkommene Gärtner-Schule*. Vienna: Binzische Buchhandlung.

Aust, Bruno, and Ulrich Stark. 1992. *Die Städtebauliche Entwicklung Berlin seit 1650 in Karten. Erläuterungsheft zum Kartenwerk*. Berlin: Institut für Angewandte Geodäsie.

Crosby, Alfred W. 1973. *The Columbian Exchange: Biological and Cultural Consequences of 1492* Westport, CT: Greenwood.

Düselder, Heike. 2009. "'Von den angenehmen ländlichen Beschäftigungen': Die Bedeutung der Gärten des Adels für Gartenkultur und Wirtschaft." In *Zeitschrift für Agrargeschichte und Agrarsoziologie* 57, no. 1: 10–26.

Döring, Detlef, ed. 2016. *Geschichte der Stadt Leipzig: Von der Reformation bis zum Wiener Kongress*, vol. 2. Leipzig: Leipziger Universitätsverlag.

Franz, Günther, ed. 1984. *Geschichte des deutschen Gartenbaues*. Stuttgart: Eugen Ulmer.

Habel, Hubertus. 2015. "Gemüsesamen für Europa: Zunftgenese und Verdichtung des Bamberger Gärtnerhandwerks 1600–1900." In Häberlein and Zink 2015, 93–124.

Häberlein, Mark, and Robert Zink, eds. 2015. *Städtische Gartenkulturen im historischen Wandel*. Stadt in der Geschichte 40. Ostfildern: Jan Thorbecke.

Haus-, Garten- und Land-Kalender [...] Auff das Jahr Christi 1712. http://digital.slub-dresden.de/id367720760-17120000. Accessed February 2, 2022.

Hiebner, Johann Christoph. 1664. *Horticultura: Das ist Kurtz- und verständliche Anleitung/ wie ein Lust- Obst- und Küchen-Garte anzulegen*. Brieg: Tschorn.

Hofmann, Jochen A. 2014. *Obstlandschaften 1500–1800: Historische Geographie des Konsums, Anbaus und Handels von Obst in der Frühen Neuzeit*. Bamberg: University of Bamberg Press.

Hofmann, Jochen A. 2015. "Zur Innovationsfunktion von Gärten in der frühneuzeitlichen Agrarlandschaft: Dargestellt an Beispielen aus Franken." In Häberlein and Zink 2015, 73–91.

Imbert, Dorothée, ed. 2015. *Food and the City: Histories of Culture and Cultivation*. Washington, DC: Dumbarton Oaks Research Library and Collection.

Landsteiner, Erich, and Tim Soens, eds. 2020. *Farming the City: The Resilience and Decline of Urban Agriculture in European History*. Vienna: Studien Verlag.

Liebster, Günther. 1984. "Der deutsche Obstbau seit dem 18. Jahrhundert." In Franz 1984, 143–205.

Meibeyer, Wolfgang. 2008. *Die Stadt Braunschweig im 18. Jahrhundert: Stadtbild und Grundbesitz in Braunschweig nach der Vermessung von Andreas Carl Haacke 1762 bis 1765*. Braunschweig: Appelhans.

Moderhack, Richard. 1997. *Braunschweiger Stadtgeschichte*. Braunschweig: Waisenhaus-Druckerei.

Müller, Siegfried. 2003. "Reichart, Christian." In *Neue Deutsche Biographie*, vol. 21, edited by F. Menges, 297. Berlin: Duncker & Humblot.

Mundus, Doris. 2016. "Alltagsleben." In Döring 2016, 592–616.

Petersen, Niels. 2020. "Städtisches Gartenland zwischen Stadt und Land (14.–16. Jahrhundert)." In *Reichsstadt und Landwirtschaft*, edited by Stefan Sonderegger, Helge Wittmann, and Dorothee Guggenheimer, 165–84. Petersberg: Michael Imhof.

Peterson, Barbara, and Peter Meindl. 2005. "Obst und Gemüse." In *Umwelt Stadt: Geschichte des Natur- und Lebensraumes Wien*, edited by Karl Brunner and Petra Schneider, 220–21. Vienna: Böhlau.

Pingel, Norman-Mathias. 1992. "Einwohnerzahlen." In *Braunschweiger Stadtlexikon*, edited by Luitgard Camerer, 66. Braunschweig: Meyer.

Reichart, Christian. 1758. *Einleitung in den Garten- und Acker-Bau*. Erfurt: Nonne.

Roeck, Bernd. 1989. *Eine Stadt in Krieg und Frieden: Studien zur Geschichte der Reichsstadt Augsburg zwischen Kalenderstreit und Parität*. Göttingen: Vandenhoeck & Ruprecht.

Rosseaux, Ulrich. 2015. "Naturgenuss und Sommerpläsier: Städtische Gärten um 1800 als Erholungs- und Unterhaltungsräume." In Häberlein and Zink 2015, 141–47.

Schaier, Joachim. 2009. "Die Erfurter Großgärtnerei J.C. Schmidt im 19. und Anfang des 20. Jahrhunderts." *Zeitschrift für Agrargeschichte und Agrarsoziologie* 57, no. 1: 59–76.

Schanbacher, Ansgar. 2019. "Umwelt und Ressourcen in der frühneuzeitlichen Stadt Mitteleuropas." In *Nachhaltigkeit in der Geschichte: Argumente – Ressourcen – Zwänge*, edited by Arnd Reitemeier, Ansgar Schanbacher, and Tanja Susanne Scheer, 111–134. Göttingen: Universitätsverlag Göttingen.

Scheinost, Marina. 2009. "Die Bamberger Gärtner: Innen- und Außensicht einer städtischen Berufsgruppe." In *Zeitschrift für Agrargeschichte und Agrarsoziologie* 57, no. 1: 27–42.

Schindling, Anton. 1999. *Bildung und Wissenschaft in der Frühen Neuzeit*. Enzyklopädie deutscher Geschichte 30. 2nd ed. Munich: Oldenbourg.

Schmölz-Häberlein, Michaela. 2015. "Außereuropäische Pflanzen in realen und imaginären Gärten des 16. Jahrhunderts." In Häberlein and Zink 2015, 39–71.

Schott, Dieter. 2014. *Europäische Urbanisierung (1000–2000): Eine umwelthistorische Einführung*. Cologne: Böhlau.

Schröder-Lembke, Gertrud. 1984. "Der Gartenbau in der Hausväterzeit." In Franz 1984, 112–42.

Schwarz, Alberto. 2016. "Architektur und Stadtbild." In Döring 2016, 685–724.

Seitz, Paul. 1984. "Der Gemüse- und Kräuteranbau und die Speisepilzerzeugung seit dem 18. Jahrhundert." In Franz 1984, 365–454.

Soens, Tim. 2020. "Urban Agriculture and Urban Food Provisioning in Pre-1850 Europe: Towards a Research Agenda." In Landsteiner and Soens 2020, 13–29.

von Thünen, Johann H. 1842. *Der isolirte Staat in Beziehung auf Landwirthschaft und Nationalökonomie*. 2nd ed. Rostock: G.B. Leopold's Universitäts-Buchhandlung.

Walker, Adam. 1790. *Ideas Suggested on the Spot in a Late Excursion Through Flanders, Germany, France, and Italy*. London: J. Robson.

Werner, Wolfram. 1967. *Goslar am Ende seiner reichsstädtischen Freiheit unter besonderer Berücksichtigung der Reformen von J.G. Siemens*. Goslar: Selbstverlag des Geschichts- und Heimatschutzvereins Goslar.

Willerding, Ulrich. 1987. "Landnutzung und Ernährung." In *Göttingen: Geschichte einer Universitätsstadt: Von den Anfängen bis zum Ende des Dreißigjährigen Krieges*, vol. 1, edited by Dietrich Denecke and Helga-Marie Kühn, 437–64. Göttingen: Vandenhoeck & Ruprecht.

Wimmer, Clemens A. 2008. "Aus der Geschichte der Gartengeräte: Werkzeuge zur Bearbeitung des Bodens." In *Gartenbaugeschichte*, no. 4: 7–37.

The City as a Driver of Regional Agriculture: Erfurt and Its Horticultural Heritage

Sibylle Küttner, Frank Lohrberg

Baumann, Martin. 2011. "50 Jahre Internationale Gartenbauausstellung iga '61 in Erfurt: Historische Entwicklung und Bedeutung als Gartendenkmal." In Baumann and Raßloff 2011, 309–40.

Baumann, Martin, and Steffen Raßloff, eds. 2011. *Blumenstadt Erfurt*. Schriften des Vereins für die Geschichte und Altertumskunde von Erfurt 8. Erfurt: Sutton.

Bischoff, Harald. 2011. "Geschichte des Deutschen Gartenbaumuseums." In Baumann and Raßloff 2011, 360–81.

Blüthner, Wolf-Dieter. 2011. "Die Firma N.L. Chrestensen." In Baumann and Raßloff 2011, 177–202.

Czekalla, Eberhard. 2011. "Gärtnerische Aus-, Fort- und Weiterbildung seit dem 19. Jahrhundert in Erfurt." In Baumann and Raßloff 2011, 271–85.

Czekalla, Eberhard, and Reiner Prass. 2011. "Christian Reichart und der Erwerbsgartenbau im 18. Jahrhundert." In Baumann and Raßloff 2011, 49–73.

Daviron, Benoit, Coline Perrin, and Christophe-Toussaint Soulard. 2019. "History of Urban Food Policy in Europe, from the Ancient City to the Industrial City." In *Designing Urban Food Policies*, edited by Caroline Brand, Nicolas Bricas, Damien Conaré, Benoit Daviron, Julie Debru, Laura Michel, and Christophe-Toussaint Soulard, 27–51. Cham: Springer.

Fischer, Ralf, Wolf-Dieter Blüthner, and Christel Bosecker. 2017. *Brunnenkresse: Gesunde Erfurter Delikatesse*. Erfurt: Landesverband Gartenbau Thüringen e.V.

Herz, Gerhard. 2021. “Ausgewählte Nachrichten aus Erfurts Vergangenheit zu Gartenbau und Pflanzenzucht.” In *Stadt und Geschichte: Zeitschrift für Erfurt*, special issue. no. 20: 10–13.

Kahl, Monika. 1985. “Zur Geschichte des Reichart-Denkmals.” In Pontius et al. 2021, 47–51.

Karn, Susanne. 2011. “Die Gartenschau in Erfurt: Von der harmonischen Kulturlandschaft zur mustergültigen ‘Lehrschau.’” In Baumann and Raßloff 2011, 286–308.

Landeshauptstadt Erfurt, Stadtverwaltung. 2011. “Beste Verarbeitungsbedingungen: Investitionsstandort Nahrungsgüterwirtschaft und Gartenbau.” 2nd ed. https://www.erfurt.de/ef/de/service/mediathek/veroeffentlichungen/2011/107526.html. Accessed January 23, 2022.

Landeshauptstadt Erfurt, Stadtverwaltung. 2021. “Wirtschaftsstandort Erfurt: Gartenbau und Nahrungsgüter.” https://www.erfurt.de/ef/de/wirtschaft/wirtschaftsstandort/gng/index.html. Accessed September 30, 2021.

Moritz, Horst. 2021. “Grünes Erfurt: Ein Überblick.” In *Stadt und Geschichte: Zeitschrift für Erfurt*, special issue, no. 20: 3–7.

Müllerott, Hansjürgen. 1991. “Das Thüringer Becken: Ein bedeutendes europäisches Waidanbaugebiet.” In *Zeitschrift für Agrargeschichte und Agrarsoziologie* 39, no. 2: 186–99.

Noll-Reinhardt, Gudrun. 2017. *Geld stinkt nicht: Erfurt und der Waidhandel*. Erfurt: Geschichtsmuseen der Stadt Erfurt.

Pontius, Hartmut, Ilsabe Schalldach, Erika Schwarz, and Ulrich Scheidt. 1985. “Christian Reichart 1685–1775. Pionier und Förderer des Erfurter Erwerbsgartenbaues.” Special issue, *Veröffentlichungen des Naturkundemuseums Erfurt*.

Reichart, Christian. 1753, *Land- und Gartenschatz: Von den zur Speise dienlichen Kohlen, Wurzeln, und Zwiebeln, deren Erziehung und Wartung nach allen Stücken aufrichtig beschrieben worden*, vol. 3. Erfurt: Johann Heinrich Nonne.

Reichart, Christian. 1754. *Land- und Gartenschatz: Von vieljähriger Nutzung der Aecker ohne Brache und wiederholte Düngung, wobey zugleich eine Anweisung die Korn- und Hülsenfrüchte, nebst dem Hanfe, Flachse und einigen Klee-Gewächsen, zu erbauen, gegeben und mit Kupfern erläutert worden*, vol. 5. Erfurt: Johann Heinrich Nonne.

Riehm, Juliane. 2021. “Brunnenkresse für Erfurt.” https://brunnenkresse-für-erfurt.de. Accessed November 18, 2021.

Schalldach, Ilsabe. 2011. “Die Familie Haage: 325 Jahre Gärtnereigeschichte,” In Baumann and Raßloff 2011, 74–107.

Selzer, Stephan. 2011. “Erfurt und Toulouse: Gemeinsamkeiten und Unterschiede zweier Waidstädte im spätmittelalterlichen Europa.” In Baumann and Raßloff 2011, 17–41.

The Role of Centralised Policy Planning for Bulgarian Urban Agricultural Heritage from the Socialist Period
Dona Pickard

Fol, Aleksandur, Vasil Gyuzelev, Nikolay Genchev, Dimitar Konstantinov Kossev, Ilcho Ivanov Dimitrov, Andrey Pantev, Milcho Lalkov, and K. Petrov. 1981. *A Short History of Bulgaria*. Sofia: Science and Arts Publishing House.

Koleva, Galina, and Dona Pickard. 2015. “Sustainable Development Values in Urban Land Use by the Example of Urban Agriculture.” In *Ecological Ethics, Nature and Sustainable Development in Bulgaria*, edited by E. Marinova, 379–91. Sofia: Sustainable Development for Bulgaria Foundation.

State Gazette. 1963. Decree No. 21 from 31 January 1963 of the Central Committee of the Bulgarian Communist Party and the Council of Ministers of People’s Republic of Bulgaria on the development of animal husbandry in the personal farms of the cooperators and using the unmanaged land near settlements.

State Gazette. 1978a. Decree No. 76 of the Council of Ministers from 5 December 1977 on the implementation of the system for self-provision of the population with fruit, vegetables, meat, milk, eggs, and fish.

State Gazette. 1978b. Regulation No. 6 by the Ministry of Agriculture and Food Industry, Ministry of Forestry and the Central Cooperative Union.

State Gazette. 1982. Decree No. 11 of the Council of Ministers from 2 March 1982 on the complete establishment of the system for self-provision of the population from the regions and the settlement systems with staple agricultural products.

State Gazette. 1987. Decree No. 26 of the Council of Ministers from 23 April 1987 on the improvement of the system for self-provision of the population with agricultural produce.

Yoveva, Antoaneta, Boriana Gocheva, Galya Voykova, Boris Borissov, and Al Spassov. 2000. “Sofia: Urban Agriculture in an Economy in Transition.” In *Growing Cities, Growing Food, Urban Agriculture on the Policy Agenda*, edited by Nico Bakker, Marielle Dubbeling, Sabine Guendel, Ulrich Sabel-Koschella, and Henk de Zeeuw, 501–18. Feldafing: DSE.

Yoveva, Antoaneta, and Plamen Mishev. 2001. “Using Urban Agriculture for Sustainable City Planning in Bulgaria: The Case of Trojan.” In *Urban Agriculture Magazine*, no. 4: 14–16.

Unpublished transcripts of interviews with:

a) Secretary of the agricultural cooperatives’ labor union in the 1970s and 1980s, who received a plot of land near Sofia under the force of Decree No. 76 of the Council of Ministers.
b) The current director of the Forestry University experimental field, former agronomist at the greenhouse production center at the Sofia thermal power station.
c) Floriculture plant selection expert at the flower production enterprise Bulgartsvet from the 1960s to the 1980s.
d) Interviews and focus groups with contemporary Urban Agriculture activists and Sofia municipality representatives.

Heritage at the Urban Fringe: Allotment Gardening in Europe as Urban Agricultural Heritage
Attila Tóth

Appel, Ilka, Christine Grebe, and Maria Spitthöver. 2011. *Aktuelle Garteninitiativen: Kleingärten und neue Gärten in deutschen Großstädten*. Kassel: Kassel University Press.

Barthel, Stephan, John Parker, and Henrik Ernstson. 2013. “Food and Green Space in Cities: A Resilience Lens on Gardens and Urban Environmental Movements.” In *Journal of Urban Studies* 52. no. 7: 1321–38.

Bell, Simon, Runrid Fox-Kämper, Nazila Keshavarz, Mary Benson, Silvio Caputo, Susan Noori, and Annette Voigt. 2016. *Urban Allotment Gardens in Europe*. Abingdon: Routledge.

Borysiak, Janina, Andrzej Mizgajski, and Andrew Speak. 2017. “Floral Biodiversity of Allotment Gardens and its Contribution to Urban Green Infrastructure.” In *Urban Ecosystems* 20, no. 2: 323–35.

Branduini, Paola, Raffaella Laviscio, Lionella Scazzosi, Jan Supuka, and Attila Tóth. 2016. “Urban Agriculture and Cultural Heritage: A Historical and Spatial Relationship.” In *Urban Agriculture Europe*, edited by Frank Lohrberg, Lilli Lička, Lionella Scazzosi, and Axel Timpe, 138–48. Berlin: Jovis.

Costa, Sandra, Runrid Fox-Kämper, Russell Good, and Ivana Sentić. 2016. “The Position of Urban Allotment Gardens within the Urban Fabric.” In Bell et al. 2016, 201–28.

Crouch, David, and Colin Ward. 1997. *The Allotment: Its Landscape and Culture*. Nottingham: Five Leaves.

Dekánek, Štefan. 1971. *Záhradkové osady: Vzorová predloha*

prednášky [Allotment colonies – patterns and models]. Bratislava: Slovenský ovocinársky a záhradkársky zväz, Ústredný výbor.

Drescher, A. W., Robert Holmer, and David Iaquinta. 2006. "Urban Home Gardens and Allotment Gardens for Sustainable Livelihoods: Management Strategies and Institutional Environments." In *Tropical Homegardens*, edited by B. M. Kumar and P. K. R. Nair, 317–38. Dordrecht: Springer.

Drilling, Matthias, Renata Giedych, and Lidia Poniży. 2016. "The Idea of Allotment Gardens and the Role of Spatial and Urban Planning." In Bell et al. 2016, 35–61.

Duží, Barbora, Attila Tóth, Mária Bihuňová, and Robert Stojanov. 2014. "Challenges of Urban Agriculture: Highlights on the Czech and Slovak Republic Specifics." In *Current Challenges of Central Europe: Society and Environment*, edited by Jan Vávra, Miloslav Lapka, and Eva Cudlínová, 82–107. Prague: Charles University.

Gilbert, Paul Robert. 2013. "Deskilling, Agrodiversity, and the Seed Trade: A View from Contemporary British Allotments." In *Agriculture and Human Values* 30. no. 1: 101–14.

Glotter, K. 2007. "The Allotment Garden House in Vienna: Future of Allotment Gardening." In *Documentation Allotment Gardens with a Future - Livable City*. Hamburg: Behörde für Stadtentwicklung und Umwelt.

Grantham, George. 1989. "Agricultural Supply during the Industrial Revolution: French Evidence and European Implications." In *The Journal of Economic History* 49, no. 1: 43–72. http://www.jstor.org/stable/2121417. Accessed April 17, 2021.

Hall, Peter, and Mark Tewdwr-Jones. 2010. *Urban and Regional Planning*. 5th ed. Abingdon: Routledge.

Keshavarz, Nazila, Simon Bell, Andis Zilans, Andrew Hursthouse, et al. 2016. "A History of Urban Gardens in Europe." In Bell et al. 2016, 8–32.

King, Heather. 2007. "Allotments as Cultural Artifacts." In *Material Culture Review*, no. 65: 47–65. https://journals.lib.unb.ca/index.php/MCR/article/view/18086. Accessed November 10, 2021.

Lawson, Laura. 2005. *City Bountiful: A Century of Community Gardening in America*. Berkeley: University of California Press.

Maćkiewicz, Barbara, Magdalena Szczepańska, Ewa Kacprzak, and Runrid Fox-Kämper. 2021. "Between Food Growing and Leisure: Contemporary Allotment Gardeners in Western Germany and Poland." In *Die Erde - Journal of the Geographical Society of Berlin* 152, no. 1: 33–50.

Pawlikowska-Piechotka, Anna. 2010. *The Tradition of Allotment Gardens in Poland*. Gdynia: Novae Res.

Supuka, Jan, Lubica Feriancová, and Attila Tóth. 2013. "Mestské po nohospodárstvo – tradície a nové cesty rozvoja" [Urban Agriculture – Traditions and New Ways of Development]. In *Životné prostredie* 47, no. 4: 237–41.

Tóth, Attila, Barbora Duží, Jan Vávra, Ján Supuka, Mária Bihuňová, Denisa Halajová, Stanislav Martinát, and Eva Nováková. 2018. "Changing Patterns of Allotment Gardening in the Czech Republic and Slovakia." In *Nature and Culture* 13, no. 2: 161–88.

Tóth, Atilla, and Axel Timpe. 2017. "Exploring Urban Agriculture as a Component of Multifunctional Green Infrastructure: Application of Figure-Ground Plans as a Spatial Analysis Tool." In *Moravian Geographical Reports* 25, no. 3: 208–18.

Tvardková, Veronika, and Eliška Rolfová. 2013. "Zahrádkové osady v Evropě i u nás: Historie zahrádkových osad." In *Zahrádkové osady: Sníny minulosti, nebo záblesky budoucnosti?*, edited by Petr Gibras et al., 29–46. Prague: Univerzita Karlova v Praze.

Van den Berg, Agnes, Marijke van Winsum-Westra, Sjerp de Vries, and Sonja M. E. van Dillen. 2010. "Allotment Gardening and Health: A Comparative Survey among Allotment Gardeners and Their Neighbors without an Allotment." In *Environmental Health* 9, no. 1: 74–86.

Russian Dachas: A Popular Urban Agricultural Heritage

Johanna Altendorf, Jay Heydecke, Katharina Christenn, Axel Timpe

Boukharaeva, Louiza, and Marcel Marloie. 2015. *Family Urban Agriculture in Russia*. Cham: Springer.

Dornblüth, Gesine. 2018. "Der Russe und seine Datscha: Kleines Glück im Grünen." In *Deutschlandfunk Kultur*, December 8, 2018. https://www.deutschlandfunkkultur.de/der-russe-und-seine-datscha-kleines-glueck-im-gruenen.1076.de.html?dram:article_id=425055. Accessed October 27, 2020.

Grimonpont, Arthur. 2019. "Les collectifs de jardins russes: une organisation résiliente" [Russian garden collectives: a resilient organization]. In *Les Greniers d'Abondance*, April 28, 2020. https://resiliencealimentaire.org/les-collectifs-de-jardins-russes-une-organisation-resiliente/. Accessed July 1, 2020.

Nikolaeva, Uliana G., and Alexander V. Rusanov. 2020. "Self-isolation at the Dacha: Can't? Can? Have to?" In *Population and Economics* 4, no. 2: 182–98. https://population-andeconomics.pensoft.net/article/54577/. Accessed March 3, 2021.

Ortar, Nathalie. 2005. "Les multiples usages de la datcha des jardins collectifs" [The Multiple Uses of the Dacha Allotments in Russia]. In *Anthropologie et Sociétés* 29, no. 2: 169–85. https://www.erudit.org/en/journals/as/2005-v29-n2-as1018/011900ar/. Accessed March 5, 2021.

Rumjanzewa, Marina. 2017. *Auf der Datscha: Eine kleine Kulturgeschichte*. Berlin: Dörlemann.

Russian Federation. 2017. "Федеральный закон No. 217-ФЗ 'О ведении гражданами садоводства и огородничества для собственных нужд и о внесении изменений в отдельные законодательные акты Российской Федерации.'" [Federal Law No. 217-FZ "On gardening and horticulture for individual personal needs"], in force January 1, 2019. http://www.fao.org/faolex/results/details/fr/c/LEX-FAOC172684/. Accessed October 27, 2020.

Semyonov, V. 2017. "Общая площадь дачных участков в России составляет десять территорий Москвы" [The total area of dacha plots in Russia covers ten territories of Moscow]. All-Russian newspaper of independent journalistic investigations *Our Version* [Наша версия], September 8, 2017. https://versia.ru/obshhaya-ploshhad-dachnyx-uchastov-v-rossii-sostavlyaet-desyat-territorij-moskvy. Accessed November 1, 2020.

Statista. 2019. "Russland: Grad der Urbanisierung bis 2019." *Statista*. https://de.statista.com/statistik/daten/studie/171395/umfrage/urbanisierung-in russland/. Accessed June 5, 2020.

Resilient Cities with Urban Agricultural Heritage: Tokyo, Japan

Giles B. Sioen, Makoto Yokohari

Armstrong, Donna. 2000. "A Survey of Community Gardens in Upstate New York: Implications for Health Promotion and Community Development." In *Health & Place* 6, no. 4: 319–27.

Elmqvist, Thomas, Heikki Setälä, Steven N. Handel, S. van der Ploeg, James Aronson, James Nelson Blignaut, E. Gómez-Baggethun, David J. Nowak, Jakub Kronenberg, and Rudolf de Groot. 2015. "Benefits of Restoring Ecosystem Services in Urban Areas." In *Current Opinion in Environmental Sustainability* 14: 101–8.

Hirohara, Takashi, Makoto Yokohari, Yoshitake Kato, and Takashi Watanabe. 2002. "A Study of the Small-Scaled Material Cyclic between Urban and Rural Land Uses in Urban Fringe Areas of Tokyo." In *The Japanese Institute of Landscape Architecture* 65, no. 5: 889–92.

Jarzebski, Marcin Pawel, Thomas Elmqvist, Alexandros Gasparatos,

Kensuke Fukushi, Sofia Eckersten, Dagmar Haase, Julie Goodness, Sara Khoshkar, Osamu Saito, Kazuhiko Takeuchi, Töres Theorell, Nannan Dong, Fumiko Kasuga, Ryugo Watanabe, Giles Bruno Sioen, Makoto Yokohari, and Jian Pu. 2021. "Ageing and Population Shrinking: Implications for Sustainability in the Urban Century." In *npj Urban Sustainability* 17, no. 1: 1–11.

Kochizu Library Co. Ltd. 2021. "Edo Kiriezu Honjo Ezuzu." Figure nos. 1–18. http://oldmap.jp/j/oldmap/edo/102.html. Accessed November 15, 2021.

Langemeyer, Johannes, Monika Joanna Latkowska, and Erik Nicolas Gomez-Baggethun. 2016. "Ecosystem Services from Urban Gardens." In *Urban Allotment Gardens in Europe*, edited by Simon Bell, Runrid Fox-Kämper, Nazila Keshavarz, Mary Benson, Silvio Caputo, Susan Noori, and Annette Voigt, 115–41. London: Routledge.

La Rosa, Daniele, Luca Barbarossa, Riccardo Privitera, and Francesco Martinico. 2014. "Agriculture and the City: A Method for Sustainable Planning of New Forms of Agriculture in Urban Contexts." In *Land Use Policy* 41: 290–303.

Lee-Smith, Diana. 2010. "Cities Feeding People: An Update on Urban Agriculture in Equatorial Africa." In *Environment and Urbanization* 22, no. 2: 483–99.

Lin, Brenda B., Stacy M. Philpott, and Shalene Jha. 2015. "The Future of Urban Agriculture and Biodiversity-Ecosystem Services: Challenges and Next Steps." In *Basic and Applied Ecology* 16, no. 3: 189–201.

Minami, Ryōshin, Kwan S. Kim, and Malcolm Falkus, eds. 1999. *Growth, Distribution and Political Change: Asia and the Wider World*. London: Springer.

Ministry of Agriculture, Forestry and Fisheries of Japan. 2011. "The Importance of Urban Agriculture." In *Ministry of Agriculture, Forestry and Fisheries*. http://www.maff.go.jp/j/wpaper/w_maff/h18_h/trend/1/t1_3_4_02.html. Accessed February 4, 2017.

Muramatsu, Naoko, and Hiroko Akiyama. 2011. "Japan: Super-Aging Society Preparing for the Future." In *The Gerontologist* 51, no. 4: 425–32.

Nakazawa, Takashi, and Shigeru Beppu. 2012. "Shifting from Emergency Food to Disaster Preparation Food to Help Disaster Survivors." In *Science and Technology Trends Quarterly Review*, no. 44: 36–52.

OECD. 2016. "Working Party on Agricultural Policies and Markets: Cross-Country Comparison of Farm Size Distribution." Paris: OECD Publishing.

Okata, Junichiro, and Akito Murayama. 2011. "Tokyo's Urban Growth, Urban Form, and Sustainability." In *Megacities: Urban Form, Governance and Sustainability*, edited by Andre Sorensen and Junichiro Okata, 15–41. Tokyo: Springer.

Rowe, John W., and Robert L. Kahn. 1987. "Human Aging: Usual and Successful." In *Science* 237, no. 4811: 143–49.

Rowe, John W., and Robert L. Kahn. 1997. "Successful Aging." In *The Gerontologist* 37, no. 4: 433–40.

Sardeshpande, Mallika, Christoph D. Rupprecht, and Alessio Russo. 2020. "Edible Urban Commons for Resilient Neighbourhoods in Light of the Pandemic." In *Cities* 109, no. 2. DOI:10.1016/j.cities.2020.103031.

Shiraishi, Masumi. 2001. "The Preservation and Use of Scarce Agricultural Land in Suburban Areas." NLI Research no. 148. Tokyo: NLI Research Institute.

Shiraishi, Yoshitaka. 2001. *Tokai no hyakushōdesu. Yoroshiku* [I'm an urban farmer. Nice to meet you.]. Tokyo: Komonzu.

Sioen, Giles, Makiko Sekiyama, Toru Terada, and Makoto Yokohari. 2017. "Post-Disaster Food and Nutrition from Urban Agriculture: A Self-Sufficiency Analysis of Nerima." *International Journal of Environmental Research and Public Health* 748, no. 14: 1–20.

Sioen, Giles, Toru Terada, Makiko Sekiyama, and Makoto Yokohari. 2018. "Resilience with Mixed Agricultural and Urban Land Uses in Tokyo, Japan." In *Sustainability* 10, no. 2: 435.

Sioen, Giles, Toru Terada, and Makoto Yokohari. 2016. "Neighborhood Self-Sufficiency in Tokyo: How Much Can Hobby Farms Contribute?" In *Growing in Cities*, edited by Simone Tappert, 440–53. Basel: University of Applied Sciences.

Slavin, Joanne L., and Beate Lloyd. 2012. "Health Benefits of Fruits and Vegetables." In *Advances in Nutrition* 3, no. 4: 506–16.

Statistics Bureau, Japan Ministry of Internal Affairs and Communications. 2016a. "2015 Population Census: Basic Complete Tabulation on Population and Households." *e-Stat*, http://www.e-stat.go.jp/SG1/estat/GL38020103.do?_toGL38020103_&tclassID=000001077438&cycleCode=0&requestSender=estat. Accessed January 15, 2021.

Statistics Bureau, Japan Ministry of Internal Affairs and Communications. 2016b. "Statistical Handbook of Japan 2016." Tokyo: Statistics Bureau, Japan Ministry of Internal Affairs and Communications.

Tahara, Shinichi, Sayaka Shioyama, Hideharu Kurita, and Toru Terada. 2011. "A Quantitative Assessment of Agricultural Production from Allotment Gardens." In *Journal of the Japanese Institute of Landscape Architecture* 74, no. 5: 685–88.

The World Bank. 2016. "Urban population (% of total)." http://data.worldbank.org/indicator/SP.URB.TOTL.IN.ZS?end=2015&locations=JP&start=1973&year_high_desc=true. Accessed February 4, 2017.

Tokyo Metropolitan Government. 2015. "Tokyo Disaster Prevention Plan: Becoming the World's Safest, Most Secure City." Shinjuku, Tokyo: Disaster Prevention Department of Tokyo.

Tokyo Metropolitan Government. 2016. "Land Use Data, Tokyo 2015." Tokyo: Tokyo Metropolitan Government.

Van den Berg, Agnes E., Marijke van Winsum-Westra, Sjerp de Vries, and Sonja M. E. van Dillen. 2010. "Allotment Gardening and Health: A Comparative Survey among Allotment Gardeners and Their Neighbors without an Allotment." In *Environmental Health: A Global Access Science Source* 9, no. 1: 74.

Wilkins, Jennifer L., Tracy J. Farrell, and Anusuya Rangarajan. 2015. "Linking Vegetable Preferences, Health and Local Food Systems through Community-Supported Agriculture." In *Public Health Nutrition* 18, no. 13: 2392–401.

Yokohari, Makoto, and Marco Amati. 2005. "Nature in the City, City in the Nature: Case Studies of the Restoration of Urban Nature in Tokyo, Japan and Toronto, Canada." In *Landscape and Ecological Engineering* 1, no. 1: 53–59.

Yokohari, Makoto, and Jay Bolthouse. 2011. "Planning for the Slow Lane: The Need to Restore Working Greenspaces in Maturing Contexts." In *Landscape and Urban Planning* 100, no. 4: 421–24.

Yokohari, Makoto, Robert D. Brown, Yoshitake Kato, and Hideki Moriyama. 1997. "Effects of Paddy Fields on Summertime Air and Surface Temperatures in Urban Fringe Areas of Tokyo, Japan." In *Landscape and Urban Planning* 38, no. 1–2: 1–11.

Belgrade's Garden Colonies: Where Memory, Nature, and People Meet

Slavica Čepić, Dragana Ćorović, Jelena Tomićević-Dubljević

Adžić, T. 2012. "Urbane baštenske kolonije na užoj teritoriji Beograda, značaj i upotreba." Master's thesis, University of Belgrade.

Barthel, Stephan, Carl Folke, and Johan Colding. 2010. "Social-Ecological Memory in Urban Gardens: Retaining the Capacity for Management of Ecosystem Services." In *Global Environmental Change* 20, no. 2: 255–65.

Blagojević, Ljiljana. 2005. "Back to the Future of New Belgrade: Functional Past of the Modern City."

Paper presented at 2005 AESOP Annual Congress, Vienna, Austria.

Čepić, Slavica, Jelena Tomićević-Dubljević, and Ivana Živojinović. 2020. "Is There a Demand for Collective Urban Gardens? Needs and Motivations of Potential Gardeners in Belgrade." In *Urban Forestry and Urban Greening* 53. DOI: 10.1016/j.ufug.2020.126716.

Crouch, David. 1989. "The Allotment, Landscape and Locality: Ways of Seeing Landscape and Culture." In *Area* 21, no. 3: 261–67.

Crouch, David. 1993. "Representing Ourselves in the Landscape: Cultural Meanings in Everyday Landscape." In *Continuities in Popular Culture: The Present in the Past & the Past in the Present and Future*, edited by Ray B. Browne and Ronald J. Ambrosetti, 26–48. Bowling Green, OH: Bowling Green State University Popular Press.

Djokić, Vladan, Jelena Ristić Trajković, Danilo Furundžić, Verica Krstić, and Danica Stojiljković. 2018. "Urban Garden as Lived Space: Informal Gardening Practices and Dwelling Culture in Socialist and Post-Socialist Belgrade." In *Urban Forestry & Urban Greening* 30: 247–59.

Gulin Zrnić, Valentina, and Tihana Rubić. 2018. "City-Making through Urban Gardening: Public Space and Civic Engagement in Zagreb." In *Narodna Umjetnost*, 55, no. 1: 159–79.

Krstić, Aleksandar. 1932. "Baštenske kolonije." In *Beogradske Opštinske Novine* 50, no. 3: 206–214.

Mendelson, Andrija. 1975. "Nova stambena naselja kao oblik razvoja Beograda." In *Urbanizam Beograda* 30: 17–21.

Olick, Jeffrey K., and Joyce Robbins. 1998. "Social Memory Studies: From 'Collective Memory' to the Historical Sociology of Mnemonic Practices." In *Annual Review of Sociology* 24: 105–40.

Slavuj Borčić, Lana, Marin Cvitanović, and Aleksandar Lukić. 2016. "Cultivating Alternative Spaces: Zagreb's Community Gardens in Transition: From Socialist to Post-socialist Perspective." In *Geoforum* 77: 51–60.

Stojanović, Bratislav. 1975. "Za analitički osvrt na dosadašnju stambenu gradnju." In *Urbanizam Beograda* 30: 22–62.

Tomić, Velimir. 1981. "Osnovne karakteristike programa društveno-ekonomskog i prostornog razvoja grada Beograda za period od 1981. do 1990. godine." *Urbanizam Beograda* 63–65: 33–42.

UNESCO. 2011. "Recommendation on the Historic Urban Landscape." https://whc.unesco.org/uploads/activities/documents/activity-638-98.pdf. Accessed November 12, 2021.

Urban Planning Institute of Belgrade. 2007. "The Key for Biotope Mapping." Belgrade: Urban Planning Institute of Belgrade.

Urban Planning Institute of Belgrade. 2019. "General Regulation Plan of the System of Green Areas of Belgrade" Belgrade: Urban Planning Institute of Belgrade.

Vuksanović-Macura, Zlata, and Dragana Ćorović. 2013. "Green Areas in Belgrade's Old Center: Transformation from Gardens to Parks." In *Stara gradska jezgra i istorijske urbane celine: problemi i mogućnosti očuvanja i upravljanja*, edited by Svetlana Dimitrijević Marković, 218–34. Belgrade: Zavod za zaštitu spomenika kulture grada Beograda.

Vuksanović-Macura, Zlata, and Dragana Ćorović. 2016. "From Ottoman Gardens to European Parks: Transformation of Green Spaces in Belgrade." In *Landscape Values: Place and Praxis*, edited by Gesche Kindermann, Nessa Cronin, Conor Newman, and Tim Collins, 382–87. Galway: Centre for Landscape Studies, NUI Galway.

From Marshes to Market Gardens: Hortillonnages d'Amiens and Marais de Bourges

Leandra Brunet, Nicole Laufhütte, Axel Timpe, Katharina Christenn

L'Association des Maraîchers de Bourges. 2009a. "La terre et l'eau." Updated 2013. http://spardasv.free.fr/joomla/index.php?option=com_content&view=article&id=6:la-terre-et-leau&catid=2:les-marais&Itemid=2. Accessed October 16, 2020.

L'Association des Maraîchers de Bourges. 2009b. "L'Association des Maraîchers de Bourges. Accueil: l'AMB." Updated 2013. http://spardasv.free.fr/joomla/. Accessed November 5, 2021.

L'Association des Maraîchers de Bourges. 2009c. "Qui sommes nous?" Updated 2013. http://spardasv.free.fr/joomla/index.php?option=com_content&view=article&id=3&Itemid=3. Accessed October 16, 2020.

L'Association des Maraîchers de Bourges. 2009d. "Les marais de demain." Updated 2013. http://spardasv.free.fr/joomla/index.php?option=com_content& view=article&id=5:les-marais-de-demain&catid=2:les-marais& Itemid=2. Accessed October 16, 2020.

Clauzel, Céline. 2008a. "Dynamiques de l'occupation du sol et mutations des usages dans les zones humides urbaines: Étude comparée des hortillonnages d'Amiens (France) et des chinampas de Xochimilco (Mexique)." PhD diss., Université Paris-Sorbonne. https://tel.archives-ouvertes.fr/tel-00351695/document.

Clauzel, Céline. 2008b. "Mutations des hortillonnages d'Amiens vers une agriculture multifonctionnelle et urbaine: Hortillonnages d'Amiens et agriculture urbaine." In *Economies et Sociétés Série Systèmes agroalimentaires* 42: 2297–307. https://hal.archives-ouvertes.fr/hal-00359445/document.

Conan, Michel. 1993. "The Hortillonnages: Reflections on a Vanishing Gardeners' Culture." In *The Vernacular Garden*, edited by John Dixon Hunt and Joachim Wolschke-Bulmahn, 19–46. Washington, DC: Dumbarton Oaks Research Library & Collection.

Donadieu, Pierre. 1999. "Des marais dans la ville." In *Zones Humides Infos*, edited by the Société nationale de protection de la nature, 2–5. https://www.snpn.com/wp-content/uploads/2016/08/ZHI-23.pdf. Accessed October 28, 2020.

Fleury, André. 1998. "Agriculture urbaine: Nature, agriculture et ville les mutations d'usage des marais cultivés au coeur des villes." Updated December 12, 2011. http://www7.inra.fr/dpenv/aurb19.htm. Accessed October 13, 2020.

Lajoinie, Guillaume. 2019. "Guillaume, un maraîcher optimiste qui plante avec le sourire!" Updated October 11, 2019. https://www.bourgesberrytourisme.com/2019/10/11/guillaume-un-maraicher-optimiste-qui-plante-avec-le-sourire/. Accessed October 16, 2020.

Les Hortillonnages d'Amiens. n.d. (a). "Association pour la protection et la sauvegarde des Hortillonnages." http://www.hortillonnages-amiens.fr/infos-pratiques/association-protection-sauvegarde-hortillonnages.html. Accessed October 11, 2020.

Les Hortillonnages d'Amiens. n.d. (b). "Histoire des hortillonnages d'Amiens." http://www.hortillonnages-amiens.fr/histoire/. Accessed October 11, 2020.

Les Hortillonnages d'Amiens. n.d. (c). "Le marché sur l'eau des Hortillonnages." http://www.hortillonnages-amiens.fr/evenements/marche-sur-eau.html. Accessed October 11, 2020.

Limouzin, Pierre. 1994. "Une agriculture périurbaine en voie de banalisation: l'exemple amiénois." In *Bulletin de l'Association de Géographes Français*, 156–59. https://www.persee.fr/doc/bagf_0004-5322_1994_num_71_2_1730. Accessed October 7, 2020.

Morris, Sandra. 1999. "Parc St. Pierre, Amiens." In *Relating Architecture to Landscape*, edited by Jan Birksted, 269–80. London: E&FN Spon.

Musset, Alain. 2003. “L’agriculture sur l’eau en milieu urbain: Les hortillonnages d’Amiens et les chinampas de Xochimilco.” In *Bulletin de l’Association de Géographes Français*: 325–37. https://www.persee.fr/doc/bagf_0004-5322_2003_num_80_3_2339. Accessed October 7, 2020.

Narboux, Roland. 2010. *Les Marais de Bourges*. Romorantin: Communication-presse-édition.

Patrimoine Marais. n.d. (a). “L’association: Présentation.” https://www.patrimoine-marais.org/associationpatrimoinemarais. Accessed October 16, 2020.

Patrimoine Marais. n.d. (b). “L’association: Nos réalisations et actions.” https://www.patrimoine-marais.org/nos-realisations-et-actions. Accessed October 16, 2020.

From Orchard to Wetland Park: Guangzhou’s Approach to Transform Urban Agricultural Heritage
Mengyun Chen, Guangsi Lin

Astudillo Miguel F., Gunnar Thalwitz, and Fritz Vollrath. 2015. “Modern Analysis of an Ancient Integrated Farming Arrangement: Life Cycle Assessment of a Mulberry Dyke and Pond System.” In *International Journal of Life Cycle Assessment* 20, no. 10: 1387–98.

Dahiya, Bharat. 2012. “Cities in Asia, 2012: Demographics Economics, Poverty, Environment and Governance.” In *Cities* 29: 44–61.

Gongfu, Zhong. 1982. “The Mulberry Dike-Fish Pond Complex: A Chinese Ecosystem of Land-Water Interaction on the Pearl River Delta.” In *Human Ecology* 10, no. 2: 191–202.

Shidong, Chen, and Yuan Qifeng. 2017. “Urban Ecosphere Structure and Its Resilience Evolution: Theoretical Framework and Empirical Analysis of Guangzhou.” In *Planners* 33, no. 8: 25–30 (in Chinese).

UNESCO. 2011. “Recommendation on the Historic Urban Landscape.” UNESCO World Heritage Centre, Paris. https://whc.unesco.org/uploads/activities/documents/activity-638-98.pdf. Accessed February 18, 2021.

Urban Agricultural Heritage of Lisbon: From the Past to the Future?
Mariana Sanchez Salvador

Barata, Ana. 2010. *Lisboa “Caes da Europa”: Realidades, desejos e ficções para a cidade (1860–1930)*. Lisbon: Edições Colibri.

Brito, Raquel Soeiro de. 1976. “Lisboa: esboço geográfico.” Special edition of *Boletim Cultural da Junta Distrital de Lisboa* 3, no. 82.

CML – Câmara Municipal de Lisboa. 2012. “Regulamento do Plano Diretor Municipal de Lisboa.” Lisbon: Câmara Municipal de Lisboa. https://informacoeseservicos.lisboa.pt/fileadmin/download_center/normativas/regulamentos/urbanismo/Regulamento_PDM.pdf. Accessed November 23, 2021.

CML – Câmara Municipal de Lisboa. 2015. “Biodiversidade na cidade de Lisboa: Uma estratégia para 2020.” Lisbon: Câmara Municipal de Lisboa. https://issuu.com/camara_municipal_lisboa/docs/biodiversidade_estrat_2020. Accessed November 22, 2021.

CML – Câmara Municipal de Lisboa. 2018. “Parques Hortícolas Municipais.” Lisbon: Câmara Municipal de Lisboa. http://www.cm-lisboa.pt/viver/ambiente/parques-horticolas-municipais. Accessed November 22, 2021.

FAO – Food and Agriculture Organization of the United Nations. 2019. “FAO Framework for the Urban Food Agenda: Leveraging Sub-National and Local Government Action to Ensure Sustainable Food Systems and Improved Nutrition.” Rome: Food and Agriculture Organization of the United Nations – FAO. http://www.fao.org/3/CA3151EN/ca3151en.pdf.

Folgosa, Rita. 2020. Interview with author, Lisbon, July 31, 2020. [Recording in possession of author.]

Gaspar, Jorge. 1994. “Génese de uma paisagem.” In *Rassegna*, no. 59 (Lisboa): 82–88.

Henriques da Silva, Raquel. 1994. “Lisboa das Avenidas Novas.” In *Rassegna*, no. 59 (Lisboa): 44–51.

Marat-Mendes, Teresa, Patrícia Bento d’Almeida, and Joana Mourão. 2015. “A legenda do levantamento da Planta de Lisboa do Engenheiro Silva Pinto.” In *Arquivo Municipal de Lisboa: Um Acervo para a História*, edited by A. A. Santos, E. M. Alberto, and M. J. P. Coutinho, 275–87. Lisbon: Arquivo Municipal de Lisboa. Câmara Municipal de Lisboa. http://arquivomunicipal.cm-lisboa.pt/pt/eventos/conferencias-jornadas/conferencias-coloquios/um-acervo-para-a-historia-ii/livro-de-comunicacoes/.

Marat-Mendes, Teresa, Patrícia Bento d’Almeida, Joana Mourão, Samuel Niza, and Daniela Ferreira. 2014. “Mapping Lisbon Agriculture (1898–1911).” EUAH Conference, https://memoproject.files.wordpress.com/2014/12/mapping-lisbon-agriculture_23_07_2014.pdf. Accessed November 22, 2021.

Marat-Mendes, Teresa, Joana Mourão, Patrícia Bento d’Almeida, and Samuel Niza. 2015. *Atlas da água e da agricultura: Região de Lisboa em 1900–1940* [Water and Agriculture Atlas: Lisbon Region in 1900–1940]. Lisbon: Instituto Universitário de Lisboa ISCTE-IUL.

Niza, Samuel, Daniela Ferreira, Teresa Marat-Mendes, Joana Mourão, and Patrícia Bento d’Almeida. 2014. “The Metabolic Behavior of Lisbon Metropolitan Area from the Pre-Industrial Period to the Present.” EUAH Conference, https://memoproject.files.wordpress.com/2014/12/niza_metabolism_lisboneuah.pdf. Accessed November 22, 2021.

Pereira, Miriam H. 1971. *Livre Câmbio e Desenvolvimento Económico*. Lisbon: Edições Cosmos.

Ribeiro, L. F. 1992. *Quintas do Concelho de Lisboa: Inventário, Caracterização e Salvaguarda*. Lisbon: Instituto Superior de Agronomia.

Trindade, María José Lagos, and Jorge Gaspar. 1973/1974. “A utilização agrária do solo em torno de Lisboa, na Idade Média, e a Teoria de Von Thünen,” In *Boletim Cultural da Junta Distrital de Lisboa* 2, nos. 79–80: 3–11.

Urban Agricultural Heritage in Benin: The Role of Traditional Coconut-Cattle Systems in Cotonou
Bossima I. Koura, Eric Boenecke, Frank Lohrberg, Luc H. Dossa

Aboh, André Boya, Kahina Mekhtoub, Souleymane Ouedraogo, Hong Hanh Pham Thi, and Angela María Rivera. 2001. *Importance, contraintes et voies de développement des élevages urbains et périurbains dans la région Sud du Bénin*. Cotonou: ICRA/GTZ/INRAB.

Adeniji, K.O. 1985. “Review of Endangered Cattle Breeds of Africa.” In *Animal Genetic Resources in Africa: High Potential and Endangered Livestock*, 20–32. Nairobi: OAU/STRC/IBAR.

Ahozonlin, Maurice Cossi, Ivan Bossima Koura, and Luc Hippolyte Dossa. 2019. “Determinants of Crossbreeding Practices by Cattle Farmers in South Benin, West Africa: Implications for the Sustainable Use of the Indigenous Lagune Cattle Population.” In *Sustainable Agriculture Research* 8, no. 2: 101–9.

Ahozonlin, Maurice Cossi, and Luc Hippolyte Dossa 2020. “Diversity and Resilience to Socio-Ecological Changes of Smallholder Lagune Cattle Farming Systems of Benin.” In *Sustainability* 12, no. 18: 7616.

Albéca, Alexandre. 1895. *La France au Dahomey*. Paris: Hachette Livre.

Childs, A. H. B., and C. G. Groom. 1964. “Balanced Farming with Cattle and Coconuts.” In *East African Agricultural and Forestry Journal* 29, no. 3: 206–7.

Cornevin, Robert. 1970. *Le Dahomey*. Paris: Presses Universitaires de France.

ECARESE. 2019. *Effets combinés des activités anthropiques et de la variabilité climatique sur les ressources naturelles et systèmes d'élevage du cordon littoral du Bénin: Rapport final du projet.* Cotonou: Fonds National de la Recherche Scientifique et de l'Innovation Technologique.

FAO – Food and Agriculture Organization of the United Nations. 1994. "Identification and Characterization of West African Shorthorn Cattle." In *World Animal Review* 78, no. 1.

FAO – Food and Agriculture Organization of the United Nations. 2012. *Growing Greener Cities in Africa: First Status Report on Urban and Peri-Urban Horticulture in Africa.* Rome: Food and Agriculture Organization of the United Nations.

Floquet, Anne, and Juste Nansi. 2005. "Plus de place en ville pour les boeufs? La filière bovine face à l'expansion urbaine à Abomey et Bohicon (Bénin)." *Cebedes, Document de travail Ecocité* no. 4, www.ecocite.org.

Herrero, Mario, Philip K. Thornton, Pierre Gerber, and Robin Reid. 2009. "Livestock, Livelihoods and the Environment: Understanding the Trade-offs." In *Current Opinion in Environmental Sustainability* 1, no. 2: 111–20.

INSAE (Institut National de la Statistique et de l'Analyse Economique). 2012. "Statistiques/Statistiques Economiques/Production agricole, Bénin." http://www.insae-bj.org/productionagricole.html. Accessed September 23, 2019.

Koohafkan, Parviz, and Miguel A. Altieri. 2011. *Globally Important Agricultural Heritage Systems: A Legacy for the Future.* Rome: Food and Agriculture Organization of the United Nations.

Koura, Ivan Bossima. 2011. "Stratégies d'alimentation des élevages périurbains de bovins au sud-Bénin: caractéristiques et dynamique sur le cordon littoral sableux des communes d'Abomey-Calavi et de Ouidah." Thesis, Université d'Abomey-Calavi.

Koura, Ivan Bossima, Luc Hippolyte Dossa, Barthélémy Kassa, and Marcel Houinato. 2015. "Adaptation of Peri-Urban Cattle Production System to Environmental Changes: Herders Feeding Strategies in Southern Benin." In *Agroecology and Sustainable Food Systems* 39, no. 1: 83–98.

MAEP-CNN. 2004. *Etat des ressources zoogénétiques: rapport national.* Cotonou: MAEP.

Msellati, Laurent, Jean-Michel Bergès, D. Delzescaux, and Dominque Planchenault, eds. 1993. *Elevage sous cocoteraie: Intégration et diversification, exemple du Vanuatu.* Montpellier: CIRAD-EMVT.

Railliet, Alcide, and Gabriel Petit, eds. 1912. *Bulletin de la société centrale de médecine vétérinaire*, vol. 66. Paris, Asselin et Houzeau.

RB-MAEP. 2021. "Aménagement de la zone balnéaire: Les pépinières de production de plants de cocotiers à Sèmè-Podji accueillent les ministres Dossouhoui et Tonato." In *Programme Gouvernemental de plantation de cocotiers le long de la côte Atlantique.* https://www.gouv.bj/actualite/1260/amenagement-zone-balneaire-pepinieres-production-plants-cocotiers-seme-podji-accueillent-ministres-dossouhoui-tonato/. Accessed November 23, 2021.

Rege, Edward, Gertrude S. Aboagye, and Chi L. Tawah. 1994. "Shorthorn Cattle of West and Central Africa II: Ecological Settings, Utility, Management and Production Systems." In *World Animal Review* no. 78 ("Identification and Characterization of West African Shorthorn Cattle").

Sandrine, Houessou O., Luc Hippolyte Dossa, Rodrigue Diogo, Marcel Houinato, Andreas Buerkert, and Eva Schlecht. 2019. "Change and Continuity in Traditional Cattle Farming Systems of West African Coast Countries: A Case Study from Benin." In *Agricultural Systems* 168: 112–22.

La Vega de Granada: A Cultural Landscape Built Around Irrigation

Anna Kerfers, Ardiana Rahimi, Axel Timpe, Katharina Christenn

Cáceres Paco. 2013. "Concha López: 'La dinamización de la vega pasa por activar la producción agraria para que sea la despensa de Granada' Agricultora Ecológia y Pionera en la Vega de Granada." https://www.otragranada.org/spip.php?article653&lang=es. Accessed November 2, 2020.

Castillo Ruiz, José. 2010. "La vega de Granada: La construcción cultural de un territorio a través de la actividad agraria." In *Revista PH*, no. 74: 20–27.

Castillo Ruiz, José, Alberto Matarán Ruiz. 2020. "La Vega de Granada: The Defence of a Paradigmatic Agrarian Heritage Space by Local Citizens." In *AgriCultura: Urban Agriculture and the Heritage Potential of Agrarian Landscape*, edited by Lionella Scazzosi and Paola Branduini, 225–43. Basel: Springer International Publishing.

García Leal, Ana. 2014. "Patrimonio Agrario en la Vega de Granada: Los regadíos del río Dílar." In *Revista electrónica de Patrimonio*, no. 14: 4–33.

Gimeno García, H., R. González Lera, and G. Guzmán Casado. 2006. "El manejo tradicional de las huertas en la provincia de Granada: Estudios de caso de la Vega de Granada y el parque natural de Castril." In *VII Congreso SEAE Zaragoza*, 1–11.

Junta de Andalucia. 2017. "Plan especial de ordenacion de la Vega de Granada: Memoria de informacion y diagnostico." Seville: Consejería de Medio Ambiente y Ordenación del Territorio.

Puente Asuero, Raúl. 2013. "La Vega de Granada: De un espacio agrario en crisis a un complejo paisaje cultural." In *Revista de estudios regionales*, no. 96: 181–213.

Trillo San José, Carmen. 2005. "A Social Analysis of Irrigation in Al-Andalus: Nazari Granada (13th–15th Centuries)." In *Journal of Medieval History* 31, no. 2: 163–83.

Zurita Povedano, Eduardo. 2015. "Nuevas aproximaciones a un paisaje agrario de interés cultural: La vega de Granada." PhD diss., Universidad de Granada.

Hidden Urban Agricultural Heritage at the Manzanares River: Toward an Agro-ecological Wedge in the Southeast of Madrid City

Nerea Morán, Marian Simón Rojo

Ayuntamiento de Madrid. n.d. "Concurso Bosque Metropolitano." https://estrategiaurbana.madrid.es/concurso-bosque-metropolitano/. Accessed November 10, 2021.

Ayuntamiento de Madrid. 2018. *Estrategia de Alimentación Saludable y Sostenible 2018–2020.* Madrid: Ayuntamiento de Madrid.

Ayuntamiento de Madrid. 2019. *Plan de Infraestructuras Verdes y Biodiversidad* (Biodiversity and Green Infrastructures Plan). Madrid: Ayuntamiento de Madrid.

Ayuntamiento de Madrid. 2020. "Metropolitan Forest Contest Guidelines."

Colding, Johan, and Stephan Barthel. 2013. "The Potential of 'Urban Green Commons' in the Resilience Building of Cities." In *Ecological Economics* 86: 156–66.

GIPL (Asociación Cultural del Grupo de Investigadores del Parque Lineal del Manzanares). 2021. "La Salmedina cristiana." http://www.parquelineal.es/. Accessed November 26, 2021.

Gómez Orea, Domingo. 2008. "Plan Maestro: Parque Lineal del Manzanares. Tramo 2." Madrid: Dirección General de Patrimonio Verde, Área de Gobierno de Medio Ambiente. Ayuntamiento de Madrid.

López García, M., A. Bonet López, and M. González Solís. 2008. *El Real Canal de Manzanares: En busca del paisaje perdido. La huella en el territorio, la huella en la historia*. Madrid: Ayuntamiento de Madrid.

Morán, Nerea. 2018. "La huella de la alimentación en la configuración urbana de Madrid/Footprints on Madrid Urban Form Configuration." In *Aproximaciones Contemporáneas al Paisaje Urbano. II Jornadas Internacionales de Investigación sobre paisaje, patrimonio y ciudad*, edited by Universidad de Alcalá de Henares, 237–38. Alcalá de Henares: Universidad de Alcalá.

Simon Rojo, Marian, Xavier Recasens, Sonia Callau, Barbora Duží, Frank Lohrberg, Sebastian Eiter, Veronica Hernandez-Jimenez, Patricia Kettle, Dona Pickard, Lionella Scazzosi, and Henrik Vejre. 2016. "From Urban Food Gardening to Urban Farming." In *Urban Agriculture Europe*, edited by Frank Lohrberg, Lilli Lička, Lionella Scazzosi, and Axel Timpe, 22–28. Berlin: Jovis.

Protection and Values of the Cultural Heritage of the Campagna Romana Between Public Policies and Movements from Below

Anna Lei

AAA Architects. 2012. "R-urban Act 1." Paris: AAA/prepav.

Arena, Gabriella. 1984. *Il verde a Roma: Dall'hortus alla villa*. Rome: il Bagatto Editrice.

Branduini, Paola, Raffaella Laviscio, and Lionella Scazzosi. 2016. "L'agricoltura urbana e il patrimonio culturale: un beneficio reciproco." *Agriregionieuropa*, no. 44: 55–58.

Braudel, Fernand. 1987. "Histoire et sciences sociales: La longue durée." *Réseaux* 5, no. 27: 7–37.

Calzolari, Vittoria, ed. 1999. *Storia e natura come sistema: Un progetto per il territorio libero dell'area romana*. Rome: Árgos.

De Certeau, Michel. 1980. *L'Invention du quotidien: Arts de faire*. Paris: Gallimard.

Corboz, André. 1983. "Le territoire comme palimpseste." *Diogène*, no. 121: 14–35.

Corner, James. 2001. "Landscraping." In *Stalking Detroit*, edited by Georgia Daskalakis, Charles Waldheim, and Jason Young, 122–25. Barcelona: ACTAR.

Costanza, Robert, Ralph D'Arge, Rudolf de Groot, Stephen Farber, Monica Grasso, Bruce Hannon, Karin E. Limburg, Shahid Naeem, Robert V. O'Neill, José Paruelo, Robert G. Raskin, Paul C. Sutton, Marjan van den Belt. 1997. "The Values of the World's Ecosystem Services and Natural Capital." In *Nature*, no. 387: 253–60.

Donadieu, Pierre. 2013. "L'immaginario dei territori agrourbani o la terra ritrovata." *Scienze del territorio* 1: 59–70.

Donadieu, Pierre. 2016. "L'architecture du paysage demain: Une démocratie des communs paysagers?" Lecture presented at the IFLA, *Tasting the Landscape*, Turin, April 22, 2016.

Erbani, Francesco. 2013. *Roma: Il tramonto della città pubblica*. Rome-Bari: Laterza.

European Commission. 2006. "Thematic Strategy for Soil Protection." COM(2006)231, September 22, 2006.

Fleury, André, and Pierre Donadieu. 1997. "De l'agriculture péri-urbaine à l'agriculture urbaine." In *Courrier de l'environnement de l'INRA*, no. 31: 45–60.

Formica, Marina, ed. 2009. *Roma e la Campagna romana nel Grand Tour*. Rome-Bari: Laterza.

Hirsch, Alison. 2012. "Facilitation and/or Manipulation? Lawrence Halprin and 'Taking Part.'" In *Landscape Journal* 31, nos. 1: 117–34.

Insolera, Italo. 1971. *Roma moderna: Un secolo di storia urbanistica*. 2nd ed. Turin: Einaudi.

Insolera, Italo. 1980. *Immagini e realtà dal X al XX secolo*. Rome-Bari: Laterza.

Istat (Instituto Nazionale di Statistica). 2011."6. Censimento Generale dell'Agricoltura 2010." Nepi: Varigrafica Alto Lazio.

ISPRA. 2017. "Consumo di suolo, dinamiche territoriali e servizi ecoistemici." *Rapporti*, no. 266.

Lei, Anna. 2019. *Agricolture urbanizzate: Nuovi paesaggi commestibili nella campagna romana*. Rome: Nuova Cultura.

Millennium Ecosystem Assessment. 2005. *Ecosystems and Human Well-Being: Synthesis*. Washington, DC: Island Press.

Municipality of Rome. 2003. Rome Town Plan, 2003. Adopted version.

Municipality of Rome. 2008. Rome Town Plan, 2008. Ratified version.

Nicolin, Pierluigi. 2012. "Il bello dell'agricoltura urbana." In *Lotus*, no. 149: 42–46.

Ostrom, Elinor. 1996. "Crossing the Great Divide: Coproduction, Synergy, and Development." *World Development* 24, no. 6: 1073–87.

Secchi, Bernardo. 2005. *La città del ventesimo secolo*. Bari: Laterza.

Sereni, Emilio. 2008. *Storia del paesaggio agrario italiano*. 18th ed. Bari: Laterza.

Urban Gardening as a Practice to Safeguard Historical Agricultural Sites in Can Cabanyes and Torre Codina (Badalona, Catalonia)

Xavier Recasens, Dolors Nieto, Clara Forn, Oscar Alfranca

Ajuntament de Badalona. 2009. "Reglament de règim d'ús dels horts de titularitat municipal i per l'atorgament de llicències d'ús privatiu del domini públic." In *Butlletí Oficial de la Província de Barcelona*, no. 245, 26–29.

Camps-Calvet, Marta, Johannes Langemeyer, Laura Calvet-Mir, and Erik Gómez-Baggethun. 2016. "Ecosystem Services Provided by Urban Gardens in Barcelona, Spain: Insights for Policy and Planning." In *Environmental Science and Policy* 62: 14–23.

Čibik, Miroslav, Attila Tóth, and Roberta Štěpánková. 2010. "Integration of the Historical Watermill into a Sustainable Peri-Urban Riverfront Redesign." In *Public Recreation and Landscape Protection with Nature Hand in Hand*, edited by Jitka Fialová, 212–16. Křtiny: Mendel University in Brno and Czech Society of Landscape Engineers.

De Silva, Wasana. 2019. "Urban Agriculture and Buddhist Concepts for Wellbeing: Anuradhapura Sacred City, Sri Lanka." In *International Journal of Design & Nature Ecodynamics* 14, no. 3: 163–77.

Egerer, Monika, Peter Bichier, and Stacy M. Philpott. 2017. "Landscape and Local Habitat Correlates of Lady Beetle Abundance and Species Richness in Urban Agriculture." In *Annals of the Entomological Society of America* 110, no. 1: 97–103.

Guitart, Daniela, Catherine Marina Pickering, and Jason Byrne. 2014. "Color Me Healthy: Food Diversity in School Community Gardens in Two Rapidly Urbanising Australian Cities." In *Health and Place* 26: 110–17.

Park, Sin-Ae, A-Young Lee, Ho-Sang Lee, Kwan-Suk Lee, and Ki-Choel Son. 2015. "A Comparison of Exercise Intensity between Two Horticultural and Four Common Physical Activities among Male Adults in Their 20s." In *Korean Journal of Horticultural Science and Technology* 33, no. 1: 133–42.

Schram-Bijkerk, Dieneke, Piet Otte, Liesbet Dirven, and Anton M. Breure. 2018. "Indicators to Support Healthy Urban Gardening in Urban Management." In *Science of the Total Environment* 621: 863–71.

Timpanaro, Giuseppe, Vera Teresa Foti, Alessandro Scuderi, Stefania Toscano, and Daniela Romano. 2018. "Urban Agriculture as a Tool for Sustainable Social Recovery of Metropolitan Slum Area in Italy: Case Catania." In *Acta Horticulturae* 1215: 315–18.

UNESCO. 2005. "Operational Guidelines for the Implementation of the World Heritage Convention." Paris: World Heritage Centre.

Villarroya i Font, Joan, ed. 1999. *Història de Badalona*. Badalona: Museu de Badalona.

Intangible Agricultural Heritage as a Resource for Sustainable Contemporary Cities
Paola Branduini

Alcántara Onofre, Saúl. 2020. "Urban Agriculture and Landscape in Mexico City: Between History and Innovation." In Scazzosi and Branduini 2020, 79–96.

Branduini, Paola. 2016. "Il patrimonio rurale nutre la città." In *Economia e Società: Oltre il ponte* 34: 40–54.

Branduini, Paola. 2020. "Engagement, Participation and Governance of Urban Agricultural Heritage." In Scazzosi and Branduini 2020, 45–62.

Branduini, Paola, and Fabio Carnelli. 2021. "The Preservation of Rural Landscapes for Building Resilience in the Context of Small Towns: Insights from Northern Italy." In *Historic Cities in the Face of Disasters*, edited by Fatemeh Farnaz Arefian, Judith Ryser, Andrew Hopkins, and Jamie Mackee, 399–416. Berlin: Springer.

Branduini, Paola, Raffaella Laviscio, and Lionella Scazzosi. 2020. "AgriCulture in Milan: The Mutual Benefit between Urban Agriculture and Cultural Heritage." In Scazzosi and Branduini 2020, 245–61.

Castillo Ruiz, José, and Alberto Matarán. 2020. "La Vega de Granada: The Defence of a Paradigmatic Agrarian Heritage Space by Local Citizens." In Scazzosi and Branduini 2020, 225–44.

Conference of the European Ministry of Territory (CEMAT). 2003. "European Rural Heritage Observation Guide." Strasbourg: Council of Europe.

Council of Europe. 2005. "Convention on the Value of Cultural Heritage for Society (Faro Convention)." Strasbourg: Council of Europe.

ICOMOS. 2019. "The Future of Our Pasts: Engaging Cultural Heritage in Climate Action." Paris: ICOMOS.

Jelinčić, Daniela Angelina, and Dragana Glivetić. 2020. *Cultural Heritage and Sustainability: Practical Guide*. Lille: Interreg Europe Programme. https://www.interregeurope.eu/fileadmin/user_upload/tx_tevprojects/library/file_1586942702.pdf.

Laviscio, Raffaella. 2020. "Is Urban Agriculture an Opportunity to Preserve Landscape Systems? Suggestions from England." In Scazzosi and Branduini 2020, 145–62.

Lennon, Jane. 2020. "Tangible and Intangible Heritage in Urban Agriculture." In Scazzosi and Branduini 2020, 97–114.

Prados, María-José, and Jesús Santiago-Ramos. 2020. "Urban Agriculture and Territorial Heritage: Keys to Resiliency." In Scazzosi and Branduini 2020, 65–78.

Scazzosi, Lionella. 2018. "Landscape as Systems of Tangible and Intangible Relationships: Small Theoretical and Methodological Introduction to Read and Evaluate Rural Landscape as Heritage." In *The Conservation and Enhancement of Built and Landscape Heritage*, edited by Elisabetta Rosina and Lionella Scazzosi, 19–40. Milan: PoliScript.

Scazzosi, Lionella. 2020. "Urban Agriculture as Heritage: Methodological Issues and Perspectives." In Scazzosi and Branduini 2020, 17–44.

Scazzosi, Lionella, and Paola Branduini, eds. 2020. *AgriCultura: Urban Agriculture and the Heritage Potential of Agrarian Landscape*. Berlin: Springer.

United Nations 2015. *Transforming Our World: The Sustainable Development Agenda for 2030*. New York: United Nations. https://sdgs.un.org/publications/transforming-our-world-2030-agenda-sustainable-development-17981. Accessed July 16, 2021.

UNESCO. 2003. Convention for the Safeguarding of the Intangible Cultural Heritage. Paris: UNESCO World Heritage Centre.

UNESCO. 2019. "Operational Guidelines for Implementing the World Heritage Convention." Paris: UNESCO World Heritage Centre.

Bamberg Market Gardeners' District – A Living Cultural Heritage for Centuries: Solutions for Dealing with Tangible and Intangible Heritage
Diana Büttner

Alberth, Patricia. 2018. "Applying a Sustainable Development Approach to the World Heritage 'Town of Bamberg' Site." In *World Heritage and Sustainable Development*, edited by Peter Bille Larsen and William Logan, 214–25. Oxon: Routledge.

Baier, Alexandra, Gerhard Hagen, and Arnd Rüttger. 2018. *Nicht nur Süßholzraspler und Zwiebeltreter*. Bamberg: sehdition.

Bamberg Gardeners' Interest Group: The Bamberg gardeners who have joined forces in an interest group work together to boost their marketing.

Büttner, Diana. 2013. "Die Bamberger Gärtnerstadt und das Modellprojekt Urbaner Gartenbau." In *Local Land & Soil News*, nos. 44/45: 18–20.

Büttner, Diana, Viktoria Piehl, and Jan Wilhelm. 2012. "Bambergs Identitätsfindung als Stadtdenkmal." In *Die Kunstdenkmäler von Bayern* 1, no. 1: 706–61.

Daftary-Steel, Sarita, Christine M. Porter, Suzanne Gervais, David Vigil, and Daryl Marshall. 2017. "What Grows in East New York: 'East New York Farms!' and Expectations of Urban Agriculture." In *Feeding the City: Improving Local Food Access, Security, and Sovereignty*, edited by Christopher Bosso, 95–112. Oxon: Routledge.

Eyink, H., and B. Heck, eds. 2017. *Weißbuch Stadtgrün*. Berlin: Bundesministerium für Umwelt, Naturschutz, Bau und Reaktorsicherheit (BMUB).

Gunzelmann, Thomas. 2019. "Umgrenzung und historisch-topographische Struktur der Theuerstadt und der östlichen Stadterweiterung." In *Die Kunstdenkmäler von Bayern* 7, no. 1: 1–10.

Kloos, Michael, and Patricia Alberth. 2018. "The Case Study of the Town of Bamberg (Germany) Concerning the Combination of Management Plans with Participation Strategies in Urban World Heritage Properties." In *Aspects of Management Planning for Cultural World Heritage Sites*, edited by Simon Makuvaza, 209–23. Cham: Springer.

UNESCO. 2019. "Operational Guidelines for the Implementation of the World Heritage Convention." Paris: World Heritage Centre.

Wilhelm, Jan. 2019. "Geschichtliche Entwicklung der Unteren Gärtnerei und der nordöstlichen Stadtentwicklung." In *Die Kunstdenkmäler von Bayern* 7, no. 1: 10–39.

Strategies to Reanimate the Urban and Agricultural Heritage of Oasis Settlements in Oman: The Case of Al Hamra
Alexander Kader

Chakraborty, Titash. 2019. "What You Should Know about Oman's Falaj System." *Oman Observer* (March 9, 2019). https://www.omanobserver.om/what-you-should-know-about-omans-falaj-system/. Accessed November 23, 2020.

Gangler, Anette. 2003. "Oasis Settlement Structures / Oman." http://sulama-intra.de/documents/publications/Gangler_2003. PDF. Accessed November 23, 2020.

Luedeling, Eike. 2007. *Sustainability of Mountain Oases in Oman: Effects of Agro-environmental Changes on Traditional Cropping Systems*. Kassel: University Press.

Nagieb, Maher, Stefan Siebert, Eike Luedeling, Andreas Buerkert, and Jutta Häser. 2004. "Settlement History of a Mountain Oasis in Northern Oman: Evidence from Land-Use and Archaeological Studies." In *Die Erde* 135: 81–106.

Su, Ming Ming, Yehong Sun, Qingwen Min, and Wenjun Jiao. 2018. "A Community Livelihood Approach to Agricultural Heritage System Conservation and Tourism Development: Xuanhua Grape Garden Urban Agricultural

Heritage Site, Hebei Province of China." In *Sustainability* 10, no. 2: 361.

Vejre, Henrik, Sebastian Eiter, Verónica Hernández-Jiménez, Frank Lohrberg, Isabel Loupa-Ramos, Xavier Recasens, Dona Pickard, Lionella Scazzosi, and Marian Simon-Rojo. 2016. "Can Agriculture Be Urban?" In *Urban Agriculture Europe*, edited by Frank Lohrberg, Lilli Lička, Lionella Scazzosi, and Axel Timpe, 18–21. Berlin: Jovis.

Chinampas of Xochimilco: Urban Agriculture from the Ancient Americas Until Today

Laura Camacho Latz, Sophie Laukemper, Katharina Christenn, Axel Timpe

AJ+ Español. 2020. "La chinampa de Xochimilco sigue activa en la pandemia." *Facebook,* https://www.facebook.com/ajplusespanol/videos/300281837976519/?vh=e&extid=0&d=n. Accessed October 15, 2020.

Aztec History. n.d. "Aztec Social Classes." http://www.aztec-history.com/aztec-social-classes.html. Accessed December 9, 2020.

Crossley, Phil. 2004. "Sub-irrigation in Wetland Agriculture." In *Agriculture and Human Values* 21, no. 2: 191–205.

González Pozo, Alberto. 2016. *Las Chinampas: Patrimonio Mundial de la Ciudad de México.* Mexico City: Universidad Autónoma Metropolitana.

Government of Mexico City. 2017. "Chinampa Agricultural System of Mexico City, Mexico: A Proposal for Designation as a Globally Important Agricultural Heritage System (GIAHS)." Mexico City: AZP.

Hirst, K. Kris. 2019. "Chinampa of Floating Gardens." *ThoughtCo.* Updated November 12, 2019. https://www.thoughtco.com/chinampa-floating-gardens-170337. Accessed October 17, 2020.
Powers, Matt. 2020. "De Las Chinampas: Ancient Aztec Floating Gardens Restored!" *Youtube*, https://www.youtube.com/watch?v=ijzL5IsF-Ow&t=2996s. Accessed December 12, 2020.

Robles, Braulio, Jorge Flores, José Luis Martínez, Patricia Herrera. 2018. "The Chinampa: An Ancient Mexican Sub-Irrigation System." In *Irrigation and Drainage* 68, no. 3: 1–8.

Salem Media. 2020. "Aztec Agriculture: Floating Farms Fed the People." *History on the Net.* https://www.historyonthenet.com/aztec-agriculture-floating-farms-fed-the-people. Accessed October 17, 2020.

The Transformation of Everyday Landscapes into Heritage: A Driver for Territorialized Agro-Food Systems in the Peri-Urban Context of Madrid

Rafael Mata Olmo, Carolina Yacamán Ochoa, Esther Sanz Sanz

Ambroise, Régis, François Bonneaud, and Véronique Brunet-Vinck. 2000. *Agriculteurs et paysages: Dix exemples de projets de paysage en agriculture.* Dijon: Éducagri éditions.

Bastian, Olaf, Karsten Grunewald, Ralf-Uwe Syrbe, Ulrich Walz, and Wolfgang Wende. 2014. "Landscape Services: The Concept and Its Practical Relevance." In *Landscape Ecology* 29, no. 9: 1463–79.

Castillo Ruiz, José. 2007. "El futuro del patrimonio histórico: la patrimonialización del hombre." In *Revista de Patrimonio Histórico*, no. 1 (digital edition).

Clark, K. and Drury P. 2002. "Du monument au citoyen: les fonctions du patrimoine culturel dans une Europe en évolution." In Council of Europe 2002, 119–24.

Council of Europe. 2000. "Council of Europe Landscape Convention (ETS No. 176)." Strasbourg: Council of Europe.
Council of Europe. 2002. *Fonctions du patrimoine culturel dans une Europe en changement.* Strasbourg: Council of Europe.

Dewarrat, Jean-Pierre, Richard Quicerot, Marcos Weil, and Bernard Woeffray. 2003. *Paysages ordinaires: De la protection au projet.* Sprimont, Belgium: Pierre Mardaga.

Di Méo, Guy. 1995. "Patrimoine et territoire, une parenté conceptuelle." In *Espaces et Sociétés*, no. 78: 16–33.

Feria, José Maria, ed. 2012. *Territorial Heritage and Development.* London: CRC Press.

Lowenthal, David. 1998. *The Heritage Crusade and the Spoils of History.* Cambridge: Cambridge University Press.

Manero Miguel, Fernando. 2017. "Spatial Heritage and Culture of the Territory." In Manero Miguel and García Cuesta 2017, 29–56.

Manero Miguel, Fernando, and José Luis García Cuesta, eds. 2017. *Territorial Heritage & Spatial Planning: A Geographical Perspective.* Navarre: Thomson Reuters Aranzadi.

Mata Olmo, Rafael. 2010. "La dimensión patrimonial del paisaje: Una mirada desde los espacios rurales." In *Paisaje y patrimonio*, edited by Javier Maderuelo, 31–73. Madrid: Abada Editores.

Mata Olmo, Rafael. 2015. "Reflexiones en torno a la valoración y gestión del paisaje en los parques agrarios." In *El parque Agrario: Una figura de transición hacia nuevos modelos de gobernanza territorial y alimentaria*, edited by Carolina Yacamán Ochoa and Ana Zazo Moratalla, 165–82. Madrid: Heliconia.

Ortega Valcárcel, José. 1999. "El patrimonio territorial: el territorio como recurso territorial y económico." In *Ciudades* 4: 33–48.

Prats, Llorenç. 2004. *Antropología y patrimonio.* 2nd ed. Barcelona: Ariel.

Sanz Sanz Esther. 2011. "Le tourisme communautaire: Un outil pour le dépassement du conflit ville-campagne: Le cas des jalq'a du district rural 8 de la ville de Sucre, au sud-est de l'altiplano Bolivien." Master's thesis, Ecole des Hautes Etudes en Sciences Sociales.

Scazzosi, Lionella. 2020. "Urban Agriculture as Heritage: Methodological Issues and Perspectives." In *AgriCultura: Urban Agriculture and the Heritage Potential of Agrarian Landscape*, edited by Lionella Scazzosi and Paola Branduini, 17–44. Berlin: Springer.

Silva Pérez, Rocío, and Víctor Fernández Salinas. 2017. "The Limitless Concept: The New Heritage Paradigm and Its Relation to Space." In Manero Miguel and García Cuesta 2017, 57–84.

Termorshuizen, Jolande W., and Paul Opdam. 2009. "Landscape Services as a Bridge between Landscape Ecology and Sustainable Development." In *Landscape Ecology*, 24: 1037–52.

Yacamán Ochoa, Carolina. 2014. "Plan de gestión y desarrollo del Parque Agrario de Fuenlabrada." Fuenlabrada: Ayuntamiento de Fuenlabrada.

Yacamán Ochoa, Carolina, and Rafael Mata Olmo. 2017. *Huertas y campos de Fuenlabrada: Un paisaje agrario con historia y future.* Madrid: Heliconia.

Yacamán Ochoa, Carolina, Irene Pérez Ramírez, Veronica Hernández, and Marina García Llorente. 2018. "La cartografía participativa de los servicios de los ecosistemas como metodología para la valorización social del paisaje agrario periurbano." In *VII Congreso Internacional de Agroecología, 30, 31 de mayo y 1 de junio de 2018.* Córdoba: Instituto de Sociología y Estudios Campesinos.

Yacamán Ochoa, Carolina, Esther Sanz Sanz, and Rafael Mata Olmo. 2020. *Agricultura periurbana y planificación territorial. De la protección al proyecto agrourbano.* Valencia: Publicacions de la Universitat de València, Colección Desarrollo Territorial.

Murs à Pêches de Montreuil: Rediscovering Urban Agricultural Heritage

Ayda Hamid Kargari, Kevin C. Wehnert, Katharina Christenn, Axel Timpe

De Decker, Kris. 2015. "Fruit Walls: Urban Farming in the 1600s." In *Low-Tech Magazine*, https://www.lowtechmagazine.com/2015/12/fruit-walls-urban-farming.html. Accessed March 4, 2021.

Deville, Damien, and Florence Brondeau. 2017. "Appropriations citoyennes et jeux d'acteurs dans un espace en devenir: Le quartier des Murs à Pêches à Montreuil." In *Géographie et cultures*, no. 103: 109–29.

Est Ensemble Grand Paris. 2020. "Plan Local d'Urbanisme intercommunal d'Est Ensemble, 6. Plan de Zonage, 7.c Montreuil – Murs à Pêches." https://www.calameo.com/read/006040198266f187c0251. Accessed February 8, 2021.

Eßlinger, Johann Georg 1767. *Herrn Decombe Ausführliche Beschreibung von den Pfirsich-Bäumen, worinnen angezeigt wird, wie solche auf unterschiedliche Weise, nützlich können erzogen, und unterhalten werden, denen Liebhabern der Gärtnerei zum Besten aus dem Französischen in das Teutsche übersetzt.* Frankfurt, Leipzig: Johann Georg Eßlinger.

Eva G. 2019. "Nouveau projet sur le site des murs à pêches de Montreuil." http://vergersurbains.org/nouveau-projet-au-murs-a-peches-de-montreuil/. Accessed November 1, 2020.

Fintelmann, Gustav Adolph. 1849. "Die Pfirsichzucht zu Montreuil bei Paris." In *Deutsches Magazin für Garten und Blumenkunde: Neue Zeitschrift für Garten- und Blumenfreunde, und Gärtner* 2: 268–308.

Fourastié, Jean. 1986. "Pouvoir d'achat du salaire (de Louis XIV à 1949)." In *En Quercy, Essai d'histoire démographique, Quercy-Recherche*. Transcription. https://www.fourastie-sauvy.org/reference/textesjean/tradition/301-de-louis-xiv-a-1949#:~:text=Le%20journalier%20de%201750%20gagnait,livres%20de%20pain%5B1%5D. Accessed March 3, 2021.

Freidberg, Susanne. 2009. *Fresh: A Perishable History*. Cambridge, MA: The Belknap Press of Harvard University Press.

Johanneau, Eloi. 1825. *Les fastes de Montreuil-les-Pêches, sa culture, ses embellissements et ses origines: épitre à M. le comte de Chabrol, ... avec des notes historiques et archéologiques*. Montreuil: C. Groubental. https://gallica.bnf.fr/ark:/12148/bpt6k6458474q/f17.item. Accessed March 3, 2021.

Lafarge, Ivan. 2012. "Les murs à palisser 'à la Montreuil.'" In *e-Phaïstos* 1, no. 1: 79–87.

Malot, Félix. 1842. "II. Culture. Rapport d'une commission spéciale, fait à la Société royale d'horticulture, sur rétablissement dune treille de feigne en espalier, dans la commune de Montreuil; par M. Malot (Félix)." In *Annales de la Société Royale d'horticulture de Paris, et Journal Spécial de l'état et des Progrès du Jardinage* 30, no. 176: 272–73.

McCusker, John J. 1974. "Les équivalents métriques des poids et mesures du commerce colonial aux XVIIe et XVIIIe siècles." In *Revue française d'histoire d'outre-mer* 62, no. 3: 349–65. https://www.persee.fr/doc/outre_0300-9513_1974_num_61_224_1773. Accessed March 4, 2021.

Mozard, Jean. 1814. *Principes pratiques sur l'education, la culture, des arbres fruitiers, et principalement du pêcher; D'après la methode de Pepin, et autres célèbres cultivateurs de Montreuil.* Paris: Bertrand.

RP. 2019. "Bienvenue." *Voyage autour du 10cts Semeuse Lignée.* http://www.cofspi.net/index.php?. Accessed March 4, 2021.

De Salaberry, Charles-Maire. 1838. "Girardot." In *Biographie universelle, ancienne et moderne. Supplément*, vol. 65, *Ga–Goz*, edited by Louis Gabriel Michaud, 401–3. Paris: Libraire-Éditeur.

Tilloy, Jean. 2021. "La Fondation du Patrimoine et Stéphane Bern accordent aux Murs à Pêches l'aide financière francilienne la plus importante des sites de maillage du Loto du Patrimoine." https://www.montreuil.fr/fil-in-fos/detail/page?tx_news_pi1%5Bnews%5D=3339&cHash=bfcc8f4f5bb5aec37fbd927098956755. Accessed February 16, 2021.

Ville de Montreuil. 2012. "Histoire des murs à pêches." https://www.montreuil.fr/la-ville/histoire-de-la-ville/histoire-des-murs-a-peches. Accessed February 16, 2021.

Ville de Montreuil. 2016. "Faisons le mur ensemble!" https://www.montreuil.fr/fileadmin/user_upload/12_Environnement/07_Les_murs_a_peches/MaisonMAP-PannoExpoA1-BDweb.pdf. Accessed March 4, 2021.

Ville de Montreuil. 2018. "Les 5 axes du projet de la ville." https://www.montreuil.fr/environnement/les-murs-a-peches/les-5-axes-du-projet-de-la-ville. Accessed March 4, 2021.

Ville de Montreuil. 2019. "Exposition Promenons nous dans les Murs à pêches, Montreuil." https://www.montreuil.fr/fileadmin/user_upload/12_Environnement/07_Les_murs_a_peches/exposition-map-sept2019.pdf. Accessed March 4, 2021.

Ville de Montreuil and Est Ensemble Grand Paris. 2018. "Plan local d'urbanisme de la ville de Montreuil, 5-1 Règlement." https://www.montreuil.fr/fileadmin/user_upload/05_Grands_Projets/10_La_revision_du_PLU_2016-2018/03_Un_projet_avec_trois_phases_distinctes/Phase_3__l_approbation_du_PLU/02_Consultation_du_PLU/05_Dispositif_reglementaire/5.1-Reglement-final.pdf. Accessed February 25, 2021.

Ville de Paris. 2019. "Murs à Fleurs." https://www.parisculteurs.paris/fr/sites/parisculteurs-saison-3/1606-murs-a-peches-de-montreuil-93100.html. Accessed November 10, 2021.

Reconnecting City and Countryside: Participatory Solutions for Hamburg

Ole Oßenbrink, Birte Mehrkens, Andreas Ulbrich, Cord Petermann

Agra Europe (AgE). 2019. "Wenig Kontakt zwischen Städtern und Landwirten." *top agrar online*. https://www.topagrar.com/panorama/news/wenig-kontakt-zwischen-staedtern-und-landwirten-10150330.html. Accessed March 2, 2022.

Altmann, Marianne, and Manfred Berndt. 2016. "Strategiepapier zur prozessorientierten Entwicklung einer 'Nachhaltigkeitsstrategie für den Produktionsgartenbau Hamburg.'" http://www.hamburg.de/contentblob/9827648/e0d0816c85c8bbb35adaae0a371bac4d/data/strategiepapier-„nachhaltigkeitsstrategie-fuer-den-produktionsgartenbau-hamburg.pdf. Accessed March 30, 2020.

Beecroft, Richard, Helena Trenks, Regina Rhodius, Christina Benighaus, and Oliver Parodi. 2018. "Reallabore als Rahmen transformativer und transdisziplinärer." In *Transdisziplinär und transformativ forschen: Eine Methodensammlung*, edited by Antonietta Di Giulio and Rico Defila, 75–100. Basel: Springer VS.

BMVBS. 2006. "Leitbilder und Handlungsstrategien für die Raumentwicklung in Deutschland." Berlin: Ministerkonferenz für Raumordnung, June 30, 2006.

Dirksmeyer, Walter, Hildegard Garming, and Sabine Ludwig-Ohm. 2013. "Situation des Gartenbaus in Deutschland sowie Möglichkeiten und Hemmnisse für seine zukünftige Entwicklung: Ergebnisse einer Befragung von Beratern und Berufsstand." Braunschweig: Johann Heinrich von Thünen-Institut.

Farhauer, Oliver, and Alexandra Kröll. 2014. *Standorttheorien: Regional- und Stadtökonomik in Theorie und Praxis*. Wiesbaden: Springer Gabler.

Heyen, T. 2018. "20 Prozent weniger Betriebe: Viele Gärtner geben auf." In *Bergedorfer Zeitung*, January 22, 2018.

Hoffmann, Gerd. 2010. "Die Vier- und Marschlande: Eine besuchenswerte KulturLandschaft." http://bergedorf-chronik.de/bergedorf-blaetter/2010_vm_kulturlandschaft.pdf. Accessed March 30, 2020.

Kleefeld, Klaus-Dieter, Peter Burggraaff, and Beate Lange. 2007. *Länderübergreifende Kulturlandschaftsanalyse Altes Land*. Cologne: Büro für historische Stadt- und Landschaftsforschung.

Marktgemeinschaft Blumengroßmarkt Hamburg eG. 2021. "Geschichte." https://www.blumengrossmarkt-hh.de/docs/4556/historisches.aspx. Accessed November 15, 2021.

Stadtentwicklungsbehörde Hamburg Amt für Landschaftsplanung. 1994. "Landschaftsprogramm Hamburg – Landschaftsbild." https://www.hamburg.de/contentblob/4626906/6cdb13944bf3b-c6034546e5214d79f18/data/landschaftsbild-broschuere.pdf. Accessed March 30, 2020.

Vogelgesang, Waldemar, Johannes Kopp, Rüdiger Jacob, and Alois Hahn. 2018. *Stadt-Land-Fluss: Sozialer Wandel im regionalen Kontext*. Wiesbaden: Springer VS.

Enhancing and Promoting Milan's Peri-Urban Agricultural Landscape as a Cultural Resource: The Case of MUSA

Andrea L'Erario, Paola Branduini, Raffaella Laviscio, G. Matteo Mai, Lionella Scazzosi, Francesco C. Toso

Bisi, Lucia. 2012. *Nutrire Milano. Storia e paesaggio dell'alimentazione in città*. Milan: Skira.

Bocchi, Stefano, and Mariella Borasio. 2013. "Politiche di sviluppo place-based e distrettualità in agricoltura, Il caso Lombardo." In *Scienze del Territorio*, no. 1: 319–22.

Branduini, Paola. 2020. "Engagement, Participation and Governance of Urban Agricultural Heritage." In *AgriCultura: Urban Agriculture and the Heritage Potential of Agrarian Landscape*, edited by Lionella Scazzosi and Paola Branduini, 45–62. Berlin: Springer.

Branduini, Paola, Giulia Giacché, and Raffaella Laviscio. 2016. "Agricoltura urbana in Italia: primi esiti di un lavoro di confronto." In *AgriregionEuropa* 44: 39–41.

Branduini, Paola, Raffaella Laviscio, Francesco Carlo Toso, and Andrea L'Erario. 2019. "Mapping Evolving Historical Landscape Systems." In *The International Archives of the Photogrammetry, Remote Sensing and Spatial Information Sciences*, XLII-2/W11: 277–84.

Branduini, Paola, Coline Perrin, Brigitte Nougarèdes, and Elena Colli. 2020. "Cultural Heritage Preservation and Resilience in Urban Agriculture through the Lens of Social Justice: A Case Study in Milan." In *Urban Food Democracy and Governance in North and South*, edited by Alec Thornton, 101–22. Berlin: Springer.

Cognetti, Francesca, and Serena Conti. 2014. "La terra della città: Milano e le sperimentazioni sociali di agricoltura urbana." In *Scienze del territorio* 2: 179–86.

Colombo, Cristina Federica, Raffaella Laviscio, and Paola Branduini. 2017. "Maps: Knowledge and Management Tools for the Cultural Heritage." In *Ecomuseums and Cultural Landscapes: State of the Art and Future Prospects*, edited by Raffaella Riva, 252–60. Santarcangelo di Romagna: Maggioli.

Council of Europe. 2000. "Council of Europe Landscape Convention (ETS No. 176)." Strasbourg: Council of Europe.

Council of Europe. 2005. "Convention on the Value of Cultural Heritage for Society (Faro Convention)." Strasbourg: Council of Europe.

European Regional Development Fund (ERDF). 2007–2013. "Protection and Enhancement of Natural and Cultural Heritage." Lombardy Region operational competitiveness program–POR, Axis 4.

Ferraresi, Giorgio, ed. 2009. *Produrre e scambiare valore territoriale: dalla città diffusa allo scenario di forma urbis et agri: Il Laboratorio del Parco Agricolo Sud Milano tra produzioni di qualità locale e consumo consapevole*. Florence: Alinea.

Laviscio, Raffaella. 2019. "Enhancement and Reuse Strategies of Rural Heritage: Experiences in the Metropolitan Area of Milan." In *Il patrimonio culturale in mutamento: Le sfide dell'uso, Proceedings of the 35th International Congress Science and Cultural Heritage, Bressanone, 1-5 July 2019*, edited by Guido Driussi, 615–25. Venice: Arcadia Ricerche.

L'Erario, Andrea. 2019. "Tutelare il paesaggio agrario periurbano attraverso la multifunzionalità: Costruzione e valutazione di una proposta di piano di conservazione e valorizzazione in area milanese." In *Aestimum* 75: 207–37.

L'Erario, Andrea, and Alessandra Oppio. 2020. "Preservation and Valorisation of Agricultural Peri-Urban Landscape: A Multi-Methodological Approach for Public and Private Governance Policies." In *Green Metamorphoses: Agriculture, Food, Ecology*, edited by Biancamaria Torquati and Andrea Marchini, 391–403. Wageningen: Wageningen Academic Publishers.

Lombard Regional Law. 2007. "Tools for the Competitiveness of Enterprises in the Lombardy Region."

Scazzosi, Lionella. 2015. "Preservare la 'Machina agraria': Per una lettura e valutazione del paesaggio rurale storico." In *Il risveglio del giardino: Dall'hortus al paesaggio*, edited by Paolo Cornaglia and Maria Adriana Giusti, 318–31. Lucca: Maria Pacini Fazzi.

Scazzosi, Lionella. 2018. "Rural Landscape as Heritage: Reasons for and Implication of Principles Concerning Rural Landscape as Heritage ICOMOS-IFLA 2017." In *Built Heritage* 2: 39–54.

Stroppa, Claudio. 1992. *La campagna in città: l'agricoltura urbana a Milano*. Naples: Liguori.

Image Credits

Urban Agriculture as Heritage
Frank Lohrberg

Fig. 1
representation: Frank Lohrberg

Early Modern Urban and Peri-Urban Horticulture in German Territories
Ansgar Schanbacher

Fig. 1a
drawing: Wikimedia Commons, URL: https://commons.wikimedia.org/wiki/File:Augsburg_Stadtkern_Kilianplan.jpg (accessed November 10, 2021)

Fig. 1b
drawing: Wikimedia Commons, URL: https://commons.wikimedia.org/wiki/File:Kilianplan_Augsburg.png (accessed November 26, 2021)

Fig. 2
representation: Ansgar Schanbacher, data: Municipal Archives Braunschweig

Figs. 3a–b
drawing: Work originally published by HAB Wolfenbüttel, URL: http://diglib.hab.de/drucke/6-4-oec-1/start.htm (accessed 10 November 2021)

The City as a Driver of Regional Agriculture: Erfurt and Its Horticultural Heritage
Sibylle Küttner, Frank Lohrberg

Fig. 1
photo: Horst Dünkel

Fig. 2
photo: Theater Waidspeicher

Fig. 3a
photo: Stadtarchiv Erfurt, 6_0_5Dreienbrunnen_035

Fig. 3b
photo: Stadtarchiv Erfurt, 5_110_B6-29_032

Fig. 3c und 8
drawing: Jay Heidecke

Fig. 4
drawing: Jay Heydecke, Katja Gadziak

Fig. 5
photo: Stadtarchiv Erfurt, 6_9_10b_027

Fig. 6
photo: Stadtarchiv Erfurt, 6_6_E04_005

Fig. 7
photo: Stadtarchiv Erfurt, 6_0_6F3_002

The Role of Centralized Policy Planning for Bulgarian Urban Agricultural Heritage from the Socialist Period
Dona Pickard

Figs. 1a–b
photo: family archive Dona Pickard

Fig. 2
photo: Dona Pickard

Fig. 3
photo: Nikolay Georgiev, Forestry University (picture of paper print)

Fig. 4
drawing: Dona Pickard, data: GIS Sofia

Heritage at the Urban Fringe: Allotment Gardening in Europe as Urban Agricultural Heritage
Attila Tóth

Fig. 1
photo: The Nordic Museum, 1915, public domain

Fig. 2
photo: Rudolf Holtappel, 1959, Fotoarchiv Ruhr Museum

Fig. 3
drawing: Howard, 1902, published in *Garden Cities of To-Morrow* in 1902, public domain

Fig. 4
drawing: Dekánek, 1971, published in Tóth et al. (2018): *Changing Patterns of Allotment Gardening in the Czech Republic and Slovakia*, p. 168

Fig. 5
photo: Attila Tóth, 2016

Russian Dachas: A Popular Urban Agricultural Heritage
Johanna Altendorf, Jay Heydecke, Katharina Christenn, Axel Timpe

Fig. 1
photo: Igor Shelaputin, Aerostatic federation of Yaroslavl region, URL: https://commons.wikimedia.org/wiki/File:Коровино-шелапутин-2016-9676.jpg (accessed 21 April 2021)

Fig. 2
drawing: Johanna Altendorf, Jay Heydecke, 2020, based on geodata from OpenStreetMap, URL: https://www.openstreetmap.org (accessed 20 December 2020)

Fig. 3
representation: Katja Gadziak, Katharina Christenn, Axel Timpe, based on representation by Johanna Altendorf, Jay Heydecke, 2020, data: Rumjanzewa (2017), Boukaraeva et al (2015)

Fig. 4
representation: Katja Gadziak, Katharina Christenn, Axel Timpe, based on representation by Johanna Altendorf, Jay Heydecke, (2020), data: Boukharaeva et al. (2015)

Fig. 5
representation: Katja Gadziak, Katharina Christenn, Axel Timpe, based on representation by Johanna Altendorf, Jay Heydecke (2020), data: Boukharaeva et al. (2015), Федеральная служба государственной статистики [Federal State Statistic Service Russia] (2019), *Сельское хозяйство в России 2019* ['Agriculture of Russia, Moscow 2019'], p. 49

Fig. 6
representation: Johanna Altendorf, Jay Heydecke, data: Boukharaeva et al. (2015), M. Rumjanzewa, (2017), G. Dornblüth, (2018), A. Grimonpont, (2019), U. Nikolaeva, , A. Rusanov, (2020), N. Ortar, (2005)

Fig. 7
painting: Valentin Gubarev (1999)

Fig. 8
photo: V. Lozovskiy (1981), RIA Novosti archive, image #487609, URL: https://commons.wikimedia.org/wiki/File:RIAN_archive_487609_Boleslav_Telichan%27s_family_at_summer_house.jpg (accessed January 15, 2021)

Resilient Cities with Urban Agricultural Heritage: Tokyo, Japan
Giles B. Sioen, Makoto Yokohari

Fig. 1
drawing: Giles B. Sioen, adapted from a drawing from Yokohari (2005), original source: Kochizu Library Co. Ltd. (2021)

Fig. 2, Fig. 5, Fig. 6
photo: Giles B. Sioen, 2012

Fig. 3
photo: Giles B. Sioen, 2015

Fig. 4
drawing: Giles B. Sioen, 2018, data: Tokyo Metropolitan Government (2016), 'Land use data, Tokyo 2015' (Tokyo)

Fig. 7, Fig. 8
photo: Giles B. Sioen, 2016

Belgrade's Garden Colonies: Where Memory, Nature, and People Meet
Slavica Čepić, Dragana Ćorović, Jelena Tomićević-Dubljević

Fig. 1, Fig. 2, Fig. 4
map: Nacionalna Infrastruktura Geoprostornih Podataka, URL: https://a3.geosrbija.rs/ (accessed November 9, 2021)

Fig. 3, Fig. 5, Fig. 6, Fig. 7
photo: Slavica Čepić, 2019

From Marshes to Market Gardens: Hortillonnages d'Amiens and Marais de Bourges

Leandra Brunet, Nicole Laufhütte, Axel Timpe, Katharina Christenn

Fig. 1, Fig. 2, Fig. 3, Fig. 6, Fig. 7
representation: Katja Gadziak, Katharina Christenn, Axel Timpe
drawing: Leandra Brunet, Nicole Laufhütte, based on Géoservices IGN, URL: https://geoservices.ign.fr/documentation/diffusion/telechargement-donnees-libres.html(accessed March 3, 2021)

Fig. 4
representation: Katja Gadziak, Katharina Christenn, Axel Timpe
drawing: Leandra Brunet, Nicole Laufhütte, based on Clauzel (2008a), p. 223; Clauzel (2008b); IGN, URL: https://remonterletemps.ign.fr/telecharger?x=323849&y=49.903965&z=13&layer=GEOGRAPHICAL-GRID-SYSTEMS.MAPS.SCAN-EXPRESS.STANARD&demat=DEMAT.PVA$GEOPORTAIL:DEMAT;PHOTOS&missionId=missions.4971500 (accessed March 3, 2021)

Fig. 5
drawing: Leandra Brunet, Nicole Laufhütte, based on Patrimoine Marais, URL: https://www.patrimoine-marais.org/fichespedagogiques (accessed December 14, 2020)

Fig. 8
photo: Institut national de l'information géographique et forestière (IGN), URL: https://www.ign.fr/ (accessed November 24, 2021)

From Orchard to Wetland Park: Guangzhou's Approach to Transform Urban Agricultural Heritage

Mengyun Chen, Guangsi Lin

Fig. 1, Fig. 3, Fig. 4, Fig. 5
Drawing: Mengyun Chen, 2019

Fig. 2
drawing: Mengyun Chen, 2019
photo: Google Earth, 2020

Fig. 6
representation: Katja Gadziak, Katharina Christenn, Axel Timpe, based on representation by Mengyun Chen, 2020

Fig. 7
photo: Haizhu District Archives Bureau, 1978

Figs. 8a–d
drawing: Mengyun Chen, 2019
photo: Google Earth, 2020

Fig. 9
photo: Mengyun Chen, 2019

Urban Agricultural Heritage of Lisbon: From the Past to the Future?

Mariana Sanchez Salvador

Fig. 1
map: Direcção Geral dos Trabalhos Geodésicos do Reino, Biblioteca Nacional de Portugal

Fig. 2
map: Water and Agriculture Atlas: Lisbon Region in 1900–1940, map no. 20, Marat-Mendes et al. (2015)

Fig. 3, Fig. 6, Fig. 9
photo: Eduardo Portugal, Arquivo Municipal de Lisboa

Fig. 4
photo: Casa Fotográfica Garcia Nunes, Arquivo Municipal de Lisboa

Fig. 5
photo: José Pedro Pinheiro Corrêa, Arquivo Municipal de Lisboa

Fig. 7
map: Silva Pinto, commissioned by Lisbon's City Council, Câmara Municipal de Lisboa, URL: http://geodados.cm-lisboa.pt/datasets/cartografiahistorica-silvapinto-1911 (accessed November 22, 2021)

Fig. 8
drawing: Mariana Sanchez Salvador

Fig. 10
photo: Paulo Guedes, Arquivo Municipal de Lisboa

Fig. 11
drawing: Katja Gadziak, Katharina Christenn, Axel Timpe, based on Câmara Municipal de Lisboa

Urban Agricultural Heritage in Benin: The Role of Traditional Coconut-Cattle Systems in Cotonou

Bossima I. Koura, Eric Boenecke, Frank Lohrberg, Luc H. Dossa

Fig. 1
drawing: Katja Gadziak, Katharina Christenn, Axel Timpe, data: Africa, URL: https://commons.wikimedia.org/wiki/File:Blank_Map-Africa.svg (accessed November 23, 2021), Benin, URL : https://download.geofabrik.de/africa/benin.html (accessed November 23, 2021), Coastline, OpenStreetMap, URL: https://www.openstreetmap.org (accessed November 23, 2021)

Fig. 2, Fig. 4
drawing: Katja Gadziak, Katharina Christenn, Axel Timpe

Fig. 3
photo: Bossima I. Koura, 2021

Fig. 5, Fig. 6
photo: Bossima I. Koura, 2017

La Vega de Granada: A Cultural Landscape Built Around Irrigation

Anna Kerfers, Ardiana Rahimi, Axel Timpe, Katharina Christenn

Fig. 1, Fig. 3, Fig. 6
representation: Katja Gadziak, Katharina Christenn, Axel Timpe
drawing: Anna-Maria Kerfers and Ardiana Rahimi, based on Junta de Andalucía, Consejería de Agricultura, Ganadería, Pesca y Desarrollo Sostenible, 'Plan Especial de Ordenación de la Vega de Granada', URL: http://www.juntadeandalucia.es/medioambiente/site/portalweb/menuitem.7e1cf46ddfz9bb227a9ebe205510e1ca/?vgnextoid=38ef09193e738310VgnVCM1000001325e50aRCRD&vgnextchannel=6657dd3bd-4f94510VgnVCM1000001325e50aRCRD (accessed November 2, 2020), historical aerial photographs provided by the Spanish National Cartography System, Obra derivada deOrto-AMS-1956-1957 195–1957 CC- BY 4.0 scne

Fig. 2, Fig. 4, Fig. 5
drawing: Anna-Maria Kerfers and Ardiana Rahimi

Fig. 7
representation: Anna-Maria Kerfers and Ardiana Rahimi, data: García Leal, A. (2014)

Hidden Urban Agricultural Heritage at the Manzanares River: Toward an Agro-ecological Wedge in the Southeast of Madrid City

Nerea Morán, Marian Simón Rojo

Fig. 1
representation: Katja Gadziak, Katharina Christenn, Axel Timpe
drawing: Nerea Morán, Marian Simón Rojo, based on data from the National Geographical Institute

Fig. 2
representation: Katja Gadziak, Katharina Christenn, Axel Timpe
drawing: Nerea Morán, Marian Simón Rojo, based on maps from Linear Park Research Group (GIPL)

Fig. 3
drawing: Ministry of Public Works

Fig. 4, Fig. 7
photo: Nerea Morán, Marian Simón Rojo

Fig. 5
map: National Geographical Institute

Figs. 6a–d
representation: Katja Gadziak, Katharina Christenn, Axel Timpe
drawing: Nerea Morán, Marian Simón Rojo, based on MTN25 (CNIG) and Map of Crops and Agrarian Uses (Ministry of Agriculture)

Figs. 8a–d
representation: Katja Gadziak, Katharina Christenn, Axel Timpe
drawing: Nerea Morán, Marian Simón Rojo, based on data from the National Geographical Institute

Protection and Values of the Cultural Heritage of the Campagna Romana Between Public Policies and Movements from Below
Anna Lei

Fig. 1
map: Frutaz, A. P. (1962), *Le piante di Roma* (vol. 3, Rome: Istituto di Studi Romani), p. 396

Fig. 2, Fig 7, Fig. 8
photo: Alessandro Cimmino

Fig. 3
image: in M. Formica (2009)

Fig. 4
drawing: Vittoria Calzolari, in V. Calzolari (1999)

Fig. 5
drawing: P. M. Giaccheri, in V. Calzolari (1999)

Fig. 6
map: Municipality of Rome (2003)

Urban Gardening as a Practice to Safeguard Historical Agricultural Sites in Can Cabanyes and Torre Codina (Badalona, Catalonia)
Xavier Recasens, Dolors Nieto, Clara Forn, Oscar Alfranca

Fig. 1
drawing: Katja Gadziak, Katharina Christenn, Axel Timpe, based on data: Pla Territorial Metropolità (2010), URL: https://territori.gencat.cat/ca/01_departament/05_plans/01_planificacio_territorial/plans_territorials_nou/territorials_parcials/ptp_metropolita_de_barcelona/index.html (accessed June 4, 2020)

Fig. 2
representation: Xavier Recasens, Dolors Nieto, Clara Forn, Oscar Alfranca, data: J. Villarroya i Font (dir.) (1999), Història de Badalona (Badalona: Museu de Badalona), Idescat, URL: https://www.idescat.cat/tema/xifpo?lang=en, (accessed June 4, 2020)

Fig. 3, Fig. 6
photo: Xavier Recasens

Fig. 5, Fig. 8
map: Área Metropolitana de Barcelona, Geoportal de Cartografia, URL: https://geoportalcarto-grafia.amb.cat/AppGeoportal-Cartografia2/index.html?locale=es (accessed June 4, 2020)

Fig. 4, Fig. 7
representation: Katja Gadziak, Katharina Christenn, Axel Timpe, based on drawing by Xavier Recasens, Dolors Nieto, Clara Forn, Oscar Alfranca, data: maps of Àrea Metropolitana de Barcelona, Geoportal de Cartografia, URL: https://geoportalcartografia.amb.cat/AppGeoportalCartografia2/index html?locale=es (accessed June 4, 2020)

Intangible Agricultural Heritage as a Resource for Sustainable Contemporary Cities
Paola Branduini

Fig. 1
photo: Paola Branduini, 2014

Figs. 2a–b
photo: Cascina Battivacco, Società Agricola Fedeli, URL: https://cascinabattivacco.it/ (accessed November 26, 2021)

Fig. 3
photo: Paola Branduini, 2015

Figs. 4a–c, Fig. 5
photo: Paola Branduini, 2021

Fig. 6
representation: Paola Branduini

Bamberg Market Gardeners' District – A Living Cultural Heritage for Centuries: Solutions for Dealing with Tangible and Intangible Heritage
Diana Büttner

Fig. 1
photo: Jürgen Schraudner, Bamberg City Archive

Fig. 2
photo: aerowest, Bamberg Municipal Building Department

Fig. 3
drawing: Diana Büttner, 2011
map: Bamberg State Library

Fig. 4, Fig. 5, Fig. 6, Fig. 9
photo: Jürgen Schraudner, Bamberg World Heritage Office

Fig. 7
photo: Steffen Schützwohl, City of Bamberg

Fig. 8
photo: Jürgen Schraudner, Bamberg Gardeners' Interest Group

Strategies to Reanimate the Urban and Agricultural Heritage of Oasis Settlements in Oman: The Case of Al Hamra
Alexander Kader

Fig. 1, Fig. 2, Fig. 3, Fig. 5
photo: Alexander Kader, 2019

Fig. 4, Fig. 7, Fig. 8
representation: Katja Gadziak, Katharina Christenn, Axel Timpe, based on representation by Alexander Kader

Fig. 6
drawing: Katja Gadziak, Katharina Christenn, Axel Timpe, based on drawing by Alexander Kader

Chinampas of Xochimilco: Urban Agriculture from the Ancient Americas Until Today
Laura Camacho Latz, Sophie Laukemper, Katharina Christenn, Axel Timpe

Figs. 1a–d
representation: Katja Gadziak, Katharina Christenn, Axel Timpe
drawing: Laura Camacho Latz, Sophie Laukemper, based on OpenStreetMap, URL: https://www.openstreetmap.org (accessed November 19, 2021), Government of Mexico City (2017), p. 109

Fig. 2
representation: Laura Camacho Latz, Sophie Laukemper

Fig. 3
drawing: Laura Camacho Latz, Sophie Laukemper, based on Government of Mexico City (2017), p. 45, National Research Council (1989), *Lost Crops of the Incas: Little-Known Plants of the Andes with Promise for Worldwide Cultivation* (Washington, DC: The National Academies Press), p. 8

Fig. 4
representation: Katja Gadziak, Katharina Christenn, Axel Timpe, based on representation by Laura Camacho Latz, Sophie Laukemper

Fig. 5
representation: Katja Gadziak, Katharina Christenn, Axel Timpe
map: Laura Camacho Latz, Sophie Laukemper, based on OpenStreetMap, URL: https://www.openstreetmap.org (accessed November 19, 2021), A. González Pozo, (2016), p. 67

Fig. 6
drawing: Laura Camacho Latz, Sophie Laukemper

Fig. 7
representation: Katja Gadziak, Katharina Christenn, Axel Timpe
map: Laura Camacho Latz, Sophie Laukemper, based on OpenStreetMap, URL: https://www.openstreetmap.org (accessed November 19, 2021)

The Transformation of Everyday Landscapes into Heritage as a Driver for Territorialized Agro-Food Systems in the Peri-Urban Context of Madrid
Rafael Mata Olmo, Carolina Yacamán Ochoa, Esther Sanz Sanz

Fig. 1, Fig. 2, Fig. 6
photo: Carolina Yacamán Ochoa

Fig. 3
photo: Portal de Archivos Españoles del Ministerio de Educación, Cultura y Deporte

Figs. 4a–i
photo: Carolina Yacamán Ochoa

Fig. 5
drawing: Carolina Yacamán Ochoa

Fig. 7
representation: Rafael Mata Olmo, Carolina Yacamán Ochoa, Esther Sanz Sanz

Murs à Pêches de Montreuil: Rediscovering Urban Agricultural Heritage

Ayda Hamid Kargari, Kevin C. Wehnert, Katharina Christenn, Axel Timpe

Fig. 1
photo: Montreuil Aux Pêches, URL: http://www.montreuilauxpeches.fr/photos/galleries/Docs_MAP/AnciennesPhotosMontreuil/f.jpg (accessed December 19, 2020)

Fig. 2
representation: Kevin C. Wehnert, 2021, data: J. G. Eßlinger (1767); J. Mozard (1814); K. De Decker (2015); I. Lafarge (2012) 'Les murs à palisser "à la Montreuil",' (e-Phaïstos), I-1, pp. 84–86, 88 (fig. 5); F. Malot (1842), 'II. Culture. Rapport d'une commission spéciale, fait à la *Société royale d'horticulture*, sur rétablissement dune treille de feigne en espalier, dans la commune de Montreuil; par M. Malot (Félix)', in *Bureau de la société d'horticulture*, and L. Bouchard-Houzard (ed.), *Annales de la Société Royale d'horticulture de Paris, et Journal Spécial de l'état et des Progrès du Jardinage* (vol. 30, no. 176, July 1842, Paris), pp. 272–73

Fig. 3
photo: Montreuil Aux Pêches, URL: http://www.montreuilauxpeches.fr/photos/galleries/Docs_MAP/AnciennesPhotosMontreuil/y.jpg (accessed December 19, 2020)

Fig. 4
representation: Katja Gadziak, Katharina Christenn, Axel Timpe drawing: Kevin C. Wehnert, 2021, data: De Sallaberry (1838); J. Mozard (1814); G.U. Fintelmann, (1849); J.G. Eßlinger (1767); map: Cartothèque numérique de la Société d'Histoire de Nanterre, France (1773)

Fig. 5
representation: Katja Gadziak, Katharina Christenn, Axel Timpe representation: Kevin C. Wehnert, 2021, data: De Sallaberry (1838); J. Mozard (1814); J.G. Eßlinger (1767); G. U. Fintelmann (1849); Maison des Murs à Pêches (2016); I. Lafarge (2012) "Les murs à palisser à la Montreuil," e-Phaïstos, I–1, 85–86, Fig. 5

Fig. 6
representation: Kevin C. Wehnert, 2021, data: J. G. Eßlinger (1767); J. Mozard (1814); G.U. Fintelmann (1849)

Fig. 7
representation: Katja Gadziak, Katharina Christenn, Axel Timpe drawing: Ayda Hamid Kargari, 2020, based on Montreuil, QGIS shape file Map-1/5000, URL: https://www.montreuil.fr/environnement/la-valorisation-et-la-protection-du-site (accessed November 10, 2021); Fruits Défendus, URL: https://www.helloasso.com/associations/fruits-defendus (accessed November 10, 2021), les Paris culteurs, URL: https://www.parisculteurs.paris/fr/sites/paris-culteurs-saison-3/1606-murs-a-peches-de-montreuil-93100.html (accessed November 10, 2021)

Fig. 8
photo: Reporterre/mursapeches.blog, URL: https://www.leparisien.fr/seine-saint-denis-93/montreuil-l-association-des-murs-a-peches-lance-unsos-20-02-2020-8263851.php (accessed November 10, 2021)

Fig. 9
photo: *in Exposition. Promenons-nous dans les Murs à pêches*, URL: https://www.montreuil.fr/fileadmin/user_upload/12_Environnement/07_Les_murs_a_peches/exposition-map-sept2019.pdf (accessed March 4, 2021)

Reconnecting City and Countryside: Participatory Solutions for Hamburg

Ole Oßenbrink, Birte Mehrkens, Andreas Ulbrich, Cord Petermann

Fig. 1
photo: Jürgen Gilles

Fig. 2
photo: Marktgemeinschaft Blumengroßmarkt Hamburg eG, URL: https://www.blumengrossmarkt-hh.de/docs/4556/historisches.aspx (accessed November 15, 2021)

Fig. 3
representation: Katja Gadziak, Katharina Christenn, Axel Timpe, based on a representation by Jan Ole Oßenbrink

Fig. 4
photo: Jan Ole Oßenbrink (2020)

Fig. 5
representation: Katja Gadziak, Katharina Christenn, Axel Timpe, based on a drawing by Jan Ole Oßenbrink, data: OpenStreetMap, URL: https://www.openstreetmap.org/copyright (accessed November 24, 2021)

Fig. 6
photo: Jan Ole Oßenbrink (2019)

Enhancing and Promoting Milan's Peri-Urban Agricultural Landscape as a Cultural Resource: The Case of MUSA

Andrea L'Erario, Paola Branduini, Raffaella Laviscio, G. Matteo Mai, Lionella Scazzosi, Francesco C. Toso

Fig. 1
drawing: Katja Gadziak, Katharina Christenn, Axel Timpe, based on drawing by Andrea L'Erario, 2020

Fig. 2, Fig. 4, Fig. 5, Fig. 7
photo: L'Erario, 2015

Fig. 3
drawing: Federico Meroni, 2015

Fig. 6
photo: National University of Milan, 2015

Fig. 8
map: PaRID-Politecnico di Milano, 2015

Inner cover
representation: Katja Gadziak, Katharina Christenn, Axel Timpe, data: Sara Jafroudi and Chloe Kiernicki, map: data from OpenStreetMap, URL: https://www.openstreetmap.org/copyright (accessed May 04, 2021)

Authors' Affiliations

Oscar Alfranca
Universitat Politècnica de Catalunya, Department of Agri-Food Engineering and Biotechnology

Johanna Altendorf
RWTH Aachen University, Faculty of Architecture

Eric Boenecke
Leibniz Institute of Vegetable and Ornamental Crops, Program area HORTSYS – Next-Generation Horticultural Systems

Paola Branduini
Politecnico di Milano, Department of Architecture, Built Environment and Construction Engineering, PaRID Lab

Leandra Brunet
RWTH Aachen University, Faculty of Architecture

Diana Büttner
City of Bamberg, World Heritage Office

Laura Camacho Latz
RWTH Aachen University, Faculty of Architecture

Slavica Čepić
University of Belgrade, Faculty of Forestry, Department of Landscape Architecture and Horticulture

Mengyun Chen
South China University of Technology, Department of Landscape Architecture

Katharina Christenn
RWTH Aachen University, Institute of Landscape Architecture; Technische Universität München, Faculty of Architecture

Dragana Ćorović
University of Belgrade, Faculty of Forestry, Department of Landscape Architecture and Horticulture

Luc H. Dossa
University of Abomey-Calavi, Faculty of Agricultural Sciences

Clara Forn
Museu de Badalona

Ayda Hamid Kargari
RWTH Aachen University, Faculty of Architecture

Jay Heydecke
RWTH Aachen University, Faculty of Architecture

Alexander Kader
German University of Technology in Oman, Department of Urban Planning and Architectural Design

Anna Kerfers
RWTH Aachen University, Faculty of Architecture

Bossima I. Koura
Université Nationale d'Agriculture, Ecole de Gestion et d'Exploitation des Systèmes d'Elevage

Sibylle Küttner
Horticultural historian

Nicole Laufhütte
RWTH Aachen University, Faculty of Architecture

Sophie Laukemper
RWTH Aachen University, Faculty of Architecture

Raffaella Laviscio
Politecnico di Milano, Department of Architecture, Built Environment and Construction Engineering, PaRID Lab

Anna Lei
Sapienza, Università di Roma, Department of Architecture and Design

Andrea L'Erario
Politecnico di Milano, Department of Architecture and Urban Studies

Guangsi Lin
South China University of Technology, Department of Landscape Architecture

Frank Lohrberg
RWTH Aachen University, Institute of Landscape Architecture

G. Matteo Mai
Politecnico di Milano, Department of Architecture, Built Environment and Construction Engineering, PaRID Lab

Rafael Mata Olmo
Autonomous University of Madrid, Department of Geography, Research Group Landscape and Territory in Spain, Mediterranean Europe and Latin America

Birte Mehrkens
Osnabrück University of Applied Sciences, Faculty of Agricultural Sciences and Landscape Architecture

Nerea Morán
Germinando Cooperative Society

Dolors Nieto
Museu de Badalona

Ole Oßenbrink
Osnabrück University of Applied Sciences, Faculty of Agricultural Sciences and Landscape Architecture

Cord Petermann
Osnabrück University of Applied Sciences, Faculty of Agricultural Sciences and Landscape Architecture

Dona Pickard
Bulgarian Academy of Sciences, Institute of Philosophy and Sociology

Ardiana Rahimi
RWTH Aachen University, Faculty of Architecture

Xavier Recasens
Universitat Politècnica de Catalunya, Department of Agri-Food Engineering and Biotechnology

Mariana Sanchez Salvador
ISCTE – Lisbon University Institute, DINÂMIA'CET-IUL – Center for Socioeconomic and Territorial Studies

Esther Sanz Sanz
French National Research Institute for Agriculture, Food, and Environment; Leibniz Centre for Agricultural Landscape Research

Lionella Scazzosi
Politecnico di Milano, Department of Architecture, Built Environment and Construction Engineering, PaRID Lab

Ansgar Schanbacher
Universität Göttingen, Institut für Historische Landesforschung

Marian Simón Rojo
Germinando Cooperative Society; Technical University of Madrid; Architecture, Urbanism and Sustainability Research Group, GIAU+S, UPM

Giles B. Sioen
National Institute for Environmental Studies, Japan; Future Earth Global Secretariat, Japan

Axel Timpe
RWTH Aachen University, Institute of Landscape Architecture

Jelena Tomićević-Dubljević
University of Belgrade, Faculty of Forestry, Department of Landscape Architecture and Horticulture

Francesco C. Toso
Politecnico di Milano, Department of Architecture, Built Environment and Construction Engineering, PaRID Lab

Attila Tóth
Slovak University of Agriculture in Nitra, Institute of Landscape Architecture

Andreas Ulbrich
Osnabrück University of Applied Sciences, Faculty of Agricultural Sciences and Landscape Architecture

Kevin C. Wehnert
RWTH Aachen University, Chair of Building Technology

Carolina Yacamán Ochoa
Autonomous University of Madrid, Department of Geography, Research Group Landscape and Territory in Spain, Mediterranean Europe and Latin America

Makoto Yokohari
The University of Tokyo, Department of Urban Engineering

Editors' Biographies

Prof. Dr.-Ing. Frank Lohrberg studied landscape architecture at Hanover University and won the Peter Joseph Lenné Award in 1990.

Beginning in 1994 he worked at the University of Stuttgart, where he received his doctorate in 2001, which dealt with urban agriculture and city planning. Since 2002 he is principal of lohrberg stadtlandschaftsarchitektur, which focuses on landscape architecture. In 2010 he was appointed as chair of the Institute of Landscape Architecture at RWTH Aachen University.

Prof. Lohrberg has chaired several national and EU-funded research projects focusing on urban agriculture and green infrastructure. Currently his institute coordinates the H2020 project EFUA-European Forum on Urban Agriculture.

Dipl.-Ing. (TUM) Katharina Christenn studied landscape architecture at Technische Universität München and Sapienza Università di Roma. She started her academic career with her doctoral research on the history of professional landscape architecture in the twentieth century at the Chair of Landscape Architecture and Transformation at Technische Universität München. As a research and teaching associate at the Institute of Landscape Architecture at RWTH Aachen University since 2016, she has been active in design studio teaching and projects in the field of co-producing green infrastructure with urban agriculture as well as the transformation of the Rhenish Mining Area. Her focus is in cultural heritage and the transformation of post-industrial landscape. Since 2022 she is coordinating the project INSUAH (Integrated Study on Urban Agriculture as Heritage) and thus deepening the research on urban agricultural heritage.

Dr.-Ing. Axel Timpe is a landscape architect trained at Leibniz Universität Hannover/DE and Centre d'Études Supérieures d'Aménagement at Université François Rabelais de Tours/FR. He started his professional career at lohrberg stadtlandschaftsarchitektur in 2003. Since 2010 he has been a research and teaching associate at RWTH Aachen University's Institute of Landscape Architecture and now is its deputy director. He accomplished his PhD thesis "Designing Productive Parks" here in January 2017. Axel Timpe is coordinating Horizon 2020 Innovation Action proGIreg, the transdisciplinary green infrastructure research project CoProGrün, and had a coordinating role in COST Action Urban Agriculture Europe. His research focus is on green infrastructure, nature-based solutions, and urban agriculture and their co-design and co-production with local stakeholders. In addition to design studio teaching at RWTH Aachen, he developed the edX MOOC "Nature-Based Urban Regeneration."

Dr.-Ing. Ayça Sancar studied architecture at Izmir Institute of Technology and RWTH Aachen University. In 2022, she completed her doctoral dissertation titled "The Stage of the State: Opera Architecture and Cultural Politics in Turkey 1923–1956" at the Department of Architectural Theory of RWTH Aachen University. She is currently working as a teaching and research associate at the Institute of Landscape Architecture of RWTH Aachen University. Her teaching and research practice is focused on the development of digital formats and tools for didactical purposes. As part of these endeavors, she coordinated the development of the massive open online course "Cultural Heritage in Transformation" and conducted seminars on the depiction of cases of urban agricultural heritage in animated videos.

Imprint

Copy editing
Keonaona Peterson

Project management
Alexander Felix, Nora Kempkens

Production
Anja Häring, Amelie Solbrig

Graphics
Katja Gadziak, Katharina Christenn, Axel Timpe, Dennis Lurtz

Layout, cover design, and typesetting
Studio Pandan (Pia Christmann, Ann Richter, Vreni Knödler), Berlin

Paper
Vivus 100, 120 g/m²

Lithography
Repromayer GmbH, Reutlingen

Printing
Grafisches Centrum Cuno GmbH & Co. KG, Calbe

Library of Congress Control Number
2022938984

Bibliographic information
published by the German National Library
The German National Library lists this publication in the Deutsche Nationalbibliografie; detailed bibliographic data are available on the Internet at http://dnb.dnb.de.

Printed on 100% recycled paper, certified with the German BLUE ANGEL eco-label.

ISBN 978-3-0356-2251-5

e-ISBN (PDF) 978-3-0356-2252-2

P.O. Box 44, 4009 Basel, Switzerland
Part of Walter de Gruyter GmbH, Berlin/Boston

9 8 7 6 5 4 3 2 1

www.birkhauser.com